THE NEW
AMERICAN
COMMENTARY

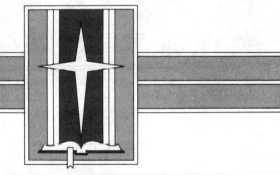

An Exegetical and Theological
Exposition of Holy Scripture

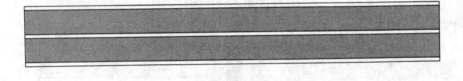

THE NEW AMERICAN COMMENTARY

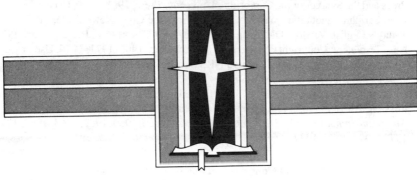

Volume
33

1, 2 THESSALONIANS

D. Michael Martin

BROADMAN
& HOLMAN
PUBLISHERS

© Copyright 1995 • Broadman & Holman Publishers
All rights reserved
4201-33
ISBN 0-8054-0133-4
Dewey Decimal Classification: 227.81
Subject Heading: BIBLE. N.T. THESSALONIANS
Library of Congress Catalog Card Number: 95–23281
Printed in the United States of America

Library of Congress Cataloging-in-Publication Data

Martin, Michael, 1952–
    1, 2 Thessalonians / Michael Martin.
       p. cm. — (The New American commentary ; v. 33)
    Includes bibliographical references and indexes.
    ISBN 0-8054-0133-4 (hardbound)
    1. Bible. N.T. Thessalonians.—Commentaries. I. Title.
II. Series.
BS2725.3.M364   1995
227'.8107—dc20

This volume is dedicated to my parents,
D. I. and Virginia Sanders Martin,
with thanksgiving to God
for the seeds of the faith which they helped plant and
which they have nurtured throughout my life

Editors' Preface

God's Word does not change. God's world, however, changes in every generation. These changes, in addition to new findings by scholars and a new variety of challenges to the gospel message, call for the church in each generation to interpret and apply God's Word for God's people. Thus, THE NEW AMERICAN COMMENTARY is introduced to bridge the twentieth and twenty-first centuries. This new series has been designed primarily to enable pastors, teachers, and students to read the Bible with clarity and proclaim it with power.

In one sense THE NEW AMERICAN COMMENTARY is not new, for it represents the continuation of a heritage rich in biblical and theological exposition. The title of this forty-volume set points to the continuity of this series with an important commentary project published at the end of the nineteenth century called AN AMERICAN COMMENTARY, edited by Alvah Hovey. The older series included, among other significant contributions, the outstanding volume on Matthew by John A. Broadus, from whom the publisher of the new series, Broadman and Holman, partly derives its name. The former series was authored and edited by scholars committed to the infallibility of Scripture, making it a solid foundation for the present project. In line with this heritage, all NAC authors affirm the divine inspiration, inerrancy, complete truthfulness, and full authority of the Bible. The perspective of the NAC is unapologetically confessional and rooted in the evangelical tradition.

Since a commentary is a fundamental tool for the expositor or teacher who seeks to interpret and apply Scripture in the church or classroom, the NAC focuses on communicating the theological structure and content of each biblical book. The writers seek to illuminate both the historical meaning and contemporary significance of Holy Scripture.

In its attempt to make a unique contribution to the Christian community, the NAC focuses on two concerns. First, the commentary emphasizes how each section of a book fits together so that the reader becomes aware of the theological unity of each book and of Scripture as a whole. The writers, however, remain aware of the Bible's inherently rich variety. Second, the NAC is produced with the conviction that the Bible primarily belongs to the church. We believe that scholarship and the academy provide an indispensable foundation for biblical understanding and the service of Christ, but the editors and authors of this series have attempted to communicate the findings of their research in a manner that will build up the whole body of Christ. Thus, the commentary concentrates on theological exegesis while providing practical, applicable exposition.

THE NEW AMERICAN COMMENTARY's theological focus enables the reader to see the parts as well as the whole of Scripture. The biblical books vary in content, context, literary type, and style. In addition to this rich variety, the editors and authors recognize that the doctrinal emphasis and use of the biblical books differs in various places, contexts, and cultures among God's people. These factors, as well as other concerns, have led the editors to give freedom to the writers to wrestle with the issues raised by the scholarly community surrounding each book and to determine the appropriate shape and length of the introductory materials. Moreover, each writer has developed the structure of the commentary in a way best suited for expounding the basic structure and the meaning of the biblical books for our day. Generally, discussions relating to contemporary scholarship and technical points of grammar and syntax appear in the footnotes and not in the text of the commentary. This format allows pastors and interested laypersons, scholars and teachers, and serious college and seminary students to profit from the commentary at various levels. This approach has been employed because we believe that all Christians have the privilege and responsibility to read and seek to understand the Bible for themselves.

Consistent with the desire to produce a readable, up-to-date commentary, the editors selected the *New International Version* as the standard translation for the commentary series. The selection was made primarily because of the NIV's faithfulness to the original languages and its beautiful and readable style. The authors, however, have been given the liberty to differ at places from the NIV as they develop their own translations from the Greek and Hebrew texts.

The NAC reflects the vision and leadership of those who provide oversight for Broadman and Holman, who in 1987 called for a new commentary series that would evidence a commitment to the inerrancy of Scripture and a faithfulness to the classic Christian tradition. While the commentary adopts an "American" name, it should be noted some writers represent countries outside the United States, giving the commentary an international perspective. The diverse group of writers includes scholars, teachers, and administrators from almost twenty different colleges and seminaries, as well as pastors, missionaries, and a layperson.

The editors and writers hope that THE NEW AMERICAN COMMEN-

TARY will be helpful and instructive for pastors and teachers, scholars and students, for men and women in the churches who study and teach God's Word in various settings. We trust that for editors, authors, and readers alike, the commentary will be used to build up the church, encourage obedience, and bring renewal to God's people. Above all, we pray that the NAC will bring glory and honor to our Lord who has graciously redeemed us and faithfully revealed himself to us in his Holy Word.

SOLI DEO GLORIA
The Editors

Author's Preface

The editors of *The New American Commentary* have observed that "the Bible primarily belongs to the church." Holding this conviction, it is appropriate that they should envision a commentary series designed "to enable pastors, teachers, and students to read the Bible with clarity and proclaim it with power." As one who shares their conviction that biblical scholarship should edify the church, I am delighted that I have been given the opportunity to participate in the production of the NAC.

Readers of the commentary should note several features in this volume consistent with the intent of the series. To begin with, the focus of the commentary is on the text of 1 and 2 Thessalonians. The unadorned message of the Scripture has amazing power. I have attempted to present that message in as straightforward a fashion as possible. Careful syntactical analysis of the Greek text of the letters forms the foundation of the study. In addition, I have worked with the conviction that an appreciation of the rhetorical strategies utilized in the letter enables readers to understand better the apostle's message. Similarly, a knowledge of the social setting in which the letters functioned provides an enhanced appreciation of the letters themselves. While dealing with these matters, however, I have avoided technical terms and debates as much as possible. Often the more technical material is referenced in the notes, but the bulk of the comments in the text focus on the message the epistles convey to the church.

Second, I am indebted to the fine scholars who have produced numerous invaluable studies of the letters and studies of related topics. Noting them all, however, would have produced far more footnotes than commentary. The footnotes that are included are intended to aid readers who wish to expand their study of a particular verse or topic. Space limitations as well as the philosophy behind the production of the NAC dictate that these notes be suggestive rather than exhaustive. Also, works in languages other than English are cited only when they are the only adequate avenue of continued study.

Third, I agree with the editors that the NIV is an excellent translation. Obviously, its translators took great care to render the biblical texts in clear, idiomatic English. The particular translation philosophy adopted by the designers of the NIV, however, often results in the creation of a less literal and more interpretive translation of the Greek text. All translations are interpretive; but the NIV is more so than many others (e.g., the NASB and the NRSV). In terms of this commentary, the translation philosophy of the NIV sometimes created situations in which the interpretive choices made by the translators of the NIV could not be discussed without reverting back to a more literal rendering of the Greek text. References to other English translations generally serve to highlight interpretive options in the Greek that are not readily apparent to the person reading the NIV alone.

Finally, I wish to express appreciation to those who have contributed in very direct ways to the production of this volume. The general and associate editors of the series have been a constant source of help and encouragement, and I must thank them for this as well as for the invitation to participate in the NAC project. I am indebted also to the library staff of Golden Gate Baptist Theological Seminary and especially to my former student and teaching assistant Kevin Compton, who assisted in the preparation of an initial working bibliography. Much of the work on the commentary was completed at Tyndale House in Cambridge, England; and I owe a debt of gratitude to the warden, Bruce Winter, and his coworkers who share with him the ministry of maintaining a world-class residential research library for biblical studies. My time in England was made possible by the generous sabbatical program maintained by the administration of Golden Gate Baptist Theological Seminary and by the funding provided by Drs. David and Faith Kim through the Kim Endowment. Last, but far from least, I am thankful to my wife, Beth, and sons, Philip and Garrett. Their assistance, support, patience, and prayers enrich my life and ministry more than words could ever express.

—D. Michael Martin

Abbreviations

Bible Books

Gen	Isa	Luke
Exod	Jer	John
Lev	Lam	Acts
Num	Ezek	Rom
Deut	Dan	1, 2 Cor
Josh	Hos	Gal
Judg	Joel	Eph
Ruth	Amos	Phil
1, 2 Sam	Obad	Col
1, 2 Kgs	Jonah	1, 2 Thess
1, 2 Chr	Mic	1, 2 Tim
Ezra	Nah	Titus
Neh	Hab	Phlm
Esth	Zeph	Heb
Job	Hag	Jas
Ps (pl. Pss)	Zech	1, 2 Pet
Prov	Mal	1, 2, 3 John
Eccl	Matt	Jude
Song	Mark	Rev

Apocrypha

Add Esth	The Additions to the Book of Esther
Bar	Baruch
Bel	Bel and the Dragon
1,2 Esdr	1, 2 Esdras
4 Ezra	4 Ezra
Jdt	Judith
Ep Jer	Epistle of Jeremiah
1,2,3,4 Mac	1, 2, 3, 4 Maccabees
Pr Azar	Prayer of Azariah and the Song of the Three Jews
Pr Man	Prayer of Manasseh
Sir	Sirach, Ecclesiasticus
Sus	Susanna
Tob	Tobit
Wis	The Wisdom of Solomon

Commonly Used Sources for New Testament Volumes

AB	Anchor Bible
ACNT	Augsburg Commentary on the New Testament
AGJU	Arbeiten zur Geschichte des antiken Judentums und des Urchristentums
AJT	*American Journal of Theology*
AJTh	*Asia Journal of Theology*
ANF	Ante-Nicene Fathers
ATANT	Abhandlungen zur Theologie des Alten and Neuen Testaments
ATR	*Anglican Theological Review*
ATRSup	*Anglican Theological Review Supplemental Series*
AusBR	*Australian Biblical Review*
AUSS	*Andrews University Seminary Studies*
BAGD	W. Bauer, W. F. Arndt, F. W. Gingrich, and F. Danker, *Greek-English Lexicon of the New Testament*
BARev	*Biblical Archaeology Review*
BBR	*Bulletin for Biblical Research*
BDF	F. Blass, A. Debrunner, R. W. Funk, *A Greek Grammar of the New Testament*
BETL	Bibliotheca ephemeridum theologicarum lovaniensium
Bib	*Biblica*
BJRL	*Bulletin of the John Rylands Library*
BK	*Bibel und Kirche*
BR	*Biblical Research*
BSac	*Bibliotheca Sacra*
BT	*The Bible Translator*
BTB	*Biblical Theology Bulletin*
BZ	*Biblische Zeitschrift*
BZNW	Beihefte zur *ZAW*
CBC	Cambridge Bible Commentary
CBQ	*Catholic Biblical Quarterly*
CCWJCW	Cambridge Commentaries on Writings of the Jewish and Christian World
CNTC	Calvin's New Testament Commentaries
CO	W. Baur, E. Cuntiz, and E. Reuss, *Ioannis Calvini opera quae supereunt omnia,* ed.
Conybeare	W. J. Conybeare and J. S. Howson, *The Life and Epistles of St. Paul*
CJT	*Canadian Journal of Theology*
CSR	*Christian Scholars' Review*
CTM	*Concordia Theologial Monthly*
CTQ	*Concordia Theological Quarterly*

ISBE	*International Standard Bible Encyclopedia*
JAAR	*Journal of the American Academy of Religion*
JANES	*Journal of Ancient Near Eastern Studies*
JAOS	*Journal of the American Oriental Society*
JBL	*Journal of Biblical Literature*
JES	*Journal of Ecumenical Studies*
JETS	*Journal of the Evangelical Theological Society*
JJS	*Journal of Jewish Studies*
JR	*Journal of Religion*
JRE	*Journal of Religious Ethics*
JRH	*Journal of Religious History*
JRS	*Journal of Roman Studies*
JSNT	*Journal for the Study of the New Testament*
JSOT	*Journal for the Study of the Old Testament*
JSS	*Journal of Semitic Studies*
JTS	*Journal of Theological Studies*
LEC	Library of Early Christianity
LouvSt	*Louvain Studies*
LS	Liddel and Scott, *Greek-English Lexicon*
LTJ	*Lutheran Theological Journal*
LTQ	*Lexington Theological Quarterly*
LW	Luther's Works
LXX	Septuagint
MCNT	Meyer's Commentary on the New Testament
MDB	*Mercer Dictionary of the Bible*
MM	J. H. Moulton and G. Milligan, *The Vocabulary of the Greek Testament*
MNTC	Moffatt NT Commentary
MQR	*Mennonite Quarterly Review*
MT	Masoretic Text
NAB	New American Bible
NAC	New American Commentary
NASB	New American Standard Bible
NBD	*New Bible Dictionary*
NCB	New Century Bible
NEB	New English Bible
Neot	*Neotestamentica*
NICNT	New International Commentary on the New Testament
NIGTC	New International Greek Testament Commentary
NIV	New International Version
NovT	*Novum Testamentum*
NovTSup	Novum Testamentum, Supplements
NPNF	Nicene and Post-Nicene Fathers
NRSV	New Revised Standard Version

NRT	*La nouvelle revue théologique*
NTD	Das Neue Testament Deutsch
NTI	D. Guthrie, *New Testament Introduction*
NTM	*The New Testament Message*
NTS	*New Testament Studies*
PC	Proclamation Commentaries
PEQ	*Palestine Exploration Quarterly*
PRS	*Perspectives in Religious Studies*
PSB	*Princeton Seminary Bulletin*
RB	*Revue biblique*
RelSRev	*Religious Studies Review*
RevExp	*Review and Expositor*
RevQ	*Revue de Qumran*
RevThom	*Revue thomiste*
RHPR	*Revue d'histoire et de philosophie religieuses*
RSPT	*Revue des sciences philosophiques et théologiques*
RSR	*Recherches de science religieuse*
RSV	Revised Standard Version
RTP	*Revue de théologie et de philosophie*
RTR	*Reformed Theological Review*
SAB	*Sitzungsbericht der Preussischen Akademie der Wissenschaft zu Berlin*
SBLDS	SBL Dissertation Series
SBLMS	SBL Monograph Series
SBLSP	SBL Seminar Papers
SEAJT	*Southeast Asia Journal of Theology*
SJT	*Scottish Journal of Theology*
SNTSMS	Society for New Testament Studies Monograph Series
SNTU	*Studien zum Neuen Testament und seiner Umwelt*
SPCK	Society for the Promotion of Christian Knowledge
ST	*Studia theologica*
SWJT	*Southwestern Journal of Theology*
TB	*Tyndale Bulletin*
TBC	Torch Bible Commentaries
TBT	*The Bible Today*
TDNT	G. Kittel and G. Friedrich, eds., *Theological Dictionary of the New Testament*
Theol	*Theology*
ThT	*Theology Today*
TLZ	*Theologische Literaturzeitung*
TNTC	Tyndale New Testament Commentaries
TrinJ	*Trinity Journal*
TRu	*Theologische Rundschau*
TS	*Theological Studies*

Contents

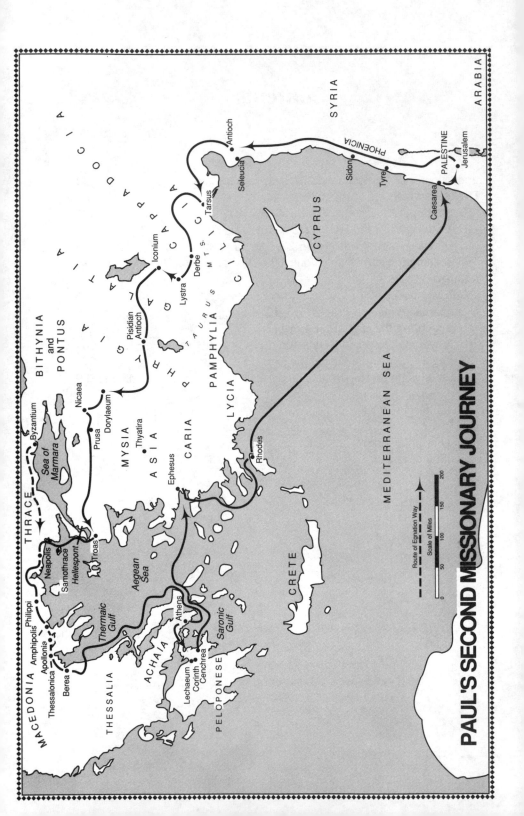

PAUL'S SECOND MISSIONARY JOURNEY

1, 2 Thessalonians

──────────── INTRODUCTION ────────────

1. Thessalonica—A Prominent City of Macedonia

The ruins of the ancient city of Thessalonica lie beneath the structures of the modern port city of Thessaloniki (Salonica). The modern city is situated on the Gulf of Salonica in northern Greece just to the west of the three-fingered peninsula of Chalcidice. The ancient city was founded in Macedonia (a region that encompassed roughly the northern half of the Greek peninsula)[1] about 315 B.C. by Cassander, who named it after his wife, Thessalonica, the daughter of Philip II and sister of

---

[1] For an excellent introduction to both the ancient and modern literature related to the province, see D. Gill, "Macedonia," in *The Book of Acts in Its First Century Setting,* vol. 2, *Graeco-Roman Setting,* ed. D. Gill and C. Gempf (Grand Rapids: Eerdmans, 1994), 397–417. For a brief introduction to the history and religions of Macedonia, see H. Koester, "Macedonia," *HBD,* or J. Finegan, "Macedonia" and "Thessalonica," *IDB,* and C. Thompson, "Thessalonica," *IDBSup.*

Alexander the Great.[2] By the time Paul visited Thessalonica, its residents (and those of Macedonia in general) could boast a long and illustrious history.

Macedonia was established as a kingdom early in the seventh century B.C. by Perdikkas I. Especially prominent among the rulers who followed was Archelaus, who ruled at the end of the fifth century B.C., strengthening the military and improving the system of roads in the region. In 359 B.C. Philip II ascended to the throne. Under his guidance Macedonia grew in prominence and strength until at the Battle of Chaeroneia in 338 B.C. it established its dominant position over the other Greek states. Soon after this, Philip planned to expand the influence and power of Macedonia further by crossing the Hellespont and waging war against the Persian forces that were threatening the Greek homeland. He sent forces into Asia Minor in 336 but was assassinated before he could join them. Alexander the Great, son of Philip II and Olympias (and a student of Aristotle), ascended to the throne at his father's death. He proceeded with his father's plans to conquer Persia but did not stop with that. In a mere decade Alexander's armies swept through the entire eastern Mediterranean world from Greece to Egypt and as far east as the Indus River, thus earning the title given him by historians, Alexander the Great.

While Alexander campaigned, regents governed the Greek states. When the regent of Macedonia, Antipater, died in 319, a struggle for control of Macedonia ensued. Antipater had named Polyperchon to succeed him, but by 316 Antipater's son Cassander had defeated Polyperchon and had begun rebuilding his war-torn realm. Numerous villages in the vicinity of Therma on the Thermaic Gulf (now the Gulf of Salonica) had been destroyed in the conflict. Cassander resettled the residents, establishing a new port city, Thessalonica. Macedonia remained under Greek control until 168 B.C. when the Roman consul Aemilius Paullus defeated the king of Macedonia, Perseus, at the Battle of Pydna.[3]

Under Roman rule Macedonia was divided into four regions. Thessalonica was the capitol of the region in which it was located. Following a failed attempt by Andriscus (the son of Perseus) to reestablish the monarchy, Macedonia was designated a Roman province in 148 B.C. By the time of Paul, Macedonia was a senatorial province governed by a

---

[2] Strabo, 7.7, frag. 21, 24.
[3] Plutarch, *Aemilius Paullus,* 16–22.

Roman proconsul who had his administrative capitol in the free city of Thessalonica. Charges of inciting insurrection against Rome (which some Thessalonians leveled against Paul, Acts 17:6–9) would have been taken seriously in such a politically significant city.

Thessalonica was not only an important city politically but also commercially. One of Rome's major east-west trade routes passed through Macedonia. The Via Egnatia originated on the Adriatic coast at both Apollonia and Dyrrachium. The two routes quickly joined and proceeded east to Thessalonica and the Aegean coast. Roughly following the coast, the road continued on through Amphipolis, Philippi, and Nicopolis to Kypsela in Thrace—a distance, according to Strabo, of 4,280 stadia (535 miles).[4] Military and commercial travel moving east/west that could not take advantage of the sea routes further south would have moved along the Via Egnatia. Paul and his coworkers traveled this road as they moved from Philippi through Amphipolis and Apollonia to Thessalonica, leaving it as they turned south toward Athens.

2. Paul and the Thessalonians

According to Acts, Paul established the church in Thessalonica (17:1–10) during his second missionary journey (15:36–18:22). As a result of his preaching in the synagogue, "some of the Jews" and "a large number of God-fearing Greeks and not a few prominent women" were converted (17:4). Some of the Jews who had rejected Paul's message determined to drive him from the city by inciting a mob to charge Paul and his coworkers with crimes against the empire (17:5–6a). When they could not find Paul, they dragged Jason and some other believers before the city officials (the politarchs[5]) and claimed: "These men who have turned the world upside down have come here also, and Jason has received them; and they are all acting against the decrees of Caesar, saying that there is another king, Jesus" (17:6b–7, RSV).[6] The believers of course would have denied the charges. The city officials faced the dual problem of the mob's charges of insurrection and their own respon-

---

[4] Strabo, 7.7.4.

[5] For introduction to the ancient and modern literature related to the politarchs, see G. Horsley, "The Politarchs," in *The Book of Acts in Its First Century Setting,* vol. 2, *Graeco-Roman Setting,* ed. D. Gill and C. Gempf (Grand Rapids: Eerdmans, 1994), 419–31.

[6] The exact nature of the charge is uncertain; see E. Judge, "The Decrees of Caesar at Thessalonica," *RTR* 30 (1971): 1–7.

sibility to keep the peace. They dealt with the situation by requiring Jason and the others to post a bond and then dispersing the mob. That night the Thessalonian believers "sent Paul and Silas away to Berea" (17:10).

Though this account in Acts is brief, it implies that the church was made up of converted Jews and God-fearers. It implies that Paul made a large enough impact in the synagogue and in the city to provoke a harsh response from unconverted synagogue leaders who viewed the gospel as a serious threat. It also indicates that certain elements of the city could be stirred to mob action against the new church with little or no evidence of wrongdoing. Paul's inability to return to Thessalonica (1 Thess 2:18) and his concern for the perseverance of the believers there (1 Thess 3:5) are certainly consistent with the image of the church's situation painted in Acts. Likewise the animosity toward the church related in Acts is consistent with the references to persecution in the Thessalonian correspondence (cf. 1 Thess 1:6; 2:14; 2 Thess 1:4–7).

The Thessalonian correspondence, however, also provides information regarding Paul's stay in Thessalonica that seems on the surface to be inconsistent with the Acts account. Acts states that Paul reasoned in the synagogue for "three Sabbath days" (Acts 17:2). But Paul was in the city long enough to work at his trade (1 Thess 2:7–9), to provide instructions (4:1–2) and an example of how a Christian should live (1:6; 2:1–12), and to establish a strong bond of affection between himself and the believers (2:17–20; 3:6). Could he have accomplished all this in three weeks, or must he have spent more time in Thessalonica?

The seam in the Acts account between 17:4 and 17:5 at least allows for the possibility of continued ministry in the city after Paul's three-week ministry in the synagogue. And Acts does not indicate how long Paul stayed in Jason's house (first mentioned in Acts 17:5) before the riot that forced his departure (17:10). Thus the possibility exists that it was in Thessalonica (not Corinth; cf. 18:5–8) where Paul first established the pattern of moving his base of operations from the local synagogue to a private residence when he was rejected by the synagogue leadership. If so, then Paul easily could have been in Thessalonica several weeks beyond the three during which he focused on converting the Jews. A longer stay is also consistent with Phil 4:16, which indicates that Paul's stay in Thessalonica was long enough for the church at Philippi to send a contribution to support his ministry there. The information in Acts does not contradict the information in 1 Thessalonians. Acts' mention of three weeks does not limit Paul's stay but is describing only three weeks of his stay.

The Thessalonian correspondence indicates that Paul maintained contact with the Thessalonian church as his evangelization of Greece continued during his stay in Athens and Corinth. Acts contains no explicit record of such contacts. After Paul and his coworkers were driven from Thessalonica, they went to Berea. Subsequently Paul was driven from Berea by opponents who followed him from Thessalonica, and so he traveled to Athens. Silas and Timothy were able to remain in Berea, but Paul instructed them to join him in Athens "as soon as possible" (Acts 17:10–15). The next mention in Acts of Silas and Timothy comes in 18:5, where they rejoined Paul in Corinth having come "from Macedonia" (not Berea). Acts does not mention Timothy in Athens nor any communication between Paul and the Thessalonian church. However, 1 Thess 3:1–2 indicates that Timothy did join Paul in Athens and was subsequently sent from Athens to Thessalonica. Timothy returned from that mission bringing good news about the church, and Paul responded by sending 1 Thessalonians to the church (1 Thess 3:5–6).

Paul also sent 2 Thessalonians to the church (from Athens or Corinth?) in response to a report received about the church (2 Thess 2:2; 3:11), but neither the source of the report (Timothy?), nor the timing of the letter (before or after 1 Thessalonians?), nor the letter carrier (Timothy?) is identified. What is clear, however, is that Paul maintained an ongoing, active concern for the churches he founded. He did not leave them to make their way alone. In the months Paul ministered in Athens and Corinth, Timothy made at least two (perhaps three) round trips as Paul's emissary between Athens/Corinth and the church at Thessalonica—each trip a journey of about a thousand miles.

3. The Authorship of 1 Thessalonians

The author of the letter identified himself as the apostle Paul (1:1, along with Silas and Timothy), and relatively few scholars dispute the letter's genuineness.[7] Pauline authorship was rejected by F. C. Baur and the Tübingen School, and for a brief period a number of scholars followed their lead.[8] But Baur's influence has faded, and supporters of his

---

[7] See, e.g., R. Scott, *The Pauline Epistles* (Edinburgh: T & T Clark, 1909), 215–33.

[8] See B. Rigaux, *Saint Paul: Les Epitres aux Thessaloniciens* (Paris: Jl. Gabalda; Gembloux: J. Duculot, 1956), 120–28, for a discussion of the attitude of nineteenth-century continental scholarship toward the authenticity of the Thessalonian correspondence.

position today would be in the distinct minority.

In discussing authorship, some scholars make much of three apparent inconsistencies between the Acts account of the Pauline mission in Thessalonica and the evidence from 1 Thessalonians.[9] First is the length of Paul's ministry there. Second, Acts leaves the impression that the church was predominantly Jewish, while 1 Thess 1:9 implies the church members were idolaters in their pre-Christian lives. Third, in Acts, Timothy remained in Berea when Paul left for Athens and later rejoined him at Corinth (17:14; 18:5). According to 1 Thess 3:1–2, Timothy was with Paul in Athens and was sent by Paul to Thessalonica while Paul himself remained in Athens.

Although it is possible to argue that the author of the letters did not know the true history of the Pauline mission reflected in Acts (and thus was not Paul), more often such seeming historical discrepancies raise concerns about the accuracy of Acts, not the authenticity of 1 Thessalonians. Even if Acts 17:1–10 is used to judge the authenticity of 1 Thessalonians, Pauline authorship is not to be disproved. The accounts differ but are far from irreconcilable (as discussed in the previous section).

On the other hand, there are numerous indications of the authenticity of 1 Thessalonians. The letter was known and affirmed as Pauline in the early church.[10] It was included by Marcion in his *Apostolicon* (A.D. 140) and is found in the Muratorian Canon (A.D. 180). Irenaeus, Clement of Alexandria, Ignatius, and Polycarp all appear to have been familiar with 1 Thessalonians as a Pauline letter.[11] Within the letter itself several features argue strongly for Pauline authorship. First, the language of 1 Thessalonians is thoroughly Pauline as J. Frame has demonstrated.[12] Second, the author of the letter wrote as though he would be alive at the coming of the Lord. A false letter written after Paul's death would certainly not have presented Paul making such an assumption.

---

[9] See D. Carson, D. Moo, and L. Morris, *An Introduction to the New Testament* (Grand Rapids: Zondervan), 344–45.

[10] For a brief discussion of 1 Thessalonians in the earliest extant MSS of the NT see R. F. Collins, *The Birth of the New Testament* (New York: Crossroad, 1993), 1–4.

[11] See E. Askwith, *An Introduction to the Thessalonian Epistles* (New York: Macmillan, 1902), 40–52, and A. Barnett, *Paul Becomes a Literary Influence* (Chicago: University Press, 1941), 178–80.

[12] J. E. Frame, *A Critical and Exegetical Commentary on the Epistles of St. Paul to the Thessalonians* (Edinburgh: T & T Clark, 1960), 28–37, whose arguments stand in contrast to those of Baur.

Third, the letter presumes the imminence of the parousia, a presumption understandable in Paul's generation of believers but which was less common as time passed. Fourth, the content of the letter cannot be attributed to a false teacher(s) promoting his particular theological perspective since no such unusual theological perspective is evident in the letter. Clearly 1 Thessalonians was authored by the apostle himself.

4. The Authorship of 2 Thessalonians

As in the case of 1 Thessalonians, the prescript of 2 Thessalonians identifies the senders as Paul, Timothy, and Silas. The letter itself contemplates the possibility (if not the fact) of the circulation of a forged letter supposedly from Paul (2 Thess 2:2). Not surprisingly, the conclusion of 2 Thessalonians also contains Paul's "signature" as an evidence of authenticity not only for this letter but also for any others the church might receive from him (3:17).[13]

These things in themselves, however, have not prevented speculation regarding the authenticity of the letter. In fact, 2 Thessalonians is not nearly so widely affirmed as Pauline as is 1 Thessalonians. This is not, however, due to inferior external evidence for its authenticity. Both 1 and 2 Thessalonians were accepted by Marcion (A.D. 140) and occur in the Muratorian Canon (A.D. 180). The evidence from several early church fathers also indicates that 2 Thessalonians was known and used by the early church as a genuine Pauline letter. Objections to its authenticity rest primarily on the basis of internal evidence: material in the letter that some scholars argue is inconsistent with if not alien to Pauline vocabulary, style, and/or theology.[14]

Several studies contain lengthy lists of words and phrases found in 2 Thessalonians but which do not occur in any other Pauline letter.[15] At the same time, some observe that several elements typical of Pauline correspondence are missing from 2 Thessalonians. The absence of diatribe and rhetorical questions gives the letter a less personal feel. Imper-

---

[13] The carrier of a letter and the character of its content also would validate its authenticity.

[14] One of the most influential studies rejecting Pauline authorship has been that of W. Trilling, *Untersuchungen zum zweiten Thessalonicherbrief* (Leipzig: St. Benno, 1972). See also J. Bailey, "Who Wrote II Thessalonians?" *NTS* 25 (1979): 131–45.

[15] Frame, *Thessalonians*, 28–32, observes that 2 Thessalonians is not as rich in specifically Pauline words as is 1 Thessalonians but that the vocabulary of 2 Thessalonians is still Pauline. Cf. Trilling, *Untersuchungen*, 48–51.

atives are relatively infrequent in 2 Thessalonians, and a collection of paraenetic material (as in 1 Thess 5:12–24) is absent. The result is that the "tone" of 2 Thessalonians is inconsistent with that of 1 Thessalonians—the former sounding less personal. Where the letters are similar, it is argued that they are too similar, indicating a likeness born of imitation, not common authorship.

Even those who make these arguments, however, recognize that none of them is conclusive. Arguments from silence (such as citing the lack of rhetorical questions or paraenetic material in 2 Thessalonians) are notoriously weak. Likewise, the presence of unique vocabulary in 2 Thessalonians is not necessarily the result of non-Pauline authorship. Numerous other factors—for example, a change in amanuensis, a difference in subject matter, or the use of preformed tradition—also could explain variations in vocabulary from one letter to another by the same author. The supposed change in tone from 1 to 2 Thessalonians rests on such distinctions as we find in the thanksgivings of the two letters. In 1 Thessalonians Paul gave thanks for the Thessalonians (1:2; 2:13; 3:9). In 2 Thessalonians he was "bound" (RSV) or "obligated" to give thanks (1:3). Does the latter phrase imply emotional distance, a greater level of respect and appreciation, or are the two statements essentially synonymous? Because discerning the tone of the letters depends on interpretations of this sort of ambiguous phrasing, conclusions regarding authorship based on such speculations are simply not persuasive.

Perhaps the most frequently cited variation between 1 and 2 Thessalonians has to do with their presentations of the parousia of the Lord. It is argued that 1 Thessalonians presents the reader with a parousia that could occur suddenly and unexpectedly at any moment (4:13–5:11). Second Thessalonians, in contrast, presents a series of recognizable events that must precede the parousia (2:1–12). It is considered inconceivable that the same author should write such incompatible accounts of the Lord's parousia. This argument against Pauline authorship is weak at several points. First, it misrepresents the teachings of 1 Thessalonians that "the Lord will come like a thief in the night" (5:2). Those for whom the coming of the Lord will be as a thief (i.e., unexpected) are unbelievers, but believers "are not in darkness"; thus that day will not surprise them as a thief (v. 4). It is the very point of 5:1–11 that believers know the Lord is coming and must therefore persist in the faith as they await his arrival (vv. 8,11).

Second, that Paul would write both of an imminent end of the world and at the same time of signs that will indicate that the end is at hand is not inconceivable. This was in fact a common feature of non-Christian apocalyptic literature of the day. Similarly, we also find the coming of the lord in judgment presented in the gospels using the image of the "thief." The thief analogy occurs there (as it does in Paul) in conjunction with signs heralding the end. Such signs do not provide a concrete time frame; thus believers must be constantly faithful and vigilant. The timing of the signs relative to one another and to the climactic event of judgment is also left ambiguous. Thus believers can know with certainty that the Lord is coming and should be able to recognize the beginning of the event. But they do not know when it will occur nor the precise duration of the event from beginning to end. It is this combination of certainty regarding the event and ambiguity regarding its precise nature and timing that is reflected in both letters to the Thessalonian church.

Third, the fact that material was presented in 2 Thessalonians that was not mentioned in 1 Thessalonians does not require that the author of 1 Thessalonians was ignorant of or had rejected these teachings about the events preceding the end. First Thessalonians 5:1–11 presupposes some prior knowledge regarding the parousia (see 5:1). The fact that signs of the end are not listed or that the man of lawlessness is not discussed may simply indicate that Paul had already given the church this material verbally. These teachings then could easily have been presupposed in Paul's presentation. And given the intent of 5:1–11 to encourage persistent faithfulness, the listing of signs is simply not a necessary part of Paul's argument. Reminding the church of the signs of the end was, on the other hand, a necessary part of the argument of 2 Thess 2:1–12 since the intent in that instance was to convince believers not to succumb to the lie that the day of the Lord had already come. Thus the absence of signs of the end from 1 Thess 4:13–5:11 does not justify the rejection of the Pauline authorship of 2 Thessalonians. The difference in content, rather, can best be explained as the result of a difference in purpose in the two letters.

Second Thessalonians is Pauline. The external evidence is in favor of an early acceptance of it in the early church as Pauline. The content has not been shown to be incompatible with Paul's other writings. The letter itself claims Pauline authorship, and rejecting that claim says more about the level of scepticism with which the interpreter approaches the text than it does about the text itself.

5. The Unity of 1 Thessalonians

W. Schmithals has argued that the Thessalonians correspondence as we have it contains the blended contents of four letters. First Thessalonians in his estimate is the product of editing together Paul's second letter to the church (which originally contained the material found in 1 Thess 1:1–2:12 and 4:2–5:28) and his fourth letter (which we now have as 1 Thess 2:13–4:1). His assessment is based primarily on the observation that the letter as we have it contains two proems (1:2 and 2:13) as well as two conclusions (3:11 and 5:23).[16] Although Schmithals helps us recognize some unusual elements in the structure of the letter, his hypothesis of multiple letters is not convincing. Paul was not obligated to follow strict epistolary conventions, so deviations from such prove nothing. There is no manuscript evidence supporting the independent existence of four letters. And if 2:13 to 4:1 was originally an independent letter, it would have included introductory and concluding remarks and a Pauline benediction. For these (especially the latter) to disappear entirely from the textual tradition is highly unlikely. All in all it is best to seek an explanation for the unusual epistolary structure of 1 Thessalonians in areas other than the splicing together of multiple documents. (See the following commentary for alternative ways of explaining the structures found in the text.)

6. The Sequence of the Thessalonian Correspondence

That Paul wrote the letters to the Thessalonians in the order in which they occur in the canon is commonly assumed. Over the years, however, several scholars have argued that the correspondence reads more naturally if we assume that 2 Thessalonians was written before 1 Thessalonians.[17] Several issues are involved in making this determination. First, the canonical order of the documents should not prejudice the discus-

---

[16] W. Schmithals, "Die Thess als Briefkompositionen," in *Zeit und Geschichte*, ed. E. Dinkler (Tübingen: Mohr, 1964), 302.

[17] See J. C. West, "The Order of 1 and 2 Thessalonians," *JTS* 15 (1913): 66–74; F. J. Badcock, *The Pauline Epistles and the Epistle to the Hebrews in Their Historical Setting* (New York: Macmillan, 1937), 46–52; T. W. Manson, "St. Paul in Greece: The Letters to the Thessalonians," *BJRL* 35 (1952): 428–47; and R. W. Thurston, "The Relationship between the Thessalonian Epistles," *ExpTim* 85 (1973): 52–56. For a recent commentator who consistently interprets the letters from this perspective see C. A. Wanamaker, *The Epistles to the Thessalonians*, NIGTC (Grand Rapids: Eerdmans, 1990).

sion of their chronological order. Canonical arrangement appears to have been determined more by the relative size of each letter than by their dates of composition. In spite of this some writers seem to assume the priority of 1 Thessalonians simply on the basis of tradition. At least they give no arguments supporting its priority. R. Jewett, on the other hand, goes beyond asserting the priority of 1 Thessalonians and provides several reasons for maintaining that the canonical order is also the chronological order.[18] Although his arguments have strong points, they are no more conclusive than many of the arguments for the priority of 2 Thessalonians.[19]

Second, 1 Thess 3:1–2 reveals that Paul sent Timothy to Thessalonica from Athens and wrote 1 Thessalonians after Timothy's return. (Whether he returned to Athens or to Corinth is impossible to know.) One might reasonably assume that Paul would not have sent Timothy from Athens to Thessalonica without sending along some kind of correspondence. If Timothy did carry a letter on that occasion, either it is now lost or it is the letter we have as 2 Thessalonians. For one of Paul's letters to be lost to us today certainly is possible. We have only two of four letters he sent to the church at Corinth (1 and 2 Corinthians and the two letters mentioned in 1 Cor 5:9 and 2 Cor 2:4,9). And if the letter to the Laodiceans (Col 4:16) is not a reference to Ephesians, then it is a lost letter as well. Although it seems likely that Timothy would have carried some message from Athens to Thessalonica, there is no proof that he did; and if he did, it might not have been 2 Thessalonians. In short, the simple fact that Timothy made the trip mentioned in 1 Thess 3:1–2 does not justify assuming he carried 2 Thessalonians on that occasion.

Third, we find the statement in 2 Thess 3:17: "I, Paul, write this greeting in my own hand, which is the distinguishing mark in all my letters. This is how I write." One might argue that it was in his first letter to a particular congregation that Paul would establish his normal procedure and call attention to his signature. However, Paul's other letters, which appear to be the first (or only) to particular locals, do not contain comparable statements regarding his signature. This would seem to imply that the statement in 3:17 was not a matter of routine for first letters but a response to the specific problem of a forged letter received by the Thessalonians (2 Thess 2:2).

---

[18] Jewett, *Thessalonian Correspondence,* 26–30.
[19] See Wanamaker's response to Jewett, *1 and 2 Thessalonians,* 40–44.

Fourth, some argue that the Thessalonians were still undergoing persecution at the time 2 Thessalonians was written (2 Thess 1:4–7; note the present tense), but by the time 1 Thessalonians was sent, the persecutions were over (1 Thess 2:14; note the past tense). The assumption is that the persecutions that began with the founding of the church would have lessened in intensity as time passed. However, Paul's assumption seems to have been that persecution was a regular and recurring event in the life of believers (1 Thess 1:6; 2:14–16; 3:4,7), who could expect perpetual "trouble" from opponents of the truth (2 Thess 1:6–7). A scenario of recurring persecution in Thessalonica, if valid, would make it impossible to determine the sequence of the letters on the basis of the use of past versus present-tense verbs describing persecution.

Fifth, Paul's statement, "We hear that some among you are idle" (2 Thess 3:11), may imply that Paul was addressing a problem new to the church. The apostle treated the problem quite seriously, calling for the church to "keep away" from such people (3:6) and advising them that those who would not work should not be allowed to share in the church's common meals (3:10). On the other hand, the problem of the "idle" is mentioned only briefly in 1 Thess 5:14. Is this because he had already addressed the problem at length in his earlier letter, so that the problem of the idle was no longer so severe? Although this is possible (and would require the priority of 2 Thessalonians), it is also possible that a minor problem mentioned first in 1 Thessalonians escalated and became a major problem that required church discipline by the time 2 Thessalonians was written.

Sixth, both letters refer either to previous instruction or to previous letters received by the congregation. Did Paul "not need to write" the Thessalonians about "times and dates" (1 Thess 5:1) because he had already sent 2 Thess 2:1–12 to them or because he had given them verbal instruction when he was first with them? Does Paul's reference to a letter from him to the Thessalonians (2 Thess 2:15) refer to 1 Thessalonians sent at an earlier date, or does the comment (along with the reference in 2:2) refer to a hypothetical letter? Neither of these questions can be answered with certainty.

Finally, arguments based on the relative maturity of the theology of each epistle are untenable unless far more time passed between the writing of the two letters than most would assume. Though these and other arguments regarding the sequence of the letters have been proposed, none have proven to be so persuasive or unassailable that they have settled the debate. Although it is clear that the priority of 1 Thessalonians has not been disproved, it is also clear that the priority of 2 Thessalonians has much in its favor. As long as this ambiguity remains, the interpreter is wise to avoid leaning heavily on any interpretation that is dependent for its validity on a particular chronological sequence for the letters.

7. The Date of the Thessalonian Correspondence

First Thessalonian is undoubtedly one of the earliest letters we have from the hand of Paul. The broad acceptance of the letter as genuinely Pauline, the content of the letter itself, and the date of Paul's encounter with Gallio in Corinth combine to validate a date for 1 Thessalonians of about A.D. 50 or 51. After evangelizing Macedonia, Paul traveled to Achaia (first to Athens, then to Corinth). While in Athens he sent Timothy to strengthen the Thessalonian congregation. When Timothy returned to Paul, it was most likely after Paul had moved on to Corinth since Paul's stay in Athens does not seem to have been protracted. First Thessalonians was written shortly after Timothy's return.

This chain of events places the composition of the letter within a few months of Paul's encounter with the proconsul Gallio in Corinth. According to an inscription from Delphi, Gallio assumed this proconsulship in June of either A.D. 51 or 52, most likely the former.[20] The latter part of Paul's eighteen months in Corinth probably overlapped the early part of Gallio's proconsulship, giving an approximate date for Paul's Corinthian ministry of spring/summer A.D. 50 to summer/fall A.D. 51.[21] First Thessalonians then would have been written in the late summer of A.D. 50, although a date several months later cannot be ruled out.

The date assigned to 2 Thessalonians depends on one's decisions regarding both its authorship and its relation to 1 Thessalonians. Assuming Pauline authorship and the traditional sequence of the letters,

---

[20] The inscription records a letter from Claudius dated no later than August 1, 52, that mentions the emperor's friend Gallio, who was proconsul of Achaia at the time. The letter implies that Gallio had been in office for some time; and since such offices were assumed in June of each year, Gallio most likely had assumed his proconsulship of Achaia in June of A.D. 51. See D. Gill, "Achaia," in *The Book of Acts in Its First Century Setting*, vol. 2, Graeco-Roman Setting, ed. D. Gill and C. Gempf (Grand Rapids: Eerdmans, 1994), 436–37.

[21] This assumes two things: first, that Paul's opponents would have brought charges against him shortly after a new proconsul arrived on the scene and second, that Paul left Corinth shortly after his encounter with Gallio. See the argument to this effect by C. Hemer, *The Book of Acts in the Setting of Hellenistic History* (Tübingen: Mohr, 1989), 119.

2 Thessalonians would be dated several months after the writing of 1 Thessalonians and toward the end of Paul's Corinthian ministry—late 50 or early 51. If, on the other hand, the priority of 2 Thessalonians is assumed, it is also reasonable to assume that Timothy took it with him when Paul sent him from Athens to Thessalonica (1 Thess 3:1–6). This would result in a date early in A.D. 50.[22]

8. Paul's Use of the Thanksgiving Form

Hellenistic letters commonly began (following the prescript) with a wish for the well-being of the recipient(s).[23] All of Paul's letters (except Galatians, 1 Timothy, and Titus) contain instead a prayer of thanksgiving for the recipients. The form of these Pauline introductory thanksgivings has received considerable attention for many years.[24] The thanksgiving in 1 Thessalonians, however, is unique among Paul's letters in that there are actually three statements of thanks in the first three chapters (1:2–5; 2:13; 3:9–13). The thanksgiving in 1:2–5 is structurally typical of those that begin most Pauline letters. It begins with a form of *eucharistein* ("to give thanks") followed by a series of three participial clauses stating the manner or basis for the thanksgiving. Normally a purpose clause would present the prayer itself for the recipients of the letter. In this first thanksgiving, however, the final clause is missing. The prayer for the readers is not stated until much later (in 3:9–13). Rather than conclude with a final clause, this first thanksgiving flows into a celebration of the way in which the Thessalonians had imitated Paul's faith and in turn had become examples of the faith to others.

The second statement of thanks (2:13) likewise leads to an affirmation of the Thessalonians' faith (2:14). The Thessalonians' life of faith imitated (i.e., was consistent with) that of Paul (1:6), the Lord himself (1:6), and faithful churches elsewhere (2:14), demonstrating its genuineness. "Imitation," as used here, has no negative connotations. It does not imply a false or shallow copy of someone else's genuine faith.

---

[22] For those who reject the Pauline authorship of 2 Thessalonians, the letter is dated much later, normally toward the end of the first century or even the beginning of the second. See the discussion of the authorship of 2 Thessalonians above.

[23] See S. K. Stowers, *Letter Writing in Greco-Roman Antiquity* (Philadelphia: Westminster, 1986).

[24] See P. Schubert, *Form and Function of the Pauline Thanksgiving*, BZNW 20 (Berlin: Töpelmann, 1939), and P. T. O'Brien, *Introductory Thanksgivings in the Letters of Paul*, NovTSup 49 (Leiden: Brill, 1977).

Good news about the church inspired a third expression of thanksgiving (3:9–13). Timothy had visited Thessalonica. On his return to Paul he had reported that in spite of the apostle's absence and in spite of the persecution the church was enduring, the Thessalonians remained true to the gospel (2:17–3:8). The news of the faithfulness of his converts inspired a statement of thanksgiving (v. 9) and the prayer that he and his associates might see the church again and supply what was lacking in their faith (3:10). This lengthy (1:2–3:10) series of three statements of thanksgivings (made lengthy by elaborating the circumstances of and reasons for the thanks) concludes with a benediction. The prayer expressed (3:11–13) takes to the throne of God the prayer concerns stated in 3:10.

The contents of 1 Thessalonians 1–3 may be explained in form-critical terms as the expansion of a thanksgiving by rather lengthy personal digressions.[25] Such an approach, however, tends to minimize the importance of the personal material by labeling it as digressions. Yet these "digressions" comprise the bulk of the first three chapters. It seems unlikely that Paul would devote so much space to reminiscences unless they were integral to accomplishing his purpose(s) for sending the letter. Thus it seems unwise to assume that the body of the letter, and so the discussion of major matters of concern, does not begin until chap. 4. Chapters 1–3 do form a unity. They are not just a disjointed collection of prayers and personal reminiscences.[26] But it is not the study of the thanksgiving form that enables us to see the aim of these chapters. Rather the aim of 1:2–3:13 is best seen through the lens of rhetorical criticism.[27]

9. Paul's Use of Rhetorical Strategies

The basic task of the Hellenistic rhetorician was the production of persuasive oral presentations. Rhetoric was a ubiquitous element in the Hellenistic world. The educated were trained in it. Even for those who were not so educated, the skills of the rhetorician were demonstrated in the speeches heard in a multitude of social situations. Understanding the

---

[25] Ibid.

[26] F. C. Baur, *Paul, the Apostle of Jesus Christ,* 2, 85, cited by F. W. Hughes, "The Rhetoric of 1 Thessalonians," in *The Thessalonian Correspondence,* BETL 87 (Leuven: University Press, 1990), 107, n. 49.

[27] For an introduction to Hellenistic rhetoric and its application to the study of the NT in general, see B. Mack, *Rhetoric and the New Testament* (Minneapolis: Fortress, 1990), and G. Kennedy, *New Testament Interpretation through Rhetorical Criticism* (Chapel Hill: University of North Carolina Press, 1984).

forms and tools a rhetorician used to persuade others allows one to follow the flow of thought and understand the arguments presented. Paul was not, as far as we know, a trained rhetorician. Yet his letters give evidence that he was aware of and utilized these persuasive structures and techniques common in his day.

Several scholars have attempted to analyze Paul's letters according to the categories and characteristics of ancient rhetoric. This of course assumes that Paul used rhetorical strategies if not rhetorical structures. It also assumes that Paul's letters were essentially substitutions for his presence and were thus written versions of what would have been presented orally were it possible. These attempts to discover "the writer's rhetorical strategies, in order to understand better the author's persuasive intent,"[28] have shed considerable light on the argument of the letter. However, the application of rhetorical criticism to 1 Thessalonians has not solved all the interpretive problems the letter presents.

Part of the problem faced by scholars applying rhetorical criticism to 1 Thessalonians is that the social setting of the Pauline letter is not the same as the social setting envisioned for any of the standard forms of rhetorical address discussed in the ancient handbooks of rhetoric. Rhetoricians were trained in judicial rhetoric, which assumed the setting of a court with its need for argument and proofs. They were trained in deliberative rhetoric, which assumed the setting of political debate and the need of a group of people to choose a course of action. They were trained also in epideictic rhetoric, which was designed to assign blame or praise in a variety of social settings. A good rhetor was expected to elaborate on these basic categories and use the strategies taught under the rubric of standard categories to address a variety of social situations. But none of the handbooks or extant examples of secular Hellenistic rhetoric assume a setting that mixes the form of a letter, the concerns of a pastor, the pronouncements of an apostle, and the passing on of authoritative religious tradition.

There is little agreement about which basic type of rhetorical discourse 1 Thessalonians represents.[29] The argument of 1 Thessalonians

---

[28] Hughes, "The Rhetoric of 1 Thessalonians," 94.

[29] For an introduction to the theory and techniques of Greco-Roman rhetoric see Mack, *Rhetoric and the New Testament*, 31–48, and its bibliography on pp. 103–10. See also G. Kennedy, *New Testament Interpretation through Rhetorical Criticism*; R. Jewett, *The Thessalonian Correspondence: Pauline Rhetoric and Millenarian Piety* (Philadelphia: Fortress, 1986); Wanamaker, *1 and 2 Thessalonians;* Hughes, "The Rhetoric of 1 Thessalonians."

does not follow precisely any of the standard rhetorical *structures* studied to date. Yet standard rhetorical *strategies* are evident in the letter.

Apparently the same Pauline creativity evident in his adaptation of the letter forms (his unique use of address, wish for well-being, etc.) was at work in his use of rhetorical strategies to meet his own needs and purposes. If this is so, then one should not expect to find complete rhetorical structures in Paul's letters because the needs of his letters dominated his use of rhetoric, just as they dominated his use of conventional letter forms. What can enlighten our understanding of the apostle's arguments, however, is the recognition of the rhetorical strategies Paul used to address the immediate needs of a congregation.

10. The Theology of the Thessalonian Letters

Letters express the theology of their authors but do so in a manner appropriate to the genre. Thus the letters to the Thessalonians present us with half of a conversation (Paul's half) excised from the middle of an ongoing dialogue. For the most part, the experiences and conversations that were part of the relationship between Paul and the Thessalonians before these letters were written are unknown to us. Yet these are the very things that shaped the letters. What is contained in them was written because of Paul's sense of the Thessalonians' needs (e.g., see 2 Thess 3:11), not to produce a balanced and nuanced expression of Christian theology. Left unstated in the letters are matters about which the Thessalonian church was already well informed (e.g., see 1 Thess 4:9–10; 5:1–2) or matters regarding which they had no urgent need at the moment.

Centuries later we who eavesdrop on this pastoral conversation struggle to understand it. Largely we struggle because we are not privy to the experiences and knowledge that Paul and the Thessalonians assumed as common knowledge. This struggle is perhaps most evident when scholars attempt to reconstruct the theology of a particular letter because an author's theology is typically bigger than his letters. Letters express teachings that are the outcroppings of theology but which rarely are intended to be complete expressions of the author's thought. A reconstruction of Pauline thought underlying, unifying, and giving balance to the specific teachings of the Thessalonian correspondence is a task that must be left to writers of Pauline theology. The following summary should be understood merely as a survey of teachings—the outcroppings of Pauline theology evident in these particular letters.

(1) Persecution and Peace

The Acts account and both letters are unified on this score: the gospel that brought salvation had also resulted in persecution of the believers. The opponents of the gospel were angry enough and persistent enough to follow the evangelists and drive them (at least their leader, Paul) not just out of the city of Thessalonica but entirely out of the province of Macedonia (Acts 17:10–15). The opponents were willing to lie about the teachings and the goals of the church (claiming it was a subversive group) in order to discredit it. They would use the legal system if they could but were not above instigating mob action if it was required to accomplish their ends (17:5–9). Paul recognized the severity of the persecution and the genuine threat it posed to the work of the gospel in Thessalonica (1 Thess 3:5).

The Thessalonian epistles were designed in large part to address this problem of persecution[30] and bring peace to the Thessalonian believers.[31] Both 1 and 2 Thessalonians begin and end with a concern for peace (1 Thess 1:1; 5:23; 2 Thess 1:2; 3:16). Peace with unbelievers is desirable, and Paul encouraged behavior that would "win the respect of outsiders" (1 Thess 4:12). But the absence of conflict is not always attainable. In fact, Paul warned the church that persecution by evil and faithless persons was inevitable (1 Thess 3:3; 2 Thess 3:2). If believers were to have peace, it must somehow be found even while experiencing persecution and suffering. It was this kind of peace that Paul sought to bring to the Thessalonians. He did so by placing their suffering in context.

Those who suffer have an understandable tendency to focus on the experience of suffering. It can become their whole world, and a genu-

---

[30] K. Donfried asserts that we should understand 1 Thessalonians "not primarily as a 'paraenetic' letter but as a 'paracletic' letter, as a consolatio" designed to console and encourage the church to persevere in spite of continued persecution ("The Theology of 1 Thessalonians as a Reflection of Its Purpose," in *To Touch the Text*, ed. M. Horgan and P. Kobelski [New York: Crossroad, 1989], 243–44). See also J. Pobee, *Persecution and Martyrdom in the Theology of Paul*, *JSNT* 6 (Sheffield: JSOT, 1985), for a broader discussion of the Pauline writings that also sees 1 Thessalonians as addressed to a church experiencing persecution.

[31] Cf. the emphasis on peace in the letters by J. Bassler, "Peace in All Ways," in *Pauline Theology, Vol. I, Thessalonians, Philippians, Galatians, Philemon*, ed. J. Bassler (Minneapolis: Fortress, 1991), 71–85. In the same volume see also "Part II: The Theology of the Thessalonian Correspondence," which provides several other perspectives on the theology of the letters.

inely bleak world it is. Paul did not attempt to diminish the severity of the Thessalonians' persecution. Rather, he sought to broaden their vision. (1) He reminded them to look back to the beginning of their Christian experience and remember that they suffered for the kingdom of God, not needlessly (1 Thess 1:5; 5:9–10; 2 Thess 1:5,11; 2:13–14). (2) He reminded them that their suffering was evidence of the genuineness of their faith and a reflection of their true imitation of God's apostles and of the Lord himself, so that they in turn became models of faith for others (1 Thess 1:6–7; 2 Thess 1:4). (3) He reminded them to look beyond the evil of the moment toward the ultimate end of the travails and to the glory and rest God reserved for his people (1 Thess 1:3,10; 3:13; 2 Thess 1:7,10). (4) He reminded them that they were not alone in their suffering. He, his coworkers, indeed the entire Judean church suffered as well (1 Thess 2:2,14; 3:7). (5) Neither did they persevere in their own strength alone but were constantly supported by the apostles and indeed by the power of God himself (1 Thess 1:6; 2:17; 3:1–3,10,11–13; 5:23–24; 2 Thess 1:11; 2:16–17; 3:3). (6) Finally, he assured them that the evil ones who were inflicting this suffering would suffer a just punishment (1 Thess 1:10; 2:16b; 2 Thess 1:6–9).

Knowledge of such truths does not make suffering disappear, nor does it mean that suffering is good or should be sought. But suffering is tolerable when it has purpose, when something of value is gained by it, and when those who inflict it do not do so with impunity. A sufferer gains comfort in the comradeship of shared suffering and can give thanks in all circumstances given the knowledge that the suffering will eventually give way to victory and reward. Peace is the result, an enduring and genuine sense of well-being even in the midst of distress.

(2) Eschatology and Endurance

The Thessalonian correspondence has much to say about eschatology. Several major passages in the letters (1 Thess 4:13–18; 5:1–11; 2 Thess 2:1–12) along with several briefer references (1 Thess 1:10; 2:19–20; 3:5,13; 2 Thess 1:6–10; 2:14) address various aspects of the end times. The details of these passages will be dealt with in the body of the commentary, but several preliminary observations may be made at this point.

First, and most importantly, the eschatological material presented was intended to serve a pastoral purpose. Paul's concern to comfort grieving believers produced 1 Thess 4:13–18. First Thessalonians 5:1–

11 reminded readers that those who know the Lord is coming must persist in faithful, godly living. The suffering of the church called forth the assurance that those who were persecuting them would suffer a just punishment (2 Thess 1:6–10). The intrusion of false teaching into the church required the apostle to remind the church of apostolic teachings already received and urge them not to listen to deceptive lies (2 Thess 2:1–15). None of these passages were presented as new information for the church. The larger system of teachings regarding eschatology of which they were a part apparently was provided to the church earlier (perhaps verbally), thus the writings do not provide complete systems of thought.

Second, we should not allow frustration with the truncated nature of the teachings to blind us to the positive purposes eschatological truths served in the first century and can serve still today. The parousia will be a day of joyous reunion. It will be a glorious day of participation in the glory of Christ. The day of the Lord promises that evil will receive its just punishment. The reminder that judgment inevitably comes to all serves as a reminder that believers must do all they can for themselves and for others to be prepared for that day. Such emphases as these dominate the presentation of eschatology in Thessalonians (as well as in the NT in general). Their usefulness for teaching the church requires no great precision regarding date or sequence of events. The fact of the events alone is sufficient to encourage believers to persevere in evangelism and godly behavior.

Third, it is impossible to be certain which letter was written first, and as a result we should not assume Paul presented the eschatological material in the letters in some particular sequence. Attempts to discern development in Paul's thought regarding the parousia are inevitably based on a presumed sequence of letters and so rest on a weak foundation. Even if the priority of one letter were proven, we should still presume that Paul gave the Thessalonians instruction regarding the end times when he was with them.[32] If this is so, then both letters presume a foundation of teachings delivered before either letter was composed.

Finally, many unresolved questions remain and undoubtedly will continue to be debated due to either a lack of information in the biblical text or to some ambiguity in the text.

1. Did Paul expect the parousia in his lifetime? Although many

---

[32] Heb 6:1–3 includes "instruction about … the resurrection of the dead and eternal judgment" among its list of "elementary teachings."

scholars answer with a confident yes, others argue that Paul hoped, but did not assert, that he would see the coming of the Lord. Witherington, for instance, ably defends the proposition that it is Paul's "beliefs about the certainty and the character of the end of human history, not some belief about its timing," that best explains his letters.[33]

2. How does the "rapture" relate to the "day of the Lord," and how does the tribulation relate to both of these events? The Thessalonian epistles refer to several particular eschatological events (e.g., parousia, day of the Lord, the taking up of the church to meet the Lord in the air, the appearance, and then judgment of the lawless one). For the most part, however, each one is treated independently, not woven into a larger chronologically ordered sequence of end-time events. We may assume some such sequence of events existed in the apostle's mind, but no elaboration of it exists in his letters, and all attempts to reconstruct it must include a fair amount of speculation.[34]

3. Who is the "man of lawlessness," who or what is the restrainer/restraining force, and to what does the "apostasy" refer? The commentary that follows illustrates the wide range of answers possible for each of these questions. The very existence of such diverse answers from acknowledged scholars is testimony to the difficulty and ambiguity of the passages that touch on these matters. If these texts are to have meaning for the church, then the meanings found must be such that they are not invalidated by the evident ambiguities of the text.

4. How do Paul's teachings mesh with those anticipating a "millennium"? The absence of the term in Paul's writings does not signify the rejection of it but reflects the apostle's point of focus. Eschatology in Paul's writings appears not as a subject for speculation but as a spur for Christian faithfulness. It provides believers with assurance of life eternal, encourages Christian deeds, and demands perseverance. In short he focused primarily on the manner of life of the believer leading up to the day of the Lord and expressed himself apart from any particular millennial scheme. As a result, understanding Paul's eschatological passages in context does not require establishing a firm millennial position.

---

[33] B. Witherington, *Jesus, Paul and the End of the World* (Downers Grove: InterVarsity, 1992), 10.

[34] For an excellent overview of recent developments in eschatology see the spring issue of *SWJT* 36 (1994) as well as two volumes by two contributors to that issue: S. Grevy, *The Millennium Maze: Sorting out Evangelical Options* (Downers Grove: InterVarsity, 1992), and C. Blaising and D. Bock, eds., *Dispensationalism, Israel and the Church—The Search for Definition* (Grand Rapids: Zondervan, 1992).

(3) Election and Faith

The certainty of the Thessalonians' future was dependent on the certainty of their relationship to God. It is not surprising then that the letters repeatedly assured the believers that (1) God had chosen them, (2) evidence of the genuineness of their relationship with God abounded, and (3) their perseverance and God's faithfulness guaranteed a sure future for them as participants in his kingdom.

From the outset of the Thessalonian letters Paul reminded believers that they were the "called out" *(ekklēsia)*.[35] This common word for various kinds of assemblies (political and religious) is given special character by its modifiers. Believers were those in their communities called out "in God the Father and the Lord Jesus Christ" (1 Thess 1:1; cf. 2 Thess 1:1). They were "chosen" *(eklogēn)* by God (1 Thess 1:4), and Paul urged them to live in a manner "worthy of God, who calls *[kalountos]* you into his kingdom and glory" (2:12; cf. 4:7). For God had "appointed" *(etheto)* them to receive salvation, not wrath (5:9), at the day of the Lord. And they could be sure of their future because the God who "calls" *(kalōn)* them for his own "is faithful" (5:24). The second letter contains the same emphases. Though the lawless one will deceive many, Paul expressed confidence regarding the Thessalonian believers. He assured: "From the beginning God chose *[heilato]* you to be saved. … He called *[ekalesen]* you to this through our gospel, that you might share in the glory of our Lord Jesus Christ" (2 Thess 2:13–14; cf. 1:11).

The *kaleō* word group dominates in the previous references and indicates a divine choice or selection *(eklog)* leading to the issuing of a divine call *(kaleō)* expressed in the form of the "gospel" proclaimed by Paul and his coworkers (2 Thess 2:14). A threefold stress results. First, the chosenness of the people conveys a sense of their great worth in the eyes of God (and contrasts with the world's rejection and persecution of them). It provided an uplifting affirmation. Second, the faithfulness of the God who selected and called them conveys a sense of security. Whatever opposition they might face, whatever temporal setbacks the church might suffer, they knew their sure victory because they knew God had chosen them for his own. Third, it served as the basis of Paul's ethical injunctions. God's people must live godly lives. Persons called

---

[35] This is, of course, true of all Paul's letters to Christian assemblies, but the fact that ἐκκλησία is the common term for the assembly of believers should not diminish the theological import of the term.

into God's kingdom are obligated to live not only anticipating their future residence in the kingdom but also live as those who are already citizens governed by the norms of that kingdom. The behavior required of believers is twice described as "God's will" (4:3; 5:18). Ethical commands are given not on the basis of Paul's personal authority but "by the authority of the Lord Jesus Christ" (1 Thess 4:2; cf. 5:27; 2 Thess 3:6). The apostles strove "not to please men but God" and recognized also that not only actions but also motivations were subject to scrutiny, for Paul reminded the Thessalonians that God "tests our hearts" (1 Thess 1:4). For the genuine child of God ethical behavior is not an option in these letters but a natural and necessary extension of each believer's relationship with the Father and Son. God's calling is a calling to a "sanctified" life (1 Thess 4:3–8).

Along with the divine initiative Paul also recognized the importance of the human response. Paul was well aware (1) that the gospel he proclaimed could encounter rejection rather than faith and (2) that those who reject the gospel are thereby responsible for their own condemnation. He thanked God that the Thessalonian believers accepted the message of the apostles as "the word of God" rather than reject it as merely "the word of men" (1 Thess 2:13). They chose to turn from idols and serve the "living and true God" (1:9), and the genuineness of their commitment was seen in their imitation of the apostles and of the Lord. It was seen as well in the fact of their perseverance in spite of suffering (1:3,6; 2:14; 2 Thess 1:4–5). Others might reject the truth and prefer to "believe the lie" (2 Thess 2:11), but such was not true of the faithful who were saved "through belief in the truth" (2 Thess 2:13). The fact that Paul worried about the church's perseverance (1 Thess 3:5), felt it necessary to urge continued obedience (1 Thess 4:1,10; 2 Thess 3:4,13), and urged the church to discipline any members persisting in flagrantly sinful behavior (2 Thess 3:6,14–15) recognizes the persistent reality of the individual Christian's volition.

The fact of divine election and the real impact of each individual's volition are equally evident in the Thessalonian correspondence. The two concepts, God's sovereignty and human freedom, seem logically inconsistent, and the relationship between the two have been debated for centuries. The content of the Thessalonian correspondence is only a small part of the scriptural evidence cited in this larger debate. It must suffice here, however, to point out that our letters do not present either divine choice or human volition in a manner that allows one to diminish the other. No attempt is made to reconcile them logically. In fact, both truths are presumed without so much as a hint that the author even acknowledged any incompatibility between them. For a modern interpreter to treat them any differently would be inconsistent with the testimony of the letters.

OUTLINE OF THE BOOKS

1 THESSALONIANS

    I. Prescript (1:1)
        1. Authors and Addressees (1:1a)
        2. Greeting (1:1b)
    II. Thanksgiving and Hope (1:2–3:13)
        1. Introduction (1:2–10)
        2. Apostolic Character while in Thessalonica Rehearsed (2:1–12)
        3. Thanksgiving for Perseverance in the Gospel (2:13–16)
        4. Apostolic Activities after Leaving Thessalonica Rehearsed (2:17–3:8)
        5. Thanksgiving and Intercessory Prayer (3:9–13)
    III. Ethical Exhortations (4:1–5:22)
        1. Introductory Call to Obedience (4:1–2)
        2. Exhortations Regarding Sanctification (4:3–8)
        3. Exhortations Regarding Brotherly Love (4:9–12)
        4. Exhortations Regarding the Dead (4:13–18)
        5. Exhortations Regarding Times and Seasons (5:1–11)
        6. Exhortations Regarding Life in the Fellowship (5:12–22)
    IV. Benediction and Conclusion (5:23–28)
        1. Benediction (5:23–24)
        2. Concluding Exhortations (5:25–27)
        3. Epistolary Conclusion (5:28)

2 THESSALONIANS

    V. Prescript (1:1–2)
        1. Recipients (1:1)

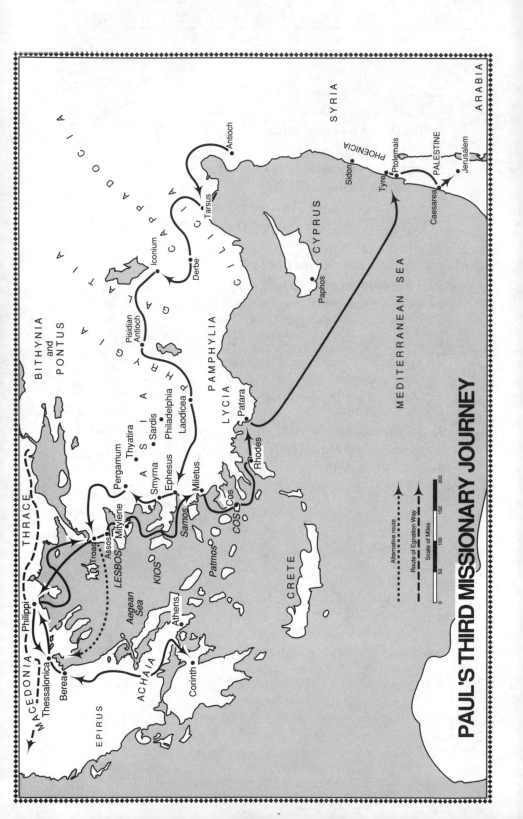

PAUL'S THIRD MISSIONARY JOURNEY

I. PRESCRIPT (1:1)
   1. Authors and Addressees (1:1a)
   2. Greeting (1:1b)

I. PRESCRIPT (1:1)

1. Authors and Addressees (1:1a)

[1]Paul, Silas and Timothy,

To the church of the Thessalonians in God the Father and the Lord Jesus Christ:

The prescript of 1 Thessalonians follows the commonly used pattern for introductions in Hellenistic letters: the sender and the recipient are identified, and a brief greeting is expressed. Any author was free to elaborate on each of these items as he or she deemed necessary, but in personal correspondence such additions were generally brief. The prescript would often lead into a wish for the health or prosperity of the recipient(s) of the letter.[1] Although the form of the prescript of 1 Thessalonians is conventional, the content of the elaborations on the form is distinctly Christian.

First and Second Thessalonians are the only two of his letters in which Paul did not add some elaboration to his name and/or to the names of his cosenders. In other letters such additions remind the recipients of Paul's apostolic status and responsibilities (cf. esp. Galatians). The absence of such additions in the Thessalonian correspondence may imply that his relationship with the Thessalonians was stable, and as a result he felt no need to stress his apostolic status. First Thessalonians is predominantly a letter of affirmation and encouragement. Although Paul seems to have found it necessary to defend himself against unidentified

---

[1] See S. K. Stowers, *Letter Writing in Greco-Roman Antiquity* (Philadelphia: Westminster, 1986), and J. L. White, *The Form and Function of the Body of the Greek Letter,* SBLDS 2 (Missoula, Mont.: Scholars Press, 1972), for more detail and for numerous examples of the Hellenistic letter.

critics in Thessalonica, the criticism does not appear to have involved a challenge to his status as an apostle so much as a criticism of his behavior (2:1–12). On the other hand, 2 Thessalonians commands the church regarding the disciplining of the idle (3:6–15), and so apostolic authority is exercised; yet the address is virtually the same as is found in 1 Thessalonians. Since 1, 2 Thessalonians are among the earliest of his extant letters, Paul simply may not yet have developed the practice of emphasizing his status as a part of the letter address.

The letter identifies three coauthors: Paul, Silas, and Timothy. Joint authorship is reflected also in the predominant use of the first-person plural "we" throughout the letter. That Paul was the leading character of the three is implied by his ability to dispatch Timothy as his emissary (3:2). Also on the few occasions when the first-person singular "I" is used in the letter it is used by Paul to refer to himself (2:18; 3:5; esp. 5:27). And in a comparable situation in 2 Thessalonians, where the same three men are identified as coauthors in the address, Paul claimed the letter as his in the conclusion without any mention of Silas or Timothy (2 Thess 3:17). The exact nature of the relationship between Paul and his various coworkers is difficult to determine. In Acts and the letters bearing Paul's name about "100 names, often coupled with a score of assorted titles, are associated with the Apostle."[2]

"Silas" (the name consistently used in Acts) is a variant of the longer "Silvanus" (the name used in the rest of the NT, including the Greek text here).[3] This Silvanus likely was the same person as the Silas mentioned in Acts who was a trusted leader of the church in Jerusalem (Acts 15:22,27). He, along with Judas (also called Barsabbas), carried a letter to the Gentile church in Antioch from the Jerusalem church. Both men also were prophets, and they ministered to the church at Antioch (15:32,34).[4] Paul later chose the same man as his companion on the sec-

---

[2] E. E. Ellis, "Paul and His Co-Workers," *NTS* 17 (1970–71): 437. Ellis includes in his article a list of the thirty-six personal names and nine titles that are most suggestive for understanding the apostle's circle of coworkers.

[3] Silvanus (Σιλουανός) may be the Latinized form of the Greek name Silas (Σιλᾶς). Considering that the first mention of the man places him in Jerusalem as a representative of the Jewish Christian church, both names may well have been derived from a Semitic original. See BAGD, s.v. "Σιλουανός" and "Σιλᾶς."

[4] V. 34 contains a variant reading explaining that Silas decided to stay in Antioch. The variant is a scribal addition inserted to explain Silas's presence in Antioch later in the narrative (15:40). See B. Metzger, *A Textual Commentary on the Greek New Testament* (New York: UBS, 1971), 439.

ond missionary journey (Acts 15:40). The need to select a missionary companion other than Barnabas resulted from the disagreement between Paul and Barnabas over John Mark. The choice of Silas to fill this role probably was motivated both by his gifts (Acts 15:32) and by the esteem in which he was held by the Jerusalem church. His participation in the Gentile mission might well have given the mission credibility in Jewish circles, where Paul was considered theologically suspect. The narrative of the mission to Greece presents Silas as an equal to Paul but Paul as the main spokesman of the team (Acts 16:19,25,29; 17:4,10,14–15; 18:5). In addition to these references in Acts, Paul named Silvanus in 1 Thess 1:1; 2 Thess 1:1; and 2 Cor 1:19 as a coworker in the mission in Greece.[5]

Timothy is a prominent character both in Acts and in the Pauline corpus. He was a resident of Lystra and a member of the church there of whom the believers "spoke well." As the son of a Jewish-Christian mother and a Greek father (probably a non-Christian), he had not been circumcised (Acts 16:1–3). After being recruited and circumcised by Paul, Timothy remained an associate of the apostle during his evangelization of Greece (Acts 17:14–15; 18:5) and his ministry in Ephesus (Acts 19:22; 20:4). He is named in six Pauline letters as a coworker (1 Corinthians; Philippians; Colossians; 1 Thessalonians; 2 Thessalonians; Philemon). Several times he served as a special emissary from the apostle (1 Cor 4:17; 16:10; Phil 2:19; 1 Thess 3:2,6).[6] In the several letters where he is mentioned, Timothy is accorded the respect of a faithful fellow worker in the gospel and at the same time lauded as a beloved son in the faith to Paul (Rom 16:21; 1 Cor 4:17; Phil 1:1; 2:19 23). He also is the named recipient of two letters.[7]

The letter is addressed to the church *(ekklēsia)*. *Ekklēsia* was not a distinctively Christian word. It means "assembly" and was used of a variety of assemblies in the first-century world—social, political, or religious. Acts 19:32,39, for instance, identifies as an *ekklēsia* the gathering of citizens in Ephesus to protest the work of Paul and the church.

---

[5] Also see B. N. Kaye, "Acts' Portrait of Silas," *NovT* 21 (1980): 13–26.

[6] See R. W. Funk, "The Apostolic Parousia: Form and Significance," in *Christian History and Interpretation: Studies Presented to John Knox*, ed. W. R. Farmer et al. (Cambridge: University Press, 1967), 249–68, for a discussion of the tasks and authority that characterized such apostolic emissaries.

[7] See T. D. Lea and H. P. Griffin, Jr., *1, 2 Timothy, Titus* (Nashville: Broadman, 1993), 19–53, for a general introduction to matters related to the authorship and the recipient(s) of 1, 2 Timothy.

Ekklēsia is also a synonym for "synagogue" *(synagōgē)* and was occasionally used of Jewish assemblies in the Septuagint. The early Christian assemblies could have described themselves as *ekklēsiai* to distinguish their Christian assemblies from the Jewish *synagōgai*. It seems more likely, however, that *ekklēsia* was chosen as a word that was both understandable to the Gentile population and at the same time general enough so as not to prejudice the uninformed hearer regarding the character of the assembly.[8] In other words, it was not so much separation from the synagogue as access to the Gentile world that made the term *ekklēsia* useful as a self-designation. Considering the degree of anti-Semitism in the first century Greco-Roman world, it would have been much easier for an inquirer to attend an *ekklēsia* than a *synagōgē*.

In this regard as in many others the early church sets the modern an excellent example. Form must serve function. Whether it is in the choosing of a name, the selection of a schedule, or the setting up of an organizational structure, a concern for the church's mission must be the priority that drives the process.

The particular assembly to which 1 Thessalonians is addressed was specified using three qualifying phrases that are both ascriptive and restrictive. The phrases distinguish this assembly from the others that would exist in Thessalonica and also remind the assembly that its very existence is an expression of their relationship to the Father and the Christ. It was an assembly "of the Thessalonians." This is the broadest of the three delimiters and identifies the members of the church as residents of one of the most prominent cities of Macedonia.[9]

Second, it was an assembly "in God the Father." Thessalonica contained numerous secular *ekklēsiai* as well as various religious groups that could have used the same designation. This phrase identified the recipients as a religious community committed to the God both Jews and Christians serve.[10] "Father" is the first designation descriptive of God in the letter. It connotes both authority and benevolent concern.

Third, the recipients were assembled "in ... the Lord Jesus Christ."

---

[8] For a more detailed discussion see K. L. Schmidt, *TDNT,* s.v. "*kaleō ... ekklēsia.*"

[9] For discussion of the city of Thessalonica see the Introduction, "Thessalonica—A Prominent City of Macedonia" on p. 21.

[10] For discussion of the phrase ἐν θεῷ πατρὶ, "in God the Father," which is unique to the Thessalonian correspondence, see E. Best, *A Commentary on the First and Second Epistles to the Thessalonians* (London: A. & C. Black, 1977), 62–62, and J. E. Frame, *A Critical and Exegetical Commentary on the Epistles of St. Paul to the Thessalonians* (Edinburgh: T & T Clark, 1960), 69–71.

This assembly acknowledged Jesus as Messiah (Christ) and as master (Lord). Such an address does more than direct the letter to its intended recipients; it reminds the recipients who they are. From these core distinctives radiate a multitude of other characteristics that both make the church what it is and distinguish it from its social context. In the letter that follows, Paul instructed the believers regarding their identity, their place among the brethren, and the way in which they should interact with one another. Such self-definition is vitally important for any faith community. The assembly in Thessalonica functioned partly to help believers define the role the church played in the larger society and their place in the present world and in the world to come. Now as then, in ways as simple as a form of address or as complex as a lengthy theological discourse, the church must help its members understand who they are, how they are like and unlike the non-Christian world, and the hope they have for the world to come.

2. Greeting (1:1b)

Grace and peace to you.

1:1b Some modern translations note that in the address a few early manuscripts add the pronoun "our" and read "God our father" (adding *hēmōn* after *patri*). The greeting "grace and peace to you" was also expanded by several scribes who added to the end of the verse "from God the Father and the Lord Jesus Christ." It is highly improbable that Paul wrote these words. A limited number of manuscripts contain the additions, and the changes lengthen the text, bringing the prescript of 1 Thessalonians into harmony with 2 Thess 1:1. Both adding pious material and harmonizing are well-documented scribal tendencies.[11]

In a play on words that produces a uniquely Pauline and distinctively Christian construction, the Greek salutation *(chairein)* "be glad" or "greeting" (which was stylized at the beginning of Hellenistic letters and had as little content in the first century as "Dear ..." has for writers today) was replaced by *(charis)* "grace." The Jewish greeting *(shalom)*

---

[11] Metzger observes accurately that "if any one of these expansions had been original, there is no reason why it would have been deleted" (*Textual Commentary,* 629). See K. Aland and B. Aland, *The Text of the New Testament* (Grand Rapids: Eerdmans, 1989), and Metzger, *The Text of the New Testament* (New York: Oxford, 1968), for discussion of scribal tendencies and the praxis of textual criticism in general.

"peace" is added in Greek *(eirēnē)*. The combined effect turns a perfunctory "hello" into a theologically meaningful salutation. "Grace" would remind the reader of the goodness of a God who gives blessings even to those who are undeserving and particularly of the preeminent work of undeserved benevolence—the giving of his Son.[12] "Peace" reflects the Hebrew wish for wellness and wholeness and ties the grace of the Christ to the foundation of the God of the Jews, the one true God.[13]

---

[12] See H. Conzelmann, "χαίρω," *TDNT* (which contains also a discussion of the Heb. equivalents of *charis* by W. Zimmerli); C. L. Mitton, "Grace," *IDB,* and Holladay, "Grace in the Old Testament."

[13] See W. Foerster, "Εἰρήνη," *TDNT.* Included in this article is a brief treatment of shalom by G. von Rad.

II. THANKSGIVING AND HOPE (1:2–3:13)

1. Introduction (1:2–10)

The first several verses of the letter introduce the topics with which the letter will deal (especially the first three chapters) and establish rapport with the readers. Rhetoricians referred to this stage of a communication as the *exordium*. Expressed in letter format, it contains the thanksgiving typical of Pauline letters and is equivalent to the wish for the well-being found at the beginning of Hellenistic letters. Here as in other letters the Pauline prayer of thanks is more involved than the expression of best wishes common at the beginning of the typical personal letter of Paul's day. The thanksgiving (vv. 2–5) is blended with an affirmation (vv. 6–10) of the church. Both together praise past actions of the Thessalonians with the intent (as becomes clear later in the letter) of encouraging the continuation and expansion of praiseworthy Christian deeds and character.

(1) The Thanksgiving (1:2–5)

²We always thank God for all of you, mentioning you in our prayers. ³We continually remember before our God and Father your work produced by faith, your labor prompted by love, and your endurance inspired by hope in our Lord Jesus Christ.

⁴For we know, brothers loved by God, that he has chosen you, ⁵because our gospel came to you not simply with words, but also with power, with the Holy Spirit and with deep conviction. You know how we lived among you for your sake.

The thanksgiving in 1:2–5 operates on several levels. First, it expresses a genuine appreciation for the faithfulness of the Thessalonian Christians. This is no expression of the kind of flattery or insincerity Paul renounced in other passages (2:3–6; Gal 1:10) as "man-pleasing." Honesty and "God-pleasing" should characterize Christian communication. Renouncing empty flattery and sly manipulation does not, however, rule out honest affirmation or the attempt to influence others through genuine praise in the hopes that their praiseworthy actions will continue and grow.

Second, the thanksgiving is a way of establishing rapport with the readers. By affirming them, Paul solidified his good relationship with them at the outset of the letter in the interest of securing a sympathetic hearing. Such a strategy is consistent with the rhetorical wisdom of the day, which advised the speaker to secure the *pathos* (goodwill) of his hearers. A good hearing requires the goodwill of the audience.

Third, the thanksgiving praises several points of Christian character that subsequently are encouraged and elaborated upon in the body of the letter. Christian labors (3:6,12; 4:9; 5:12), persistent anticipation of the return of the Lord (1:10; 5:1,8–11), a genuine faith proven in persecution (2:14; 3:4–6), the imitation of the apostle of the Lord (1:6; 2:9–11), and the example or witness believers provide to others (1:7–10; 5:14) are all lauded. By mentioning these as a part of the thanksgiving, Paul brought to his readers' attention matters he would write about further. In this way the thanksgiving foreshadows the discussions to come.

1:2 All but one of Paul's letters begin with thanksgiving. The one exception (Galatians) begins with a reprimand of wavering Christians and a curse upon those who seek to pervert the true gospel. Galatians 1:6–9 demonstrates that the apostle was quite capable of forgoing the expression of thanks if it were not genuinely felt or appropriate.

The writers' prayer of thanks for the Thessalonian believers was not just a momentary event. Verse 2 stresses the continuity of concern and the constancy of the prayers offered up by the apostolic band on behalf of their churches. Paul took seriously the efficacy of prayer as is evidenced by his requests for prayer for himself and for his apostolic mission (2 Thess 3:1–3a). The verb tense used implies a recurring thanksgiving as do the modifiers "always" and "continually." "Continually" may be taken with v. 3 as in the NIV or with v. 2 and translated "continually mentioning you" (RSV).[1]

The main statement, "We always thank God," is elaborated upon with the use of three participial clauses: "mentioning ..." (v. 2b), "we continually remember ..." (v. 3), and "for we know ..." (vv. 4–5). This structure is obscured somewhat because it is difficult to translate the three clauses in a parallel fashion. The first participle (in v. 2b) expresses the mode or manner in which the thanks occurs. While engaged in "our prayers," the apostle remembered and expressed thanks. Of the several words for prayer in the New Testament the one in v. 2 *(proseuchōn)* is perhaps the most generic. If it is used with any nuance, it refers to prayer expressing worshipful praise (in contrast to, for instance, a prayer of petition or intercession). In this context of worshipful prayer Paul recalled the works of faith done by those whom God has chosen and empowered through his Spirit. Worship is enriched by the celebration of God's work in the lives of his children.

1:3 Paul gave thanks because (or "when"; the participle may be temporal or causal) he recalled the work, labor, and endurance demonstrated by the Thessalonians. Faith, love, and hope are not the focal points in this verse, though Paul frequently cited them as prime Christian virtues (cf. 5:8; 1 Cor 13:13; Col 1:5).[2] As subjective genitives

---

[1] L. Morris, *The First and Second Epistles to the Thessalonians,* NICNT [rev.] (Grand Rapids: Eerdmans, 1991), 39, and E. Best, *A Commentary on the First and Second Epistles to the Thessalonians* (London: A. & C. Black,1977), 66 take "continually" with "mentioning" (v. 2); J. E. Frame (*A Critical and Exegetical Commentary on the Epistles of St. Paul to the Thessalonians* [Edinburgh: T & T Clark, 1960], 75) and Wanamaker (*1 and 2 Thessalonians,* 74) argue that it is better taken with v. 3. Best's observation that "there is nothing in Pauline usage to determine" whether the adverb should go with what precedes or with what follows is accurate and should be kept in mind whichever option one chooses; and as I. H. Marshall observes, the decision does not significantly affect the sense of the verse "since the two activities are simultaneous" (*1 and 2 Thessalonians,* NCB [Grand Rapids: Eerdmans, 1983], 51).

[2] Best confuses the situation with his statement that "each of the triad (faith, hope, and love) is qualified by a word that suggests activity" (*1 and 2 Thessalonians,* 67) since it is the triad of virtues that qualifies the "work," "labor," and "endurance," not the opposite.

"faith," "hope," and "love" in this sentence identify that which motivates and produces Christian actions. But the actions themselves are what is stressed. Paul remembered the "work," "labor," and "endurance" of those who were in the church. Visible Christian deeds and perseverance in spite of difficulty give witness to a genuine and enduring faith. Thus Paul gave thanks for a faith that was shown to be real by the evidence visible in the lives of the believers.

"Work" and "labor" are synonyms. The latter *(kopou)*, however, is a slightly more intense word indicating strenuous work in contexts where a contrast with the former *(ergou)* is implied. This verse presents no conflict with Paul's rejection of the works of the law as a basis of salvation (Gal 3–4). The "work of faith" lauded here is the Christian life, the deeds that result from the indwelling Spirit (Gal 5:16–26; cf. Eph 2:10). These are not prerequisites of salvation but the results of salvation in the lives of those transformed by Christ (1 Cor 6:1–4; 12:1–2). Exactly which works and labors Paul had in mind is not stated at this point in the letter.

Paul also thanked God for the "endurance" *(hypomonē)* of the Thessalonians. *Hypomonē* is often used of a church's persistence in the faith in spite of persecutions (e.g., Rom 12:12; Heb 10:32; 1 Pet 2:20), and that is evidently what Paul had in mind here (cf. 1 Thess 1:6; 2:14). Believers are able to endure because of the hope they have in the Lord. "Hope" does not express a baseless wish but a confident expectation of the Lord's future work. That Christians live expectantly (in hope) is evidence of the genuineness of their commitment to and confidence in the Lord. It is this proof of a genuine faith that Paul was celebrating in his thanksgiving. When in our churches' faith and love are evidenced in word and deed, when hope enables endurance, our leaders have cause for joyful thanksgiving and an obligation to affirm the fellowship.

"Before our God and Father" is used by the NIV to describe Paul's position in prayer.[3] Wanamaker has argued that the same phrase used in 3:9 of prayer before God refers back to 1:3 and implies that the phrase relates to the participle "remembering."[4] But an inference drawn from a passage over two chapters' distant is less persuasive than the structure of Paul's sentence in 1:3. The phrase "before our God and Father" occurs at the end of the verse in the Greek text and more naturally depicts God as the witness of the Thessalonians' acts of faith. In other

---

[3] Cf. Best, *1 and 2 Thessalonians,* 70.
[4] Wanamaker, *1 and 2 Thessalonians,* 76.

words, it is not only before Paul but before God himself that their work, labor, and endurance has testified to the genuineness of their faith.[5]

1:4–5 The third participle modifying "We … thank God" introduces the content of vv. 4–5. Verse 4 is not the beginning of a new sentence (NIV) but continues the thought begun in v. 2. Paul thanked God for the Thessalonians because he was sure of their election by God.[6] The language of calling *(kaleō)* and election *(eklogē)* is featured prominently in 1 Thessalonians (1:4; 2:12; 4:7; 5:24), but it is not a focal point of the letter. No attempt was made to explain the concept, but it was clearly intended to provide both assurance and admonition for the church. Paul had seen evidence in their lives that they were part of the called people of God. Evidence of a genuine faith, along with a belief in the faithfulness of God, provides assurance. At the same time those called of the Lord are expected to live in a manner appropriate to their calling. Thus the fact of election both reminds the church of its special relationship to God and at the same time admonishes them to live in the way that this calling demands.

The elect church is "loved by God." The verb used implies an established state of being, not a momentary benevolence on God's part. The phrase "is one of many examples of language originally applied to Israel (Dt 32:15; 33:12; Is 44:2) which is now reapplied to the Christian church."[7] Paul's intent in the use of the phrase alongside the terminology of election was not to assert anything about the manner or nature of God's choosing but to encourage the church with the assurance that "they belong to God's people and are the present objects of his love." So alongside a celebration of the Thessalonians' choice to obey the gospel and live faithful Christian lives (v. 3), Paul also rejoiced in God's choice of them on the basis of his love. The apostle expressed thanks for both the Thessalonians' commitment and for God's election. There is no indication in the Thessalonian correspondence that Paul considered these two truths incompatible.

The verbal form translated "for we know" implies knowledge gained

---

[5] Cf. F. F. Bruce, *1 and 2 Thessalonians,* WBC (Waco: Word, 1982).

[6] A full treatment of the issue of election in Paul is outside the scope of this commentary. For two recent enlightening discussions that touch both on election in Paul and the evidence in the Thessalonian correspondence, see J. M. G. Wolf, *Paul and Perseverance,* WUNT 2, 37 (Tübingen: Mohr, 1990), and I. H. Marshall, "Election and Calling to Salvation in 1 and 2 Thessalonians," in *The Thessalonian Correspondence,* BETL 87 (Leuven: University Press, 1990), 259–76.

[7] Marshall, "Election and Calling to Salvation in 1 and 2 Thessalonians," 262.

by past experience. The *hoti* ("for") clause that begins v. 5 could be treated as an epexegetical clause (translated "that is, ..." and used to describe the manner of the election)[8] or as a causal clause (translated "because ..." and used to explain the basis for Paul's confidence that they were indeed part of the elect people of God).[9] If Paul's concern in the passage was to affirm that the church was chosen and beloved by God, then it seems best to take v. 5 as a causal clause. Paul knew the Thessalonians were part of the chosen people of God because he knew the character of the gospel the Thessalonians received (v. 5) and saw the observable results of conversion in their lives (vv. 6–10).

Four qualifiers explain the manner in which the gospel came to the Thessalonians. It did not come "in word only." There is no hint here that Paul was discounting the spoken word.[10] His assertion, rather, is that the gospel was communicated verbally and more. Demonstrations of power, the work of the Holy Spirit, and the full conviction of the messengers worked with the words to provide the Thessalonians with a cogent and convincing presentation of the gospel. Thus the gospel presented in Thessalonica came "with power, with the Holy Spirit, and with deep conviction." But how were these three experienced so that they were more convincing than words alone? Several passages in Paul's letters (Rom 15:17–19; 2 Cor 12:12) and in Acts (14:3; 16:17–18; 19:6,11–12) record the miraculous events that accompanied the Pauline gospel. The word used for "power" *(dunamis)* is also one of the words used in the Gospels for Jesus' miracles. It was God's power, not Paul's, that was demonstrated among the Thessalonians.

The second phrase, "with the Holy Spirit," broadens the statement to more than the miraculous.[11] The Spirit's power to call, convict, enlighten, transform, assure, and comfort far more effectively than mere words alone distinguishes the coming of the gospel from the arrival of eloquent conjurers. In this sense the work of the Spirit is the guarantor of truth.

"Deep conviction" (or perhaps "profound assurance") may refer either to the conviction demonstrated by the missionaries or the assurance that developed in the hearers of the gospel. In fact, all four phrases

---

[8] See Best, *1 and 2 Thessalonians*, 73, for arguments supporting this use of ὅτι.

[9] See Wanamaker, *1 and 2 Thessalonians*, 78, for arguments supporting this treatment of ὅτι.

[10] The contrast between human logic and divine truth was part of the Pauline message (1 Cor 1:18–2:16), but nothing in the Thessalonian correspondence suggests a situation in Thessalonica that would require Paul to address this issue.

[11] So also Best, *1 and 2 Thessalonians*, 75.

could be understood as descriptions of the Thessalonian reception of the gospel. They heard the words of the gospel, miracles occurred in their midst, the works of the Spirit were evident, and evidence was seen that they were fully persuaded of the truth of the gospel.[12] The missionaries, if that is what Paul had in mind, demonstrated their conviction through a willingness to undergo the rigors of travel by persistence in the face of opposition and by their willingness to work night and day without material remuneration from their converts (1 Cor 9:3–17; 2 Thess 3:7–9). Such are not the acts of charlatans. Each is evidence of Paul's conviction that the gospel is truly the power of God that offers salvation.

The assurance of the converts, if that is what Paul had in mind, might have been demonstrated by their willingness to endure persecution even after Paul was run out of the city. Certainly Jason revealed the profound level of his faith at the hearing where charges were leveled against the Christian missionaries (Acts 17:6–9). Conviction is invisible without action. Paul's conviction as well as that of the Thessalonians (seen in their respective actions) testified to the genuine relationship that each had with the God who chose them (v. 4).

Understanding vv. 4–5a as descriptive of the Thessalonians (not descriptive of the way Paul presented his gospel) fits well in the context of the comparative clause that concludes v. 5. The comparative adverb *(kathōs)* "just as," which should introduce the last statement ("you know how ..."), is not translated in the NIV. The result is to obscure the intended comparison between vv. 4–5a and v. 5b. The apostle asserted in these verses, "We know" (v. 4a) the genuineness of your faith because we have seen its impact in your lives, just as *(kathōs)* "you know" (v. 5b) what sort of lives we lived while we lived among you. This is in fact the first in an impressive series of references in 1 Thessalonians reminding the church of the way the apostles lived and what they taught while in Thessalonica (2:1–2,5,11; 3:3–4; 4:2; 5:2).

Just as the apostle knew the impact the gospel had on the Thessalonians (and so knew the reality of their faith), so also the Thessalonians knew what sort of men the missionaries were when they were in Thessalonica. The true character of Paul and company was revealed by the lives they lived in the midst of and for the benefit of the young Thessal-

---

[12] Bruce takes the first three phrases as descriptive of the missionaries' presentation of the gospel and the final phrase as a reference to the church's reception of the gospel and the evidence that they were deeply committed to its truth (*1 and 2 Thessalonians*, 14). See also Best, *1 and 2 Thessalonians*, 76.

onian Christians. The lives the missionaries lived demonstrated the genuineness of their gospel and at the same time gave the new converts a flesh-and-blood example of what it meant to live as a follower of Jesus. Today's ministers are called to the same demanding work: proclaiming the faith in word and life. History, both ancient and modern, all too often documents how easily orthodox theology is negated by aberrant ethics. We must live as examples of what we proclaim lest our actions invalidate our message in the minds of our hearers.

At this point in his letter Paul left the thanksgiving form behind to expand on the affirmations of the church's faith referred to in generalities in vv. 4–5. In doing so he both encouraged the church to continue along the good path they had begun and expressed his goodwill toward the church. Paul no doubt hoped the church would respond with goodwill and thus be open to hear not only the compliments and encouragements in the letter but also the admonitions and corrections.[13]

By mentioning the behavior of both the missionaries and the church (vv. 4–5), the letter leads into an affirmation of the church as faithful imitators of the apostolic faith. An imitator *(mimētēs)* is to modern minds one who lacks creativity and depth. An imitation sounds like something that is not a genuine article and is therefore inferior. Such concepts do not apply to the manner in which Paul used *mimētēs*. In virtually every letter Paul presented himself as an example[14] and called upon his readers to imitate his faith and his life.[15] Such exhortations were appropriate, not arrogant. It is the character of life that separates true from false prophets (Matt 7:15–20). Persons in both the religious and philosophical communities of the first century felt that the only teachers worth a moment's attention were those who taught with their lives as well as with their words.[16] Thus Paul clearly understood that just as he sought to imitate Christ, so also he was obligated to serve as

---

[13] An *encomium* (a rhetorical introduction) served to foreshadow the topics to be treated subsequently and at the same time build rapport with the audience. Verses 2–10 accomplish both of these tasks.

[14] For Paul as type or example (τύπος) see Rom 5:14; 6:17; 1 Cor 10:6; Phil 3:17; 1 Thess 1:7; 2 Thess 3:9.

[15] For encouragements to imitation (μιμεόμαι or μιμητής) see 1 Cor 4:16; 11:1; Eph 5:1; 1 Thess 1:6; 2:14; 2 Thess 3:7,9.

[16] See A. J. Malherbe, *Moral Exhortation, A Greco-Roman Sourcebook,* LEC 4 (Philadelphia: Westminster, 1986), 34–40, for examples that illustrate the philosophers' recognition that one's life must validate one's moral exhortations.

an example of the Christian life to others. And the true disciple of Paul became an example of the faith for others as well.

(2) An Affirmation (1:6–10)

6You became imitators of us and of the Lord; in spite of severe suffering, you welcomed the message with the joy given by the Holy Spirit. 7And so you became a model to all the believers in Macedonia and Achaia. 8The Lord's message rang out from you not only in Macedonia and Achaia— your faith in God has become known everywhere. Therefore we do not need to say anything about it, 9for they themselves report what kind of reception you gave us. They tell how you turned to God from idols to serve the living and true God, 10and to wait for his Son from heaven, whom he raised from the dead—Jesus, who rescues us from the coming wrath.

1:6–7 On the basis of the gospel they received and the lives of the missionaries they observed (v. 5), the Thessalonians disciplined their own lives. They became what the words and the lives of the apostle and his company revealed that a follower of Jesus should be. They understood that by following Paul's teachings and example they were following the Lord. They became imitators in that their lives reflected the teaching of the Lord and his apostles.

The second clause in v. 6, "in spite of severe suffering," translates a participle that the NIV takes as a concessive statement. In other words, the believers "welcomed the message" although it entailed suffering. Others see the same clause as an explanation of the Thessalonian "imitation" of Paul and the Lord: "You became imitators of us and of the Lord, for you received the word in much affliction" (RSV). That is, the Thessalonians, just like Paul and the Lord, received the word with affliction and joy. In other contexts Paul did write of sharing the suffering of the Lord (Phil 3:10). But if the aorist participle "receiving …" alludes to the evangelization of the Thessalonians, then the parallel between Paul, the Lord (especially), and the Thessalonians is difficult if not impossible to make. Thus it is better to take the participle as concessive with the NIV.

Their reception of the word of the gospel was not an easy experience. It was accompanied by "suffering" *(thlipsei)*. The church suffered "persecution" (another translation of *thlipsei*) at the hands of "their own countrymen," who were opposed to the spread of the gospel (see 2:14 and 3:3–4). The intensity of the opposition is reflected in Acts by the persecutors' persistence. They followed the missionaries from Thessalonica to Berea and agitated against the gospel there just as ardently as they had in their own city (17:10–15). But overt aggression is not the only kind of suffering a believer might experience.

Malherbe has argued that the "affliction" (the RSV's translation of *thlipsei*) Paul had in mind was not primarily persecution but the distress of alienation.[17] Conversion to Christianity entailed a significant change in a person's social life. It was capable of dividing families (1 Pet 3:1–2) and alienating believers from some social functions (1 Cor 8:1–13). Their adoption into the Christian "family" no doubt served to alleviate some of the separation trauma new believers must have experienced. But the inner struggle produced by conversion for most if not all Gentile converts must have been an affliction every bit as difficult as any external persecution.

In spite of these afflictions[18] the Thessalonians' reception of the gospel was accompanied by Spirit-inspired joy. The presence of the Spirit signified membership in the new people of God (Acts 2:16–21). The Spirit provided gifts with the power to console, instruct, strengthen, and heal the community of faith (1 Cor 12). The Spirit was both evidence of the fact of salvation and the assurance of the ultimate deliverance yet to come. Although conversion meant temporary affliction, it also promised eternal rejoicing. Thus the Thessalonians persevered. They did not allow persecution to paint Paul and the gospel as a source of trouble. Rather, they were sources of good news to be celebrated and shared. Because they realized this and lived accordingly, they became examples for others experiencing the suffering and joy of the faith.

Those who had imitated the example or "model" *(tupon)* of Paul and the Lord in turn became models for other churches (v. 7). This is high praise. Although Paul frequently used the terminology of imitation (implicitly complimenting those who were worthy of imitation), he nowhere else wrote to a particular church that their faith was a pattern or type that inspired the discipleship of others.

"All the believers in Macedonia and Achaia" covered a lot of terri-

---

[17] See Malherbe, *Paul and the Thessalonians* (Philadelphia: Fortress, 1987), 46–52.

[18] Wanamaker probably is right when he argues (against Malherbe) that the affliction Paul had in mind in 1:6 was persecution, not alienation (*1 and 2 Thessalonians,* 81–82). But there is no need to reject Malherbe's suggestion entirely. The Thessalonians likely experienced both social alienation and persecution. In fact the latter would be an expression of and would exacerbate the former.

tory. Macedonia was the Roman province in the northeast section of Greece. The Macedonian churches of which we are aware included those in Philippi, Thessalonica, and Berea. Achaia was the Roman province directly south of Macedonia. In it were churches in the cities of Athens and Corinth. North to south the two provinces stretched for several hundred miles and contained all of the churches established on the second missionary journey (Acts 16:6–18:22).

1:8–10 The Thessalonians became both models (v. 7) and messengers (v. 8) of the gospel. In word and in life they helped to spread "the Lord's message"[19] throughout their province, impacting the entire region of Macedonia and Achaia[20] as well as territories beyond. In what sense did the "message ring out" from them? There is no mention of the church sending anyone as an assistant to Paul or as an independent missionary (though such would happen later in the apostle's ministry). Eventually Paul's missionary strategy did involve using the main cities of each province (e.g., Ephesus, Acts 19:10) as a base for evangelizing outlying regions, but we have no evidence of this practice prior to Paul's ministry in Corinth (assuming the Corinthian church established the church in the neighboring port town of Cenchrea, Rom 16:1).

Apparently Paul did not mean that the Thessalonian church had sent out messengers but that the story of their faith had circulated widely. This was no doubt facilitated by Thessalonica's status as an important port city and by its location on the Via Egnatia. Paul's affirmation of the church reached its grandest scale with this boast in their behalf: the "Lord's message rang out" not only in Achaia and Macedonia but "everywhere" their faith toward God had gone forth. "Rang out" (v. 8) is used only here in the New Testament and indicates a resounding report that is widely heard. "Everywhere" (lit., "in every place," *en panti topō*) probably refers to Christian places of assembly,[21] where news of new churches, persecution, and perseverance would be shared by traveling Christian merchants and missionaries. Assuming this letter was written during Paul's ministry in Corinth (Acts 18:1–18) shortly after his work in Thessalonica (Acts 17:1–9), Paul himself had not trav-

---

[19] Lit., "the word of the Lord." The NIV is correct to take the genitive as subjective, as is seen by use of the phrase in the LXX to refer to a message from Yahweh, not a message about Yahweh.

[20] The two place names share a single article here, indicating that the apostle was grouping them together in this statement over against the spread of the message beyond these provinces.

[21] Acts 4:31; 1 Cor 2:1; 2 Cor 2:14.

eled out of Achaia.[22] But he would have encountered numerous travelers moving through the commercially busy region of Corinth.

Discerning how widely the Thessalonians' reputation had spread would not have posed a problem. Whether or not Paul's words of praise are hyperbolic, his comments still functioned to affirm the church. The story of the Thessalonians was so impressive that others already were telling it as they traveled among the congregations. Such retelling constituted high praise and encouraged the Thessalonian church's faith and promoted the characteristics Paul hoped the Thessalonians would continue to exhibit.

The content of the Thessalonians' story, as told by others, is detailed in vv. 9–10. The verb "they report" ("they" is emphasized) has two objects. They reported (1) the "reception" the Thessalonians gave the missionaries, and they reported (2) "how you turned from idols." The term "reception" (eisodon) refers to the "entrance" of the apostles into the Thessalonian community. But in context the reference extends beyond the moment of contact to the way the missionaries were accepted by those who became believers. Giving a sympathetic hearing to a popular speaker is not especially problematic and so is not especially laudable. Hearing positively and extending hospitality to missionaries about whom controversy swirls is much more difficult. The social pressure to disown Paul and his companions must have grown more intense with each day. The difficulty associated with Paul's work in the city makes the reception given by those who became believers all the more laudable. The rejection of the apostle by the Jews and subsequent attempts to undermine the gospel must have made it quite difficult for Gentile converts to remain loyal to Paul and his companions. Minds open to the truth of the gospel and loyal believers who endure persecution earn affirmation from their leaders. The leader who will not pay it robs the people of God and undermines his own ministry.

Second, the nature of the Thessalonians' conversion is commended. Conversion is pictured here as a willful act of turning from one path and proceeding in another direction. The nature of their turning is further described by two phrases and two infinitival clauses. The choice of terminology in these statements descriptive of conversion, coupled with

---

[22] Acts does not detail all of the apostle's travels (nor do his letters), but there is no clear evidence indicating (as Morris seems to) that Paul traveled widely enough during his Corinthian ministry for that to serve as the basis for his statement that the Thessalonians' faith was known in every place (Morris, *1 and 2 Thessalonians,* 52).

the lack of distinctively Pauline emphases, has led several commentators to conclude that these are non-Pauline, Jewish-Christian phrases descriptive of the conversion of Gentiles.[23] Best may go too far with his attempt to see the comments as a pre-Pauline unit of tradition and to set them out in two three-line stanzas, but he is certainly correct that such summaries of the gospel are not Pauline in origin. The statements are Pauline, however, not in origin but by adoption.

The Thessalonians had turned "to God" and "from idols." The phrase describes well the Gentile mission as a whole. It also enlightens us about the composition of the Thessalonian church. The brief account in Acts 17:1–10a leaves the impression that Paul had a three-week ministry focused on the synagogue and was then driven from the city. Yet here we hear only of turning from idols to serve the living God—a description not appropriate for Jews or even God-fearers converted to Christianity. It seems likely from this that Paul's three weeks of synagogue preaching was only the first part of his stay in Thessalonica. First Thessalonians 1:9 implies that between his synagogue preaching (Acts 17:1–3) and the troubles that drove him from the city (Acts 17:5–10a) Paul spent several more weeks cultivating Gentile converts in the faith.

If the persecution that drove Paul away continued, the believers who remained in Thessalonica must have faced pressures to leave the faith and return to the other gods of the city. By praising the Thessalonians and bragging that their faith was known and celebrated throughout the church, Paul encouraged continued perseverance. He would not allow the church to hear only the voice of its detractors. In addition, by raising the specter of the false worship they had turned from in the past, Paul reminded the converts that turning from the gospel would mean returning to alternatives they had already dismissed as unsatisfying. Who has the words of life? If the Thessalonians had found in the past that idols did not, then they still do not.

The report of the conversion of the Thessalonians was further described with two infinitival clauses. They "turned ... to serve ... and to wait." The first infinitive commends the church for serving the true and living God. This differs from the preceding phrases only in the addition of the idea of service. The present infinitive "to serve" describes the current character of their lives more than the past moment

---

[23] For a presentation of this passage as a pre-Pauline fragment originating from the Jewish-Christian church, see Best, *1 and 2 Thessalonians,* 85–87. See Wanamaker, *1 and 2 Thessalonians,* 84–89, for a response to Best's work.

of conversion. It expresses the result of genuine conversion—a life of service to "the living and true God." Although "God" in this clause does not have the article, the statement does not lack for specificity. The "living and true" God is the God of Jewish monotheism, the Father of the Christian faith.

With the second infinitive Paul commended the church's persistent expectation of the return of the Lord. This is also the result of genuine conversion—perseverance to the end. That for which Paul expressed thanks (the endurance of the church that was inspired by hope, 1:3) was also lauded by churches everywhere. This second infinitive parallels the first, and both verb tenses imply continuity of action. The activity of service is conducted in the context of persistent anticipation. Commending their patient expectation in the past served to encourage continued endurance.

They awaited "the Son." The treatments of the parousia later in the letter are anticipated in the references here to heaven, resurrection, and wrath. They await the son "from heaven." It is an exalted Lord they anticipate (Phil 2:9–11; 1 Thess 4:16–17), whose abode is that of the true and living God. They await a Son whom the true God "raised from the dead," and one who has conquered death himself can conquer death on behalf of others (1 Cor 15; 1 Thess 4:13–14). They await Jesus, who rescues them "from the coming wrath" (cf. 1 Thess 5:9). Believers live anticipating a coronation (2 Tim 4:8) rather than a condemnation.

This passage (1:2–10) began as an expression of thanks to God (1:2–5). The affirmations growing out of Paul's prayer of thanks explained the basis for his thankfulness. But beyond this, and more importantly for the message of the letter, the recital of examples of faithfulness on the part of the Thessalonians were calculated to (1) support the good already evident in the Thessalonian church, (2) strengthen existing goodwill between Paul and the church, and (3) anticipate the message contained in the remainder of the letter. The need, especially for the second of these items, is evident as Paul reviewed his behavior in Thessalonica. If in doing this he was responding to critics, then certainly they were critics attempting to drive a wedge between the apostle and his converts. And success in discrediting the apostle might well have led to the discrediting of the apostle's message. In the verses that follow, Paul defended himself in order to defend his message.

2. Apostolic Character while in Thessalonica Rehearsed (2:1–12)

In this section Paul presented a summary of his motivations and actions during his ministry in Thessalonica. This narrative material in chaps. 2–3 is interwoven with several statements of thanksgiving. This has resulted in some scholars' interpreting the entirety of 1:2–3:13 as a thanksgiving containing personal digressions. If this is true, and since the *paraenesis* (exhortation) of the letter begins in 4:1, it would appear that Paul wrote a letter that has no body but skips directly from thanksgiving to exhortations. If in reading these chapters we overemphasize the thanksgivings, there is the danger that the narrative sections will be treated as mere digressions and not given their proper weight in the argument of the letter.

Our treatment of the narratives may follow either of two paths. First, we might assume that Paul was responding to opponents who not only were attacking the gospel but also the messenger of the gospel. Presumably they would suppose that by discrediting Paul they could weaken the influence he exerted in founding and then maintaining the congregation. Paul's description of his ministry, in such a case, would serve as an apology. But is this scenario credible? Did such opponents exist in Thessalonica?

Acts tells us that Paul and his companions were driven out of Thessalonica by those who rejected the gospel. The strong feelings of the gospel's opponents were indicated by their compulsion to follow him to the neighboring city of Berea and to drive him out of the region of Macedonia entirely. Such ardent opponents would certainly have tried to undermine Paul's work in his absence. It is reasonable, therefore, to presume that forces in Thessalonica would attempt to rid the city of Paul's influence. But who might these people have been, and what strategy did they utilize?

Acts presents Jewish opposition to the gospel. Thus we might expect arguments "from the Scripture" refuting Paul's assertions that "the Christ had to suffer and rise from the dead" (Acts 17:2–3). Yet the letter does not seem to counter this kind of argument. It presents no proofs from the LXX or citations of eyewitness testimony defending the messianic role of Jesus. There is no argument as in the Epistle to the Romans detailing the lostness of the Jews or regarding the limitations of the law as in Galatians. Although Paul did mention the Jewish persecution of the church (1 Thess 2:14–15), there is nothing in the letter to counter Jewish arguments against the content of the gospel. The arguments presented, rather, concern only Paul's *ethos,* his character. Unless we are to believe that the letter responds to a Jewish attack that was purely *ad hominem* (an unlikely scenario), we should look elsewhere for the occasion of Paul's narrative in chaps. 2–3.

A second approach sees it not as a response to attacks but as a description of the apostolic *ethos*—that is, not as an apology but as an exemplar of the Christian life. The *ethos* of a teacher or philosopher referred to his behavior or lifestyle and was expected to serve both as an illustration and a validation of his teachings.

Malherbe, expanding on the work of M. Dibelius, has compared Paul's self-description in 1 Thessalonians 2 with that of the late first-century A.D. Cynic philosopher Dio Chrysostom.[24] Dio described himself in part by criticizing other Cynic philosophers of the day. He accused them of error, flattery, preaching for glory or for money, and allowing the laudable trait of boldness to degenerate to bluntness without gentleness. An ideal philosopher should rather speak with purity, without guile, without concern for glory or financial gain, and should demonstrate a boldness of speech tempered with a genuine and gentle concern for his hearers. Both the vocabulary and the mood of Dio's assertions bear remarkable similarity to Paul's assertions in chap. 2.[25]

Was it necessary for Paul to be under attack for him to produce the statements in 2:1–12? Probably not. The setting of the Hellenistic city with its many competing claims for the attention and devotion of the people required Paul to distance himself from disreputable teachers and to present himself and his message in a positive light. It was necessary not only for Paul but for the disciples in Thessalonica as well if they were to carry the same message to their own city and beyond. Thus Paul's presentation of his own *ethos* could have served the dual purpose of self-definition (over against competitors and opponents) and exhortation to the church that was to imitate him.

In both the rhetoric and the epistolography of the age, examples of laudable behavior were held up for emulation as a way of instructing and encouraging one's audience. The praise of exemplary character and

---

[24] Malherbe, "Gentle as a Nurse," *NovT* 12 (1970): 203–17.

[25] Ibid., 214–17. Although the parallels observed by Malherbe are impressive, it is also important to heed his concluding caution: "To point out that Paul had the same practical concerns as Dio, and that he used the same language in dealing with them, does not imply that he understood these words to mean the same thing they did to Dio" (ibid.). The context in which these words are found in 1 Thessalonians (both religiously and syntactically) remains the best indicator of Paul's meaning.

the condemnation of poor behaviors was especially the concern of epideictic rhetoric. Although the setting of this letter is not that envisioned for epideictic rhetoric and the concerns are distinctly Christian, chaps. 2–3 might well be understood as the application of the persuasive strategies of epideictic rhetoric to a pastoral setting. The thanksgiving (1:2–10) does double service as epistolary introduction and *encomium* (rhetorical introduction). The matter of the imitation of the faith foreshadowed in the *encomium* (1:6–7) is developed through a *narratio*—a narration of apostolic motives and behavior (2:1–3:10). The function of the narration, in this view, is not to respond to critics but to provide an example of proper Christian behavior both in negative (e.g., 2:3,5–6) and positive (2:2,7–12) terms.

Whether Paul was responding to attacks on his person or using himself and his companions as models for the church to emulate, he called upon the Thessalonian Christians themselves as witnesses to his behavior to follow his example. Six times in the space of twelve verses Paul reminded the Thessalonians of what they themselves knew (vv. 1–2,5,11) and called them to remember (v. 9) or to witness (v. 10) regarding his character among them. He also reminded them that they were not testifying regarding a stranger but their brother (v. 1). He had cared for them like a mother and father would their own children (vv. 7,11), and he still counted them so dear that he would have given his life for them (v. 8). The passage is full of verbiage expressive of a loving, familial relationship.

The very fact that the readers are members of God's "kingdom and glory" (v. 12) also testifies to the character of Paul's apostolic ministry. His visit was not a "failure" (v. 1); therefore he, as God's emissary, could not be a fraud. Not only this, but the opposition he endured repeatedly (v. 2), the hardships he accepted (v. 9), and his refusal to benefit at their expense (vv. 6,9) are surely not indicative of a religious shyster seeking to exploit a gullible public. The cost had been too high and the material rewards too meager to justify the thought that Paul was a crook manipulating people for his personal benefit.

(1) Denials (2:1–6)

¹You know, brothers, that our visit to you was not a failure. ²We had previously suffered and been insulted in Philippi, as you know, but with the help of our God we dared to tell you his gospel in spite of strong opposition. ³For the appeal we make does not spring from error or impure

motives, nor are we trying to trick you. ⁴On the contrary, we speak as men
approved by God to be entrusted with the gospel. We are not trying to
please men but God, who tests our hearts. ⁵You know we never used flattery, nor did we put on a mask to cover up greed—God is our witness. ⁶We
were not looking for praise from men, not from you or anyone else.
As apostles of Christ we could have been a burden to you,

2:1 Paul emphasized the fact that the readers themselves must testify to his character. "You know" is emphatic in the Greek text. If Paul
was combating critics, he did so by calling on the Thessalonians as
defense witnesses. These witnesses, however, were not only responsible
to witness to Paul's behavior but also to copy Paul's behavior. Whether
or not Paul was fending off an attack against the gospel, his narrative
was intended to serve a paraenetic function. It encouraged the church to
live as he had taught them to live.

Paraenesis typically reminds its recipients of things they already
know. Introductory formulae such as "you know" are to be expected
and have no great import in themselves. A connective particle, "for"
(gar), not translated in the NIV (cf. the RSV) connects the narration
that begins in 2:1 with the introduction in the preceding verses. The particle is important because it connects the introduction's emphasis on
imitation (1:5b–9a) with the narration of the missionaries' activities.

The repetition of the term "visit" *(eisodon)* does the same. It repeats
the word used in 1:9 of the "welcome" the missionaries received from
the Thessalonians. This initial visit "was not a failure" *(kenē). Kenos*
refers to an activity that is without profit or without effect. That which
is *kenos* is ineffective, worthless, or useless.²⁶ If Paul had been a fraud
and his gospel a clever myth, then his message would have had no
power and the believers would not have benefited from it. The believers' encounter with him would have been *kenos.* The fact that they did
benefit demonstrates the validity and value of the Pauline mission. The
enduring benefit of the gospel is also implied by the use of a perfect
tense verb in the clause "was not a failure."

2:2 This gospel of great value was not brought to Thessalonica
without cost or without opposition. The main verb of the verse pro-

---

²⁶ It seems best to understand Paul's use of κενῶς as broadly as possible in this context
of transition from a passage (1:2–10), where the truth (1:5, not mere "words") and the
power (1:5, with "power") and the benefit (1:10, deliverance from "wrath") of the evangelization of the Thessalonians (the "visit") are emphasized. Cf. Best, *1 and 2 Thessalonians,*
89–90; Marshall, *1 and 2 Thessalonians,* 62–63.

claims that the missionaries "dared" or "were given courage" (author translation) to speak the gospel.[27] The source of their courage was their God, implying that the source of their message was God as well (cf. v. 4). The reason Paul needed to claim divine encouragement (and by implication divine authority) is not seen until v. 3. Other itinerant teachers of Paul's day taught false wisdom for false motives, and opponents might have accused Paul and company of doing the same. But any such accusation was unfounded, and the behavior of the missionaries was evidence of the purity of their motives and the truth of their words.

In spite of persecution in Philippi, the missionaries faithfully proclaimed the message God had entrusted to them. Faithfulness in adverse conditions is one proof of pure motives. What charlatan would suffer so much abuse for so little (cf. v. 9) reward? Only true believers commissioned and emboldened by God would persevere in the face of persecution. Paul and his associates dared to share the gospel in Thessalonica although they had "suffered and been insulted" (these two concessive participles modify the main verb "we dared") in Philippi for just the same activity (see Acts 16:11–40). The fact that Paul, a Roman citizen, was flogged and jailed without due process certainly constituted "insult." The verb (hybristhentes) implies abuse or shameful treatment and may allude to the illegality that accompanied their physical suffering. "As you know" indicates that someone, perhaps Paul himself, had told the church in Thessalonica of the missionaries' experience in Philippi.

Their work in Thessalonica was conducted in spite of "strong opposition." The word translated "opposition" (agōni) was used of the "struggle" of the athlete engaged in training or in a contest and was used frequently as a metaphor for moral struggles.[28] It connotes the strenuous effort required to overcome an opponent. The opponent is not identified here. No doubt the Thessalonians did not have to be reminded of the struggles encountered in the early days of their own congregation.

2:3 "For" links the denials in v. 3 to the assertions in v. 2. The missionaries had willingly faced opposition in more than one city. They had paid a high price to carry the "appeal" of the gospel forward. They did this because the message they carried was God's message. Behind the

---

[27] The verb used, παρρησιάζομαι, connotes freedom of speech, but the context here stresses the exercise of free speech in spite of abusive opposition, hence boldness of speech. See W. C. van Unnik, "The Christian's Freedom of Speech in the New Testament," *BJRL* 44 (1961–62): 466–88.

[28] See V. C. Pfitzner, *Paul and the Agon Motif,* NovTSup 16 (Leiden: Brill, 1967).

denials of vv. 3–4 is the assumption that some teachers brought to these Hellenistic cities "appeals" that were human in origin and motivation. Paul here distanced himself from teachers who were simply earning a living by their wits, peddling so-called wisdom in the Hellenistic marketplaces.[29] He wanted the Thessalonians to understand that the appeal of the gospel was not like that of these peddlers. His motives were not personal enrichment; his message was not tailored for mass appeal. The message he proclaimed was divine truth, not human invention.

Paul's message was not of error *(planēs)*, impurity *(akatharsias)*, or deceit *(dolō)*. The Greek sentence has no verb stated and may equally apply to the origin of the message (e.g., "does not spring from") or its character. The former is the more probable emphasis in light of the subsequent statement (v. 4) that the message originated with God, who entrusted it to the missionaries.

The apostle's appeal did not originate from "error." The word could be translated "deceit" but would then be redundant with the third assertion in the series, that is, that he was not "trying to trick" *(dolō)* them. One type of "error" from a Judeo-Christian perspective is idolatry. But in this context Paul had no need to deny that his message had any connection to idols. Another type of error is intellectual confusion. It is always possible that a teacher may simply be wrong, and that seems to be what Paul was denying here. His message did not spring from faulty reasoning (a charge that the Jews might have made against his understanding of the Messiah; cf. Acts 17:2–4). Yet how could his readers be certain of the truth of the missionaries' message? Paul's certainty was not based on a claim of intellectual flawlessness or a claim that his gospel was unassailably logical (1 Cor 1:18–25). Human logic does not guarantee the discovery of truth. No, his hedge against "error" was the fact that the message he proclaimed came to him by divine revelation. Paul's gospel contained no human error not because of Paul's personal infallibility but because it was not of human origin.

The apostle's appeal did not spring from "impure motives." The term *akatharsia* refers literally to filth or refuse. It was applied metaphorically to that which was ritually or morally unclean, especially sexual sins. It is unlikely that Paul was denying that his appeal was motivated

---

[29] See Malherbe, "Gentle as a Nurse," 214–17, for a description of the popular preachers of the Hellenistic cities. L. Morris agrees that "the accusation that Paul was no better than the usual run of wandering preachers clearly underlies his defense of his position in this verse" (*The Second Epistle to the Thessalonians* [Grand Rapids: Eerdmans, 1959], 70).

by improper sexual desire. There is no hint in the letter or in the Acts account that Paul and his associates had been accused of sexual impropriety or ritual prostitution as Morris supposes.[30] The specific references that follow this verse contain denials of greed, man pleasing, and manipulative flattery. It is likely that these rather than sexual impropriety were the activities Paul was denying.

The third phrase, "nor are we trying to trick you," is a rendering of a prepositional phrase that differs from the first two. The preposition with the first two terms implies the origin *(ek)* or source of the appeal. This third term *(dolōs)* is used with *ev,* implying the manner in which the appeal was brought. Paul did not use deception or trickery in his preaching.

2:4 The strong adversative "on the contrary" *(alla)* indicates that the positive statements of v. 4 were intended to serve as a contrast to the denials of v. 3. The missionaries spoke not from any wrong motive but because God had approved them to be entrusted with the gospel. He chose them. He entrusted them with a message. Commissioned by God, they concerned themselves with pleasing the God who sent them with his message. For it was God who judged them trustworthy to carry his gospel, the same God who continued to judge their words, their actions, and their very hearts.

"Approved by God" (v. 4a) translates a verb *(dokimazē)* that connotes the approval of something as the result of careful examination. The perfect tense of the verb implies a past event of testing or examination resulting in a current state of approval. Approval implies some standard of judgment. In this context that which was being judged was the reliability of the missionaries. Entrusted with a vital message, would they carry it faithfully? Were they trustworthy? The manner in which God tested them is not a concern in this passage, and Paul may not have had any particular event in mind since he later wrote, using the same verb, of the God who "tests our hearts." The point is that even the most subtle improper motives (which men might not be able to discern) cannot escape divine examination. When God examined the hearts of the missionaries, he found that they were trustworthy. Thus he "entrusted" them "with the gospel," terminology that Paul used elsewhere of his God-given responsibility to take the good news to the Gentiles (cf. Gal 2:7).

A person obligated to speak for one who can judge the heart would be foolish to change the message in order to please the hearers. Such an

---

[30] Morris, *1 and 2 Thessalonians,* 62.

act would comprise a breach of trust. Thus it was impossible in the mind of the apostle to be a person pleaser and a God pleaser at the same time (cf. Gal 1:10). This does not mean that one must be insensitive or offensive when dealing with people. Paul elsewhere made it clear that he attempted to present the gospel so as to enhance its appeal to a variety of people ("all things to all men" in 1 Cor 9:22). But he was obliged to do so without altering the message entrusted to him. The verb translated "who tests" in the latter part of v. 4 is the same word translated "approved" in the preceding sentence, only the tense is changed. The God who examined and approved the missionaries when they were entrusted with the gospel was ever the judge of their hearts.

2:5–6 *Ad hominem* arguments are common in the course of human debate. Although they usually are unfair, they also frequently are persuasive. The effective Christian worker must always remember that flaws in his or her character can be used by opponents to discredit the gospel. Paul reminded the Thessalonians of what they themselves saw of his behavior. He also called on God (who judges the heart, v. 4) to witness that his actions were not motivated by greed. The claims that the missionaries did not come with "flattery" (v. 5a) nor were motivated by "greed" (v. 5b) are matched by the evidence that they did not seek praise from anyone (v. 6a) even though they could have exerted their apostolic authority and rights (v. 6b). Instead, they treated the Thessalonians with parental love (vv. 7–8).

The past tense "we never used" (v. 5) shifts the focus of the passage from the general statements of v. 4 back to the details of the evangelists' first visit to Thessalonica mentioned in v. 1. A series of three negative assertions begins in v. 5 and extends through v. 6 (the relationship of v. 6a to v. 6b and these to the verses following is obscured by the versification and punctuation of the NIV). The first two assertions (both in v. 5) terminate with the calling of a witness to the truth of the statements, first the Thessalonians, then God himself. The third denial begins in v. 6 and carries through the paragraph division in the NIV. The denial of v. 6, "We were not looking for praise," is then balanced by the positive statements beginning with v. 7, "We were gentle among you."

The denial "We never used flattery" in v. 5a is followed in the Greek text by the call for witness, "as you know." A parallel structure is used in v. 5b, "or a cloak for greed, as God is witness" (RSV). "Flattery" *(kolakeia)* does not refer primarily to saying nice things about people as a modern reader might presume. It was the practice of tailoring truth to fit popular opinion. It is the opposite of the boldness *(parrēsia)* given the missionaries by God (v. 2), by virtue of which they would "dare" *(parrēsiazomai)* to proclaim the gospel message even though it was not popular and might result in public abuse. It was the effort to "please men" (v. 4) that was condemned even by the secular writers of Paul's day.[31] Paul called on the Thessalonians as his witness in this regard. It was clear that he was not a "flatterer." They had seen Paul risk abuse from his hearers for speaking difficult truths in a setting where those truths were unpopular.[32]

The missionaries also did not "put on a mask to cover up greed *[pleonexias]*." Greed involves more than the desire for money, though that is included. In a later letter Paul equated *pleonexia* with idolatry (Col 3:5), implying that it signified for him a lust for possessions that could dominate all else. "Mask" *(prophasei)* in the NIV refers to a motive, either actual or false depending on the context.[33] Translations such as the NIV's or the RSV's ("a cloak for greed") assume that Paul was denying that his stated godly motives were simply a pretext for greed. Wanamaker's suggestion that we understand *prophasei* as a positive motive and translate the sentence "we did not act with a motive of greed" is preferable since it is true to the meaning of *prophasis* and produces a more understandable phrase.[34] Motive is a matter of the heart. Since it is God who judges the heart, the apostle called on God to testify regarding his true motive. In doing so he placed himself in the path of the judgment of God as an assurance to his readers that he was not lying.

The verb in the first clause of v. 5 *(egenēthēmen)* is assumed in the second clause and again at the beginning of v. 6. Translating it "use" obscures the link between these verses in which Paul asserted, "We neither *[oute]* came with words of flattery ... nor *[oute]* with a motive of greed ... nor *[oute]* seeking praise" (author translation). Following each denial, proof is offered of the truth of Paul's statements. The apostles came neither with flattery, "as you know" (RSV), nor motivated by greed, "God is our witness," nor seeking praise, "though we could have been a burden." This last statement is also a form of proof. In effect it called on the Thessalonians again to testify that the apostle did not demand the recognition due an apostle.

---

[31] Cf. Dio Chrysostom, *Oration* 32.5f.; Plutarch, *Moralia* 48e–74e.

[32] The term Paul used for "insulted" in 2:2 was also used by Dio of the "abuse" that might be heaped on a "bold" speaker by an angry audience (Dio, *Oration* 32).

[33] BAGD, s.v. "πρόφασις," 722.

[34] Wanamaker, *1 and 2 Thessalonians*, 97.

"Praise" *(doxa)* refers to the honor or respect a speaker might gain from his audience. The same word is used elsewhere with the more positive, religious meaning "glory," but here the context limits the meaning of the word to secular praise or respect. It is the wage for which a flatterer will sacrifice the truth. Paul, on the other hand, exercised boldness both inside and outside the congregation of believers. He shared the truth in love.

The verse and paragraph divisions of the NIV break the flow of the text at this point.[35] Verse 6b (which is v. 7a in the Greek text) is not the beginning of a new thought as the English punctuation indicates. Rather, v. 6b begins with a participle that continues the thought of v. 6a. The apostles did not come to Thessalonica "looking for praise" (v. 6a), although as apostles of Christ they had the authority to command respect (v. 6b). In other words they could have demanded honor (and even financial support) if they had wished to assert their rights as apostles of Christ. The fact that the apostles did not even take that which was their legitimate due indicates even more clearly that their motive was not the acquisition of either fame or fortune. They chose not to "burden" the church.

The term "burden" is used by Paul elsewhere of the financial burden that apostles could lay on the churches they served (see 1 Cor 9:3–18; 2 Cor 11:7–11; 2 Thess 3:8).[36] Material support in return for spiritual or philosophical instruction was common both in the church and in the Hellenistic world in general. It was not considered improper. In this context the term indicates more than simple financial support. It refers to the weight of authority that might manifest itself either as a demand for financial support or as a demand for respect. It identifies the apostles as individuals of importance who were "able to make demands"[37] on

---

[35] The text as Paul wrote it, of course, contained neither punctuation nor paragraph divisions. These are editorial decisions that reflect the way the editor of the text understood the flow of thought. In the discussion that follows, vv. 5–6 are taken as a unit in which three denials are accompanied by three evidences of the truth of the denial (as stated earlier). This impacts the verses that follow. It means that v. 6 should end with a period, and v. 7 should mark the beginning of a new sentence. Following the negative statements (vv. 5–6) introduced by "for we never used" (οὔτε ... ἐγενήθημεν), a series of positive statements (v. 7f.) are initiated with a strong adversative and the repetition of the same verb as in v. 5a, "but we were" (ἀλλὰ ... ἐγενήθημεν).

[36] See also J. G. Strelan, "Burden-Bearing and the Law of Christ: A Re-examination of Galatians 6:2," *JBL* 94 (1975): 266–76.

[37] Bruce, *1 and 2 Thessalonians*, 30.

others. The plural "apostles" applies easily to Paul and Silas. Whether or not it applies to Timothy is uncertain. It is difficult to know how narrowly Paul used the term.[38]

In the first six verses of the chapter we find negative statements for the most part. Paul denied that his behavior was characterized by failure, error, impure motives, trickery, man-pleasing, flattery, or greed. He consistently called corroborating witnesses or cited evidence supporting his denials. By contrast the next several verses (vv. 7–12) describe the character of the missionaries in predominantly positive terms.

If greed and manipulation did not characterize the actions of the missionaries, then what did? They lived lives of gentleness (v. 7); love and a desire to share the good things of the gospel (v. 8); hard work and financial independence (v. 9); and holiness, righteousness, and blamelessness (v. 10) among the Thessalonians. Paul's intent was not to exploit but to encourage, comfort, and urge godly living (v. 12). What evidence could Paul give that his claims were true? As both the Thessalonians and God were called to witness to the truth of the denials in vv. 1–6 (see v. 5), so both the Thessalonians and God himself are cited as eyewitnesses of the truth of Paul's positive statements (see v. 10).

(2) Affirmations (2:7–12)

**[7]but we were gentle among you, like a mother caring for her little children. [8]We loved you so much that we were delighted to share with you not only the gospel of God but our lives as well, because you had become so dear to us. [9]Surely you remember, brothers, our toil and hardship; we worked night and day in order not to be a burden to anyone while we preached the gospel of God to you.
[10]You are witnesses, and so is God, of how holy, righteous and blameless we were among you who believed. [11]For you know that we dealt with each of you as a father deals with his own children, [12]encouraging, comforting and urging you to live lives worthy of God, who calls you into his kingdom and glory.**

2:7 The interpretation of the first clause of this verse (the second clause in the Greek text) hinges on a decision regarding a textual variant. The word at issue is translated "gentle" in the NIV. Extant Greek manuscripts have one of two words at this point, either *ēpioi,* meaning "gentle," or *nēpioi,* meaning "babes." The only difference between the

---

[38] See the discussion in Wanamaker, *1 and 2 Thessalonians,* 99.

way the two Greek words are written is the *nu* (comparable to an English *n*) at the beginning of the word meaning "babes." To complicate matters the word immediately before *ēpioi/nēpioi* is *egenēthēmen*, which ends in a *nu*. In Paul's day Greek texts were written without any spaces between the individual words. Thus the variant could have resulted either from the accidental doubling of the *nu* at the end of *egenēthēmen* (thus changing *egenēthēmen ēpioi* to *egenēthēmen nēpioi*) or the accidental omission of a *nu* (thus changing *egenēthēmen nēpioi* to *egenēthēmen ēpioi*). These particular scribal errors could occur in a scriptorium where the words were being read aloud and multiple copies made (a hearing error) or as the result of a single scribe either dropping or doubling a *nu* (a visual error).

Did Paul write that the missionaries were "gentle" *(ēpioi)* or that they were "infants" *(nēpioi)?* External evidence (matters related to the number, character, and date of manuscripts) is somewhat stronger for "infants" than it is for "gentle."[39] Internal evidence (arguments derived from known scribal tendencies and tendencies of the author) is not decisive. On favor of "infants" it may be observed that in the preceding context the apostle denied that he engaged in flattery or deceit. What can be more guileless than a babe? Also Paul used "infant" twelve times in other letters, but "gentle" occurs only in 2 Tim 2:24. In addition, the image of an infant could logically lead to an image of a "mother" (lit., "nurse"). The sudden shift in images (i.e., "we were babes among you, like a mother") is difficult enough to make it improbable that a scribe would intentionally create such a mixed metaphor. But faced with this mixed metaphor a scribe might have been tempted to change "infant" to "gentle" on the assumption that an earlier scribe had miscopied the text. Finally, passages such as Gal 4:19 and Eph 2:19–22 make it clear that Paul was perfectly capable of creating blatant mixed metaphors.

In favor of the reading "gentle," we should observe that the external evidence is far from decisive, and v. 6b with its stress on apostolic authority would logically need "gentle" as a balancing concept. Also "gentle" removes the unlikely and sudden shift in image from "infant" to "mother." More significantly, although Paul did use "infant" elsewhere, he always used it to describe others, never himself. Finally, the repeated Pauline use of "infant" could have resulted in a scribal ten-

---

[39] See the listing of individual MSS involved and a brief discussion in F. F. Bruce, *The Text of the New Testament,* 2d ed. (New York: Oxford University Press, 1968), 230–33.

dency to harmonize and read the frequently occurring "infant" *(nēpioi)* in a place where Paul had actually used the rarer "gentle" *(ēpioi)*. Thus we, along with the NIV, prefer the reading "gentle."[40]

A second difficulty in relation to v. 7 is its punctuation. Should v. 6 end with a period (RSV) or a comma (NIV)? The choice of a comma implies that the apostle's decision to be gentle with the new converts (v. 7a) is to be contrasted with his determination not to exert his authority (v. 6b). However, the structure of vv. 5–6 (i.e., three assertions each followed by a supporting proof, the last proof being v. 6b) suggests that v. 6b should be taken with what precedes it. Verse 7 then begins a new sentence.[41] It is also uncertain whether v. 7 should end with a period (NIV) or should extend to include the participle and pronoun at the beginning of v. 8.[42] Extended into v. 8a the sentence beginning with v. 7 would read, "Like a mother cares for her children, that's how much we cared for you" (author translation). If the beginning of v. 8 is taken with v. 7b, then "we were delighted to share with you" should be understood as the beginning of a new sentence. Taking v. 8a with what precedes rather than what follows also eliminates the redundancy that occurs if v. 8 begins, "We loved you so much" and ends "because you had become so dear to us." (See chart on next page for results of the various revisions in punctuation.)

Flattery, greed, and exploitation did not characterize the apostles in Thessalonica. The Thessalonians knew this, God is witness of this, and their behavior proved this (vv. 5–6). Rather than these, Paul and his coworkers demonstrated guilelessness and a parental gentleness born of love (vv. 7–8). The word translated "mother" *(trophos)* literally refers to a woman who is nursing a child. It may be translated "wet nurse" rather than "mother," but most likely Paul chose the term to convey tenderness, not to distinguish between a mother and a nurse. The children are also identified as her "own" *(heautēs)* children (not her "little" children). Thus the image is that of a nursing mother caring for her own infant. The fact that this woman is nursing her own children rather than acting as a hired wet nurse implies a parental bond that goes beyond

---

[40] In support of "gentle" see Bruce, *Text of the New Testament,* 232. Contrast with this Morris, who finds the evidence rather evenly balanced but prefers the reading νήπιοι, "infants" (*1 and 2 Thessalonians,* 76–79).

[41] The editors of the UBS text also place a period at the end of v. 6.

[42] Frame asserts that "no punctuation is necessary before *houtēs*" (the first word of v. 8; see *1 and 2 Thessalonians,* 101).

mere gentleness and bridges well to the assertions of love in the following verse.[43]

Assertion	Proof
v. 5 οὔτε γάρ ποτε ἐν λόγῳ κολακείας ἐγενήθημεν οὔτε ἐν προφάσει πλεονεξίας We never used flattery, nor did we put on a mask to cover up greed	καθὼς οἴδατε, You know θεὸς μάρτυς, God is our witness
v. 6 οὔτε ζητοῦντες ἐξ ἀνθρώπων δόξαν οὔτε ἀφ' ὑμῶν οὔτε ἀπ' ἄλλων We were not looking for praise from men, not from you or anyone else	v. 7a δυνάμενοι ἐν βάρει εἶναι ὡς Χριστοῦ ἀπόστολοι As apostles of Christ we could have been a burden to you
v. 7b ἀλλα' ἐγενήθημεν νήπιοι ἐν μέσῳ ὑμω"ν, ὡς ἐάν τροφὸς θάλπῃ τα' ἑαυτῆς τέκνα' But we were gentle among you, like a mother caring for her little children	v. 8a οὕτως ὁμειρόμενοι ὑμῶν. We loved you so much
v. 8b εὐδοκοῦμεν μεταδοῦναι ὑμῖν οὐ μόνον το' εὐαγγέλιον τοῦ θεοῦ ἀλλα' καὶ τας ἑαυτῶν ψυχάς that we were delighted to share with you not only the Gospel of God but our lives as well	διότι ἀγαπητοι' ἡμῖν ἐγενήθητε because you had become dear to us.

2:8 The primary statement of the verse, "we were delighted to share with you ...," is bracketed by two assertions. The verse begins with a causal clause in Greek (lit.), "since we had such warm feelings *[homeiromenoi]* for you." It ends with another causal clause, "because you became beloved *[agapētoi]* to us." As explained, the redundancy created by applying both clauses to "we were delighted" is eliminated by taking the first of these clauses as an elaboration on the preceding

---

[43] "The point of the new metaphor is love" (Frame, *1 and 2 Thessalonians*, 100–101). The image of maternal care was used as a positive image in a variety of ancient contexts symbolizing love for one's hearers or for fellow worshipers. See Donfried, "Cults," 238–40, and Malherbe, "Gentle as a Nurse," 211–14.

verse (v. 7). "We loved" translates a rare word *(homeiromoi)* connoting the bond between a parent and a beloved child,[44] which is the focus of v. 7b. Thus in vv. 7b–8a the apostles stated that like a nurse taking care of her children, so (translated "so much" in the NIV) "we loved you."

Paul and his companions brought the Thessalonians the gift of the gospel of God. By proclaiming the message that God had entrusted to them, they were fulfilling their divine commission (2:4). The missionaries' willingness to go beyond the God-given task of sharing the gospel demonstrated the strength and genuineness of the love they had for the Thessalonians. "We were delighted to share ... our lives as well," asserted Paul. The verb "delighted" is a present tense (lit., "we are delighted"). The act of sharing the gospel was clearly a reference to ministry in Thessalonica in the past, but it was an ongoing commitment as well. Sharing their "lives" *(pseuchas)* indicates close personal involvement with the believers. Paul's work was not carried out with detached professionalism. Although Paul did not shrink from the idea of his own death (Phil 2:23–24), it is unlikely that this particular statement refers to death.[45] Paul and his coworkers could not stand aloof from the people of the Thessalonian church because the church had become "so dear" *(agapētoi,* lit., "beloved") to them. A gospel messenger who stands detached from his audience has not yet been touched by the very gospel he proclaims. The gospel creates a community characterized by love. Reminding the Thessalonians of this not only clarified Paul's motivation but also schooled the readers in the true character expected of them if they would work in the name of Christ.

2:9 In addition to gentle affection born of Christian love, the evangelists also modeled for the church an unmistakable spirit of industry and self-reliance, a spirit diametrically opposed to the charlatans who sold religion in the marketplace, as well as at odds with the idle who lived off the generosity of others (1 Thess 5:14; 2 Thess 3:6–15). It was Paul's apostolic right to place the financial "burden" on the young congregation of requiring both respect and material support (cf. 2:6b). Rather than do this, Paul and company opted to support themselves with their own labor. Paul called on the church to remember (*mnēmoneuō,*

---

[44] See *TDNT* s.v. "ὁμείρομαι," which describes the verb as " 'to feel oneself drawn to something,' with strong intensification of the feeling" (v. 5, 176). Similarly see MM, s.v. "ὁμείρομαι."

[45] See J. E. Frame, *A Critical and Exegetical Commentary on the Epistles of St. Paul to the Thessalonians* (Edinburgh: T & T Clark, 1960), 102.

cf. 1:3) the missionaries' toil *(kopos,* cf. 1:3) and labor *(mochthos)*.[46] It is unlikely that the repetition of these terms from the introductory thanksgiving was an accident. Paul's remembrance and thanksgiving for the Thessalonians' "labor of love" should have been matched by equal recall and gratitude on the church's part. It appears that even the apostle Paul was unappreciated on occasion.

A second statement clarified Paul's meaning. At the same time that the missionaries were proclaiming the gospel, they were also working to pay for their own subsistence. The typical artisan had to work a full day, sunrise to sunset, to earn enough for food and lodging. If Paul worked by day [47] at a craft and then worked additional hours at his ministry, it is little wonder that he could comment, "I have labored and toiled, and have often gone without sleep" (2 Cor 11:27).[48] Obviously Paul did not work around the clock. But the phrase "night and day" describes a long and exhausting daily schedule. The reason for working night and day was to avoid being "a burden to anyone." The negative purpose clause utilizes an infinitive *(epibarēsai)* that echoes the noun "burden" *(barei)* in v. 6 (Gk. v. 7). Here the authority is narrowed to the right to financial support, a right that Paul and his coworkers voluntarily surrendered. It was an act that clearly expressed the concern of the missionaries for the unhindered advance of the gospel (cf. 1 Cor 9:7–12) and their love for the members of the church. It was an act that just as clearly proclaimed that the missionaries were not like those making a living by selling religion to the gullible in the marketplace, caring less about their audience than they did about their daily income.

2:10–12 Again Paul called upon the church and upon God himself as witnesses (cf. v. 5). While among the Thessalonians he and his coworkers lived "holy, righteous, and blameless" lives. Paul used three adverbs here to describe the way the missionaries lived. He did not ask

---

[46] The same combination of terms for labor occur in 2 Cor 11:27 and 2 Thess 3:8. Κόπος and μόχθος are synonyms; the use of the two in combination is for emphasis.

[47] If Paul engaged in discourse during daylight hours (Acts 19:9), he would presumably have to have started work before sunrise or perform part of his work in the evenings if he worked the ten to twelve hours expected of an artisan.

[48] Paul's letters tell us he worked with his own hands (1 Cor 4:12). Acts tells us that in Corinth, Paul worked with Aquila and Priscilla as a leather worker (σκηνοποιός). See R. F. Hock, *The Social Context of Paul's Ministry: Tentmaking and Apostleship* (Philadelphia: Fortress, 1980), and the articles published earlier by the same author, "Paul's Tentmaking and the Problem of His Social Class," *JBL* 97 (1978): 555–64, and "The Workshop as a Social Setting for Paul's Missionary Preaching," *CBQ* 41 (1979): 438–50.

the church to affirm things they could not know (matters of inner purity) but things they saw daily for weeks or even months. "Holy" *(hosiōs)* and "righteous" *(dikaiōs),* in a Hellenistic setting, were used in tandem to refer to the keeping of both the laws of God and the laws of man. That Paul intended this usage is not certain,[49] but such an understanding makes sense following a call upon God and men as witnesses.[50] Paul's behavior was both pious and legal. These two positive assertions are reinforced with the negative "blameless" *(amemptōs).* If the first two adverbs indicate behavior that conforms to the standards set by man and by God, this last adverb asserts that no charge that he was in violation of these standards could be justified. The evangelists' behavior is further described in a lengthy construction including an analogy (v. 11), a series of three participles (v. 12a), and a purpose clause (v. 12b).

"For you know" continues the overt reference to the apostles' past history with the Thessalonians. Paul's behavior was not only exemplary while he was with them but it was also fatherly. Verses 9–10 paint a picture of a self-reliant, considerate, and righteous missionary. The use of another familial (cf. the analogy of the nursing mother, v. 7), that of a good father, adds warmth and a personal touch to the depiction of his relationship with the church.[51] Translation of the verse is complicated by the absence of a main verb. "Each one of you ... as a father ... his own children" expresses the ellipsis found in v. 11. The sentence may be translated into English in two ways. Some translators opt to add a verb to v. 11 that seems to fit the context and then use the participles of v. 12 as expansion of v. 11. The NIV does this, supplying the verbs, "We dealt with [each of you as a father] deals [with his own children]." The participles of v. 12, "encouraging, comforting and urging," then describe the manner in which a father deals with his children. Other translators do much the same, only varying the verb supplied in v. 11.[52] A second way to approach the problem is to use the participles of v. 12 as the primary verbal statements of the construction, creating a translation like the RSV's "like a father with his children, we exhorted each

---

[49] See Bruce, who argues that "the classical distinction between the two terms was blurred in Hellenistic Greek" (*1 and 2 Thessalonians,* 36).

[50] Wanamaker, *1 and 2 Thessalonians,* 105.

[51] For other instances of the father image see Gal 4:19; 1 Cor 4:14–21; 2 Cor 6:11–13.

[52] Best suggests "we counseled" (*1 and 2 Thessalonians,* 106); Wanamaker suggests "we brought up" or "we trained" (*1 and 2 Thessalonians,* 106). It is also possible to assume that Paul intended to repeat the verb from v. 10, ἐγενήθημεν, but this verb is difficult to fit into the syntax of v. 11.

one of you and encouraged you and charged you." Though the syntax of the verse is difficult and translations vary accordingly, the sense of the verse is relatively clear. Paul intended the analogy to convey to his spiritual children both his affection and his authority.

The emphasis in the Greek implicit in the phrases "each of you" and "his own children" strengthens the impression of personal and individual concern. The authority of the father in the family was supreme in Greco-Roman society. He was responsible for arranging for the training of his children. He, or those he assigned the task of rearing the children, would educate and/or discipline as needed.[53] Conversion to Christianity brought the converts into a new family and a new way of life. Adapting to this new life was no doubt difficult for the person who did not live in a society familiar with Christianity. Such people needed fatherly guidance then even as they do today.

"Encouraging" (parakalountes) and "comforting" (paramythoumenoi) are synonyms. Both the verbs we find here and the related nouns were often used by Paul in tandem. Both verbs indicate the act of encouraging or cheering someone. The first word more frequently than the second carries the connotation of exhortation, yet both are also used in contexts of admonition. The combination in Paul seems to indicate a positive encouragement to Christian living. "Urging" (martyromenoi) connotes the delivery of truth and was likely meant to convey the more directive functions of a father. A good father encourages and provides guidance. Yet Paul did not claim ultimate authority over his children. He did not appoint himself their father, nor was he free to act whimsically (as an earthly first-century father might), requiring of them what he willed. Rather, Paul's function as their Christian father was to train believers in order that they should "live lives worthy of God." It was not Paul's own will but the Heavenly Father's that governed both his actions and the guidance he gave to the church.

"To live" (lit., "to walk") implies continuity of conduct. The purpose of the fatherly encouragement and exhortation is to produce lives "worthy of God." A "worthy" life is a life that is appropriate or suitable and was commonly followed by the genitive of the person or thing that served as the point of reference. To live "worthy of God" makes God the focal point, the one who determines what is appropriate and what is

---

[53] F. Lyall's discussion of Roman law draws numerous parallels that might have been operative in the mind of the hearers of Paul's family analogies (Slaves, Citizens, Sons— Legal Metaphors in the Epistles [Grand Rapids: Academie, 1984], 119–30).

not. It means to live in a manner consistent with the commands and character of God. This was the very behavior Paul himself sought to model for the young Thessalonian believers.

In its historical setting Paul may have written 2:1–12 as an apostolic apology defending the missionaries' behavior or as an apostolic admonition presenting their *ethos* for the church to emulate. For modern readers the latter element dominates. Christian leaders of every era must recognize that life and faith cannot be separated (cf. Mal 2:6–8). The character of our lives impacts our ability to share the gospel effectively. Both the truth of our words and their implications are known by the way we live. An immoral (v. 2), deceitful (v. 2), manipulative, and self-centered (vv. 4–5) so-called minister is a fraud and ultimately will be recognized as such. As damning as his personal sin may be, the sin of misleading the faithful is worse (Matt 18:6). Paul encouraged the church to imitate him and in turn to become models of Christian behavior for others. If those to whom we minister were to live as we live, what kind of church would result?

This passage presents us with a great warning but also with a great opportunity. It reminds us that the power of our words can be multiplied if only the character of our lives is consistent with the gospel. It assures us that our critics can do no worse than spread blatant and transparent lies if the character of our actions is above reproach (v. 10). And it gives us the hope that by sowing a just, selfless, and loving example among those we lead we can expect to reap just, selfless, and loving behavior from those who follow.

Those called by God must live in a manner appropriate to that call, anticipating his kingdom and glory. The present participle "who calls" looks not to the conversion of the Thessalonians in the past but focuses on the ongoing calling that anticipates the future dawning of the age to come. The future hope, the anticipation of the coming kingdom and glory of God, is presented in 1 Thessalonians as a motivation for perseverance in the Christian life. Paul's statement here anticipates the paraenesis of chaps. 4–5 and echoes the thanksgiving of 1:3. It is not surprising that it is followed by the second of the three thanksgivings found in chaps. 1–3.

3. Thanksgiving for Perseverance in the Gospel (2:13–16)

This section of the letter begins with the second thanksgiving in a series of three (1:2–5; 2:13; 3:9–13) that dominate the tone of the first three chapters. They overlap in content; the first and second both utilize the concept of "imitation." The first thanks leads to an affirmation of the Thessalonian imitation of the apostles and of the Lord as they received and began to live out the implications of the gospel. This second prayer of thanks leads to an affirmation of the Thessalonian imitation of the Judean churches as they persevere in the face of persecution. Thus the themes of the "work produced by faith," "labor prompted by love," and "endurance inspired by hope" (1:3) introduced in the introductory thanksgiving are given specific content. The first two (work of faith and labor of love) are featured following the first thanksgiving, the third (endurance inspired by hope) following this, the second thanksgiving.

This thanksgiving also serves as a transition from 2:1–12 to 2:17–3:8. The former passage focuses on the character of the apostle during the time he was with the Thessalonians. The latter explains the actions of the apostle after he was driven out of the city.

The expanded section of thanksgiving in 2:13–16 celebrates both the Thessalonian reception of the faith (2:13–14) and their endurance in spite of violent Jewish opposition (2:15–16). It connects the two by reference to the Thessalonian imitation of the faith. The faith imitated in this passage, however, is not that of the apostle (as following 1:6) but that of the Jewish-Christian churches in Judea (2:14). By highlighting the Jewish opposition the Thessalonians suffered, Paul reminded his readers of the circumstances of his own departure (cf. Acts 17:5–10). He did not leave voluntarily but was "torn away" from the church. He longed to return. His prolonged absence was not a sign that he did not care about them but the result of satanic opposition blocking his path (2:17–18).

Even as it serves as a transition, the passage also functioned as additional affirmation and encouragement to the church. It compares the predominantly Gentile Thessalonian believers favorably to the Jewish-Christian churches in the cradle of Christianity. Also it reminded the Thessalonians that they were not alone in the experience of suffering. Even in suffering (perhaps especially then) there is comfort in companionship. In addition, it assured the church that their persecutors would eventually reap the wrath of God (2:15–16). Drawing comfort from the anticipation of God's judgment on the persecutors may seem harsh, but the Psalms reflect a lengthy history of making the bitter taste of suffering more palatable by predicting the destruction of the wicked.

This passage is not anti-Semitic. Paul did not condemn the Jews as a people, nor does the passage condemn those Jews who simply rejected the faith. The harsh words in vv. 15–16 were directed specifically at the persecutors of the faithful. That Paul was railing specifically against the persecutors of the church is clearly seen in the comparison of the Jewish persecution of the Judean church to Gentile persecution of the Macedonian church ("you suffered from your own countrymen," v. 14). The wrath of God was earned not by the Jewish nation in general but by persecutors obstructing the advance of the gospel. Although this passage does not allude to the fact, we should also remember that even persecutors are not beyond the reach of the grace of God. Paul, himself a former persecutor of the church, both knew and celebrated this truth.[54]

(1) Thanksgiving (2:13)

[13]And we also thank God continually because, when you received the word of God, which you heard from us, you accepted it not as the word of men, but as it actually is, the word of God, which is at work in you who believe.

2:13 Elements of the thanksgiving form used in 1:2 are repeated here. "We thank God" and the adverb translated "continually" (shifted into 1:3 in the NIV) are identical. The "and … also" in the NIV uses the first of two *kai*'s to mark a transition. The second *kai* ("also") may imply either a second instance of thanksgiving or that the missionaries also (in addition to the Thessalonians) gave thanks. The latter is unlikely and requires the supposition that Paul was responding to news that the Thessalonians were thankful that Paul had brought them the gospel.[55] More likely the second *kai* reminds the reader that Paul was a

---

[54] Several scholars have disputed the authenticity of 2:13–16 on various grounds. In terms of the structure of the letter, 2:13–16 interrupts a narrative that could easily flow uninterrupted from 2:12 to 2:17. W. Schmithals accepts the Pauline authorship of 2:13–16 but argues that its placement here is the result of the redaction of four Pauline letters into the two we have today (*Paul and the Gnostics* [Nashville: Abingdon, 1972]). See also H. Boers, "The Form Critical Study of Paul's Letters: 1 Thessalonians as a Case Study," *NTS* 22 (1975–76): 140–58. In addition, the apparently anti-Semitic tone, the presence of unusual grammar and syntax, and the reference to a judgment that had fallen on the Jews (Jerusalem's destruction?) have led some to consider 2:13–16 (especially vv. 15–16) an interpolation. See B. A. Pearson, "1 Thessalonians 2:13–16: A Deutero-Pauline Interpolation," *HTR* 64 (1971): 79–94, and D. Schmidt, "1 Thessalonians 2:13–16: Linguistic Evidence for an Interpolation," *JBL* 102 (1983): 269–79. Contrast with these the arguments of Wanamaker, *1 and 2 Thessalonians*, 29–37, 108–10.

[55] So F. F. Bruce suggests in the basis of the word order καὶ ἡμεῖς εὐχαριστοῦμεν (*1 and 2 Thessalonians*, WBC [Waco: Word, 1982], 44).

second time taking up the theme of thanksgiving.

The NIV combines *dia touto* and the causal particle *oti* into a single statement that presents the remainder of the verse as the reason for giving thanks. The "for this" in the RSV (*dia touto*) at the beginning of v. 13 could refer to the preceding verse or to what follows. The ordinary sequence for a Pauline thanksgiving places the reasons for giving thanks after the verb of thanksgiving. Although this thanksgiving is not in the ordinary location at the beginning of the letter, still the pattern seems to hold, as the *oti* ("because") following "we thank God" also indicates. The apostle identified the Thessalonians' recognition of the gospel as the word of God as the cause for thanksgiving in v. 13.

"When you received" translates the participial form of a verb commonly used of the reception of tradition (cf. 1 Cor 11:23; 15:1,3; Gal 1:9,12; 1 Thess 4:1). Likewise "heard from us" makes clear that Paul was thinking about the apostolic gospel that the missionaries passed on to the Thessalonians. Yet it was the divine origin of the message that Paul wished to emphasize, leading to the addition of "of God" in an unusual location at the end of the clause in the Greek text.

A similar clarification occurs when the apostle inserted the clause "as it actually is" into the statement "you accepted it not as the word of men, but as the word of God" (cf. Rom 1:5; Gal 1:8–9; 2 Cor 13:3; 1 Tim 2:7).[56] Though the verse does not flow smoothly due to these insertions, the intent is clear. Paul was praising the Thessalonians for their spiritual wisdom. They recognized and accepted the gospel as a word from God himself, not the product of debatable human wisdom. The fact that this word "is at work in you who believe" serves as further validation both of the truth of the gospel and of the Thessalonian faith. The present tense participle "believe" shifts the focus of the verse from the event of the Thessalonians' conversion to the present state of their faith. As in 1:5 it is the power of God at work in the believers that validates the gospel message and distinguishes the people of God.[57]

---

[56] W. A. Grudem notes ("Scripture's Self-attestation and the Problem of Formulating a Doctrine of Scripture," in *Scripture and Truth* [Grand Rapids: Zondervan, 1983], 45) that "there is abundant evidence of God's speech through human lips" and cites along with this text Matt 10:19–20; Luke 10:16; John 17:8; Acts 2:41; 4:29,31; 2 Cor 13:3; Gal 1:8–9,10–11 (besides passages referring to Jesus' words).

[57] Ἐνεργεῖται is generally used of supernatural activity. Paul did not indicate what manifestations of divine power he had in mind but included the clause in the context of a comparison between the Thessalonian and the Judean churches. We are left to assume that God worked in both in similar fashion.

(2) Affirmation (2:14–16)

[14]For you, brothers, became imitators of God's churches in Judea, which are in Christ Jesus: You suffered from your own countrymen the same things those churches suffered from the Jews, [15]who killed the Lord Jesus and the prophets and also drove us out. They displease God and are hostile to all men [16]in their effort to keep us from speaking to the Gentiles so that they may be saved. In this way they always heap up their sins to the limit. The wrath of God has come upon them at last.

2:14–16 "For" implies that what follows is in some measure evidence of the working of God in the midst of the Thessalonians. The "you" is emphatic. The proof of their acceptance of the gospel is again their "imitation" of fellow believers (cf. v. 6). But this time it was not Paul or even the Lord who supplied the pattern of faithfulness; it was the churches of God in Judea. As in the introduction of the letter, "churches" *(ekklēsiōn)* is clarified. They are "God's" assemblies "in Christ Jesus." Geographically they were the Christian assemblies "in Judea." Paul used this phrase in Gal 1:23 of the Jewish-Christian churches in the vicinity of Jerusalem. These churches suffered at the hands of fellow Jews, their countrymen, who did not believe. Likewise, Paul pointed out to the Thessalonians, "you suffered from your own countrymen." This particular "imitation" hardly could have been intentional. The Thessalonians' knowledge of the Judean churches would not have been firsthand, and nowhere did Paul encourage the seeking of persecution in order to imitate the suffering of the faithful. The Thessalonians suffered because suffering is all too often the lot of a righteous community in an unrighteous world.

Who were these countrymen *(symphyletōn)* who persecuted the Thessalonians? The earlier indications that the church was predominantly Gentile (1:9) and the contrast here between "your countrymen" and "the Jews" may indicate that Paul was thinking of Gentile persecution of the church. But *symphyletōn* is not a synonym for "Gentiles." It refers to the fellow residents of one's city or of a particular district of a city.[58] If the incident recorded in Acts 17:5–9 was the beginning of the persecution Paul had in mind, it involved Jews, "some bad characters from the marketplace," the "mob"; and it was moderated by the "city officials." Subsequent persecutions probably were not exclusively Gentile affairs. It seems more likely that "countrymen" should be under-

---

[58] C. Maurer, *TDNT* 9, s.v. "φυλή."

stood as a reference to fellow Thessalonians (Gentile and Jew).

Acts presents a Judean church that suffered at the hands of Rome because Rome considered it a disruptive influence (Acts 12:1–4; 21:33–34) and suffered Jewish persecution as a cult that demeaned Moses and the temple (Acts 6:8–14). The exact character of the persecution that followed Stephen's death is uncertain. Mob violence and some form of official imprisonment are probable.[59] Paul's involvement as one of the persecutors of the church at that time (Acts 8:3; Gal 1:13,22–24; Phil 3:6) lends a certain poignancy to the comparison.

It is unnecessary to pinpoint a particular persecution as the basis for Paul's comparison because the experience of Thessalonian Christians need not have paralleled the Judean experience exactly for the comparison to work. The primary feature of Paul's comparison is suffering at the hands of one's countrymen. Whatever mob-inspired (Acts 17:5) or officially sanctioned (Acts 17:6–9) punishments were meted out, that which both the Thessalonian and the Judean communities experienced was social rejection and the painful isolation that can result. Yet in spite of these, the Thessalonians, like the Judeans before them, persevered. Both the persecution suffered and the perseverance demonstrated provide evidence of a genuine faith. The gospel was worth suffering for. The Thessalonians' willingness to suffer persecution without relinquishing the faith demonstrated the great esteem in which they held this "word of God." Paul gave thanks for the genuineness of their faith proven in the crucible of persecution.

2:15 The Jews who opposed the gospel were condemned soundly. A series of ascriptive participles castigate the Jews who killed Jesus, killed the prophets, drove out the apostles, who were not pleasing to God, and were enemies (the one descriptive adjective used in the midst of several adjectival participles) of all humanity in that they attempted to prevent the spread of the gospel that is the salvation of humanity. This is the only instance in which Paul charged "the Jews" with the death of Jesus (cf. 1 Cor 2:8). In 2 Cor 11:24, however, Paul did use the same term, "the Jews," referring to the Jewish opponents of Christianity at whose hands he received "forty lashes minus one." Here, as is often the case in the Gospel of John (5:18; 7:1; 18:14,31; cf. 11:45,54), "the Jews" is used as a reference not to the people as a whole nor even to

---

[59] See also Bruce's suggestion that "we should think here of a more recent persecution associated with the increase of Zealot activity in Judea around the time of Ventidius Cumanus's arrival as procurator in A.D. 48 (*1 and 2 Thessalonians*, 46).

those who remained Jews religiously but to those Jews who actively opposed the spread of the gospel.[60]

The compactness of the litany of offenses gives it a harsh, angry texture. The first accusation is that these Jews killed the Lord Jesus and the prophets. Paul did not write that they crucified Jesus, and, strictly speaking, it was the Romans who executed Jesus on Golgotha. But the culpability of the religious leaders particularly, and in some measure the people who did not cry out for Jesus' release when Pilate offered it (Acts 3:13–15; 4:10; 7:52), was plain in the eyes of the church. A simpler explanation for Paul's choice of terms, however, is that "Jesus" and "the prophets" are the object of the same verb, and "killed" is general enough to apply to both objects.

"The prophets" may be taken either with what precedes (as in the NIV) or with what follows, "and persecuted both the prophets and us" (author translation). The ambiguity is aggravated by uncertainty regarding the identity of the "prophets." Most commentators argue that Paul was thinking of the Hebrew prophets. The Jews are castigated in the New Testament for rejecting and killing God's prophets (Matt 23:29–37; Acts 7:52). And it seems more likely that Paul would link the death of Jesus to the killing of the Hebrew prophets (who predicted his coming) than to the martyrdom of "prophets" in the early church. Only by presuming a chronological sequence in v. 15 does it make more sense to understand the prophets to be persons such as Stephen and James (who were killed) or Philip, Peter, and Paul (who were persecuted). The sequence in the first half of v. 15 then would flow from the killing of Jesus to the persecution of the prophets of the early church and of the Apostle to the Gentiles. Whether the prophets are Hebrews or Christians, still their persecutors displeased God and were hostile to all men in that they hindered the advance of God's message of salvation.

"Killed" is an aorist participle that reflects specific events in the past. "Drove us out" (ekdiōxantōn) or "persecuted"[61] is also aorist, which may indicate that Paul was thinking of specific instances of persecution, which had already concluded, rather than opposition in general, which

---

[60] Contrast E. Best, *A Commentary on the First and Second Epistles to the Thessalonians* (London: A. & C. Black, 1977), 114. This usage does not distinguish between those who were "Jews both by race and religion" and those who were "Jews by race but Christians by religion." It is not Judaism that is condemned in these verses but active Jewish opposition to Christianity.

[61] Ibid.

continually confronted his ministry. With the next condemnation, "they displease God," Paul switched to a present participle, implying that he had left the realm of historical reflection and begun characterizing the opponents of the gospel more generally. Though this is a shift in the thought, it is not the beginning of a new sentence (NIV) but a continuation of the description of "the Jews."

Paul often wrote of persons pleasing or not pleasing God. Those who do not please God are controlled by their sinful nature (Rom 8:8). They are more concerned with themselves than they are with the things of God or the needs of others (Rom 15:3; 1 Cor 7:32–34; 10:33; Gal 1:10). Pleasing God means living in a manner consistent with his commands (1 Thess 4:1). By opposing the will of God (the spread of the gospel) the Jews demonstrated that they did not please God. In the same way, they made themselves enemies of humanity. With the words "hostile to all men" Paul echoed the charge of antisocial behavior brought against the Jews by numerous Hellenistic writers.[62] Tacitus, for example, wrote that the Jews "regard as profane all that we hold sacred; on the other hand, they permit all that we abhor." In addition to condemning the religion of the Jews, he observed that "the Jews are extremely loyal toward one another and always ready to show compassion, but toward every other people they feel only hate and enmity. They sit apart at meals, and they sleep apart. They adopted circumcision to distinguish themselves from other people."[63] But Paul's condemnation had nothing to do with Jewish monotheism or Jewish exclusivism (characteristics the Christians shared and for which they also were criticized). Paul's condemnation of the Jews rested exclusively on the foundation of their active attempts to block the advance of God's gospel.

2:16 "In their effort to keep us from speaking" is linked to what precedes. It provides the last in a series of ascriptive modifiers (all participles but one) in vv. 15–16 descriptive of the Jews, "who killed ... Jesus and the prophets, and drove us out, and displease God, and oppose all men, by hindering us from speaking" (RSV). The present tense of the participle "hindering" implies that the Jews' opposition to the gospel was not occasional but manifested itself regularly (cf. Acts 13:45–50; 14:2,19; 17:5–10,13; 18:12; 21:10–14; 23:12–15; 24:1–9). "Hindering ..." is not linked to the preceding sequence by a conjunction and is best understood as Paul's explanation of the charge that the Jews

---

[62] See M. Whittaker, *Jews and Christians: Greco-Roman Views,* CCWJCW (Cambridge: University Press, 1984), for sample quotations.

[63] Tacitus, *Histories* 5.5.

were enemies of humanity. "Speaking to the Gentiles so that they may be saved" is a summary of the Pauline mission. By hindering Paul's mission, the Jews would keep the saving power of the gospel from a needy humanity and in this were "hostile to all men."

What a condemnation![64] Paul's rhetoric here slops blame with such a broad brush stroke that he could easily be read as anti-Semitic. Yet Paul was a Jew addressing a church that included Jewish Christians. He no more meant to say that the Jews, as a people, were enemies of humanity than he would have said that all Gentiles were enemies of God. What Paul did assert was that the Jewish opponents of Christianity are enemies of humanity. This is not an ethnic comment. Paul's castigation of the Jewish opponents of the church of Judea is part of a comparison. The Thessalonian Christians, he observed, have survived similar opposition to that which afflicted the Judean churches. If the exact actions (e.g., killed Jesus) cannot be attributed to the Thessalonians' countrymen, still, the apostle had in mind the settled and sometimes violent opposition experienced by the Gentile church. These countrymen might be Jews or Gentiles. Paul made no attempt to classify them ethnically. The vital point of comparison was the opposition that afflicted the church and would rob humanity of the message of salvation.

Though v. 16b starts a new sentence in the NIV, in the Greek sentence it is a result clause that modifies the participle in v. 16a [65] In other words,

---

[64] Wanamaker attempts to minimize the anti-Semitic tone of vv. 14–16 by stressing the social function of this type of rhetoric *(vituperatio)*. Vilification of others served as a form of differentiation. It stressed the bad in a competing social group as a way of strengthening both the self-awareness and the commitment of the writer's group. Although this is a helpful insight on the passage, it leaves the impression that Paul's passage pits Jews against Christians. It does not. The two groups envisioned behind the rhetoric of vv. 14–16 are those who accept and promote the gospel (inc. Paul and, by inference, Jewish-Christian churches of Judea and Thessalonian believers) and those who reject and actively oppose the gospel (inc. "the Jews" and, by inference, certain of the Jewish and Gentile "countrymen" of the Thessalonians). See Wanamaker, *Commentary on 1 and 2 Thessalonians,* NIGTC (Grand Rapids: Eerdmans), 118–19, and the work of A. Y. Collins, "Vilification and Self-Definition in the Book of Revelation," *HTR* 79 (1986): 308–20, and S. Freyne, "Vilifying the Other and Defining the Self: Matthew's and John's Anti-Jewish Polemic in Focus," in *Christian, Jews, "Others" in Late Antiquity* (Atlanta: Scholars Press, 1985): 117–43.

[65] Εἰς τὸ ... may indicate either a result or a purpose clause. Most often in Paul's writings it is the latter. In many instances, however, purpose and result are two sides of the same coin and are difficult to differentiate. From the perspective of the Jews, their actions resulted in filling up their quota of sins. The idea of a full measure of sins, however, anticipates divine judgment; and seen from the perspective of the divine plan, the persecution of God's messengers serves the purpose (εἰς τὸ) of filling up their measure of sins and justifying the ultimate wrath of God (v. 16c).

the result of the Jews' opposition to the advance of the gospel (v. 16a) is that "they always heap up their sins to the limit" (v. 16b). Yet the clause implies more than opposition to the Gentile mission. Although the infinitive "heap up" is aorist, it probably was intended to encompass all the events of v. 15, as the adverb "always" implies. If Paul here was alluding to the long history of Jewish opposition to God's messengers (as "prophets" might indicate, v. 15) as a part of God's grand plan of salvation, then his words might imply their anticipated restoration as well (cf. Rom 11:25–32).[66] The final sentence in v. 16, however, makes this unlikely because it is a word of judgment, not restoration.

"The wrath of God has come upon them at last" is perhaps the most difficult statement in this passage. God's wrath is predominantly an eschatological event in Paul. Evil done by Jews or Gentiles earns God's wrath, which will be executed on the day of wrath—a fate avoided by those saved through Jesus (Rom 2:5; 5:9; 1 Thess 1:10; 5:9). Yet the wrath of God can also be manifested before that final day, even through pagan agency (Rom 1:18; 13:4–5). But what was the wrath "that has come upon" the Jews? The aorist verb would appear to refer to an event Paul was interpreting as a manifestation of divine wrath. He could have had reference to the fall of Jerusalem,[67] the expulsion of Jews from Rome by Claudius (Acts 18:2), the famine of A.D. 46 (Acts 11:28), or some combination of these and/or other events. On the other hand, the verb could indicate the arrival of wrath without including the arrival of punishment.[68] This interprets the statement to say that the Jews had earned God's wrath, and God holds it in store for them (cf. Rom 2:5) but leaves the execution of that wrath to a future date. In any event, even if Paul were referring to some tragedy that had befallen the Jewish opponents of the gospel, he would have considered it no more than a limited foretaste of the judgment awaiting them at the ultimate day of wrath.

The Greek behind "at last" *(eis telos)* also presents us with options. If the sentence is translated assuming a terrible event had befallen the

---

[66] At this early stage the ultimate fate of Israel may not have been a settled issue for the apostle. See W. D. Davies, "Paul and the People of Israel," *NTS* 24 (1977–78): 4–39.

[67] This would of course require that 2:13–16 be an interpolation into the letter after the fall in A.D. 70. See B. A. Pearson, "1 Thessalonians 2:13–16: A Deutero-Pauline Interpolation," *HTR* 64 (1971): 81–84.

[68] See the discussion and references for this possible reading of φθάνω in E. Best, *A Commentary on the First and Second Epistles to the Thessalonians* (London: A. & C. Black, 1977), 119.

Jews, then "at last" is appropriate. This temporal use of *eis telos* is also implied by the parallel structures of v. 16b and v. 16c; that is, a temporal "always" calls for a temporal "at last." The alternative translation "fully" or "forever" is lexically possible and reflects the LXX usage but runs afoul of Pauline passages that hold out hope for the eventual salvation even of Jewish opponents of the gospel who repent.

A third alternative is to understand *telos* as a reference to the end of the age. The resultant meaning is that wrath had accrued to the Jews in anticipation of the end, when God's judgment will fall on all who persist in disobedience. Such a reading allows for a temporal meaning of *telos* and avoids presuming that Paul was referring to some unnamed tragedy.

The Thessalonians had received the word of God and persisted in their Christian commitment in spite of persecution comparable to that inflicted on the churches of Judea (vv. 13–16). For this Paul gave thanks. In the thanksgiving he praised the Thessalonians for their endurance in the face of determined enemies of the kingdom of God. The praise was more than giving the faithful their due. It was also a way of encouraging the continuation of the church's endurance. But if persistence in the face of opposition is a virtue, one might well have asked why the apostle had not returned to Thessalonica himself. Why had he left them, his new children in the Lord, to face the trials alone? If he cared as much as he claimed, why did he not return to lend them his support and assistance? Paul was obliged to answer the charge that his absence made a lie of his claims of great love and concern. The thanksgiving of 2:13–16 serves both as an encouragement to the church and as a transition to a discussion of the apostle's behavior relative to the church since his turbulent departure many months earlier.

4. Apostolic Activities after Leaving Thessalonica Rehearsed (2:17–3:8)

Paul was aware of the stress the Thessalonian church was under. He himself had been run out of town and then chased out of Macedonia. He certainly was aware of the persistence of opposition to the gospel in Thessalonica. He thanked God for the perseverance of the Thessalonians (v. 3) in spite of their severe suffering (v. 6). But did it seem incongruous to some members of the church that Paul encouraged them to stand firm when he himself had left town when faced with opposition? Did some doubt his professions of parental care (vv. 7–8,11–12)?

His "children" were suffering, yet he had not even returned to support and encourage them.

Even if some church members themselves may not have been disillusioned by the apostle's prolonged absence (see 3:6), it seems likely that Paul's opponents in Thessalonica would have attempted to take advantage of the situation. His detractors might well have reasoned that if the apostle's professions of Christian love were shown to be false, then they could more easily argue that his gospel was false as well (see 3:5). Paul's comments in these verses were intended to detail the feelings and actions of his missionary team in an effort to assure the Thessalonians of the genuineness of his love and reinforce the good relationship reported by Timothy.[69]

(1) Expressions of Concern (2:17–3:5)

[17]But, brothers, when we were torn away from you for a short time (in person, not in thought), out of our intense longing we made every effort to see you. [18]For we wanted to come to you—certainly I, Paul, did, again and again—but Satan stopped us. [19]For what is our hope, our joy, or the crown in which we will glory in the presence of our Lord Jesus when he comes? Is it not you? [20]Indeed, you are our glory and joy.

[1]So when we could stand it no longer, we thought it best to be left by ourselves in Athens. [2]We sent Timothy, who is our brother and God's fellow worker in spreading the gospel of Christ, to strengthen and encourage you in your faith, [3]so that no one would be unsettled by these trials. You know quite well that we were destined for them. [4]In fact, when we were with you, we kept telling you that we would be persecuted. And it turned out that way, as you well know. [5]For this reason, when I could stand it no longer, I sent to find out about your faith. I was afraid that in some way the tempter might have tempted you and our efforts might have been useless.

2:17 Paul used emotionally charged language to describe his absence from Thessalonica. The missionaries were "torn away" (lit., "orphaned") from the church. The aorist participle alludes to the apos-

---

[69] This section of the letter is an excellent example of what R. W. Funk has called the implementation of the apostolic parousia. R. Funk's form-critical study highlights the importance of passages that might otherwise be skimmed over as mere travelogues when in fact they are expressions of Paul's apostolic authority. See "The Apostolic 'Parousia': Form and Significance," in *Christian History and Interpretation: Studies Presented to John Knox,* ed. W. R. Farmer, C. D. F. Moule and R. R. Niebuhr (Cambridge: University Press, 1967), 249–68.

tle's departure from the city under duress. The strong bond between Paul and the church, comparable to the bond between loving parent and beloved child, made separation a distress to the apostle although he had only been away from them "for a short time." And although a physical separation (separation "in person") had been forced upon him, they were never apart from him "in thought" (lit., "in heart"). Paul's description of his separation from the church was designed to express clearly that his absence did not result from indifference on his part.

Since the separation was involuntary and a source of distress to the apostle, it follows that he and his coworkers "made every effort" to return. The "we" of the main verb of v. 17, "we made every effort," is emphatic. In addition, Paul's "effort to see" the Thessalonians face to face was qualified in such a way as to give it the greatest possible emphasis. In fact, it is difficult to translate the sentence without sounding redundant. Paul endeavored (RSV) "the more eagerly" (*perissoterōs*—the comparative of "abundantly" used as a superlative) and "with great desire" (*epithumia*—one of the few positive uses of the normal Pauline word for "lust") to see them "face to face" (a repetition of *prosōpon*, "in person" from earlier in the verse).

2:18 "Again and again" Paul wanted to travel to Thessalonica (v. 18).[70] The phrase is best taken to modify Paul's desire: repeatedly he wanted to visit the Thessalonians. (This fits the context better than understanding the verse to say that Paul wanted to make several trips.) "I, Paul" is emphatic and stresses that the desire to visit was intensely personal on his part. He did not stay away by choice, but his earnest and frequent efforts to see the Thessalonian Christians were thwarted by Satan (v. 18). Elsewhere Paul wrote of Satan as the tempter (1 Cor 7:5), who by deception or any other means (2 Cor 11:14; 12:7) seeks to oppose and defeat the work of Christ (1 Cor 5:5; 2 Cor 2:11). The work of the man of lawlessness will be according to the power of Satan (2 Thess 2:9), but ultimately both will be defeated by God (Rom 16:20; 2 Thess 2:8).[71] How Satan "stopped" (*enekopsen*)[72] the apostle we are not told. Illness (Paul's thorn in the flesh?) and continued opposition by the authorities in Thessalonica are both possibilities, but we have too

---

[70] Lit., "once and twice," an idiom signifying repeated effort. See L. Morris, "Kai ...," *NovT* 1 (1956): 205–8, for a note on this phrase in the LXX.

[71] For a fuller discussion of σατανᾶς see W. Foerster, *TDNT,* s.v. "σατάν," vol. 7, 151–63.

[72] Cf. Gal 5:7 and Rom 15:22, where the same verb occurs.

little information to know what hindrances he had in mind.[73] What Paul did communicate clearly is that it was not lack of desire or lack of love that prevented his return to Thessalonica, and apparently that was what the church needed to hear.

2:19 In addition to the emotional, familial bond Paul felt toward his spiritual children, they also were his pride and joy. "For" indicates that what followed served as the basis of Paul's desire to see the Thessalonians again. He longed to see them not out of a sense of obligation but because of the joy, the hope, and the sense of pride their existence generated within him. The question asked in v. 19 is rhetorical and thus tantamount to a statement: "For you are our hope."[74] There is no verb in the Greek sentence (the NIV supplies "is"), a structure that highlights the nouns "hope," "joy," and "crown." The "or" that connects "crown" to the other two nouns is a disjunctive particle used in this context to add another element to the rhetorical question. Though the NIV does not indicate it, the same particle connects "hope" and "joy," creating a three-word sequence. The particle serves to highlight each word and make it stand out in the sentence, but it does not necessarily indicate that Paul intended to contrast the three.[75]

"Hope" in Paul commonly has eschatological overtones and is based on God's activity in Christ. It was unusual for Paul to identify believers as his hope, especially in a context anticipating the parousia. Bruce suggests that the hope indicated here is the hope Paul harbored for the Thessalonians, a "hope that the divine work so well begun in them will increase to maturity."[76] Yet hope in this passage does not look to a process but seems to have the parousia as its focal point and is connected by Paul to the bestowal of a "crown in which we will glory." Paul's hope then was the hope that he would not have run in vain (cf. 3:5) but that the Thessalonians would persevere and his labors in the service of the gospel would be validated by their persistent faith.

"Joy" is a characteristic of mature faith, even in the midst of suffering (cf. 5:16). It is linked here with "crown of boasting" (RSV) and seems to indicate not joy derived from the knowledge of what God has

---

[73] See Bruce, *1 and 2 Thessalonians*, 55–56, who lists several such suggestions only to dismiss them.

[74] The two questions printed in the NIV are actually a translation of a single rhetorical question that provides its own answer by inserting, "Is it not you?" parenthetically in the middle of the sentence in the Greek text.

[75] For the copulative function of ἤ see BDF, par. 446.

[76] Bruce, *1 and 2 Thessalonians*, 56.

done but joy derived from the faithfulness of the Thessalonian believers, who were evidence of Paul's faithful service to God. Thus the believers were for Paul and his coworkers the "crown in which we will glory."

The crown *(stephanos)* was a wreath signifying victory. Sometimes it was placed on the head of victorious military leaders. But Paul's frequent use of athletic imagery (cf. the "opposition" mentioned in 2:2) would indicate that he had in mind the victor's wreath bestowed at the athletic contests held throughout the Greco-Roman world. Though Paul rejected human arrogance before God (1 Cor 1:26–31), he recognized that God's servants may either serve him well or serve him poorly (1 Cor 3:10–15) and be rewarded appropriately. Thus it is not only proper but necessary to differentiate between deeds (or a life) of which one should be ashamed and those of which one should be proud. At the time of judgment when all would be laid bare, Paul aspired to hear his Lord proclaim "well done" (cf. 1 Cor 4:1–5). Such an aspiration is not pride or arrogance. It is the desire to be judged a good steward by God.

"In the presence of our Lord Jesus when he comes" modifies hope, joy, and crown. Paul's concern was not so much with the present as with the future. "In the presence" connotes a face-to-face encounter with the Lord and is clarified with the temporal "when he comes." This latter phrase includes the first occurrence of *parousia* in the letter (see also 3:13; 4:15; 5:23; 2 Thess 2:1,8; and of the coming of the man lawlessness, 2 Thess 2:9), but not the first allusion to the event (see 1 Thess 1:3,10). This context focuses on the parousia as a time of judging for the faithful. Subsequent references will emphasize resurrection and reunion (1 Thess 4:13–18), endurance of believers to the end (1 Thess 5:23–24), or the vanquishing and judgment of evil (2 Thess 2:1–12).

Parousia refers to a presence or to the advent of a presence. Paul used the word to refer both to his own visits to his churches (see 2 Cor 7:6; cp. 1 Cor 16:17; Phil 1:26) and in the more technical sense of a divine or regal visitation (as when referring to the coming of the Lord; see earlier discussion). As a technical term in Hellenistic religions the word could describe the coming of a hidden divinity whose presence was then celebrated in the worship of the cult. In the realm of politics the term was used of the visit to a region by an important dignitary.[77] The grandeur of the Lord, the honor due him at his arrival, and the significance of his coming for both his enemies and his friends are all

---

[77] BAGD, s.v. "παρουσία."

implicit in the technical use of the term *parousia*.

2:20 The answer to Paul's rhetorical question was clear, yet Paul stated it explicitly. The Thessalonians were the beloved result of his ministry, his pride and joy. The pronoun "you" is emphatic, as in this statement both it and the verb of being, "you are," are present. Rather than repeat the three terms in the question, Paul substituted "glory and joy" in the place of "joy and crown." Thus "glory," indicative of honor or respect, should be thought of as a synonym for "crown," which was a symbol of respect bestowed upon the wearer. The present tense of the verb also makes clear that both at present and at the coming of the Lord the Thessalonian believers were a source of joy and pride.

Paul expressed these feelings to assure the church that he had not forgotten them as he moved on to other venues of ministry. They continued to be dear to him, and by stating his feelings so emphatically the apostle sought to solidify and strengthen the bond between them. A clear demonstration of the genuineness of his concern for the church was his decision to send Timothy to Thessalonica.

"So," or "therefore" (RSV), is inferential, looking back at the emotions of 2:17–20 as the basis for the actions detailed in 3:1–5. Time and again in this narration Paul expressed his great concern for the Thessalonians. At the beginning and at the end of this passage (vv. 1,5) he wrote that his concern reached a level that he could no longer bear. Thus when Paul could no longer endure the uncertainty, he decided to send Timothy back to Thessalonica.

3:1 The use of the plural "we thought it best" seems incongruous with "to be left by ourselves [lit., "alone," *monos*] in Athens." Was Paul left by himself (in which case the "we" of v. 1 is an epistolary plural and a parallel to the "I" of v. 5), or does the "we" of the verb indicate that Timothy left Paul and Silas by themselves in Athens while he went to Thessalonica?

The Acts account offers little help at this point. We are told that Jewish opposition drove Paul from Thessalonica to Berea and then to Athens (Acts 17:1–15). Acts 17:14–15 indicates that Timothy and Silas stayed in Berea when Paul fled to Athens, but they were expected to join Paul in Athens as soon as possible. Acts barely mentions any phase of Paul's ministry in Athens except for his marketplace sermon that led to his witness before the Areopagites. Silas and Timothy are not mentioned again until Paul is in Corinth (Acts 18:5), where they join him, having come from Macedonia. When did Timothy join Paul in Athens? Did Silas join him in Athens as well? When Paul sent Timothy from

Athens to Thessalonica, did he at the same time send Silas elsewhere—
to Berea or Philippi perhaps? Was it a great sacrifice to send Timothy
away (a) because Silas was also gone and Timothy's departure left Paul
alone or (b) because Timothy was so important to Paul that his absence
created difficulties even if Silas was still with Paul? (The clause "to be
left by ourselves" [kataleiphthēnai ... monoi] implies being left without needed assistance.) How long did the three of them stay in Athens,
and why did Silas and Timothy go back to Macedonia while Paul proceeded to Corinth? Unfortunately neither Acts nor Paul's letters provide
an answer to these questions.

3:2 When Paul "could stand it no longer" (v. 1), he "sent Timothy
who is our brother and God's fellow worker in spreading the gospel of
Christ" (v. 2). It seems remarkable that Timothy's credentials were
recited for a church that certainly knew him well. "Brother" is a term
widely used in Paul's epistles and may do no more than identify a fellow Christian. "Fellow worker" is a term characteristic of Paul (outside
of Paul's writings in the NT it occurs only once, 3 John 8). Writing to
the Roman church Paul would call Timothy "my fellow worker" (Rom
16:21), but the designation "God's fellow worker" (used in 1 Cor 3:9 of
Apollos) seems to have been chosen to present Timothy as one who has
a ministry in his own right. The phrase seems to convey a high status to
Timothy, approaching equality with Paul.[78] The work in which they
both were engaged was that of "spreading the gospel of Christ." If Timothy at a later date was not received with respect in some churches (due
to youth or some other cause, cf. 1 Cor 16:10–11), it might have been
necessary (even at this early date) for the apostle to make clear his high
opinion of his associate. The import of these descriptive phrases is to
depict Timothy as a valued apostolic emissary,[79] not an underling lacking authority. He was not a mere postman. By stressing the status of
Timothy, Paul also stressed that the Thessalonians were important to
him. The importance of the emissary sent reveals that Paul's inability to
visit Thessalonica himself did not imply that he considered the Thessalonians unimportant.

---

[78] The textual variants at this point change "God's fellow worker" to simply "fellow
worker" (i.e., of Paul) or "God's servant." These are likely the result of scribes who were
uncomfortable assigning Timothy such exalted status.

[79] The structure of the apostolic parousia detailed by Funk "reveals the rank of the apostolic emissary: he substitutes for the apostle himself, while the letter is at best written
authority for what the emissary has to say" ("Apostolic 'Parousia,'" 260).

The purpose for which Timothy was "sent" (cf. 1 Cor 4:17; Phil 2:19) is described in 3:2–3a. Three infinitival clauses explain Timothy's mission. The first two make positive statements (v. 2); the third reveals what the apostle was concerned to prevent (v. 3a). Timothy was sent to "strengthen" *(stērixai)* and "encourage" *(parakalesai)* the faith of the Thessalonians. Similarly, Paul prayed in a later letter that God would "strengthen" the church (Rom 16:25; 1 Thess 3:13; 2 Thess 2:17). He also used the term as the goal of his own visit to the Roman church (Rom 1:11). The verb *parakaleō* occurs frequently in Paul's writings of his own ministry of encouragement or exhortation (1 Thess 2:12). He also used the word of the activities of other ministers as here and of believers' ministries toward one another (1 Thess 4:18; 5:11).

3:3a So strengthened and encouraged, Paul hoped, none of the church would be "unsettled" *(sainesthai)* by the afflictions they were experiencing.[80] *Sainesthai* is used only here in the New Testament and not at all in the LXX. Both this context and the uses of the word outside the Bible indicate a literal meaning of "to shake" and a metaphorical meaning of "to upset" or "to agitate."[81] The potential seriousness of such agitation is reflected by Paul's fear that his efforts among the Thessalonians might have been "in vain" (3:5). "These trials" or "afflictions" (RSV) apparently refer back to the Thessalonians' suffering at the hands of their countrymen (see 2:14).

---

[80] Wanamaker expresses surprise that few commentators have linked this passage with the unsettling of the brethren in 2 Thess 2:2. But even if 2 Thess were written first, as Wanamaker argues, the link between 1 Thess 3:3 and 2 Thess 2:2 is weak. Both passages do express concern regarding the stability of the church. However, the threat envisioned in 1 Thess 2:17–3:5 is non-Christian opposition to the gospel; the threat in 2 Thess 2:1–12 is heresy from within the broader Christian community (2 Thess 1:5–10 does address non-Christian persecution of the faithful, but the topic changes at 2:1). Though the two verbs used (σαλευθῆναι in 2 Thess 2:2 and σαίνεσθαι in 1 Thess 3:3) are synonyms, that fact does not indicate that the situations discussed in the two passages are one and the same.

[81] The original literal application of σαίνω to the wagging of a dog's tail also generated the metaphorical meaning of "fawning or beguiling." Morris argues for this meaning, supposing that "while the Thessalonians were in the middle of their troubles, some of their enemies might by fair words wheedle them out of the right way" (*1 and 2 Thessalonians,* 96). The meaning is possible, but this context is one envisioning conflict, not gentle persuasion. See also *TDNT* 7, 54–56, s.v. "σαίνειν"; H. Chadwick, "1 Thess. 3:3, σαίνεσθαι," *JTS* 1 (1950): 156–58; and E. Bammel, "Preparation for the Perils of the Last Days: 1 Thessalonians 3:3," in *Suffering and Martyrdom in the New Testament: Studies Presented to G. M. Styler by the Cambridge New Testament Seminar,* ed. W. Horbury and B. McNeil (Cambridge: University Press, 1981): 91–100.

3:3b Paul inserted a parenthetical comment at this point (vv. 3b–4), which breaks the flow of the passage. As a result v. 5 repeats (with some variation) the assertions of vv. 1–3a in order to set the stage for the story of Timothy's return in v. 6. "You yourselves know" (RSV) is emphatic. The Thessalonians already knew that they were destined (*keimetha*) for afflictions. The shift to the first plural "we were destined" includes Paul and apparently the whole of the church. "Destined" here has more the sense of inevitability than predetermination—the New Testament testifies repeatedly that the lot of the Christian is to experience affliction (Matt 10:17–42; Acts 9:16; 14:22; Rom 8:17–18,35–39; 1 Pet 1:6–7; 4:12–19). Christians are set on the path of following a Savior who suffered at the hands of evil men; therefore they should expect the same treatment that he received.[82]

3:4 The Thessalonians knew to expect affliction. Paul reminded them, "We kept telling you" to expect persecution "when we were with you." The use of an imperfect tense (*proelegomen*, "we kept telling") indicates repeated warnings during the time the missionaries were in Thessalonica. It is unlikely that Paul intended the first plural "we" to refer only to himself and his coworkers. The import of the passage overall is that Paul was concerned about how the Thessalonians would hold up when persecuted by their countrymen.[83] Rather, the first plural places Paul's and the Thessalonians' affliction in the larger context of Christian suffering. "We" included the followers of Christ in general and the Thessalonians in particular. Paul warned them beforehand to expect affliction—an affliction that had come to pass. The very fact that "it turned out that way" (i.e., Paul's prediction came to pass) was a confirmation of the truth of Paul's message. Persecution then was not to be a cause for falling away from the faith but a reason for adhering to it with even greater tenacity.

3:5 After the parenthesis of vv. 3b–4 the apostle returned to his narrative. In v. 5, however, Paul shifted to first-person statements giving an even more personal sound to a message already conveyed in vv. 1–3a. "For this reason" (i.e., because the predicted affliction had come to pass) and when he personally "could stand it no longer" (the separation

---

[82] Matt 5:11–12,44; see also C. S. Lewis, *The Problem of Pain* (London: Macmillan, 1940).

[83] The infinitive translated "be persecuted" (θλίβεσθαι) connects the warning about persecutions in v. 4 with the "trials" (θλίψεσιν) in v. 3 that concerned the apostle and led to the sending of Timothy.

and the resulting ignorance as to their fate), Paul sent Timothy. In v. 2 the stated purpose of Timothy's visit was to strengthen and encourage the faith of the church and prevent the members from being "unsettled" by their trials. Verse 5 adds to these the fact-finding function: "to find out about your faith." Timothy was sent not just for the benefit of the Thessalonians but also for the benefit of Paul, as an expression of his intense personal concern for the church.

"I was afraid" is not expressed in the Greek but is derived from *mē pōs* (lest ...) and the general context of concern. The participle "the tempter" and the main verb of the clause "tempted" are different forms of the same word, *peirazō*. In later letters Paul would use this verb to refer to God or others putting someone to a test (1 Cor 10:9,13; 2 Cor 13:5) or the tempting of someone to do evil by Satan (1 Cor 7:5) or circumstances (Gal 6:1). The Satan who had hindered Paul from visiting the Thessalonians (2:18) was also the tempter who sought to undermine the Thessalonians' faith.[84] Paul feared that the members of the church might have succumbed to the temptations of the tempter and as a result his "efforts" (or "labor," *kopos*, cf. 2:9)—the proclamation of the gospel to them—had been "useless" (or "in vain," *kenon*, cf. 2:1).

Paul was confident that his labor *(kopos)* had not been unproductive (something no worker would relish, cf. 2:1). On the other hand, the Thessalonians could fail to benefit from the gospel for reasons unrelated to the quality of Paul's labors. The believers faced both affliction (3:3) and temptation (3:5), related but not necessarily identical challenges to the faithful. The seriousness of both is reflected in Paul's expressions of concern and in his decision to send Timothy to strengthen the church. Satan, the tempter, is active and will be until the end (cf. 2 Thess 2:9). Only foolish arrogance would dismiss such danger lightly. Paul wanted to know that the church persisted in its commitment. He wanted to feel that he had engaged in useful and lasting labor. So he was delighted to hear from Timothy that both were indeed the case.

(2) Timothy's Report Received (3:6–8)

⁶But Timothy has just now come to us from you and has brought good news about your faith and love. He has told us that you always have pleasant memories of us and that you long to see us, just as we also long to see you. ⁷Therefore, brothers, in all our distress and persecution we were

---

[84] Cf. Matthew's use of Satan, the tempter, and the devil as synonyms 4:3,5,8,10.

encouraged about you because of your faith. **⁸For now we really live, since you are standing firm in the Lord.**

In the lengthy sentence that makes up these verses, the primary statement is "we were encouraged" (v. 7). The news brought by Timothy (v. 6) was the cause of the encouragement. The distress and persecution of the apostle was the context into which it came (v. 7a), and the hopeful expression in v. 8 is its outgrowth. One of the purposes of Timothy's visit was to "encourage" (the same verb is used in v. 2 and v. 7) the faith of the Thessalonians. Timothy's return with good news encouraged the missionaries. Mutual encouragement implies mutual concern, respect, and a capacity to minister to one another.

3:6 Paul was encouraged at Timothy's return. His enthusiasm is conveyed by the speed with which he responded to the news from Thessalonica. "Timothy has just now come" implies that Paul had made a high priority of responding to the good news brought by his associate. Even more striking is the use of a participle of "brought good news" *(euangelizō)*. Although this word was commonly used in nonbiblical Greek with the sense of proclaiming welcome news, this is the only such use of the verb in Paul's writings. Paul's use of it in this context probably was intended to signify news that was especially welcome.[85] The good news Timothy brought concerned the "faith" and the "love" of the Thessalonian church. The combination of the two terms may simply refer to the Christian walk of the Thessalonians in general. But the verses that follow imply that a distinct meaning was intended for each. First, in v. 6b the apostle celebrated the love of the Thessalonians. Though he may well have rejoiced in hearing that the church continued in living out Christian love in general, the concern in this context is the attitude of the church toward the missionaries. Second, the apostle celebrated the fact that they were standing firm in the faith (vv. 7–8).

In light of the persecution that the faith brought into their lives, the apostle might have feared that the Thessalonians would remember him as a troublemaker. If the presentation of his *ethos* in chap. 2 was in response to attacks on his character (either actual or potential), he might have worried that the Thessalonians would remember him as one who deceived and exploited them. But instead of these, they "always" had "pleasant memories" of the missionaries. These memories *(mneian,* cf.

---

[85] Best's suggestion that the use of εὐαγγελίζω signifies the preaching of the gospel to Paul requires the application of the word as a religious technical term in a context where the nontechnical, secular meaning makes perfect sense (*1 and 2 Thessalonians,* 140).

1:2–3) regarding Paul and his company remind one that Paul also treasured fond memories of the church in Thessalonica. Although no form of *agapē* occurs in v. 6b, the passage does suggest the intensity of the Thessalonians' love for the apostle.[86] The members of the church had not been alienated by their suffering for the Gospel nor by any criticisms aimed at Paul and his associates. In fact, they longed[87] to see Paul just as much as he longed to see them.

3:7 The missionaries welcomed the encouraging news from Thessalonica (cf. the response to good news from Corinth, 2 Cor 7:5–7). Good news provided a moment of relief to those in the midst of "distress and persecution" (v. 7, cf. 2 Cor 7:4). The two terms are *thlipsei* and *ananke*. The first has been used of the Thessalonians' own "affliction" (1:6; 3:3–4). The second is a synonym (cf. 1 Cor 7:26). Both words can indicate the imposition of either emotional or physical distress and are used in tandem in the LXX (see Job 15:24; Pss 25:18; 119:143 in the NIV) and again by Paul in 2 Cor 6:4. Such distress is the lot of believers (3:4), is satanic in nature (2:18; 3:5; 2 Thess 2:9), and anticipates the final judgment when persecutors will be judged and the righteous given rest (2 Thess 1:4–10).

Paul was not specific about the distress the missionaries were experiencing. According to Acts his ministry in Corinth certainly had its share of difficulties (cf. Acts 18:5–6,9–13). But a list of afflictions is not necessary to remind the Thessalonians that (a) he shared with them the experience of suffering for Christ, (b) he cared so much for them that he worried about them even in the midst of his own suffering, and (c) for their sakes he was even willing to send Timothy to them, though it meant he was left "alone" in his affliction. Paul revealed his own need as a way of conveying the great love he felt for his spiritual children. He gave of himself and his resources to them, even when he himself was in need.

3:8 In the midst of his own suffering Paul was encouraged when Timothy returned with good news regarding the love and faith of the Thessalonians. The last phrase of v. 7, "because of your faith," picks up

---

[86] Bruce comments of the Thessalonians that "the present language (esp. επιπο-θοῦντες, "eagerly longing, yearning") suggests the intensity of their ἀγάπη (*1 and 2 Thessalonians*, 66).

[87] The verb ἐπιποθέω is an emphatic form of ποθέω and indicates a strong emotional bond between Paul and the Thessalonians (cf. 2 Cor 5:1–3; Phil 1:7–8; 2:25–26). See LS, s.v. "ποθεω" and "επιποθεω."

the mention of the faith of the Thessalonians in v. 6 and leads to the emotional outburst of v. 8. Paul's love for the church was such that their perseverance in the Lord impacted his very life. "Since you stand firm" (NIV) suggests certainty and sounds like a statement about past perseverance. The sentence, however, is conditional and might better be rendered "if you stand fast" (RSV), implying a future expectation rather than a statement about the past. The verb *stēkō* is used repeatedly as a call for continued perseverance (cf. 1 Cor 16:13; Gal 5:1; Phil 4:1).

The translation in the NIV "for now we really live" implies (by the insertion of "really," which is not in the Greek text) that the issue is quality of life. Paul "really lives"; that is, joy in living was enhanced by the knowledge that his converts persevered in the faith. But the sentiment is much stronger if it is taken not as a statement about quality of life but as hyperbole. The loved one who hears her lover say "I don't think I could survive without you" accepts the sentiment as genuine if (hopefully) not literal. Here, near the end of the section expressing his thankfulness for and his hopes for his spiritual children, is an appropriate place for such a grandiose statement by the church's spiritual father.

5. Thanksgiving and Intercessory Prayer (3:9–13)

For the third and final time Paul expressed his thanksgiving for the Thessalonians. In terms of form this expression of thanks is the conclusion of the thanksgiving begun in 1:2.[88] Also this thanksgiving differs structurally from those occurring earlier in the letter. First, it is expressed as a rhetorical question that seems to remind the reader that this is only the latest in a series of expressions of thanks for the church. At the same time it asserts that even this lengthy period of thanksgiving[89] does not sufficiently express the fullness of the apostle's feelings for the believers in Thessalonica.

This thanksgiving is also distinguished from the first two in that it contains an expression of the apostle's prayer (cf. 1:2–5; 2:13). Structurally, it is in two parts, each part sounding the same themes. The first is an assurance that the missionaries consistently pray that they might

---

[88] See P. T. O'Brien, *Introductory Thanksgivings in the Letters of Paul,* NovTSup 49 (Leiden: Brill, 1977), 156–66, and P. Schubert, *Form and Function of the Pauline Thanksgiving,* BZNW 20 (Berlin: Toepelmann, 1939), 21–27.

[89] Assuming it stretches from 1:2 to 3:13, this is clearly the longest thanksgiving in any of Paul's letters.

see the Thessalonians again and have continued ministry for their benefit (v. 10). The second, in the form of a benediction, is the prayer itself
requesting that God would clear the way for reunion, increase the
church's love, and strengthen their hearts (vv. 11–13). The content of
the prayer reminds us of the function of the thanksgivings and the narratives interspersed among them. Together the expressions of thanks and
the narratives reaffirm the positive relationship between the apostle and
his children in the faith. This relationship is the foundation on which
continued religious instruction stands and from which it derives. The
recitation of the events of the past remind the readers of the good
behavior they should emulate as they continue to persevere in spite of
opposition.

(1) Thanksgiving (3:9–10)

⁹**How can we thank God enough for you in return for all the joy we
have in the presence of our God because of you? ¹⁰Night and day we pray
most earnestly that we may see you again and supply what is lacking in
your faith.**

3:9 This third statement of thanksgiving is formed as a question
and does not use a verb for giving thanks but a noun. An inferential particle "for" (the NIV does not translate the particle *gar* but opts to begin
a new sentence with v. 9; cf. the RSV) connects the thanksgiving to
Paul's preceding assertions that he and his coworkers were encouraged
by the Thessalonians' faithfulness and love (v. 7) and the immensely
important part they played in his life (v. 8). He could not thank God
enough for them (v. 9) because of the encouragement and meaning they
had given him (vv. 7–8). The rhetorical question "How can we thank
God enough?" assumes the impossibility of the task. Paul's gratefulness
to God for the joy his relationship with the Thessalonians brought him
was beyond expression.

"How can we thank?" may also be rendered "What thanksgiving are
we able to give?" The infinitive "to give" (*antapodidōmi*) implies an
obligation to repay a debt. The debt is owed to God. It was God who
received the thanks, not the Thessalonians. For it was only by the grace
and power of God that they were part of the family of faith. Just as it
was only by the same grace that Paul became the Apostle to the Gentiles and their father in the faith. What thanksgiving could conceivably
be adequate repayment for all that God had done? The implication is
that any thanks offered to God for this benefit would be pitifully inade-

quate. That which is the basis of the thanksgiving is the "joy that we have in the presence of our God because of you." The phrase "in the presence of God" is an indication that the giving of thanks envisioned here is in the context of prayer (cf. 1:3), not simply a moment of pleasant reflection.

3:10 At the same time that thanks is offered, requests are also expressed (v. 10). The word translated "we pray" is a verb often used of prayer that means "to ask." The genuineness of the requests is stressed by the constancy implied in the present tense participle "asking" *(deomenoi)*, by the reference to time ("night and day"), and by the reference to manner ("most earnestly"). The latter is an emphatic compound that indicates the doing of something "quite beyond all measure."[90] "Night and day" does not imply unceasing prayer but the consistent inclusion of intercessions for the Thessalonians whenever Paul and his coworkers pray. Such intercessions in Paul not only express concern for the readers but also serve to highlight the central concerns of the letter and "anticipate its main paraenetic thrust."[91]

A Pauline thanksgiving generally includes a statement of the request(s) made on behalf of the readers (cf. Phil 1:9–11). It is this very feature (the statement of requests) that is missing from the two thanksgivings earlier in the letter (cf. 1:2–5; 2:13). Its inclusion, finally, in this place, along with the beginning of the paraenetic passages at 4:1, marks these verses as the conclusion of the thanksgiving.[92]

The requests so regularly and earnestly voiced in Paul's prayers center on two desires. One was the wish to see the Thessalonian church again face to face. Paul had already written that he had made every effort to visit the church again and that this was his earnest desire (2:17–18). He was delighted by the news that the feeling was mutual (3:6). And he continued to pray that they would soon be reunited. The second part of his prayer was that this reunion might enable him to "supply what is lacking" in the faith of the believers. To "supply" *(katartizō)* generally connotes completing or improving the condition of something (cf. Gal 6:1).[93] If that is true here, the word implies not pro-

---

[90] BAGD, s.v. "ὑπερεκπερισσοῦ." Cf. 1 Thess 5:13; Eph 3:20.

[91] See G. P. Wiles, *The Significance of the Intercessory Prayer Passages in the Letters of Paul*, SNTSMS 24 (Cambridge: University Press, 1974), 229.

[92] This lengthy thanksgiving (1:2–3:13) resulted from the adaptation of the thanksgiving form for rhetorical purposes.

[93] BAGD, s.v. "καταρτίζω."

viding something new but rather strengthening and or enhancing a faith already in existence.

"What is lacking" translates a word *(hysterēmata)* that may connote a natural growth toward completion or, more negatively, may connote a deficiency or inadequacy that needs to be rectified. What Paul wished to do in person he was forced to do through his representative, Timothy, and through his letter. Thus the content of 1 Thessalonians itself may indicate what Paul felt the church "lacked" and what he wished to "supply" to meet this need. The overall positive nature of Paul's comments in chaps. 1–3 would argue that Paul saw the need for continued growth in godliness in the church, not a need to correct some fatal flaw. The church was well founded and was both following the example of the apostle and serving as an example to others (1:4–10). They had survived persecution with both their faith and their appreciation for Paul intact (2:1–3:8). Chapters 4–5 do not change the impression that the church was doing well. Exhortations to live morally upright lives (4:3–8), exhibit brotherly love (4:9–10), win the respect of outsiders (4:11–12), and so on (5:12–24) are presented as encouragements to continue living as they were already (4:1–2). The only major departure from typical Pauline paraenesis are the two lengthy passages encouraging hope and faithfulness in light of Jesus' coming parousia. Overall the letter reflects a church firmly committed and a faith that needed only to be encouraged and refined.

(2) Prayer (3:11–13)

[11]Now may our God and Father himself and our Lord Jesus clear the way for us to come to you. [12]May the Lord make your love increase and overflow for each other and for everyone else, just as ours does for you. [13]May he strengthen your hearts so that you will be blameless and holy in the presence of our God and Father when our Lord Jesus comes with all his holy ones.

At this point Paul finally stated his "wish-prayer" for the church. A "wish-prayer" is an intercessory prayer that utilizes optative verbs to express the wish or desire the person praying is voicing to God.[94] This prayer both reiterates themes already expressed and anticipates what is to come in the letter. By expressing these concerns in prayer, Paul not

---

[94] See Wiles, *Intercessory Prayer Passages,* 22–107, for a treatment of the origin and development of this form of intercession as it relates to Paul's letters.

only illustrated his genuine concern for the church but also provided a transition from the narrative material in chaps. 2–3 to the paraenetic material in chaps. 4–5.[95] The three sentences in the NIV translation of 3:11–13 are in Greek one lengthy statement consisting of two main requests (vv. 11–12) followed by a purpose clause (v. 13) that in effect expresses a third desire for the church.

3:11 The prayer is addressed to "our God and Father himself and our Lord Jesus." The verb that follows this compound subject is singular, but it was not uncommon for compound subjects to take singular verbs in Greek sentences. What is more significant is the linking of the Father God and the Lord Jesus as the objects of petition. Traditional Jewish prayer directed petitions to God alone. Assuming a date of composition for 1 Thessalonians of A.D. 52, this statement is one of the earliest examples of a theologically significant change in the prayer language of Jewish-Christians. It places Jesus on a par with the Father, assigning him position and authority formerly held only by Yahweh.[96]

The first request (v. 11) that God would "clear the way," corresponding to the first infinitive of v. 10 to "see you again," expressed Paul's desire to visit the church personally. The verb used here (an optative of *kateuthunē*) may mean either "make straight" or simply "direct." The former meaning "make straight" would imply the need to remove obstacles and seems more likely to be Paul's intent in this context. Some spiritual hindrance had kept them from visiting the Thessalonians: "Satan stopped us" (2:18). Spiritual power is required to remove a spiri-

---

[95] Cp. the work of H. Boers, "The Form-Critical Study of Paul's Letters: 1 Thessalonians as a Case Study," *NTS* 22 (1975–75): 152, and R. Funk, "The Apostolic 'Parousia': Form and Significance," in *Christian History and Interpretation: Studies Presented to John Knox*, ed. W. R. Farmer, C. D. F. Moule, and R. R. Niebuhr (Cambridge: University Press, 1967), 249–68, whose studies deal with 3:11–13 as the conclusion of the material that precedes it, with the assertion of R. Jewett (*The Thessalonian Correspondence: Pauline Rhetoric and Millenarian Piety* [Philadelphia: Fortress, 1986] and Wanamaker (*1 and 2 Thessalonians*, 140) that 3:11–13 is a *transitus*, a transition that summarizes the themes of the preceding *narratio* and introduces the themes that will be taken up in the next section.

[96] Wanamaker points to 2 Thess 2:16 (another wish-prayer), where the Lord is invoked before the Father, implying that "the order was not fixed and that Christ was placed on the same honorific plane as God" (*1 and 2 Thessalonians*, 141). R. E. H. Uprichard argues that the Christology of 1 Thess is fully formed though not prominently displayed in the letter. In passages such as 1 Thess 1:1 and 3:11 "the elevated station granted to our Lord implies his divine nature" (see "The Person and Work of Christ in 1 Thessalonians," *EvQ* 53 [1981]: 112; published earlier in *IBS* 1 [1979]: 19–27).

tual hindrance. Therefore it only makes sense to ask in prayer that God might "clear the way," allowing Paul another visit to Thessalonica. According to the travels recorded in Acts, this did not happen for several years, not until after the Ephesian ministry (20:1–6). Acts, however, only records those travels pertinent to the telling of its own story. Paul may well have found his way to Thessalonica sooner.

3:12 The second petition was directed to "the Lord." Using two optative verbs Paul prayed that the Lord might cause the believers to "increase and overflow" in their love for one another and for others. (The object of the verbs is not "love" but "you," i.e., the Thessalonians.) "Increase" *(pleonazō)* and "overflow" *(perisseuō)* are synonyms. The former connotes growth that produces an abundance. It can indicate numerical increase, but that is unlikely in this context. The latter term, used of persons, implies a wealth or overabundance of some possession or quality. Together they form an emphatic prayer-wish for the spiritual growth of the Thessalonians. Following the assertion that Paul's desire was to visit the church and "supply what is lacking" in their faith (v. 10), the prayer requests divine power to accomplish the visit (v. 11) and to provide the growth that will supply all that the church is lacking and more (v. 12).

Paul prayed that the church would abound in love. Paul thought that love was the cardinal Christian virtue (cf. Rom 13) from which all other Christian virtues grow. Love reflects the character of God revealed in Christ. The church was taught by God to love one another (see 4:9–10), and following the example of Christ requires loving even those who are unbelievers and opponents of the faith. Thus Paul prayed that the church would abound in love both "for each other and for everyone else." Love "for everyone else" (lit., "for all") is a reference to persons outside the church and would include even those persecuting the Thessalonian believers.

The parenthetical comment "just as ours does for you" (i.e., may your love abound for one another and for others just as our love abounds for you) is not a part of the prayer itself. Rather, it is yet another of the numerous assertions found in these first three chapters that the missionaries loved the Thessalonians. The assertions are so frequent and so rigorously defended that one wonders if this was the essence of the problem that generated Timothy's visit and the writing of this letter. Attracted by Paul's gospel of love, were the Thessalonians now facing critics who claimed that Paul's gospel was as false as his professions of concern for them? If this were the charge, the apostle answered it fully on the basis of his actions. He had labored, sacrificed, and endured hardship and dangerous opposition for their sakes. He had treated them like a loving, gentle parent would his own children. He preferred to burden himself excessively rather than burden them at all. He did all this for their benefit, seeking no earthly reward at all. If they needed proof of the genuineness of his love, they had it in his own actions. If they needed a flesh-and-blood example of love to guide their own growth in love, the apostle had supplied this too in abundance.

3:13 Verse 13 does not start a new sentence in the Greek text. Although it does express an additional desire for the Thessalonians (which apparently explains the translation in the NIV), syntactically v. 13 continues the thought of v. 12 by providing a purpose statement. Paul desired that the church abound in love (v. 12) so that the Lord might establish their hearts blameless in holiness (v. 13).

Maintaining a close link between these two clauses is essential: blameless, sanctified hearts can only grow and bloom in the soil of a genuine and abundant love. In this the teachings of the apostle echoed the words of Jesus: "The entire law is summed up in a single command: 'Love your neighbor as yourself'" (Gal 5:14); and again, "He who loves his fellowman has fulfilled the law" (Rom 13:8; cf. Matt 22:34–40). The church today needs this message as well. But it is a message they must see their leaders live, not just hear them proclaim. To be true to the Scriptures, today's apostles must demonstrate by their actions that loveless Christianity is an oxymoron, that a gospel lacking love is a heresy, and that true Christian maturity is measured by the character of one's love, not the complexity of one's theology.

"Blameless" *(amemptous)* is a concept descriptive of something or someone judged acceptable before God in sacrificial worship. "Holy" *(hagiōsunē)* is a noun describing the state of that which is sanctified *(hagiadzō)* or consecrated as God's special possession. Both words (but esp. the latter) connote a relationship to the divine that also has ethical implications. God's saints, or holy *(hagioi)* ones, are those dedicated to him and his service. Thus their lives should reflect the values and character of the Father. If the Father is love, so must his children love, or they are not his blameless holy ones (cf. 1 John 4:7–12). "Blameless in holiness" is a more literal translation of Paul's phrase and indicates a closer link between the two words than the NIV implies with "blameless and holy." Paul prayed that the Lord would produce in the Thessalonians a wealth of love for others (both inside and outside the church), and as a result they would live lives God would judge acceptable.

Paul's prayer envisions present growth in love (v. 12) anticipating a future time of judgment (v. 13). The two phrases "in the presence of our God and Father" and "when our Lord Jesus comes" are parallel, both looking to the parousia. The established or strengthened heart is one that is so firmly grounded in love that it perseveres to the end. Thus the "endurance inspired by hope" that the believers had already evidenced and that is praised in the first thanksgiving (1:3) is here projected into the future. Endurance for a time is not enough. Endurance to the end is required.

Thankful for their endurance to this point, Paul now prayed that the Thessalonians might endure to the coming of the Lord "with all his holy ones" (v. 13). Paul regularly used "holy ones" *(hagioi)* to refer to believers in the churches (Rom 1:7; 8:27; 12:13; 15:25; 1 Cor 1:2; 6:1–2; 14:33; Phil 1:1). These holy ones, however, are depicted as coming with Jesus at his parousia. In 4:16–17 Paul indicated that both living saints and those who had died would rise to meet Jesus, who will descend "with the voice of the archangel" (cf. 2 Thess 1:7). It is unlikely therefore that the holy ones of 3:13 who descend with Jesus are the saints who have passed away. It is more probable that Paul here was using *hagioi* as it often is used in the LXX, of Yahweh's angels (see esp. Zech 14:5).

Paul's lengthy thanksgiving has served both to encourage and to instruct. His affirmations of the faith, love, and perseverance of the Thessalonian believers encouraged them to continue as they had begun. Reminding them of his behavior in their midst both provided them with a concrete example to follow in their Christian walk and also provided a counter to any accusations that opponents might aim in his direction. Paul's affirmations also served to express the bond of love he felt for the church and which they felt for him as well. Thankful for their faith in the present and hopeful regarding their faith in the future, Paul turned to exhortation regarding their Christian lives in the days ahead.

III. ETHICAL EXHORTATIONS (4:1–5:22)
1. Introductory Call to Obedience (4:1–2)
2. Exhortations Regarding Sanctification (4:3–8)
3. Exhortations Regarding Brotherly Love (4:9–12)
4. Exhortations Regarding the Dead (4:13–18)
5. Exhortations Regarding Times and Seasons (5:1–11)
    (1) Introduction (5:1)
    (2) The Manner of the Lord's Return (5:2–3)
    (3) The Christian Life Anticipating the Return (5:4–11)
6. Exhortations Regarding Life in the Fellowship (5:12–22)
    (1) Leaders and Followers (5:12–13)
    (2) The Weak and the Strong (5:14 15)
    (3) Optimists and Pessimists (5:16–18)
    (4) The Cynical and the Gullible (5:19–22)

III. ETHICAL EXHORTATIONS (4:1–5:22)

These final two chapters of 1 Thessalonians contain a variety of ethical exhortations. The first two verses (4:1–2) serve as an introduction for the two chapters that follow. The introduction includes a general encouragement to continue in godly living and a claim that the commands derive their authority from Jesus himself.

A comparison of Paul's letters to the typical form of a Hellenistic letter would reveal that the body of the letter should stand between the introductory thanksgiving and the concluding salutations. The body of the Pauline letters to the Romans and to the Galatians for instance begins with doctrinal concerns and then with little transition moves to ethical exhortations or paraenesis.[1] The shift from one to the other can

---

[1] Grouped admonitions as in chaps. 4–5 were common in the ancient world. The name for them, from the Greek, is *paraenesis,* meaning "exhortation." Paraenetic passages are typically made up of brief exhortations familiar to readers. References abound indicating the Thessalonians were aware of these imperatives (4:2,6,9,11; 5:1–2). Since the material was familiar, the author of the paraenesis generally did not feel the need to elaborate on it. Paraenetic passages generally consist of several brief exhortations that contain a common key word or develop a common theme of concern to the author. They reminded readers of commitments made earlier and encouraged continued faithfulness.

be abrupt, and their interconnectedness is often neglected. This ought not to be so. The structural separation of doctrinal and ethical material in Paul's letters should not be allowed to minimize the connection in Paul's gospel between doctrine and ethics. Doctrine without ethics is hypocrisy; ethics without doctrine lacks firm foundation.

Schubert's form-critical study of 1 Thessalonians argues that the lengthy thanksgiving of 1:2–3:13 comprises the body of the letter, which is brought to its conclusion with a collection of exhortations in chaps. 4–5.[2] Boer's study, on the other hand, sees the thanksgiving of chaps. 1–3 followed by the body of the letter in chaps. 4–5.[3] Assuming that the designation "body" is given to that which is the primary concern of the letter, then these two studies reflect alternative points of emphasis that influence our perception of the relative importance of various sections of the letter.

Rhetorical-critical studies likewise observe the shift in the text at 4:1 but assume more continuity between the two sections of the letter. The narrative *(narratio)* of the early chapters (chaps. 2–3), it is pointed out, provides essential foundation for the specific exhortations (the *probatio*) in the final chapters (chaps. 4–5). The narrative, according to one such study, has the "philophronetic intention of reestablishing Paul's relationship with his converts" and contains "a considerable amount of implicit paraenesis."[4] The *probatio* (4:1–5:22) then contains a "set of proofs demonstrating the contention in 4:1f that the Thessalonians know how to behave and to please God so they must continue to live as they have been instructed by Paul, but with renewed fervor."[5] It is this purpose that gives the passage its paraenetic character. In paraenetic material the exhortations are intended to remind the audience of teachings already learned and commitments already made and encourage them to continue on the path they have begun.

Analysis of the form of the rhetoric of 1 Thessalonians recognizes the transition that occurs as the reader moves from chap. 3 into chap. 4. On the basis of either analysis it is clear that these two major sections (chaps. 2–3 and 4–5) ought not be treated in isolation from each other.

---

[2] P. Schubert, *Form and Function of the Pauline Thanksgiving, BZNW* 20 (Berlin: Toepelmann, 1939).

[3] Boers, "Form Critical Study," 156.

[4] C. A. Wanamaker, *Commentary on 1 and 2 Thessalonians,* NIGTC (Grand Rapids: Eerdmans, 1990), 146.

[5] Ibid.

Rather, the reader should expect the two to illuminate each other.

1. Introductory Call to Obedience (4:1–2)

¹Finally, brothers, we instructed you how to live in order to please God, as in fact you are living. Now we ask you and urge you in the Lord Jesus to do this more and more. ²For you know what instructions we gave you by the authority of the Lord Jesus.

"Finally, …" marks a major transition point in the letter. The Greek word (unlike the English) does not necessarily signify an approach to the end of the entire discussion. Nor does it connote a transition to material less important than or secondary to what came before. What follows does not even introduce a range of new subjects but develops several themes introduced in the first three chapters of the letter.[6] What the transition does mark is a shift from declaration to exhortation. Predominantly declarative structures in the first three chapters give way to frequent imperatives in the last two. A corresponding shift in temporal perspective also occurs. Emphasis on the past and present in the first three chapters gives way to focus on the present and future in the last two. Understanding the transition in terms of temporal perspective and grammatical structure allows the reader to maintain the continuity of the theological concerns that underlie both this (the paraenetic) and the earlier (the narrative) sections of the letter.

The first two verses of chap. 4 introduce the paraenetic passages that follow. They identify the authority behind the teachings as the Lord and thus stress the importance of obeying them. At the same time they identify a positive goal of obedience, the goal of pleasing God. The readers were affirmed by being called "brethren." The apostle also affirmed them by acknowledging that they were in fact currently living according to the Christian teachings he had given them earlier. The brethren were reminded that the commands that followed were not new; they knew these already. So while affirming the readers, the apostle also challenged them to live lives "more and more" pleasing to God.

An additional connection between chaps. 3 and 4 may be the reverse

---

[6] W. Schmithals' suggestion that this is the editorial seam created by the joining of two letters is not supported by textual evidence or by any significant shift in content. See his chapter "Die historische Situation der Thessalonischer-Briefe," in *Paulus und die Gnostiker* (Hamburg: Bergstedt, 1965); or in English "The Historical Situation of the Thessalonian Letters," in *Paul and the Gnostics* (Nashville: Abingdon, 1972), 123–218.

(chiastic) repetition of love and holiness—love in 3:12; 4:9–12 and holiness in 3:13; 4:3–8.

4:1 "We ask you and urge you in the Lord Jesus" comes immediately after "Finally, brothers" in the Greek sentence, providing a sense of urgency to Paul's words and creating anticipation on the part of the readers. "Ask" and "urge" are synonyms, but Paul showed a marked preference for the later verb (*parakaleō,* "to urge" or "encourage").[7] The addition of "we ask" *(erōtaō)* simply provides emphasis to a common Hellenistic Greek command formula Paul often used (cf. Rom 12:1; 1 Cor 1:10). A first-person form of *parakaleō* ("I/we urge you") typically introduces the command, and an infinitive (as in Rom 15:30, "I urge you ... to join me in my struggle") or a *hina* clause (I urge you "that" you ...) states the command itself. Thus the central exhortation of vv. 1–2 is the statement "we ask you and urge you ... to do this more and more." "This" refers to living in a manner (a) consistent with apostolic instruction and (b) pleasing to God. The persons so encouraged (the "brothers") and the authority behind the command ("in the Lord Jesus") also are identified.[8]

"We ask you and urge you" are modified by the phrase "in the Lord Jesus." This is the first of two references to the authority of Jesus in the span of only two verses. This first phrase expresses the sphere in which the commands are given and received. Both the apostles and the Thessalonians functioned as servants of the resurrected Christ subject to his authority and will. The second phrase ("by the authority of the Lord Jesus," v. 2) expresses the agency or authority by which the commands were given.[9] It may refer to teachings of Jesus conveyed by his apostles or apostolic teachings validated by the authority granted the apostles by the Lord Jesus. The NIV prefers the latter as is indicated by the insertion of "the authority of," which does not occur in the Greek.

Whether the teachings themselves are attributed to Jesus or the authority to teach is attributed to Jesus, the impact is much the same. The commands the Thessalonians had received in the past and the exhortations Paul was about to deliver were not to be taken lightly.

---

[7] "Urge" (παρακαλέω) is used eight times in 1 Thess compared to only two occurrences of the verb "ask" (ἐρωτάω).

[8] See C. J. Bjerkelund, *Parakalo: Form, Funktion und Sinn der Parakalo-Satze in den paulinischen Briefen, Bibliotheca Theologica Norvegica* 1 (Oslo: Universitetsforlaget, 1967), for a full investigation of the παρακαλέω command sentences.

[9] This distinction between ἐν κυρίῳ and διὰ τοῦ κυρίου is not absolute, but if Paul did not intend some such distinction, then a rationale for the second phrase is lacking.

They are not the commands of human teachers. They are the commands of the one whom believers have accepted as their Lord. Throughout these two chapters references to the divine origin (and thus the divine authority) of the exhortations abound: 4:1,2,3,8,9,15; 5:12,18.

The statement "we ask and urge you ... to do this more and more" lacks specificity. Paul used two comparative clauses to express that which the Thessalonians were to do. "Just as you received from us [NIV, "we instructed you"] how you ought to walk and please God" (the NIV drops the comparative to simplify the English sentence) and "just as you are also walking" were inserted in the middle of the primary command in the Greek text. The clause "we instructed you" translates a verb commonly used of the passing on of religious tradition in Judaism. The instruction guided the new believers in how they were "to live" and "to please God." The present tense of both infinitives implies that consistent behavior was expected, not occasional acts of obedience.

The type of instruction to which Paul referred may be reflected in the letter from the Jerusalem Council to the Gentile churches (Acts 15:29), or ethical injunctions such as the instructions to households (Eph 5:22–6:9; Col 3:18–4:1), and virtue/vice lists (Gal 5:19–23; Col 3:5–17), as well as theological instruction (Col 1:15–20; 1 Tim 1:15; Phil 2:6–11).[10]

The Thessalonians had received instruction regarding how they were to live and "to please God." One pleases God by proclaiming the gospel while living a just Christian life (1 Thess 2:4–6), while those who oppose the gospel (1 Thess 2:15) or live in the flesh (Rom 8:8) can never please God. The NIV translation "to live in order to please God" recognizes that the "and" (*kai*), which they translate "in order to," is consecutive. Thus the way in which a Christian ought to live is in the way that is pleasing to God. The concepts overlap but are not identical. The latter gives expression to the ultimate basis for Christian behavior that the former leaves unexpressed. The believer lives not simply to obey traditions but to please God.

"As in fact you are living" is the second comparative clause in the verse. Paul was encouraging the Thessalonians to make more and more strides in living the lives they had been instructed to live. Yet Paul's challenges to continue in Christian growth never demean the strides the people had already made toward living out the implications of the gos-

---

[10] The *kenosis* hymn is admittedly used in Phil 2 for an ethical purpose, but its content reflects an origin as a Christological catechism.

pel. Throughout the letter he affirmed those he sought to spur on to greater heights of obedience to the Lord's commands. Even in the absence of the apostle and his coworkers, the Thessalonians could continue to grow in obedience as those who please God because they had received sufficient instruction already.

4:2 "For" connects the instructions the Thessalonians received in the past to the command just given to live as they had been taught. Paul implied here that the things he was about to write were not new commands but reminders about commands the Thessalonians had already received in person. The term "instructions" does not derive from the same Greek word as was used in v. 1. This is a stronger noun connoting authority and commanding obedience. It was used in military contexts of orders issued to subordinates. The Thessalonians knew the commands the apostle had given them "by the authority of the Lord Jesus." Continuing to live in a way that pleased God did not require the return of the apostle or the revelation of new traditions. It required obedience to the commands already received and already known to the church. It required obedience to the commands of Jesus. The verses that follow provide some specific content in places the apostle apparently felt the Thessalonians were in need of clarification or encouragement.

2. Exhortations Regarding Sanctification (4:3–8)

[3]It is God's will that you should be sanctified: that you should avoid sexual immorality; [4]that each of you should learn to control his own body in a way that is holy and honorable, [5]not in passionate lust like the heathen, who do not know God; [6]and that in this matter no one should wrong his brother or take advantage of him. The Lord will punish men for all such sins, as we have already told you and warned you. [7]For God did not call us to be impure, but to live a holy life. [8]Therefore, he who rejects this instruction does not reject man but God, who gives you his Holy Spirit.

4:3a The divine origin and authority of the instructions already received is restated in v. 3. This first (4:3–8) of several paraenetic sections begins with the statement that what follows is "God's will." The same section concludes with the solemn warning that the one who disregards these commands "does not reject man but God" (4:8).

The phrase "this is God's will" occurs again at 5:18 accompanying a very different set of exhortations than are found in 4:3–8 (cf. *thelēma theou* in Rom 12:2; Eph 6:6; Col 4:12; 1 John 2:17; cf. a comparable construction using the verb "will" in Jas 4:15).[11] Peter also used the phrase as a formula for encouraging godly behavior (1 Pet 2:15). Clearly the need for sanctification and the specific regulations defining godly behavior given in 4:3–8 reflect one narrow segment of the "will," not an all-encompassing statement of it.[12]

Popular discussions of the "will of God" often center on the major decisions of life. The choice of a vocation, the choice of a spouse, and other pivotal moments in life certainly are times when divine guidance is needed. But seeking the will of God ought not be relegated only to such momentous and occasional events. I sometimes wonder why people would seek the will of God at a pivotal moment in life if they have been ignoring God's will in their daily lives. Should God speak, would such a person listen? I rather doubt it. One who is not faithful in the small moments is unlikely to be faithful in the great.

A frequent assumption is that God's will is something hidden and difficult to discern. In some situations this may be so. But vv. 3–8 address matters of daily ethical living. Here we see God's will neither hidden nor difficult to discern. It is that we live moral lives avoiding the excesses of the godless. It is that a believer not abuse or exploit others. It is sanctified daily living that is God's will for our lives. Though we may not know all, we do know this much; and we do well to remember that doing God's will begins with doing that will which he has already revealed and called us to do daily. The paraenesis of chaps. 4–5 reminded the Thessalonians of this very responsibility—the responsibility of each believer to live lives guided daily by the commands of Christ and pleasing to God.

Although the concern of the entire paraenesis is for the will of God, the specific theme of vv. 3–8 is a call to sanctification *(hagiasmos)*. A concern for sanctification brackets the specific injunctions. The repetition of the term is evident in the Greek text. The noun *hagiasmos* is the Greek noun behind the NIV translation "be sanctified" in v. 3, "in a way that is holy" in v. 4, and "a holy life" in v. 7. In addition, the believers were reminded that the Spirit God gave them is a "Holy" *(hagion)* Spirit (v. 8). "Holy" (the adjectival form of the noun "sanctified") was commonly used with

---

[11] Paul used the same phrase of the sacrifice of Christ (Gal 1:4), his own calling as an apostle (1 Cor 1:1), and his personal circumstances (Rom 1:10; 15:32).

[12] The absence of the article with θελημα is consistent with Paul's intent to state not "the total extent of that will but its relevance to one sphere of conduct" (E. Best, *A Commentary on the First and Second Epistles to the Thessalonians* [London: A. & C. Black,1977], 159); but the absence of the article may simply be a Semiticism or the result of the use of θελημα in a formula with θεου, which provides as much specificity as could an article.

"Spirit," but here it is emphasized by its unusual position in the sentence.

Hagiasmos is not an easy word to translate, in part because it has both an ontological and an ethical import. The translations "consecration" or "dedication" express well the idea that whatever or whoever is sanctified is dedicated to God. This is the ontological reality—sanctification designates the Christian as one possessed by God and/or dedicated to the service of God. Since this God has expressed his character and his will, however, sanctification also has ethical implications. A person dedicated to God should act in a manner consistent with the character of God. Thus it is not surprising that sanctification in this passage (and in many others) is related to the way a Christian is to live, that is, is ethical in emphasis.

What does it mean, specifically, to live a sanctified life? The definition related to ethical actions just offered—living in a manner consistent with the character and commands of God—leaves a lot of room for interpretation. The rubric of sanctification (like that of the "will of God") could be used to open a discussion of almost any area of Christian living. The specific commands in vv. 3b–6 are examples of sanctified living, but they certainly do not exhaust the possible applications of the concept of sanctification. In fact, the range of these commands is very narrow indeed, if they are all understood as injunctions related to sexual purity. The limited scope of vv. 3–8 implies the intent to be illustrative rather than exhaustive. To some degree the scope of the passage also must have been dictated by the needs of the church. The paraenesis lacks specificity, and Paul's praise of the church (1:3,7; 3:6) implies that problems within the congregation did not exist on a large scale. Yet these were matters that the apostle wished to stress for the Thessalonians.

The interconnectedness of the various commands and their connection to the will of God and sanctification is reflected by the sentence structure Paul used. "Your sanctification" ("that you should be sanctified" in the NIV) in v. 3 is placed in apposition to "God's will." What follows is a series of four infinitives placed parallel to "sanctification" and also in apposition to "will." These are "to abstain ..." (v. 3), "to know ..." (vv. 4–5), "not to transgress ... nor to defraud" (v. 6). Translating these infinitives into English requires using them as various types of English clauses that may not appear to be parallel,[13] but the Thessalonian hearers

---

[13] The translators of the NIV attempted to indicate this parallel structure. The colon after "you should be sanctified" (v. 3a) points to three parallel clauses: "that you should avoid ..." (v. 3b), "that each of you should learn ..." (vv. 4–5), "and that in this matter ..." (v. 6).

of the letter would have found the repetition of infinitives in the passage a distinct indicator of its organization. In this context three aspects of sanctification are highlighted: one who is sanctified "should avoid sexual immorality" (v. 3), should know how "to control his own body" (vv. 4–5), and should not "wrong his brother or take advantage of him" (v. 6).

4:3b The first infinitive (expressing an ethical imperative) is "that you should avoid sexual immorality." The word "immorality" (*porneia*) was used frequently in Judeo-Christian literature where it could refer to premarital or extramarital intercourse, prostitution, incest, and any other type of sexual impropriety. Used metaphorically it could refer to the practice of idolatry.[14] An act defined as improper in one society, however, might not be so defined in another. Hellenistic society was not monolithic. Social ethics varied, with a few groups (e.g., Stoics) preaching virtues similar to those affirmed in Christian circles.[15] On the whole, however, Hellenistic society's definition of acceptable sexual behavior differed considerably from that of first-century Jews or Christians. As a result the Jews considered the Gentiles on the whole to be immoral and idolatrous. The admonition given the Gentile church from the Jerusalem Council is consistent with this conviction (see Acts 15:29).[16] Apparently many Jewish Christians feared that Gentile converts might not change their sexual habits if they were not subject to the law.

Much behavior that was tolerated among the Gentiles was considered immoral in the church. The casual use of prostitutes and the practice of ritual sexual intercourse in certain cults was common in Hellenistic cit-

---

[14] See J. Jensen, "Does *Porneia* Mean Fornication? A Critique of Bruce Malina," *NovT* 20 (1978): 161–84, for the application of πορνεία to "prebetrothal, noncommercial, noncultic heterosexual intercourse." For a broader introduction to first-century sexual mores see W. A. Meeks, *The Moral World of the First Christians,* LEC 6 (Philadelphia: Westminster, 1986).

[15] O. L. Yarbrough provides numerous examples of Greco-Roman philosophical and rhetorical treatments of the τόπος "concerning marriage" (*Not Like the Gentiles: Marriage Rules in the Letters of Paul,* SBLDS 80 [Atlanta: Scholars Press, 1985], 31–63). Many of the individuals cited advised fidelity in marriage. Jews and Christians were not the only groups calling for sexual activity to be restricted to the marriage relationship. Yet it is clear, even from the treatises that frowned upon extramarital sex, that for many in the Hellenistic world homosexuality, prostitution, orgiastic religious rituals, and the keeping of courtesans and slaves for sexual use were considered acceptable sexual behaviors.

[16] Even the terminology of v. 3 is similar to that in Acts 15:29: ἀπέχεσθαι ... πορνεία. Silas was one of the emissaries from the Jerusalem church who carried the letter containing the ruling of the apostles that accepted the Gentiles into the church but also warned them against immorality, idolatry, and uncleanness.

ies.[17] Far from limiting sex to the bounds of marriage, it was common for a man of means to have a mistress, and it also was acceptable for him to make use of his slaves for sexual gratification. Entering the church made such behavior taboo. Obviously, Gentile converts to Christianity had to struggle with the demands of what was to them a new sexual ethic, while continuing to live in a permissive society. One of the greatest challenges for a new convert, no doubt, was living according to the truth that God's word, not Hellenistic norms, must govern the behavior of God's followers. The application to the sexual behavior of the believer today is obvious, and the challenge has not changed. Living sanctified lives still means living counterculturally in many instances. Believers live by God's standards regardless of how they compare to societal norms.

4:4–5 Understanding the second infinitival clause in this passage is complicated by several factors. First, it is uncertain whether Paul intended vv. 4–5 as an elaboration of v. 3b or as a second illustration of sanctified living. "Avoid sexual immorality" (v. 3b) is a very general, negative exhortation. The command to "control" one's own "body" (v. 4) is not much more specific. It differs from the preceding in that it is a positive statement and represents a shift in the focus from the sin to the sinner. In this way it states a comparable exhortation to that in v. 3b but does so in a more positive and personal manner. However, if the alternative translation of v. 4 ("each one of you must know how to take a wife for himself in sanctification and honor," RSV; cf. the NRSV) is adopted, then the topic has shifted so significantly as to comprise a second illustration of sanctified living. If this latter translation is preferred, then vv. 4–5 add a command related to the character of the marital relationship following v. 3b's counsel to avoid improper sexual relations outside marriage.

A second factor influencing the interpretation of vv. 4–5 is the translation of the word *skeuos* ("body" in the NIV). The word literally means "object," "container," or "vessel."[18] In v. 4 *skeuos* is obviously

---

[17] R. Jewett emphasizes the cult of the Cabiri (*The Thessalonian Correspondence: Pauline Rhetoric and Millenarian Piety* [Philadelphia: Fortress, 1986], 126–32); see also C. Edson, "Cults of Thessalonica (Macedonia III)," *HTR* 41 (1948): 153–204. K. P. Donfried, "The Cults of Thessalonica and the Thessalonian Correspondence," *NTS* 31 (1985): 336–56, highlights the immorality in the Dionysian rites.

[18] The references to a person as a vessel in the NT are not examples of platonic anthropology. They are, rather, more in line with Jeremiah's image of the Potter emphasizing humanity's nature as created beings shaped by God, fragile beings with a limited life span or creations intended for some divinely determined use (see Rom 9:22–23; 2 Cor 4:7; 2 Tim 2:21; 1 Pet 3:7).

used metaphorically. The two most common translations of *skeuos* in this context are "body" and "wife."[19] Scholars have argued these alternatives since the patristic age,[20] and modern commentators are still divided over the issue.[21] Both meanings for *skeuos* are well documented in antiquity—vessel as a reference to body is predominant in Greek writings; vessel as a reference to a woman or wife, more prominently in Jewish writings. Maurer is correct when he observes that "the parallels to *skeuos* (in ancient literature) do not offer convincing support either one way or the other."[22]

The decision regarding the proper translation of *skeuos* must be made in tandem with another interpretive choice. *Skeuos* is the object of an infinitive *(ktasthai)* of *ktaomai,* which normally means "to acquire."[23] It is also possible to translate *ktaomai* "to possess," though this meaning is rare in the New Testament if it occurs at all.[24] The common meaning of the verb, "to acquire," militates against understanding "vessel" in the sense of "body." Obviously people do not acquire their bodies; they already are in possession of them. To translate *skeuos* as

---

[19] J. Whitton points out that σκεῦος was used as a euphemism for the male organ ("A Neglected Meaning for *Skeuos* in 1 Thess 4:4," *NTS* 28 [1982]: 142–43). But Whitton's note does not suggest a third alternative translation. Rather, it provides additional support for the translation "body," with emphasis on the sexual concerns of the verse, which are also clear from the context (v. 5).

[20] See *TDNT,* s.v. "σκεῦος" VII, 365, n. 48, for a list of church fathers who preferred the translation "body" and n. 49 for a list of several who preferred "wife."

[21] In favor of "wife" are R. F. Collins, "'This Is the Will of God: Your Sanctification' (1 Thess 4:3)," in *Studies in the First Letter to the Thessalonians* (Louvain: Peeters, 1984), 311–17; J. E. Frame, *A Critical and Exegetical Commentary on the Epistles of St. Paul to the Thessalonians* (Edinburgh: T & T Clark, 1960); Best, *1 and 2 Thessalonians;* T. Holtz, *Der erste Brief an die Thessalonicher,* EKKNT 13 (Zurich: Benziger, 1986); C. Maurer, *TDNT* VII, s.v. "σκεῦος"; and Yarbrough, *Not Like the Gentiles,* 66–87. Some commentators who argue for "body" are F. F. Bruce, *1 and 2 Thessalonians,* WBC (Waco: Word, 1982), 83; M. McGehee, "A Rejoinder to Two Recent Studies Dealing with 1 Thess 4:4," *CBQ* 51 (1989): 82–89 (which attempts to refute Collins and Yarbrough); L. Morris, *The First and Second Epistles to the Thessalonians,* NICNT, rev. (Grand Rapids: Eerdmans, 1991), 120–21; B. Rigaux, *Saint Paul: Les Epitres aux Thessaloniciens* (Paris: Jl. Gabalda; Gembloux: J. Duculot, 1956), 504–6; and Wanamaker, *1 and 2 Thessalonians,* 152–53.

[22] Maurer, *TDNT,* 365. He goes on to argue from the "larger linguistic context" that Paul was reflecting a Hebrew phrase that meant "to possess a woman sexually" and intended σκεῦος κτᾶσθαι to have the meaning "to live with his wife" (p. 366).

[23] BAGD, s.v. "κτάομαι." Cf. Matt 10:9; Luke 18:12; 21:19; Acts 1:18; 8:20; 22:28; 1 Thess 4:4.

[24] This may be the meaning of κτῶμαι in Luke 18:12; "to control" in v. 4 of the NIV is an extension of the idea of possession.

"body," the infinitive of *ktaomai* must be understood to mean "possess" in the sense of acquiring mastery or control over something. In v. 4 it would mean something like "control your body" in the sense of controlling sexual desires or actions. This is possible,[25] though such a usage occurs nowhere else in Paul's writings. Using the infinitive to mean "to control" is highly unusual, but not impossible.

The alternative is to translate it as "acquire" (its more normal use) and understand *skeuos* to mean "wife." In rabbinic usage the Hebrew equivalent of *skeuos* sometimes was used to refer to a woman, specifically as a sexual partner.[26] It is possible that Paul here was reflecting Hebrew idiom. In Pauline usage elsewhere, however, *skeuos* is never used to refer to one's wife. Paul's references to a "wife" follow the common Hellenistic pattern of using *gunē* ("woman"), often modified by a possessive (cf. 1 Cor 7:2–4).

Whether *ktasthai* has as its object a wife to be obtained or a body to be controlled remains debatable. Though the precise conduct commanded is a bit vague to us today, the character of the conduct commanded is clear and is applicable to the church regardless of the exact interpretation of *skeuos*. The Christian must behave "in a way that is holy and honorable." Expanding on these positive elements is the negative "not in passionate lust like the heathen who do not know God." Thus living according to the commands of Christ "attunes [the church] to the will of God, distinguishes them from the surrounding world, and ensures good order within the family of God."[27]

The phrases that further describe the manner of behavior Paul was prescribing form an important part of these verses. Yet they are often given scant attention in the scramble to interpret *skeuos ktasthai*. Christians are to conduct themselves in a distinctly Christian way. Their behavior should be "holy" (lit., "in holiness/sanctification"), reminding the reader of the theme of the paraenesis. A life lived in sanctification is one that is dedicated to reflecting the character and commands of the Lord. The body is the temple of the Holy Spirit and is not meant for

---

[25] When used in the perfect tense, κτάομαι can be translated as a present indicating that one "possesses" something as a result of an earlier acquisition. See also MM, s.v. "κτάομαι" for evidence that the present tense of the verb occasionally had the same meaning in the papyri.

[26] Maurer concludes that while "כְּלִי" is used of the woman only in a figurative sense ... the underlying phrases 'to use as a vessel,' 'to make one's vessel,' etc. are to be regarded as established euphemisms for sexual intercourse" (*TDNT*, s.v. "σκεῦος," VIII, 362).

[27] Yarbrough, "Not Like the Gentiles," 67.

union with prostitutes or for any other type of sexual immorality (cf. 1 Cor 6:12–20). Such activities comprise a misuse of the believer's body, which is sanctified to the service of God (cf. Belshazzar's misuse of temple objects and the results in Dan 5:22–28). "Honorable" behavior does not show disrespect for the sanctity of the self or demean the value of others. The use of the body (a body created by God) for immoral purposes both degrades the person and dishonors the Creator (cf. Rom 1:24, where "degrading" translates a negated verbal form of the same word).

A contrast to sanctified and honorable behavior is provided in v. 5 and helps clarify Paul's meaning. The opposite of holy, honorable living is the exercise of "passionate lust," in the manner of the Gentiles "who do not know God." In the Greek phrase "lust" *(epithymias)* modifies "passion" *(pathei)*. Ungodly, lustful passions should not dictate Christian actions. The word translated "passionate" had a different connotation to the ancient Greeks from the one it has today. It was a word much used in ethical discussions and referred to strong emotions, sexual and otherwise.[28] Paul consistently used the word in the negative sense of strong sexual urges contrary to the will of God (Rom 1:26; Col 3:5). Paul commonly (though not always, see 1 Thess 2:17) used "lust" to depict a strong ungodly sexual desire also. The combination *pathei epithymias* with the preposition *ev* warned believers that the will of God, not an unbridled libido, should dictate their actions. For "those who belong to Jesus Christ have crucified the sinful nature with its passions *[pathmasin]* and desires *[epithymiais]"* (Gal 5:24). On the other hand, Paul never argued that sexual desire itself is evil. The goal for Paul was not the destruction of physical desire but the sanctifying of it.

Behavior contrary to God's laws is perhaps to be expected from people who do not know God, but such certainly was not to be condoned among those who did know him. The "heathen" *(ethnē)* who do not know God are the Gentiles. The behavior that Paul condemned here the Jews condemned as well. The clause "like the heathen who do not know God" serves a double purpose. On the one hand, it adds the qualifier "ungodly" to the lustful desire condemned in v. 5a, making it even clearer that it was not sexual desire in general but the unrestrained lust that led to ungodly actions that Paul was condemning. On the other hand, the clause draws a dividing line between the church and the non-Christian world on the basis of sexual behavior. It reminded believers

---

[28] See W. Michaelis, *TDNT*, s.v. "πάσχω."

that they were God's people and it was right that their Christian character be conspicuous, evidenced by a sexual ethic different from that of a pagan world, which refused to acknowledge God (cf. Rom 1:21–32).

4:6a The third exhortation is expressed by two infinitives that prohibit sins against one's brother. The person who lives a sanctified life must not "wrong his brother or take advantage of him." To "wrong" a brother translates a word used only here in the New Testament. It indicates action that transgresses a law (the word is a compound meaning "go beyond"). If the law is thought of as a boundary circumscribing accepted behavior, this word depicts a person stepping beyond the bounds of legal or proper behavior. The word does not connote any specific category of sin, sexual or otherwise. To "take advantage" means "to defraud or cheat someone." It occurs in 2 Cor 7:2 and 12:17–18 in the context of the improper exploitation of a legitimate position. This implies more than simple dishonesty. It seems to connote the violation of a trust. The same is implied in the offending of a brother. When one Christian exploits and abuses a fellow Christian, dishonesty is compounded by the violation of the trust between brothers. The resultant loss of trust (even more than the dishonest act itself) has the potential to damage a fellowship severely. The first verb, "wrong," connotes an offense against a law (and the God who gave it; cf. v. 8). The second verb, "take advantage of," highlights an offense against a person. The Christian is neither to transgress God's laws nor cheat other people. The exact character of the act(s) of which the apostle was thinking, however, is still not clear, and the modifying phrase "in this matter" does not appreciably make it clearer.

Most commentators argue that "in this matter" *(en tō pragmati)* refers back to the discussion of sexual morals in the preceding verses. But some are convinced that *pragmati* in conjunction with "take advantage" *(pleonektein)* refers to business practices, not sexual behavior.[29] In favor of the latter interpretation is Paul's use of *pleonektein* for acquiring material gain inappropriately but never (if not here) for sexual

---

[29] R. Beauvery, *"Pleonektein* in I Thess 4, 6a," *VD* 33 (1955): 273–86. The NIV translation "in this matter" implies a continuation of the topic under discussion in earlier verses. But the "this" is the NIV's way of rendering the definite article in this instance. Just as valid a translation is the one in the margin of the RSV: "defraud his brother in business." M. Dibelius's suggestion that the "matter" is a lawsuit (cf. 1 Cor 6:1) lacks contextual support in 4:3–8. See *Die Briefe des Apostels Paulus. II. Die Neun Kleinen Briefe,* HNT (Tübingen: Mohr, 1913); also H. Baltensweil, "Erwagungen zu I Thess 4:3–8," *TZ* 19 (1963): 1–13.

abuses (see 2 Cor 7:2; 12:17–18). Also *pragma* was used by other authors to refer to business affairs (and perhaps has this meaning in Rom 16:2; 1 Cor 6:1; and 2 Cor 7:11). In addition, the two infinitives to "wrong ... or take advantage" are set off from the preceding text by the use of the article (the infinitives in vv. 3–4 do not have articles), which implies a change of topic. The warning in v. 7 that God did not call believers to be "impure" (*akatharsia*) may refer to "impure motives" rather than sexual impurity. (Cf. the NIV translation of the same word, *akatharsia*, in 2:3.) Finally, *pleonektein* and *pragmati* seem strange terms to apply to sexual behavior.

In favor of "this matter" continuing the discussion of sexual self-control, we should note that Paul did not use *pleonektein* only of financial matters (see 2 Cor 2:11). Also *pragma* was used of more matters than just of business affairs, and if it were used of business in v. 6, one would expect a plural form of the noun, not the singular. The presence of the article with the infinitives does not mandate a change in topic. And the reference to impurity in v. 7 may not prove but does imply that Paul did not intend a change of subject in v. 6. (Paul normally used *akatharsia* in contexts dealing with sexual immorality; see Rom 1:24; 2 Cor 12:21; Gal 5:19; Eph 4:19; 5:3; Col 3:5.) Finally, the possibility of defrauding (*pleonekteō*) a brother through immoral actions is not at all unreasonable. Adultery in the first century was considered a defrauding of the woman's husband, "discussions of which frequently included the treatment of *pleonexia*."[30]

In the absence of a clear indicator that Paul intended to shift the discussion to integrity in business matters, it is best to proceed with the understanding that v. 6 continues the series of exhortations related to sexuality. At the same time, we must not forget that sanctification is the theme of the passage, not immorality. *Porneia* occurs only once, whereas the *hagios* word group occurs four times. Yet the sexual overtones do seem to dominate, and so the sanctification of one's sexual self deserves to be highlighted. Various aspects of sexual activity are presented in these verses. Verse 3b presents a broad general statement, vv. 4–5 address sexuality in relation to oneself (assuming *skeuos* means "body"), and v. 6, looking outside the self, warns against immorality as an offense against God and others.

While some specifics of the sins that vv. 3–6a forbid may be uncertain, the following verses make it abundantly clear that ignoring the

---

[30] Yarbrough, *Not Like the Gentiles*, 76.

commands of God condemns one to certain punishment. Verses 6b–8 present a fourfold warning. The warnings are directed not to the pagan but to those members of the church who choose to live in a manner that denies the God they claim to serve. First, sinful behavior will be punished by the Lord, who is the "avenger" concerning "all these things" (RSV). Second, such sins are inconsistent with the sanctified life ("holy life") that should characterize Christians. Third, to deny that such actions are in fact sins is to reject God himself. And finally living an unsanctified life is inconsistent with the character of the Holy Spirit who indwells the believer.

4:6b "The Lord will punish men for all such sins" is a causal clause in Greek.[31] Though it may modify the infinitives of v. 6a alone, the breadth indicated in "all such sins" justifies connecting it to all the exhortations in vv. 3–6a. "All such sins" is literally "all these things," obviously meaning the ungodly behavior just described. The clause contains no verb and through this economy of words emphasizes that the Lord is the "avenger" (cf. Rom 13:4) concerning all these things.

The objects of this divine retribution are the members of the church who have violated God's commands and wronged the brethren (cf. 1 Cor 11:30–32). It is not clear whether the "Lord" Paul had in mind was Yahweh (cf. Deut 32:35; Ps 94:1; Mic 5:15) or Jesus (2 Cor 5:10) or whether the retribution was in this life (1 Cor 11:30–32) or in the future (1 Cor 3:13–15; 4:5). The difference here, however, is immaterial since the point is that divine judgment is inescapable—even for those who are in the church. Salvation does not grant believers the right to sin without suffering the consequences. Paul had previously warned the Thessalonians of this. Paul used two verbs in this last clause of v. 6 to emphasize the element of warning, "as we have already told you and warned you." The first verb provides a temporal frame and strengthens "we warned you." This latter verb means "to bear witness or testify to the truth of something." The combination of verbs implies a previous warning that was not given nonchalantly but was heavily stressed—the kind of warning that should not be readily forgotten or discounted.

4:7 The warning of judgment is followed by a reminder of the nature of the divine call. The particle "for" and the mention of a "holy" *(en hagiasmō)* life connects v. 7 to vv. 3–6. The fear of punishment alone might motivate some to proper behavior. But moral Christian

---

[31] The NIV does not translate διότι, which connects the clause to the preceding exhortations.

behavior should flow not from fear of judgment but out of the basic nature of the Christian calling. "God did not call us to be impure, but to live a holy life." Paul included himself and the other missionaries in the "us" of his assertion. He did not apply a standard of behavior to the Thessalonians that he was unwilling to share.

The "call" seems to be a look back to their initial commitment to follow Christ. Both the nature of that call and the purpose to which God called them (cf. 2:12; 5:24) require not impurity but sanctification. "To be impure" is literally "for uncleanness" and uses a noun that generally refers to sexual immorality in Paul's letters (e.g., Rom 1:24; 2 Cor 12:21; Gal 5:19). The contrasting phrase "to live a holy life" is literally "in holiness/sanctification" and links the call of God with sanctification, just as v. 3 identifies sanctification as God's will for believers. A positive response to God's calling requires a commitment to live in a manner consistent with the character and commands of God. The reality of such a commitment is seen in a sanctified life, a life obedient to the commands of God and empowered by the Spirit of God.

4:8 "Therefore" translates a strong inferential particle. Since God called believers to sanctified rather than immoral behavior, living immorally constituted a rejection of God. "He who rejects" *(athetōv)* is a present participle implying a settled attitude, not a single incident of disobedience. It does not have a stated object in the Greek text (i.e., "God," or "us" or "our teaching"). The NIV supplies "this instruction" as the understood object and probably is correct to do so since from the apostles' perspective it was the message rather than the messengers that suffered rejection (cf. Mark 9:37; Luke 10:16; John 12:44). This understanding of the role of the messenger did not originate with the church but had Old Testament antecedents (cf. Exod 16:8; 1 Sam 8:7).[32] The rejection of instructions given "by the authority of the Lord Jesus" (v. 2) was not a rejection of the messenger but of the God who sent the message. Thus time and again Paul stressed for his readers the divine origin of that which was preached (1:5; 2:4; 4:9; 5:18). Its authority did not rest with him and his intellectual qualifications or eloquence but with the God from whom the message came (cf. 1 Cor 2:1–5).

---

[32] For discussions of such representatives as they were understood within Judaism and then in the church see C. K. Barrett, "Shaliah and Apostle," in *Donum Gentilicium: New Testament Studies in Honor of David Daube*, ed. E. Bammel, C. K. Barrett, and W. D. Davies (Oxford: Clarendon, 1978), 94–102; and K. H. Rengstorf, *"apostolos," TDNT* 1.413–45.

God not only sent a message but also "gives you his Holy Spirit." Paul normally used the aorist ("gave") of the giving of the Spirit, implying a specific event rather than the durative one that the present tense ("gives") implies. The present tense participle in this verse highlights the dynamic work of God in the church, not a repeated giving of the Spirit.[33] He is the God who gives his Holy Spirit, and to live an immoral lifestyle is to reject God's gift. The unusual word order used by Paul (lit., "who gives the Spirit of him, the holy one, to you") emphasizes the holiness of the Spirit who is at work in the lives of God's people. The work of a holy *(hagios)* Spirit must be evident in the sanctified *(hagiasmos)* living of the church (see Gal 5:16–26). This is the will of God for his people (cf. v. 3). To live immorally is to give evidence of the Spirit's absence (cf. Gal 6:21).

3. Exhortations Regarding Brotherly Love (4:9–12)

⁹Now about brotherly love we do not need to write to you, for you yourselves have been taught by God to love each other. ¹⁰And in fact, you do love all the brothers throughout Macedonia. Yet we urge you, brothers, to do so more and more.

¹¹Make it your ambition to lead a quiet life, to mind your own business and to work with your hands, just as we told you, ¹²so that your daily life may win the respect of outsiders and so that you will not be dependent on anybody.

The theme of love for fellow Christians is featured in vv. 9–10. The associated theme of relating to non-Christian society is featured in vv. 11–12, and it is, as Morris notes, "artificial to separate these verses."[34] The two are connected logically and grammatically. Together these four verses present a brief exhortation of Christian relationships both inside and outside the church. The topic is introduced in vv. 9–10a. The exhortations begin in v. 10b. The only directive in the passage, *parakaloumen* ("We urge ..."), is completed by the object "you" and a series of infinitives plus a final clause ("so that ...") that carry the reader through v. 12. Using the infinitives, the apostle urged the church to love the brethren even more (v. 10b), to aspire to live a quiet life, to mind their own affairs, and to work with their own hands (v. 11). The final clause

---

[33] It probably was concern over this point that led a few scribes to replace the διδόντα with the aorist participle δόντα. See NA26 for the manuscript evidence.

[34] Morris, *1 and 2 Thessalonians*, 127.

(v. 12) gives the intended outcome of such Christian living: so that you may both "win respect" and "not be dependent."

The change in topic from sanctification (4:3–8) to that of brotherly love is reminiscent of the changes in topic found in 1 Corinthians. The shift is abrupt. There is no stated link between the two adjacent sections. The new topic is simply announced using the *peri de* ... ("now concerning ...") formula found elsewhere in Paul (cf. 1 Cor. 7:1; 8:1; 12:1).[35] The teachings that follow are introduced with the observation that these are matters with which the church members were already familiar (see vv. 9,11). Again the divine source of the teaching is highlighted (cf. 4:1–3,8). The teachings themselves are presented in brief, without elaboration or specific application. All of this is consistent with the character of paraenesis and can be seen in other authors as well (e.g., James).[36]

4:9–10a Obviously the matter of "brotherly love" *(philadelphias)* was not a new topic to the church. The grammar of v. 9 is difficult at points, but the implication is clear. Paul was complimenting the church by observing that they had no "need" (i.e., no lack in this area) that required him to write about exercising love for fellow Christians. Such statements were common in paraenetic passages. They functioned to introduce a topic without implying a deficiency on the part of the readers.[37] Paul both affirmed the church's demonstrations of love to date and introduced an exhortation to grow in love even more. Outside the New Testament both Greek and Jewish writers used "brotherly love" primarily of love within actual families, not of love within religious groups.[38] In the New Testament, however, it is always used as it is here, of love between members of the Christian family (Rom 12:10; Heb 13:1; 1 Pet 1:22; 2 Pet 1:7).

---

[35] The περὶ δὲ formula in 1 Cor organizes material written in response to a letter Paul sent to the Corinthian church (see 7:1). First Thess 4:9–12,13–18; 5:1–11 (sections introduced with a περὶ δὲ) may be a response to a letter from the Thessalonian church (as Frame suggests, *1 and 2 Thessalonians,* 140) or to questions delivered to Paul orally by Timothy (as Wanamaker mentions, *1 and 2 Thessalonians,* 159), but 1 Thessalonians makes no mention of such a letter, and the περὶ δὲ formula by itself does not require the existence of one.

[36] For an excellent summary of the form and function of paraenesis applicaple not only to James but to Paul's epistles as well, see L. G. Perdue, "Paraenesis and the Epistle of James," *ZNW* 72 (1981): 241–56.

[37] See A. J. Malherbe, *Moral Exhortation, A Greco-Roman Sourcebook,* LEC 4 (Philadelphia: Westminster, 1986), 124–25; and S. K. Stowers, *Letter Writing in Greco-Roman Antiquity* (Philadelphia: Westminster, 1986), 103.

[38] H. F. von Soden, "ἀδελφός," *TDNT* 1.146.

Paul also asserted that whatever he might have had to add in this area was doubly redundant because the Thessalonians themselves were "taught by God to love *[agapan]* each other." "You yourselves" indicates emphasis. Although the context implies that the Thessalonians were taught previously (as the NIV's "have been taught" indicates), the only verb ("you are") is actually a present tense. "You are God-taught" indicates that their education in Christian love was ongoing. Learning to love is a never-ending discipline, as Paul's exhortation to love "more and more" (v. 10) shows. "Taught by God" translates a single compound word *(theodidaktoi)*. This is the only occurrence of the word in the New Testament and the earliest known occurrence in any body of Greek literature. It may well have been coined by Paul himself. The closest biblical phrase is in the LXX text of Isa 54:13 (quoted in John 6:45). It predicts a day when "all your sons will be taught by the Lord." A hallmark of the new covenant in the New Testament is the presence of the Spirit with each believer (Acts 2:16–18; Gal 4:6) and the resultant internal witness to the will of God (cf. Jer 31:34; Heb 8:10–11). Apparently this was what Paul meant to signify with *theodidaktoi*. If this is so, then the fuller implications of being "taught by God" can be seen in Paul's references to the work of the Spirit of God within the believer (e.g., Gal 5:16–26).

They were God-taught "to love each another." Paul used an infinitival purpose clause to specify God's objective: mutual Christlike love *(agapan)*. Paul considered love for fellow Christians the prime Christian virtue (1 Cor 13) and the essential foundation for proper social interaction in the church (Rom 13:8–10; Phil 2:1–11). The same emphasis on love occurs in the teachings of Jesus recorded in the Gospels (Mark 12:28–31; Matt 22:34–40). Love for fellow believers is elevated to the status of a test of true Christianity in 1 John (2:9–11; 3:10; 4:7–8) and is reflected in the important practice of providing hospitality *(philoxenia)* to fellow Christians (Rom 12:13; 3 John 10; 1 Tim 3:2; Titus 1:8).

Paul was not implying that the Thessalonians had heard but not assimilated his and others' teachings about love. Their acts testified that they were apt students. Paul affirmed them by acknowledging that they did indeed "love all the brothers throughout Macedonia." But the nature of Christian love is such that it is always practiced, never mastered. The compliments the apostle paid the church were no doubt meant as encouragements to continued growth and serve as the basis for the exhortations in vv. 10b–12.

4:10b–12 This section (vv. 9–12) began with the apostle stating that he saw no need to write the church about love for fellow Christians (vv. 9–10a). He then addressed four exhortations to the church in a single lengthy sentence (vv. 10b–12). "We urge you ..." *(parakaloumen)*[39] is completed by a series of four infinitives that state the specific commands: (a) to abound more (in love), (b) to aspire to live a quiet life, (c) to attend to their own business, and (d) to work with their own hands (vv. 10b–11). The sentence concludes with a purpose clause. The church was to live in this manner in order to "win the respect of outsiders" and "not be dependent on anybody" (v. 12). Thus a series of commands that begins with a concern for growing, mutual Christian love concludes with a concern for the church's relationship to the non-Christian community.

First, the church was urged "to do so more and more." What the apostle wanted the church "to do" is not explicitly stated, but brotherly love is the overarching topic in vv. 9–12. Also this is the same verb *(perisseuō)* used in Paul's prayer in 3:12 that the Lord would cause the Thessalonians' love to "overflow" for one another. Assuming this first exhortation was to abound in love, we might also assume that the exhortations that follow in v. 11 tell the church "how to excel in love."[40] If this were the case, however, one would expect statements about kindness, patience, generosity, enduring wrongs, or helping the weak (cf. 1 Thess 5:14–15; 1 Cor 13:4–7; 1 Tim 6:17–19). But the exhortations that follow are not of this nature, and their stated purpose is not growth in love but gaining respect from non-Christians and avoiding need. As a result it seems likely then that these verses blended a concern for proper behavior among the brethren and proper behavior in relation to the secular society in which the brethren lived. At the very least Paul had in mind the impression left with outsiders by behavior in the congregation.

The second exhortation urged the Thessalonians, "Make it your ambition to lead a quiet life" (v. 11). Both infinitives that make up this command, "to aspire" and "to live quietly" (RSV), are present tense (as are all the others in vv. 10b–11), implying continuity in the church's behavior. Due partly to the brevity of these commands, there is considerable disagreement regarding the specific situation Paul was addressing. Schmithals' suggestion that Gnostic enthusiasts were creating

---

[39] See the discussions of παρακαλέω, pp. 84, 102, 118.
[40] Best follows this approach (*1 and 2 Thessalonians,* 174).

problems similar to those in the Corinthian church has few supporters today.[41] Most commentators understand these verses in light of 2 Thess 3:6–13 and the eschatological confusion evident in both letters. They argue that a number of the Thessalonian believers used the expectation of an immanent return of the Lord as an excuse to abandon all work.[42] Although this is a popular position, its weakness is that it is based on a connection between idleness and eschatology that Paul never made. Neither 1 nor 2 Thessalonians makes an explicit link between the refusal to work and eschatological expectations. In addition, it is not even clear from a reading of 1 Thessalonians alone that idleness was a major problem in the church at the time Paul wrote this particular letter.[43]

It is possible to understand the exhortation "to lead a quiet life" as a general call to tranquility and the following exhortation, "to mind your own business" (more lit., "mind your own things"), in a complementary fashion. Morris has proposed two possible disruptions to the peace of the congregation, neither of which would require a background of errant eschatology (though Morris does seem to presuppose eschatological confusion). Rather than minding their own affairs, perhaps some in the church had a "tendency to interfere in the running of the church" though they were not church officers.[44] This could also explain the exhortation to "respect those ... over you in the Lord" and "live in peace with each other" (5:12–13). Or Paul may have written these words thinking of the idle busybodies he mentioned in 5:14 and 2 Thess 3:11–13.[45] In either case the focus of the passage is on the congregation itself and maintaining peace within it, a peace that would deprive outsiders of anything to criticize.

R. F. Hock presents another alternative to an eschatological understanding of these verses. He argues that the commands "to lead a quiet life" and to "mind your own business" were encouragements to political quietism. By avoiding political activism and working at respectable occupations, the church would gain the approval of their non-Christian

---

[41] Schmithals, *Paul and the Gnostics,* 158–60.

[42] See Best, *1 and 2 Thessalonians,* 174–77; Bruce, *1 and 2 Thessalonians,* 91; Rigaux, *Saint Paul,* 519–21.

[43] Idleness is not presented any more prominently in 5:14 than are timidity, weakness, or a lack of patience.

[44] Morris, *1 and 2 Thessalonians,* 132.

[45] Ibid. Verse 11 urges readers to aspire to live quietly (ἡσυχάζειν). In 2 Thess 3:12 the idle are admonished to work in quietness (μετὰ ἡσυχίας).

neighbors.⁴⁶ Some of the terms Paul used in these verses were indeed used by various Greco-Roman philosophers to encourage withdrawal from public life.⁴⁷ Such encouragements would make sense in light of the apostle's past experience in Thessalonica. After all, Paul was charged with causing social and political unrest in the city (Acts 17:6–7) and might have responded by advising the church to avoid political entanglements.

There is no other indication in the Thessalonian correspondence, however, that the church was engaging in political activism or holding public office. Most people in the church probably were not wealthy enough to involve themselves in public life even if they had been so inclined.⁴⁸ Also the exhortation seems to be addressed to the church as a whole, not to the few who might have had the personal wealth and leisure required by public office. Thus Paul's advice may have had political implications, but it was primarily an encouragement to avoid public controversy in a more general sense than Hock proposes. By avoiding conflict with the authorities, the church could continue spreading the gospel with as little social or political opposition as possible. If this is the case, then these verses are concerned not with conflict within the church (e.g., caused by idlers) but with the relationship between the church and the society in which it operated. The positive side of this coin is then seen in the subsequent purpose clause (v. 12), which expressed the goal of cultivating the respect of the society in which the church lived and sought to minister.

It should be clear from Paul's own history, however, that living quietly did not mean the church should tone down its proclamation of the gospel. On the contrary, Paul consistently encouraged boldness in this regard. The church was not to live so quietly that they failed to function as witnesses of Christ both in word and deed. As a result, Paul and his churches found themselves engaged in the delicate task of proclaiming divine rule while living under Roman rule. Under Roman rule agitation

---

⁴⁶ R. F. Hock, *The Social Context of Paul's Ministry: Tentmaking and Apostleship* (Philadelphia: Fortress, 1980), 46–47.

⁴⁷ Hock observes that "withdrawal from politics is often termed 'quietism' (ἡσυχία), and taking part in politics is often termed 'attending to public affairs' (πράσσειν τὰ κοινά)" (ibid.). Paul advised his readers to aspire "to live quietly" (ἡσυχάζειν) and "to mind your own affairs" (πράσσειν τὰ ἴδια).

⁴⁸ Those who held public office in Greco-Roman cities were expected to fund various public works personally. The cost of holding office excluded all but the wealthy, and the Pauline church generally did not include many such people (1 Cor 1:26).

for social change as we know it in modern democratic civilizations was not an option available to the masses. Obedience or rebellion were the alternatives available, and Rome dealt with rebels in summary and violent fashion.

Paul did not encourage Christians to be social revolutionaries. In fact, the missionaries denied such charges when they were leveled against them (Acts 17:6–9). Earthly governments were, after all, part of the temporal economy of God (Rom 13:1–7). They were a part of the old world that was passing away, but it was not Paul's intent that the church disrupt society or overthrow governments. Rather, he encouraged Christians to be good citizens and exemplary members of their families and of their society but to do so in a manner consistent with the teachings of Christ. Only in this sense was the Pauline gospel intended to change society. It set out to change the individuals who made up society while awaiting that climactic event when the power of God would truly change the world forever.

Finally, the members of the church were urged, "Work with your hands." It is not surprising that such an exhortation should come from one with a Jewish background. Working for one's living "was often understood by the rabbis to be divinely commanded; together with the study of the Law, it was a mainstay of life."[49] The Greek attitude was quite different. Manual labor was considered slavish and demeaning for one who had the means to dedicate himself to loftier cultural pursuits.[50] Yet manual labor did have its place and was accorded appropriate respect by many Greek moralists.[51] Thus engaging in respectable forms of manual labor could have the intended results of garnering the respect of outsiders (Jewish and Greek) and fending off need. However, Paul's intent here was not to praise manual labor per se. This is not a command to the wealthy to take up a trade but an encouragement to each individual to do his own work and so be a self-supporting, contributing member of the church and so also of his city. Paul himself attempted to set a good example in this regard (2:9; 2 Thess 3:7–9). The opposite was to live a life of idleness and dependence. Paul reasoned that a person capable of working should do just that. At the same time, the church was to continue engag-

---

[49] G. Agrell, *Work, Toil and Sustenance,* trans. S. Westerholm (Lund: Verbum Hakan Ohlssons, 1976), 57.

[50] See M. I. Finley, *The Ancient Economy* (Berkeley: University of California Press, 1973), 35–61.

[51] See Hock's discussion, *Social Context,* 44–46.

ing in benevolence to those truly in need (2 Thess 3:11–13). Once again Paul stressed that these were not new commands[52] but were comparable to that which the apostle had "told" the church previously.

The intended result of living as is commanded in vv. 10b–11 is stated in v. 12. The *hina* ("so that") that introduces the clause has two objects. The first goal expressed is that the church members should "walk worthily toward those outside" (literal translation). The object is that non-Christians might observe their proper and respectable manner of life. The term "worthily" *(euschēmonōs)* assumes certain social norms or expectations. People who live in such a way that they are counted as respectable members of society, who engage in respectable pursuits,[53] are living *euschēmonōs*.

This did not mean giving up Christian distinctives. The church should not gloss over the stumbling block of the cross or surrender Christian sexual ethics in an effort to fit into society. In short, where clear Christian principles conflicted with societal norms, the Christian was to obey Christ, not appease society. Yet the church was not to alienate itself from society. In order to be a witness in the world, the church had to remain in it and in dialogue with it. Christians had to live lives that gained them a measure of respect—even if it was given grudgingly. The respect they gained from the world impacted the world's opinion of the gospel. Thus the church had to walk the fine line of neither alienating nor imitating non-Christian society. To do either was to fail in their God-given task of sharing the good news.

The second goal of the exhortations in vv. 10b–11 was that the church [or believers?] would "not be dependent on anybody" (v. 12b). The clause is literally "not have need *[chreian]* of anyone" or possibly "of anything."[54] *Chreian* ("dependent") echoes v. 9 (where the church has no "need" that Paul should write to them about brotherly love) and so helps to tie the section together.

Avoiding material need *(chreian)* may benefit the church in several ways. It would prevent them from getting a reputation as lazy, noncontributing members of society and thus lowering non-Christian citizens'

---

[52] "Just as we told you" translates a verb (παρηγγείλαμεν) that signifies the giving of a command.

[53] See Hock's discussion of employment involving unseemliness (ἀσχημοσύνη) versus occupations that were respectable (εὐσχημόνως; *Social Context*, 45).

[54] Μηδενὸς could be masculine or neuter, but the difference is minor. A church in need of some "thing" is also a church in need of some "one" who can provide it.

opinion of the church. It would prevent willfully needy individuals from becoming a drain on the church's resources and allow more funds to be available to persons who were unavoidably in need (cf. 1 Tim 5:16). A church in need is inhibited from contributing to the needs of others. A productive congregation, on the other hand, is in a position to help even with needs outside their own congregation (cf. 1 Cor 16:1–4; 2 Cor 8:1–4; 1 Tim 5:3–8,16). Clearly Christians of any era should avoid need lest they inhibit their ministry and damage their witness.

4. Exhortations Regarding the Dead (4:13–18)

[13]Brothers, we do not want you to be ignorant about those who fall asleep, or to grieve like the rest of men, who have no hope. [14]We believe that Jesus died and rose again and so we believe that God will bring with Jesus those who have fallen asleep in him. [15]According to the Lord's own word, we tell you that we who are still alive, who are left till the coming of the Lord, will certainly not precede those who have fallen asleep. [16]For the Lord himself will come down from heaven, with a loud command, with the voice of the archangel and with the trumpet call of God, and the dead in Christ will rise first. [17]After that, we who are still alive and are left will be caught up together with them in the clouds to meet the Lord in the air. And so we will be with the Lord forever. [18]Therefore encourage each other with these words.

A *peri* … formula ("concerning …") similar to those that introduce the preceding (4:9) and the following (5:1) sections, introduces the central topic of these verses.[55] Paul's words here (vv. 13–18) concern "those who fall asleep," that is, those Christian who have died. His primary intent in the passage was to comfort the living in the face of death and enable them to use his teachings to comfort one another (v. 18). Thus a primary question the modern reader should bring to this text is, What is said in these verses that would comfort a Christian who has lost a loved one?

The believer's grief in the face of a fellow Christian's death is addressed by highlighting the hope of resurrection (v. 13). The return of the Lord, by itself, is not the salve Paul applied. Rather, the reunion of the dead with the living and their shared glory in the presence of the Lord is crucial (v. 17). The living and the dead will be reunited and will be together with the Lord forever. It is this expectation that makes Christian

---

[55] Contra F. F. Bruce, *peri* … does identify the topic of this passage though it does not occur first in its sentence (*1 and 2 Thessalonians,* WBC [Waco: Word, 1982], 95).

grief the grief of temporary separation. It is still grief, but it is grief moderated by the anticipation of a certain and joyous reunion in Christ.

A problem inherent in the passage and quite difficult to solve is that of identifying more precisely the cause of the Thessalonians' distress regarding those who had died. Was someone misleading them with false teachings? Schmithals suggests that Gnostics had infiltrated the church and were denying the reality of a bodily resurrection in favor of a spiritual "resurrection" only for those who were enlightened by Gnostic insights. Since believers who had already died did not have access to these newly revealed insights, the Thessalonians were concerned that they might miss resurrection altogether.[56] In response Paul assured the Thessalonians that the dead will partake in the resurrection (thus Gnostic insights are invalid) and warned them to be prepared for the Lord's arrival (4:13–5:11). Schmithals' theory could also be used to explain the affirmation of church leaders in 5:12–13 (who were in conflict with Gnostic leaders) and the warning to test everything (5:21–22), as well as the content of 2 Thess 2:1–12. However, the early date of 1 Thessalonians makes a Gnostic heresy improbable, and Paul's response in 4:13–5:11 was rather mild and indirect if he was consciously combating Gnostic heretics.[57]

If heresy was not the problem, then perhaps ignorance was. Ludemann defends the proposal that "Paul did not deal thematically with the resurrection of the dead during his founding proclamation, owing to the expectation of an imminent parousia."[58] Such a proposal is credible only with the unusually early dating of the letter Ludemann proposes. In addition, the early stage at which martyrdom became a reality in the church (Acts 7:54–60; 12:2) and the early circulation of such Jesus material as Paul cited in 4:16 (see following comments) make it unlikely that Paul would have omitted such teachings from the earliest stages of gospel proclamation or training of new converts.

---

[56] Schmithals, *Paul and the Gnostics,* 160–67. See also W. Harnish, *Eschatologische Existenz. Ein exegetischer Beitrag zum Sachanliegen von 1 Thessalonicher 4, 15–5, 11* (Göttingen: Vandenhoeck & Ruprecht, 1973), 16–51.

[57] For a more detailed refutation of Schmithals' proposal see G. Ludemann, *Paul, Apostle to the Gentiles, Studies in Chronology* (London: SCM, 1984), 206–9, trans. F. S. Jones from the German *Paulus, der Heidenapostle, vol. 1: Studien zur Chronologie,* FRLANT 123 (Göttingen: Vandenhoeck & Ruprecht, 1980). Also M. L. Peel has shown that not all Gnostic groups denied the resurrection. See "Gnostic Eschatology and the New Testament," *NovT* 19 (1970): 141–54.

[58] Ludemann, *Paul, Apostle to the Gentiles,* 212–38.

What seems most probable is that the church simply had not under-stood the teachings regarding the resurrection that Paul must have given during the weeks the church was being founded (cf. 5:1). H.-A. Wilcke suggests for instance that the church was unclear on the timing and sequence of events. They feared that the living would participate in the parousia but the dead would be raised later—after the joy of the parousia or even after the millennial reign. Such fears would explain Paul's asser-tion "we [who remain alive] will certainly not precede those who have fallen asleep."[59] The view of Plevnik is similar. He proposes that utilizing assumption imagery, Paul presented the taking up of the faithful at the parousia. In the context of Jewish apocalyptic thought such imagery assumes, however, that the one taken up is alive. As a result the church was not certain that the dead would participate at the parousia. Paul's assurance that the dead "will rise first" brings them back to the same sta-tus as the living and allows them to participate fully at the parousia.[60]

Such confusion in the church regarding the relative timing of the parousia and the resurrection is certainly a possibility. And some Jewish apocalyptic literature does depict the in-breaking of God and the resur-rection of the dead in different time frames (cf. *2 Esdr* 7:25–44; 13:24; *2 Apoc Bar* 29–30). But given a traditional chronology for the ministry of the apostle, it is difficult to believe that by the time of his second mission-ary journey Paul had not discovered the importance of fully and clearly presenting matters related to death and resurrection. It also seems unlikely that Paul would have called the distress caused by a delayed res-urrection "sorrow" like the sorrow of those "who have no hope."

Marshall takes a slightly different tack by arguing that it is "one thing to have a theoretical belief in resurrection and quite another to maintain that belief in the actual presence of death."[61] The problem reported by Timothy may not have concerned theological content as much as the appropriation of theology into life. Out of a pastoral concern for their grief, Paul reminded the church of the theological basis of their hope of reunion. Thus the climactic image in vv. 13–18 is that of the dead reunited with the living in the presence of the Lord forever (4:17).

---

[59] See esp. H.-A. Wilcke, *Das Problem eines messianischen Zwischenreiches bei Pau-lus,* ATANT 51 (Zurich: Zwingli-Verlag, 1967).

[60] J. Plevnik, "The Taking Up of the Faithful and the Resurrection of the Dead in 1 Thessalonians 4:13–18," *CBQ* 46 (1984): 274–83.

[61] Marshall, *1 and 2 Thessalonians,* NCB (Grand Rapids: Eerdmans, 1983), 120–21.

If we understand the passage as an attempt to comfort the grieving, we find the passage is complete. If, on the other hand, we approach the passage expecting an eschatological treatise, we experience frustration. We find ourselves disappointed that Paul did not explain his thought more fully or provide more details regarding the eschaton. The brevity of his comments and their location in the paraenetic section of the letter indicate the intent to admonish and encourage, not educate. Paul's pastoral concern was to guide the way the Thessalonians were living, not provide them with eschatological gnosis. This is not a passage about the parousia but a passage about grieving for the dead. This does not mean that it is improper to mine these words for insight into the coming of the Lord (any more than it is wrong to study the Christological content of Phil 2:6–11). First Thessalonians 4:13–18 and 5:1–11 are classic texts, useful for the study of Pauline eschatology. We must not, however, allow interest in last things to blind us to the use for which these verses were intended—as a word of encouragement to a church dealing with death.

4:13 "We do not want you ignorant" was a formula that could introduce new material (e.g., travel plans; cf. Rom 1:10; 15:32) or an elaboration on familiar material (cf. 1 Cor 10:1; 12:1; 2 Cor 1:8). The use of the formula here in a paraenetic passage probably introduces a review of familiar material. Also one would expect that teachings regarding death, resurrection, and the parousia would be a part of the instruction of any church at an early stage in its establishment (cf. 1:10; 14–15). Thus, in this instance, the formula probably did not introduce totally new material but explained or elaborated on teachings previously shared with the church (cf. 5:2).[62]

The theme of the passage is identified at the outset using the preposition *peri* (cf. 4:9 and 5:1). Paul was about to address the matter of "those who fall asleep" *(tōn koimōmenōn). Koimaō,* a common word for "sleep," was often used as a euphemism for death in Greek, Jewish, and Christian writings as well as in Paul's epistles.[63] There is nothing in the context to indicate that Paul used the word here in any way other than the conventional fashion. To read the term as an ontological assertion regarding the state of believers in the interim between death and

---

[62] Cf. the positive formula "I wish you to know …" (θέλω δὲ ὑμᾶς εἰδέναι) in 1 Cor 11:3, a formula common in the papyri (G. Milligan, *St. Paul's Epistles to the Thessalonians: The Greek Text with Introduction and Notes* [London: Macmillan, 1908], 55).

[63] E.g., Homer, *Iliad* 11.241; Sophocles, *El.* 509; Gen 47:30; Isa 14:8; John 11:11–14; 1 Cor 7:39; 11:30; 15:6,51; 2 *Macc* 12:45.

resurrection is to import ideas not supported by this context.[64]

The apostle stated his reason for raising this issue in v. 13b. Paul's statement (which the NIV introduces with "or") is a negative purpose (*hina mē,* "lest") clause: he did not want the believers to be ignorant so that they who have the hope of resurrection might not grieve *(lupēsthe)* as unbelievers "who have no hope" (v. 13b).[65] The difference between the two groups is not that unbelievers grieve and Christians ought not grieve. For Paul told the Philippians that he would have had "sorrow upon sorrow" *(lupēn epi lupēn)* had their messenger and his coworker Epaphroditus died (Phil 2:27). Both Christians and non-Christians rightly express grief at the loss of a loved one. The distinction that is highlighted in v. 13 is that the non-Christian has "no hope."

In what sense did the non-Christians not have hope? A contrast between the believers and "the rest of men" might imply that Paul had in mind a singular belief system. But the whole of non-Christian humanity did not share a common religion or a common belief about life after death. For some in the first century death was considered an absolute termination of existence. This was not universally true, however, because the ancient world did in fact have an abundance of beliefs regarding an afterlife. Among these the character of life after death varied considerably from the Hades of the Homeric myths to the immortality taught by various philosophers to the salvation offered by the mystery religions. How thoroughly such teachings actually impacted the common person, if they did at all, is uncertain. But that such teachings did exist indicates that Paul was not denying their existence but their validity. The hopelessness of the non-Christian world stemmed from the one fact they all shared: they did not possess the one true hope, the Christian hope, which Christ validated by his resurrection.

4:14 The basis of this Christian hope is now stated. If we believe that Jesus died and rose, we can believe also in the resurrection of the

---

[64] See O. Cullmann's *Immortality of the Soul or Resurrection of the Dead* (London: Epworth, 1958), 48–57; and O. Michel's contrasting opinion in "Zur Lehre vom Todesschlaf," *ZNW* 35 (1936): 285–90. R. E. Bailey enters into a dialogue with both authors and finally asserts that the NT position is simply that "the Christian is one whose life is hid with Christ in God from where he awaits ... the Parousia" ("Is 'Sleep' the Proper Biblical Term for the Intermediate State?" *ZNW* 55 [1964]: 161–67). He concludes by quoting with approval D. P. Althaus: "We know nothing before the resurrection (but) that death and the dead are in God's hand. That is sufficient."

[65] Could λυπῆσθε ... ("to grieve for the dead") be a reference to pagan funeral services in which Paul did not want the Christian to participate?

Christian dead (v. 14). The "for" *(gar)* that connects v. 14 to what precedes is not translated in the NIV, nor is the conditional particle "if" that introduces the protasis. "For if we believe that Jesus died and rose again" (NASB) is a more literal rendering of the Greek text. However, this particular conditional ("if ...") structure assumes the truth of the condition (hence the RSV translation "for since we believe").

The assertion "Jesus died and rose again" probably is part of a creedal formula that summarized Christian proclamation. Paul used a similar formula in 1 Cor 15:3–7. I. Havener points to the introductory formula "we believe," the unusual use of "Jesus" without any title, and the infrequency of the term translated "rose again" *(anestē)* in Paul's writings as indicative of a pre-Pauline formula.[66] If he is correct, this must have been one of the earliest formulas in the church and so highlights for us the centrality of the death and resurrection in the apostolic gospel. The point at which the creedal citation stops is uncertain, but it is unlikely that v. 14b continues the original formula.[67]

Rather than continue the citation, Paul applied it to the situation at hand using an argument anticipatory of 1 Cor 15:20–23. He reasoned from Christ's experience to that of those who belong to Christ. We believe Christ rose, "and so we believe that God will bring with Jesus those who have fallen asleep in him." This second half of the verse is difficult to translate. The NIV inserts a second "we believe" in v. 14b, which may lead a reader to assume that Paul was arguing that one who believes in Christ's resurrection should also believe in a general resurrection. But the focal point is divine consistency, not theological consistency. The God who raised Jesus will also raise Jesus' followers. It is Jesus' resurrection that validates the gospel and guarantees the believers' resurrection (cf. 1 Cor 15:17–20).

In addition to the choice of "bring" rather than "raise" as the main verb in the clause, the placement and meaning of the phrases "with Jesus" and "in him" create difficulties. Again the NASB rendering is more literal, "Even so God will bring with Him those who have fallen asleep in Jesus." (In a footnote the editors indicate that "in Jesus" is lit.,

---

[66] I. Havener, "Pre-Pauline Formulae Christological Creedal Formulae of 1 Thessalonians," SBLSP 20 (1981): 111–13. See also Best, *1 and 2 Thessalonians,* 186–88.

[67] If it did, one would expect some parallel expression in the second clause (e.g., the repetition of ἀνίστημι) or a statement of purpose as Wanamaker suggests (*1 and 2 Thessalonians,* 168–69). Havener argues that the original formula began with "πιστεύομεν ὅτι ... ("Pre-Pauline Formulae," 113).

"through Jesus.") The use of "bring" rather than "raise" shifts the focus of the saying from a resurrection like Christ's (the emphasis one would expect after v. 14a) to involvement along with the living saints in the parousia brought about at the Father's initiative (Mark 13:32). This is done in anticipation of vv. 15–17, which depict the manner in which the dead will be brought together with the living in that day. For it is the anticipation of reunion as a feature of resurrection that provides comfort to those grieving the loss of a loved one (vv. 17–18).

The Greek prepositional phrases that are literally "with Him" and "through Jesus" are both difficult phrases.[68] "With Him" *(syn autō)* could mean "with God" or "with Jesus." Neither its form nor its placement in the sentence excludes either alternative. Its reference to God (as the NASB translates it) is favored by its proximity to "will bring" in the Greek text and the redundancy created if both phrases modify "will bring" and yet refer to Jesus. However, if "through Jesus" *(dia tou Iēsou)* modifies "those who have fallen asleep," the redundancy is moderated. The sentence then asserts that those who died "through Jesus," God will bring back with Jesus.

"Through Jesus" may modify the verb "will bring" and indicate the agent through whom God accomplishes the salvation and ultimately the resurrection of believers. Bruce argues that such a translation makes the verb "overweighted," supporting two prepositional phrases whose meaning would then be essentially the same.[69] But the phrases are not redundant if "through Jesus" is a statement of agency and "with him" (i.e., Jesus) is a statement of association. The alternative is to take "through Jesus" with "those who have fallen asleep." To do so, however, creates a phrase unique in Paul, who normally referred to the dead "in" Christ (cf. v. 16), not "through" Christ. Attempts to explain what it might mean to die "through Jesus" include suppositions that Paul was referring to martyrdom or that the phrases "through" and "in" Christ are equivalent. After discussing and rejecting several such possibilities, Best accurately observes that "the ultimate meaning of v. 14 is not really greatly affected" by this decision since what is all important in the passage as a whole is that "the Christian dead will be brought back

---

[68] In the Greek sentence "through Jesus" (διά τοῦ Ἰησοῦ) is placed between "those who have died" (τους κοιμηθέντας) and "will bring" (ἄξει). "With him" (σύν αὐτῷ) comes at the end of the sentence: οὕτως καί ὁ θεὸς τοὺς κοιμηθέντας διὰ τοῦ Ἰησοῦ ἄξει σὺν αὐτῷ.

[69] Bruce, *1 and 2 Thessalonians*, 97.

to appear *with* Jesus at the time of his parousia together with the Christian living. This is why the Thessalonians were not to be sorrowful; this is why Paul can comfort them (v. 18)."[70]

4:15–16   Several revelations are made in the verses that follow: (a) the dead will rise and join the Lord prior to the living joining him (v. 15), (b) the Lord's descent will be with "a loud command, with the voice of the archangel, and with the trumpet call of God" (v. 16), (c) those who were dead and the those living "will be caught up together" (v. 17), and (d) all believers will be with the Lord forever (v. 17). Paul validated these assertions with an appeal to divine authority (v. 15). Whether the "Lord's own word" *(en logō kyriou)* was a reference to the teachings of the earthly Jesus or to later revelation, it confirmed the accuracy of what follows.

In the statement that initiates v. 15, literally, "For this we say to you" (cf. NASB), the "for" indicates that the "word of the Lord" that follows is the basis for the assurances given in v. 14. "This" looks forward to the teaching expressed in vv. 15b–17. Paul assured the church that what he was about to say was "according to the Lord's own word." It was not human speculation but divine revelation (cf. 4:8). They could depend on its truth. But where does the "word" begin—with v. 15 or v. 16, and how far does it extend—through v. 17? Is the "word" a quotation of the earthly Jesus, or is it a revelation given by the exalted Jesus? Was it given directly to Paul, or did he receive it through the agency of another prophet?

First, vv. 15–17 do not contain a quotation from the earthly Jesus that occurs in any other extant source. If it is a saying passed from Jesus' earliest disciples to Paul, it was not recorded in any of the Gospels.[71] It might have originated as a revelation from the exalted Jesus (either to Paul or to another prophet),[72] but if this is so, the very nature of the event precludes our knowing about it without more background than the apostle provided. And apart from a clear knowledge of the source of the word we cannot know whether the content of vv. 15–17 is a quotation or a summation of the Lord's teaching.

Second, the exact boundaries of the word are debatable. Is v. 15b the

---

[70] Best, *1 and 2 Thessalonians,* 189.

[71] See J. Jeremias, who includes this passage in his study of dominical *agrapha* (*Unknown Sayings of Jesus* [London: SPCK, 1964], 64–66).

[72] R. F. Collins argues that Paul was citing a *"dictum* of early Christian prophecy" rather than an *agraphon* ("Tradition, Redaction and Exhortation," in *Studies in the First Letter to the Thessalonians* [Louvain: Peeters, 1984], 330).

saying and vv. 16–17 an apostolic elaboration? Is v. 15b an introductory summary statement that is followed by the word of the Lord itself in vv. 16–17? Or does the word occupy the whole of vv. 15b–17? The unique contribution of vv. 15b–17 is the observation that the dead will be raised first at the parousia, then the living will be taken up. No other extant saying of Jesus makes this explicit assertion. This sequence is first revealed in v. 15b and then detailed in vv. 16–17. The repetition of this point implies that v. 15b is an introductory summary leading to the citation of the word itself in vv. 16–17.[73] Also only these latter verses contain terms similar to the sayings of Jesus recorded in the Gospels (cf. Matt 24:29–31).

Though the issues of the origin of the text and the boundaries of the saying are important, the debates in these areas should not be allowed to obscure the central assertions of vv. 15–17. The dead will be raised at the parousia, then the living will be taken up. Ultimately, those who have died and those living at the parousia will join the Lord as a single great company. "And so we will be with the Lord forever" (v. 17). By identifying these teachings as "the Lord's own word," Paul intended to instill confidence in this hope and assuage grief.

Paul asserted in v. 15b that we who are alive at the time of the parousia will not precede those who have died. The subject "we" is emphatic and is clarified by the clause "who are still alive, who are left till the coming of the Lord." A point of considerable interest to those seeking to understand Pauline eschatology is whether or not the fact that Paul used the first person, "we," meant that he expected the Lord to return in his lifetime. The assumption has generally been that this was indeed the case.[74] Others find evidence that Paul initially expected the Lord to come during his lifetime but that as the years passed revised his position and accepted the possibility that the Lord's return might be further in the future than he originally anticipated.[75] Witherington, on the other

---

[73] Ibid.

[74] A. Schweitzer's position that "from his first letter to his last Paul's thought is always uniformly dominated by the expectation of the immediate return of Jesus" has enjoyed broad support among subsequent scholars (*The Mysticism of Paul the Apostle,* trans. W. Montgomery [New York: Holt & Co., 1931], 52). See A. L. Moore, *The Parousia in the New Testament* (Leiden: Brill, 1966), 109, n. 7, for a listing of like-minded authors.

[75] J. Becker observes of Paul that "whereas he expects to be alive at the Parousia in 1 Thess. 4:15 and 1 Cor. 15:50–52, he seems to contemplate his death before its occurrence in Phil. 1:20 and possibly in 2 Cor. 5:1–11 (cf. 2 Cor. 1:9)" (*Paul the Apostle* [Philadelphia: Fortress, 1980], 178). Cf. Best, *1 and 2 Thessalonians,* 195.

hand, makes a strong case that Paul believed the end could come at any time but did not presume to predict its timing. When speaking of the end and envisioning himself in relation to it, Paul normally cast himself in the category of the living since he was alive at the time he wrote, but this was a convention, not a prediction.[76]

Paul stated emphatically that at the parousia the living "will certainly not precede those who have fallen asleep." This may indicate that the church feared that the dead would be raised at some time after the parousia and so miss the glories of that day.[77] But it is far from certain that this was the problem in the church. It seems safer to find the emphasis in Paul's words on his statement of the problem in v. 14 and his climactic statement in v. 17. In these verses the emphasis does not seem to fall on the sequence of the participation of the living and the dead but on the understanding that the dead will in fact participate in the parousia. This need not mean that Paul previously had not taught this in Thessalonica. The problem may well have been the difficulty of appropriating the doctrine of the resurrection into the way that enabled these Gentile believers to manage the trauma of death. Paul wanted to spare believers the sorrow of hopeless loss so common to the pagan world. He did so by reiterating truths in traditional language and applying them to immediate needs.

Some of the Thessalonian Christians may have died shortly after receiving the gospel. Yet the letter was written only a few months after the initial evangelization of the city. The text reads as though several deaths had occurred, but was this necessarily the case? Might this passage have been intended as a preventative rather than curative? The short time between the evangelization of the city and the writing of this letter would militate against the possibility of multiple deaths in the congregation in the interim. Although the letter refers to persecutions, there is no reference to deaths in Christ's service. Considering the extremes to which Paul went to affirm the faith of the church, failure on his part to highlight faithfulness to the point of death seems incredible. The references to "those who have fallen asleep" are references to all the faithful who had died, not specifically Thessalonian Christians who had died.

Finally, the command to "encourage each other" (v. 18) could antici-

---

[76] B. Witherington, *Jesus, Paul and the End of the World* (Downers Grove: InterVarsity, 1992), 10, 23–35. See also the five arguments given by Moore that Paul held an "*undelim-ited*" hope (*Parousia,* 110).

[77] See Moore, *Parousia,* 108–9.

pate future need as easily as it could be an attempt to meet a current need. In other words vv. 13–18 may well contain admonitions appropriate to any congregation rather than being proof of a problem particular to the church at Thessalonica. The problem is the grief resulting from a death (v. 13). The word of encouragement is that the Lord will reunite the living and the dead at his return (vv. 14,17). Celebrating that reunion required recounting a depiction of the parousia (vv. 16–17).

A summary description of the parousia is given in vv. 16–17. Its brevity is evident. Detail is lacking. Also the sequence of events is truncated. Believers are "caught up ... to meet the Lord in the air," but what happens to them after that? The modern reader (and perhaps the ancient one as well) is left wondering what comes between the gathering of the saints at the beginning of the parousia and living "forever" in his presence.

Verse 16 begins with a *hoti* ("for") clause, indicating that what follows was presented as verification of the assertion (vv. 14–15) that the dead will participate in the parousia. The sequence of events is presented in four steps. First, the Lord will descend, and then the dead will rise (v. 16). Following that the living will be caught up, and finally all believers will be together with the Lord forever (v. 17). The point clearly made is that those who die before the parousia will participate in it along with those who are alive when he comes, and both will enjoy the life with the Lord that follows.

The two primary statements in v. 16 are "the Lord himself will come down" and "the dead in Christ will rise." The disciples witnessed Jesus' ascent into the clouds and were told he would return in the same way (Acts 1:9–11; cf. Mark 13:26). Stephen saw the heavens open and Jesus, the Son of Man, "standing at the right hand of God" (Acts 7:55–56). The Thessalonians demonstrated their faith by eagerly awaiting the coming of Jesus, the Son of God, from heaven (1 Thess 1:3,10). Eventually the long-awaited Jesus will descend—this time not as a babe but with grand display and heavenly entourage as befits the heavenly Lord himself. He comes "with a loud command, with the voice of the archangel and with the trumpet call of God." The three phrases are parallel, each introduced by the preposition *ev*. The second two are joined by "and" (*kai*), which Frame takes as an indication that the latter two phrases explain the first. He suggests the translation "At a command, namely, at an archangel's voice and at a trumpet of God."[78] But the

---

[78] Frame, *1 and 2 Thessalonians*, 174. Cf. 1 Cor 15:52, where three prepositional phrases with ἐν also announce the resurrection.

presence of the *kai* does not make this certain, and the three events also may be viewed as separate and distinct or as a threefold description of a single occurrence.

"A loud command" translates a single noun used only here in the New Testament.[79] It was relatively common in nonbiblical Greek,[80] and in general it indicates an order or a signal given to subordinates. Neither the origin nor the nature of this particular command is clear. The command could be issued from Jesus to the dead to arise (cf. John 5:28–29), from Jesus to his entourage to proceed (cf. 2 Thess 1:7), or from the archangel as either a cry of announcement (like the trumpet, cf. Rev 1:10) or an order to the heavenly host.

The phrase "with the voice of the archangel" connotes the involvement of the heavenly host. Mark also recorded that Jesus will come "with the holy angels" (Mark 8:38) and that he will send them to "gather his elect from the four winds" (13:26–27). The reference to an "archangel" implies a ranking of heavenly beings that was a common feature of Hellenistic Judaism.[81] Although New Testament authors did not involve themselves in the elaborate naming and ranking of the heavenly host in general, the New Testament does refer twice to archangels (here and Jude 9) and names two angels. Michael is called an archangel (Jude 9; cf. Dan 10:13; 12:1), and Gabriel is an angel who "stands in the presence of God" (Luke 1:19). Implied with the use of the term "archangel" is both status and the existence (if not the presence) of subordinates. The Lord is not alone but is accompanied by an angelic entourage. The archangel functions either as the herald proclaiming remarkable news—the arrival of the Lord—or calls the angelic army to advance with the Lord.

The Lord's descent is also "with the trumpet call of God." A trumpet call was used for a variety of purposes in the ancient orient but "was not much used as a musical instrument; its main task was to give signals."[82] It could herald a great event or issue a warning to the people (1 Sam 13:3; Jer 4:5). It was often used in military settings (Josh 6:4–5; Judg 6:34; Neh 4:19–20; cf. 1 Cor 14:8). It signaled the Hebrews' encounter with Yahweh at Sinai (Exod 19:16,19) and was used as part of the pageantry at religious festivals (Num 10:10; Lev 23:24; 25:8; Ps 81:3; cf.

---

[79] Also only once in the LXX, Prov 30:27.
[80] See Bruce, *1 and 2 Thessalonians*, 100, for several examples.
[81] Cf. D. M. Martin, "Angels," *HBD*.
[82] G. Friedrich, "σάλπιγξ," *TDNT* 7.73.

Matt 6:2). Finally, both Jewish and Christian images of God's arrival at the end to gather his people, execute judgment, and establish his kingdom include the announcement of his arrival with the trumpet (Isa 27:13; Zech 9:14; Ezra 6:23; *Apoc. Mos.* 22; Rev 8:2–12; 9:1,13; 11:15). Used in conjunction the voice of the archangel and the shout of command and the trumpet depict a grand fanfare. No one will be able to miss the event. No one will fail to realize that something remarkable is about to occur.

At the command, the voice, and the trumpet "the dead in Christ will rise." There is no mention of non-Christian dead in these verses (cf. 2:16; 2 Thess 1:6–10). Likewise there is no discussion of the resurrection body or of the manner in which the living are translated (cf. 1 Cor 15:35–54). Paul was presenting information to comfort a church grieving like those who had no hope. So that which claimed all his attention was the fact that the resurrected Christian dead will join with the Christian living at the parousia and together they will share the presence of the Lord on that day and forever. "First" is the final word of v. 16. "After that" *(epeita),* the first word of v. 17, "does not have a strong temporal sense."[83] It indicates a sequence of events, but almost immediately the two events are blended into a single occurrence as the resurrected dead join the living and both are "caught up ... to meet the Lord."

4:17 The verb "caught up" *(harpazō)*[84] is the same one found in Acts 8:39 when the Spirit suddenly "took Philip away" and when Paul was "caught up to the third heaven" (2 Cor 12:2–4). The subject "we" is modified by "who are still alive and are left" (the identical clause in v. 15). "Will be caught up" is modified by three phrases: "together with them" (i.e., the resurrected saints), "in the clouds," and "to meet the Lord in the air." The first phrase, "together with them" *(hama sun autois),* refers to those Christians who have been resurrected. Though *hama* ("at the same time") used with *sun* ("with") seems redundant, in this context "the force of the preposition *sun* is strengthened by the preceding *hama.*"[85] This emphasis on the unity of the event for the living and the dead stresses two points. First, the living have no advantage

---

[83] Best, *1 and 2 Thessalonians,* 197.

[84] The Latin verb *rapio* was used to translate *harpaz,* and from this derives the use of the English term "rapture" for the event described in vv. 16–17.

[85] Bruce, *1 and 2 Thessalonians,* 102. Cf. 1 Thess 5:10, the only other occurrence of ἅμα σύν.

over the dead in the end. Both groups will experience reunion with the Lord together. Second, the dead and the living will themselves be reunited—a reunion that will know no end. For "we will be with the Lord forever."

Together all believers will be caught up "in the clouds." In Old Testament theophanies clouds commonly shrouded the presence and glory of God (Exod 19:16; 24:15–18; Ezek 1:4,28; Isa 19:1; cf. Ps 97:2). It is understandable that movement to or from the presence of God might be described as movement to or from "the clouds of heaven" (Dan 7:13). Thus clouds received Jesus at his ascension (Acts 1:9), the church was told that the Son of Man will "come in clouds with great power and glory" (Mark 13:26), and those going out to meet him "in the air" as he descended from heaven to earth would encounter him "in the clouds."

"To meet" the Lord translates a term used only two other times in the New Testament. In the parable of the ten maidens the maidens are called out to "meet" the groom and join the marriage procession (Matt 25:6). Outside Rome some Christian brethren came to "meet" Paul and escort him back into the city (Acts 28:15). In secular Greek the word *(apantēsis)* was a technical term for meeting a visiting dignitary. A delegation honored the visitor by going outside the city and meeting him and his entourage on the road. Together the entire party would then proceed back into the city with great pomp and fanfare.[86]

What happens after believers meet the Lord in the air? The conclusion of the passage, "we will be with the Lord forever" (v. 17), speaks to believers' eternal state but leaps over any end-time events between parousia and eternal state. Considering Paul's purpose of comforting believers regarding the eternal state of the dead in Christ, v. 17 provides an appropriate conclusion to the narrative. But for those interested in end-time events this conclusion seems abrupt and leaves much unsaid. The events of vv. 16–17, for instance, are not placed in a larger tempo-

---

[86] See Cicero, *Ad Att.* 8.16.2; 16.11.6; Josephus, *Ant.* 2.327f.; *Bell.* 7.100; *Polyb.* 5.26.8; *Ditt. Or.* 332. Frame notes and agrees with Moulton's assertion regarding ἀπάντησιν that "the special idea of the word is the 'official welcome of a newly arrived dignitary'" (*1 and 2 Thessalonians,* 177). The reading of ἀπάντησιν as a technical term was subsequently supported by many writers, notably E. Peterson, "*Die Einholung des Kyrios,*" *ZST* 1 (1930): 682–702. In a recent article M. Cosby reviews the evidence and points out that ἀπάντησιν was not always used as a technical term and that its use as one in 4:17 remains an open matter, though he himself is convinced that "the Parousia in Paul's mind included divine reward of the righteous and judgment of the wicked" ("Hellenistic Formal Receptions and Paul's Use of APANTHSIS in 1 Thessalonians 4:17," *BBR* 4 [1994]: 15–33).

ral context. Other events associated with the end, such as a period of tribulation, the judging of humanity, or a millennial reign, are not mentioned. The state of the dead who rise to meet the lord is not discussed (cf. 1 Cor 15:35–49; 2 Cor 5:1–9), nor is the transformation of the living (cf. 1 Cor 15:50–58).

The event described in vv. 16–17, commonly termed the "rapture," holds a prominent place in all eschatological schemes. But it is not understood in the same way in all of them. Postmillennial and amillennial perspectives generally understand the rapture as a part of the day of the Lord when Jesus will return to gather his people to him and execute judgment on all (cf. 5:1–11). This event is variously termed the "coming" *(parousia),*[87] the "revelation" *(apokalypsis),*[88] or the "appearance" *(epiphaneia)*[89] of the Lord. Also in some forms of premillennialism it is believed that the church will remain on the earth until the final judgment (including a period of severe tribulation near the very end). For these the coming of the Lord, the rapture of the church, and the final judgment are all facets of a single event at the end of time.

In some premillennial schemes, however, the rapture is separated from the day of the Lord by the great tribulation, a seven-year period of intense, unbridled evil. Adherents to this perspective argue that the church will not remain on the earth during this time of the tribulation. Rather, the Lord will remove (or rapture) his followers either at the beginning of the tribulation or at its midpoint.[90] Such a scheme separates the rapture from the parousia by several years.

Although we cannot settle such far-reaching matters in this context, we must note that our present passage does not seem to present the event depicted in vv. 16–17 as one preceding and separate from the parousia, the day of the Lord (cf. 5:4–9). First, in v. 15 Paul explicitly termed the event he was describing the "coming" (parousia) of the Lord and linked the same term with final judgment (2 Thess 2:8; cf. 1 Thess 2:19). Since Paul did not predict two parousias, then the one event must encompass both the gathering of the church and final judgment. Second, v. 17 does not require the removal of the church from the world. It is in fact open-ended, describing nothing beyond the gathering of the church

---

[87] Cf. 1 Thess 2:19; 3:13; 4:15; 1 Cor 15:23; 2 Thess 2:8.

[88] Cf. 1 Cor 1:7; 2 Thess 1:7; 1 Pet 1:7,13.

[89] Cf. 2 Thess 2:8; 1 Tim 6:14; 2 Tim 4:1,8; Titus 2:13.

[90] E.g., J. F. Walvoord, *The Thessalonian Epistles* (Findlay, Ohio: Dunham, 1955), 80–83.

other than the fact of continuing in the presence of the Lord. Finally, vv. 15–17 seem to be cast in language and images depicting the arrival of a grand dignitary. The heralds announce his coming. The crowds surge out of their city to meet him and celebrate his arrival. At this point such a dignitary would not take the crowd with him and leave. Rather, the crowd would escort him into the city. In other words, the most likely way to complete the scenario Paul painted is by assuming that after assembling his people Christ would not leave but would proceed with his parousia. What our passage depicts is not the removal of the church but the early stages of the day of the Lord. The passage ends as it does because Paul's central concern at this juncture was not the recounting of the events of the day of the Lord but the assuaging of grief.

4:18 Paul presented vv. 13–17 as words of encouragement even as he had sent Timothy to encourage *(parakalesai)* the church (cf. 3:2). He also intended believers to encourage *(parakaleite)* "each another" with these words. In the midst of distress, comfort often comes in the form of the presence of one who cares. The one who cares may not be able to solve the problem afflicting the one suffering any more than Paul could end persecution, vanquish death, or eliminate loss. But just as joy shared is joy intensified, paradoxically suffering shared is suffering diminished. Just as the Thessalonians were called to comfort one another, so also believers of every age are called to "rejoice with those who rejoice" and "mourn with those who mourn" (Rom 12:15).

But it is not only the presence of an empathetic fellow sufferer that is comforting. The "word" can comfort also. The word Paul shared in vv. 13–17 does not eliminate loss, but it does put it in a larger context. The sufferer often can see only his suffering; it becomes his entire world. The presence of a fellow sufferer broadens that world and lets the sufferer know that he is not alone. Hand in hand with the comfort of Christian companionship, the gospel provides the comfort of Christian hope. The hope expands our world beyond the moment of mourning by placing it in the context of eternity. The moment of loss is seen in the context of certain future reunion and eternal togetherness in the presence of the Lord. The loss remains a reality, but it is a temporary reality. The grief is real, but it is no longer grief without hope. The harsh reality of separation is joined by the joyous promise of reunion as the fact of death is transformed by the promise of life eternal. Therefore encourage one another with these words.

5. Exhortations Regarding Times and Seasons (5:1–11)

Chapter 5 continues the discussion of the coming of the Lord but with a shift in emphasis. With the fate of the Christian dead clarified (4:13–18), Paul turned to the responsibility of the living. The living should remain alert and prepared for that day (vv. 6,8), for they (unlike the unbelievers, v. 3) are fully aware that it is coming (v. 4).

Some understand that the shift from a discussion of *parousia* (4:15) to a discussion of the "day of the Lord" (5:2) indicates that Paul was writing about two different events. Although this is possible, it is not the only way to explain the shift in terminology. The topic of 4:13–18 is resurrection; the topic of 5:1–11 is judgment. The intent in 4:13–18 is to comfort believers who have experienced a loss through death. The intent in 5:1–11 is to challenge believers to live faithfully and expectantly in anticipation of future judgment. These variations alone are sufficient to explain the use of *parousia* in the former and "day of the Lord" in the latter passage.

(1) Introduction (5:1)

¹Now, brothers, about times and dates we do not need to write to you,

5:1 Utilizing a *peri* ... formula, "about times and dates" (cf. 4:9,13), Paul announced his next topic.[91] The use of the formula may indicate that Paul was responding to a query from the Thessalonians.[92] "Times and dates" (v. 1) translates two Greek words for time. In contexts where distinctions are made between them, the first *(chronos)* connotes time as a sequence, and the second *(chairos)* connotes an event or an epoch in time.[93] But the two apparently formed a stock phrase in the church's teachings about the end times (cf. Acts 1:7), and the pair may have been stereotyped to the point that they were used as a couplet without regard to the meaning of the individual words.[94]

The syntax behind "we do not need to write to you" is difficult, but

---

[91] The importance of the περὶ δὲ formula in this instance is denied by T. L. Howard, who stresses the unity of 4:13–18 and 5:1–11. See "The Literary Unity of 1 Thessalonians 4:13–5:11," *GTJ* 9 (1988): 163–90.

[92] See the comment at 4:9.

[93] The distinction noted by Augustine (*Ep* 197.2) and numerous commentators after him was common in the classical era, but not in the first century A.D.

[94] See J. Barr, *Biblical Words for Time, SBT* 33 (London: SCM, 1962). Note that the eschatological character of "times and dates" was so well established that the phrase by itself was a sufficient title for Paul's paraenesis.

the meaning of the clause is clear. After identifying the topic in v. 1a, Paul acknowledged that the readers were already familiar with Christian teachings regarding the end times (vv. 1b–2a). The implication is that the church did not need to be reminded of the facts but of the implications these facts held for their actions. The formula is comparable to the one Paul used in 4:9. He did not need to write about Christian love because the church was God-taught to love one another. He did not need to write about times and dates because they already knew what they needed to know. Apparently Paul had taught them about the day of the Lord during the establishing of the church.[95] In the verses that follow the apostle in fact said little about the timing of that day. Rather, he reminded that church that its coming is inevitable, it will surprise unbelievers, and believers in contrast must remain alert and prepared.

The remainder of the exhortation falls into three sections. In the two verses (vv. 2–3) that follow the introduction, the church was reminded of the manner of the Lord's return. It is this which they apparently already knew, and Paul did not elaborate greatly in this area. The bulk of the passage (vv. 4–10) focuses on the way believers should live in light of this knowledge. The final verse (v. 11) provides a concluding exhortation.[96] Unbelievers are in the dark and live accordingly. But the church must not live like unbelievers. Since they anticipate the Lord's return, they should live in the manner of a people prepared for it.

(2) The Manner of the Lord's Return (5:2–3)

[2]for you know very well that the day of the Lord will come like a thief in the night. [3]While people are saying, "Peace and safety," destruction will come on them suddenly, as labor pains on a pregnant woman, and they will not escape.

5:2–3 The reason Paul did not need to write concerning "times and

---

[95] It is also possible that Paul was referring to 2 Thess 2:1–12, though that too would have been in addition to earlier teachings delivered orally (see "The Sequence of the Thessalonian Correspondence" on p. 30).

[96] It is possible to subdivide vv. 4–10 into treatments of "the call for watchfulness" (vv. 4–8a) and "Christian existence" (vv. 8b–10; see Bruce, *1 and 2 Thessalonians,* 108; and B. Rigaux, "Tradition et redaction dans I Thess 5:1–10," *NTS* 21 [1975]: 318–40), but this should be done with caution. The calls for watchfulness and a consistent Christian life (cf. 4:8 and 1:3) are tightly intertwined in the paraenesis. Watchfulness apart from preparedness is futile, and preparedness is only deemed necessary by those who are aware the day is coming and thus watch for it. Also syntactically it is unlikely that Paul intended a break in the middle of v. 8 since the participial clause "putting on" (v. 8b, ἐνδυσάμενοι) continues the hortatory "let us be self-controlled" (v. 8a, νήφωμεν; cf. Collins, "Tradition," 334–42).

dates" was because ("for," *gar,* connects v. 2 to v. 1) the Thessalonians already knew about the manner of the Lord's coming. The "you" of "for you know" is emphatic (cf. NASB "you yourselves"). The fact that they knew "very well" *(akribōs)* what Paul was about to discuss did not mean there was no need for clarification or elaboration. Apollos taught about Jesus "accurately" *(akribōs,* Acts 18:25), but Priscilla and Aquila still found it necessary to explain the way of God to him "more adequately" *(akribesteron,* Acts 18:26). The mention of accurate knowledge in the context of "times and dates" makes it sound as if Paul intended to discuss a sequence of events or a timetable of sorts. This is not, however, what he went on to discuss. If what the church knew of times and dates is epitomized in vv. 2–3, then they had little knowledge regarding the precise timing and nature of events leading to the day of the Lord.[97] What they knew well was that "the day of the Lord will come like a thief in the night." The remainder of this passage does not go much beyond this insight and its implications for Christian living.

Actually, two analogies are used in vv. 2–3. The first is that of the thief in the night. The second is that of the pregnant woman. The thief in the night analogy has enjoyed the lion's share of attention. The analogy of the pregnant woman is largely ignored. Like most analogies, these are open to multiple meanings if taken in isolation from their context. If, on the other hand, analogies are interpreted within the bounds set by their immediate literary context, they are less likely to be allegorized and used to say things the author did not intend.[98]

Both analogies were used to illuminate the coming of the "day of the Lord," a phrase full of meaning to anyone familiar with the Jewish Scriptures.[99] The day of the Lord in the Old Testament is a day of judgment. Yahweh will punish the evil within Israel (Amos 5:18–20) on that day, and the wicked among the nations will face a day of terrible wrath (Isa 13:6–13; Obad 15). Those who have not repented will face

---

[97] Additional information is of course contained in 4:13–18 and 2 Thess 1:5–10 but about the event itself, not about times and dates leading up to it. It is 2 Thess 2:1–12 that is the best indicator of the content of Pauline teachings to the Thessalonians in this area (see esp. 2:5).

[98] See M. Martin, "Pauline Metaphors Describing Christian Leadership," Ph.D. diss., Southwestern Baptist Theological Seminary, 1980, for a discussion of methodology for the interpretation of metaphorical language in Paul's writings.

[99] For a discussion of the day of the Lord in the OT see H. H. Rowley, *The Faith of Israel* (London: SCM, 1956), 177–201; B. K. Smith, "Obadiah," in *Amos, Obadiah, Jonah,* NAC (Nashville: Broadman & Holman, 1995), 195–201.

"destruction from the Almighty" (Joel 1:13–15). Yet the punishment of the evil is at the same time the deliverance of the righteous (Joel 2:31–32; Zech 14:1–21; Mal 4:5). In the New Testament, Jesus is the Lord whom God has appointed to judge the world (Acts 17:31), so the day of the Lord (2 Thess 2:2; 1 Cor 5:5; 2 Pet 3:10) is the day of the Lord Jesus Christ (1 Cor 1:8; 2 Cor 1:14; Phil 1:6,10; 2:16).[100] The same dual emphasis on judgment and deliverance at the day of the Lord that is seen in the Old Testament also is evident in Paul's writings and in the New Testament as a whole.

The Thessalonians were reminded that the day of the Lord would come as a thief in the night. The image of the thief also occurs as a description of the coming of the Lord in the Gospels (Matt 24:36–43; Luke 12:35–40) and in 2 Pet 3:10 and Rev 3:3; 16:15. The most consistent element in these passages is the call for constant readiness, since the specific timing of the coming is unknown. The meaning of the image in 5:1–12 is best seen in the literal statements of v. 3, which apply the image. It will be unexpected (destruction will come suddenly upon people whose bywords are "peace and security"). Also Paul did not apply the implication of the thief analogy to believers. They were, in fact, specifically excluded. The Lord's coming will not be as a thief in the night for members of the church (v. 4). Believers expect it, though they do not know when the day will arrive.[101]

Only unbelievers will be taken by surprise by the fact of the Lord's return. The clause "while people are saying, 'peace and safety' " is not a prediction of a particular time in human history so much as a prediction of an attitude.[102] The words need not describe idyllic times but arrogant or self-deceived people. They are like the prophets and priests who disputed Jeremiah's warnings of impending destruction and cried "peace, peace" when in fact Babylon was about to destroy the city (Jer 6:14). Ezekiel mocked such people by likening them to fools whose response to finding a weak wall is to whitewash it to make it look good. It will

---

[100] See also Paul's references to "the day" (Rom 13:12; 1 Cor 3:13; 1 Thess 5:4) or "that day" (2 Thess 1:10).

[101] Those who believe the rapture of the church will precede the tribulation and thus the day of the Lord believe the reason the day of the Lord will not come upon them unexpectedly is that it will not come upon them at all. See J. F. Walvoord, *The Blessed Hope and the Tribulation* (Grand Rapids: Zondervan, 1976), 108–21.

[102] The use of ὅταν plus the present tense λέγωσιν also indicates that Paul was thinking generally of the character of the people, not of a particular end-time event for which the aorist would be more appropriate.

collapse when the storm comes and expose their folly (Ezek 13:10–12). These are people who tell themselves they are secure and in control. They are not expecting God to invade their world.

Two of the words in v. 3, "safety" *(asphaleia)* and "suddenly" *(aiphnidios),* occur only here in Paul's writings; the verb behind "will come" *(ephistēmi),* occurs only here and in 2 Tim 4:2,6. Also "peace" as a synonym for "safety" is unusual for Paul as is the impersonal "people say" (lit., "they say"). The unusual vocabulary and usage together with the proverbial quality of the saying may indicate that Paul used existing apocalyptic material and then "reworked the tradition in accordance with his own purposes."[103] "Suddenly" *(aiphnidios)* occurs first in its clause so is emphasized by the sequence of the sentence.

The destruction *(olethros)* that comes upon the unbeliever at the end is sudden, but it is surprise not speed that is the point. In 2 Thess 1:8–9 Paul proclaimed the everlasting "destruction" *(olethros)* of "those who do not know God and do not obey the gospel." Those who refuse to acknowledge or obey God live in self-imposed ignorance not only of the God who is but also of the God who will judge them. Their moment of judgment comes as a shock, befalling a people who feel secure. It is like the arrival of a thief, unexpected and surprising. These are the very characteristics of that day that should not apply to the church, for the church knows a day of judgment is approaching (v. 4) and therefore should remain faithful and vigilant (vv. 5–11).

A second feature of the day of the Lord is stressed in v. 3. The analogy of the pregnant woman is less celebrated but should carry just as much impact as that of the thief. The emphasis of this second image is clearly not that the event is a surprise. To what pregnant woman does labor come as a surprise? The prophets used the image of labor as an analogy for distress and disaster (Isa 37:3; Jer 6:24), sometimes in a context of divine judgment (Jer 22:23) and destruction at the day of the Lord (Isa 13:6–8). Paul, however, did not use the image to depict terror or anguish. The phrase associated with the woman experiencing the onset of labor is the last clause of v. 3, "and they will not escape." The statement is emphatic. The certainty of judgment is stressed with a double negative, identical to that translated "will certainly not" in 4:15. When genuine labor begins, there is no avoiding its conclusion. The judgment of that day once begun will carry through to its finale, and

---

[103] For evidence that "the articulation of the motifs is Pauline even if the motifs themselves are traditional, see Collins, "Tradition," 337.

there is no circumventing it.

The verses that follow draw distinctions between believers and nonbelievers in relation to the day of the Lord. Believers are excluded from the implications of the image of the thief. In contrast the church is not excluded from the implications of the image of the woman in labor. That day is expected by the church; and thus though the timing may be unknown, the fact of the parousia will not come as a surprise. But for the Christian, as for the non-Christian, the beginning of that day will lead unavoidably to its conclusion.[104] There will be no delay, no opportunity to take care of neglected business. There will be no second chance, no opportunity for additional preparation before meeting the Lord. It is this very point that is the basis of the exhortations to be alert and prepared in vv. 4–11.

(3) The Christian Life Anticipating the Return (5:4–11)

⁴But you, brothers, are not in darkness so that this day should surprise you like a thief. ⁵You are all sons of the light and sons of the day. We do not belong to the night or to the darkness. ⁶So then, let us not be like others, who are asleep, but let us be alert and self-controlled. ⁷For those who sleep, sleep at night, and those who get drunk, get drunk at night. ⁸But since we belong to the day, let us be self-controlled, putting on faith and love as a breastplate, and the hope of salvation as a helmet. ⁹For God did not appoint us to suffer wrath but to receive salvation through our Lord Jesus Christ. ¹⁰He died for us so that, whether we are awake or asleep, we may live together with him. ¹¹Therefore encourage one another and build each other up, just as in fact you are doing.

Now that Paul had highlighted those facets of the day of the Lord of which he wished to remind the Thessalonians, he could draw from them pertinent conclusions. The first of these is not stated explicitly but underlies the entire passage. It is that the day of the Lord divides humanity into two distinct camps—those who are ready and destined for salvation and those who are not ready and are destined for wrath. This distinction is seen repeatedly in vv. 4–6, which describe Christians in contrast to non-Christians. Verses 7–11 then use this distinction and the specter of the day of judgment as a basis for urging faithfulness and perseverance.

---

[104] Even those exhorted to watch so that they might "escape all that is about to happen" will ultimately "stand before the Son of Man" (Luke 21:36) and clearly do not escape the event of judgment altogether.

5:4–5 The non-Christians are "in darkness" (v. 4); they "belong to the night" (v. 5). Later in the passage they are depicted as "asleep" (v. 6) and "drunk" (v. 7) on the basis that night, sleep, and drunkenness go together. These all have one point in common. They depict people who are blind. They cannot or will not see clearly and are therefore unprepared for what lies ahead. Christians are described with opposing terminology. They are "not in darkness" (v. 4), are "sons of light" and "sons of day" (v. 5a), and "do not belong to the night or to the darkness" (v. 5b). During the day people are expected to be "alert and self-controlled" (v. 6).

Paul's reference to the thief is the only one in the New Testament that includes a reference to "the night." Although this modifier contributes to the sense of surprise at the thief's coming, it also enabled Paul to use the images of night and day to contrast believers and unbelievers in connection with the coming of the day of the Lord. "But you brothers …" (v. 4) takes up this contrast and makes it explicit by emphasizing the "you" who are believers. Those who are a part of God's family "are not in darkness." Darkness was commonly used in the ancient world as a negative image. Within Judaism it symbolized persons and powers ignorant of or opposed to Yahweh, as is reflected both in the Old Testament (Job 22:9–11; Ps 82:5; Prov 4:19; Isa 60:1–3), in the Qumran community's Manual of Discipline (1QS 1:9–10; 3:13–4:26), and in their scroll dedicated to the conflict between the sons of light and sons of darkness (see 1QM 1:1–3; cf. v. 5). Similarly, in the New Testament darkness symbolized the current sinful and rebellious age (Col 1:13) and those in it captured by the powers opposed to God (Rom 13:12; 1 Cor 4:5). Such darkness is dispelled by the coming of the gospel in the hearts of believers and ultimately by the coming of the Christ in glory (2 Cor 4:4–6; 6:14; 1 Pet 2:9). Though believers live in this age of darkness, their lives are to reflect the light of God (Eph 5:8–11; 1 John 1:5–7).

Since the gospel has enlightened believers; they are not in darkness. They know the day of the Lord is coming, thus its arrival will not "overtake"[105] (NASB) them like a thief. It is unlikely Paul meant that they were aware of the time of the coming as a result of teachings received in the past. Even teachings such as those in Mark 13 and 2 Thessalonians 2

---

[105] The verb καταλαμβάνω, "to overtake" or "to seize with hostile intent," has a more negative connotation than the NIV "surprise" conveys, especially in conjunction with the image of a thief. See BAGD, s.v. "καταλαμβάνω."

were meant to provide a warning and encouragement, not a date (Mark 13:32–37; 2 Thess 2:13–15; cf. 2 Pet 3:8–12). It was the fact of the coming of the day, not its timing, to which Paul referred. Thus his encouragement to them was to be alert and prepared at all times.

The true basis of Paul's confidence in the church and his exhortations to them was not the signs they had been taught but the birth they had experienced. They were "all sons of the light and sons of the day" (v. 5).[106] "Day" in this verse is not a direct reference to the day of the Lord. Sons of the day do await the dawning of the day of judgment. In this verse, however, "day" is parallel in structure and thought to "light" and the antithesis of night and dark. Thus it refers to daytime, not the day of judgment. "Son of ..." was a Hebraism commonly found in the New Testament to ascribe some quality to the person named (cf. Mark 3:17; Luke 10:6; 16:8; John 17:12; Acts 4:36).[107] It is certainly true that Christians should possess the qualities of an enlightened people. But the new creation and adoption terminology in Paul (Gal 3:26; 2 Cor 5:17) indicates that he did not use the language superficially. Children of light are true children of God. They have undergone a transformation that makes a new life (a life in the light) inevitable, not just preferable. Godliness for true sons of the light is not just a matter of appropriate actions; it is an outgrowth of their essential nature, their relationship to God.

The uniqueness of the Christian community over against all others is stressed by adding to what they are (sons of light and day) a statement that circumscribed everyone else (sons of night and darkness).[108] "Night and darkness" symbolize willful ignorance of God and imply certain judgment apart from repentance and entrance into the realm of light. As the Gospels divide all peoples at the judgment into wheat and tares or sheep and goats, so Paul placed the whole of humanity in two camps. The lines are drawn sharply, and no middle ground is contemplated.[109] Christianity is not a religion in which one can dabble. It is not possible to hedge the bet by belonging to both the church and another religious group. One is either of the light or in darkness.

---

[106] "Sons of day" is not used elsewhere in the NT.

[107] The NIV translates the "son of ..." idiom with various English idioms. Cf. the NASB or RSV in the passages cited. See also BDF 162.6, and N. Turner, *A Grammar of New Testament Greek, Vol. III, Syntax* (Edinburgh: T & T Clark, 1963), 207–8.

[108] The structure is chiastic, i.e., the sequence used for the first couplet (light, day) is reversed when their antithetical parallels are listed (night, darkness).

[109] Cf. the distinction between believers and "others" in v. 6, "those" who sleep and "we" of the day in vv. 7–8, and those who suffer wrath and we who receive salvation in v. 9.

5:6 Believers are different from unbelievers in terms of heritage (they are sons of light) and in terms of true insight (they can see because they are in the light). Thus they must also live differently. Verse 6 begins with an emphatic double inferential, *ara ouv,* "so then," used elsewhere in Paul's writings to indicate a transition in his text (cf. Rom 8:12; 2 Thess 2:15). It links the statements of who believers are (vv. 4–5) with exhortations regarding how believers must live (vv. 6–10).

Since believers know that the day of the Lord is coming, they should not act like people who are unaware of this fact. Paul included himself in the injunction "let us not sleep" (NASB),[110] a present subjunctive *(katheudōmen)* implying consistency in the Christian's behavior.[111] In Mark 13:32–37 the disciples were also warned not to let the master find them "sleeping" *(katheudontas)* when he returned (v. 37). The "others" who do sleep are unbelievers oblivious to the approaching day of judgment and so unprepared (cf. "the rest of men," 4:13). In contrast, believers should remain "alert and self-controlled" (v. 6). Both of these verbs are also present hortatory subjunctives; Paul was appealing for consistent vigilance. The first word, translated "let us be alert," means "to stay awake." Literally, it is that which is expected of a watchman who must not sleep at his post. It was often used metaphorically of the preparedness of those awaiting the Lord's return (Luke 12:37; Matt 24:42–43; 1 Pet 5:8; Rev 3:2–3; 16:15).

The same verb *(grēgoreō)* is used in Mark 13:35 ("keep watch") as the alternative to being found asleep.[112] The second exhortation, "be ... self-controlled," literally means "to remain sober," but in the New Testament it is only used figuratively. Like *grēgoreō* it can indicate one who is aware of his surroundings, and if that is its meaning here, it serves to strengthen the exhortation to alertness. But more likely Paul intended to exhort Christians to live in a self-controlled fashion (cf. 2 Tim 4:5; 1 Pet 4:7; 5:8). Neither he nor they should engage in the irresponsible or outrageous behaviors associated with drunkenness. As believers watch for the day of the Lord, they must behave in a way that lets them view that day with hope rather than with dread.

---

[110] A different verb for sleep (κοιμάω) was used in 4:13–18. But the use of καθεύδω in 5:1–11 probably has more to do with the intent to echo the saying of Jesus recorded in Mark than any attempt to draw a distinction between these two synonyms.

[111] Paul did not write "let us not be like others" but "let us not sleep as others" (i.e., as non-Christian do).

[112] Cf. the literal use of the term in Mark 14:34,37–38 and the disciples' inability to "watch" while Jesus prayed.

5:7 Verse 7 inserts a saying that reinforces the link between sleep, drunkenness, and the night. The saying is a generalization about the way people live. Night is the time for sleep, and it is after the labors of the day that people find the leisure to drink and become drunk. In light of the comments in vv. 4–6, however, Paul was clearly drawing an analogy to the spiritual world. Blindness to the things of God and immoral behavior are activities characteristic of spiritual darkness.

5:8 Verse 8 draws the contrast. Those of the night are asleep and are drunk, "but since we are of the day, let us be sober" (v. 8, NASB). The "we" of v. 8 is emphatic, placed first in the Greek sentence. Verses 8–10 are dominated by the exhortation "let us be self-controlled" (the same verb used in v. 6). This call to sober living is modified by two participial clauses. The first, "since we belong to the day," reminds believers of who they are. The second, "putting on ... the breastplate, and ... a helmet" (NASB) reminds believers of how they must live. Christians live "sober" lives because as children of the day (cf. v. 5) a life of darkness is inherently alien and offensive. Yet the church exists in the midst of darkness and should expect that they will come in conflict with it. They need, then, to be prepared for such conflict.

Living as "sons of light" in a world of darkness requires preparation. The second participle modifying "let us be self-controlled" presents a brief military analogy. The logical link with the images of light and darkness is not explicit but probably is to be found in the implicit conflict between these two contradictory realms. Elsewhere the church was exhorted: "Put on the full armor of God. For our struggle is not against flesh and blood but against the powers of this dark world" (Eph 6:11–12). In his letter to the Romans, Paul mixed many of the same elements that are found here. In preparation for the Lord's coming, believers must not sleep, must put aside deeds of darkness, put "on the armor of light," and behave decently "as in the daytime" (see Rom 13:11–14).

The Thessalonians likewise were encouraged to live sober lives, putting on "the breastplate of faith and love, and for a helmet the hope of salvation" (RSV). Isaiah 59:17 may have been Paul's inspiration for the image, but if so, he adapted Isaiah's picture by placing the armor not on God (as Isaiah did) but on the believer. Gentile readers probably would have thought first not of Isaiah 59 but of the ubiquitous Roman soldier. Whatever the origin of the image, a breastplate and helmet certainly were prominent and vital pieces of armor, and this may be the reason Paul used them. However, a soldier's belt, heavy sandals, or shield are just as vital pieces of equipment (cf. Eph 6:14–16). Since it is impossible to be certain why Paul chose the breastplate and helmet for his analogy, it is unwise to allegorize the equipment. It is also unnecessary. As armor was essential and was characteristic of a soldier, so the essential virtues of faith, love, and hope (as well as the behaviors they imply, cf. 1:3; Rom 13:12–14) must characterize the Christian.

Believers prepare for the day of the Lord by persevering in the faith, love, and hope that were the starting point of their Christian life. The participle translated "putting on" *(endusamenoi)* is aorist and implies an action antecedent to the action of the main verb, "let us be self-controlled." Putting on the armor is not a matter of doing something new but rather a matter of continuing in one's original commitment. Committed and equipped, the Christian soldier stands firm in the faith, stands firm in the face of opposition, stands firm until the end (cf. Eph 6:13–14,18).

"Putting on" is also used of "putting on Christ" and of living according to Christian ethical standards (Rom 13:14; Gal 3:27; Eph 4:24; Col 3:10). It does not connote shallowness (as a garment might hide the person underneath) but evident and genuine transformation (cf. 1 Cor 15:53,54). The recognizable garb of the Christian ought to be behavior expressive of faith, love, and hope. These central Christian virtues are foundational for the living of a distinctly Christian life. "Faith and love" are placed together as modifiers of "breastplate." "Hope" is the lone referent for "helmet" and is itself refined by the phrase "of salvation." This serves to highlight hope and bring the reader's attention back to the future deliverance that is the theme of this section. Paul's point here is that those who are on the road to ultimate salvation should behave differently from those on the road to destruction.

5:9 Christians live in anticipation of future salvation, which is the culmination of the work begun in them in Christ. Christ's death (vv. 9b–10) and God's judgment (v. 9a) serve as the two touchstones of Christian existence. Believers live life on a trajectory leading from one event to the other. "Let us be self-controlled" (v. 8) is modified by a causal clause that begins with v. 9. The Thessalonians lived as enlightened, self-controlled children of God, possessing the "hope of salvation" because of ("for") what God had done for them in Christ.

"For God did not appoint us to suffer wrath" reflects the divine initiative in deliverance.[113] A fate "appointed" by God is a reality, even if

---

[113] Several scholars are convinced that the saying on election in v. 9 reflects the use of a pre–Pauline tradition (cf. Plevnik, "Parousia as Implication," 85–87; Havener, "Pre-Pauline Formulae," 115–21; Rigaux, "Tradition," 333).

the full reception of that reality is not yet seen. The Thessalonians were to live in accord with their future fate. The reality of the future salvation of God must shape the believers' present actions, just as the past work of Christ calls for a life of Christlikeness. The second half of the verse adds that this deliverance was "through our Lord Jesus Christ who died for us" (NASB). The addition of a purpose clause, "so that ... we may live together with him" (v. 10), and the encouragements to persevere throughout the letter reflect the responsibility of believers in the experience of salvation to choose life by committing themselves to Christ.

Though it is not stated explicitly, it is implied that ultimately non-Christians must face the "wrath" of God (cf. 2 Thess 1:8–10; Rom 2:5,8; 5:9). Christians ought not exhibit behavior deserving of wrath because their destiny is different. They are not destined "for wrath" but "for obtaining salvation" (NASB). The two phrases are parallel in the Greek text, both introduced by "for" *(eis)* and linked by a strong adversative "but" *(alla)*. Salvation is placed last to facilitate the elaboration on it in vv. 9b–10. Thus it is "obtaining salvation" that Paul highlighted as a positive conclusion to vv. 4–10, leading to the exhortation to encourage and edify one another in v. 11. Salvation is here presented as a future event, contrasted with the reception of wrath on the day of judgment. Paul, in fact, presented the deliverance of the Christian in three time frames: past (e.g., Eph 2:5,8), present (e.g., 1 Cor 1:18; 15:2; 2 Cor 2.15), and future (e.g., Rom 2:7; 5:9).

5:10 Salvation is obtained through our Lord Jesus Christ, "who died for us so that ... we might live with him" (RSV). Similar "interchange" formulae can be found in other Pauline writings (cf. Rom 14:9; 2 Cor 5:15,21; Gal 1:4).[114] The formula is so brief here that one can only suppose Paul had covered this ground with the church earlier and that there had been no subsequent confusion regarding the significance of the work of Christ. This is the one time in the letter Paul explicitly mentioned Christ's death on behalf of believers. That this was a basic part of the church's instruction of converts, however, is seen in the formulae cited in 1 Cor 15:3–4: "For what I received I passed on to you as of first importance: that Christ died for our sins ... and was raised on the third day." And this well-documented fact (he appeared to Peter, the twelve, and five hundred of the brothers, vv. 5–6) provides the believer

---

[114] For a discussion of the relation of interchange formulae and the Pauline concept of atonement see M. D. Hooker, "Interchange and Atonement," *BJRL* 60 (1977–78): 462–81; and "Interchange in Christ," JSNTSup 22 (1971): 349–61.

with the assurance of resurrection. For if "Christ has been raised from
the dead, how can some of you say that there is no resurrection of the
dead?" (1 Cor 15:12). Christ's burial and resurrection, included in the
citation of the tradition in 1 Cor 15:3–4, is not explicitly mentioned
here; but resurrection is assumed in v. 10b.

Christ died so that those who believed in him "might live together
with him." The mention of life together with Christ does more than simply complete a common formula in this context. The double preposition
"together with" *(hama sun)* echoes 4:17, "caught up together with them
… to meet the Lord in the air." The life anticipated in 5:10 is eschatological life. Paul was reminding the Thessalonians that Christ died as a
part of God's plan to give believers life forever with him. The gift of
life at the cost of Christ's death should inspire gratitude and encourage
obedience to such a benevolent God. The prospect of eternal life as well
should have encouraged the Thessalonians to live lives "alert" and
"self-controlled," anticipating the day the Lord will judge humanity and
grant his disciples eschatological salvation.

The dual conditional clause "whether we are awake or asleep" (v. 10)
is problematic. The term for awake echoes the earlier use of the same
word in v. 6, where readers are admonished to "be alert." The alternative, to be "asleep," was presented as a characteristic of unbelievers in
the preceding verses (vv. 6–7). Paul was certainly not saying here that
both the "sons of the light" who are "alert" and the non-Christians who
are "asleep" and who "belong to the night" will live in Christ. But what
was he saying?

One possibility is that this verse takes up a thread from 4:13 and ties
together the two discussions of the end times. If this is so, then "asleep"
in 5:10 is a reference to death. A difficulty with this interpretation is that
the two passages (4:13–18; 5:1–11) use different verbs for sleep. When
he used sleep as a euphemism for physical death (4:13–18), Paul used
koimaō. For sleep as spiritual blindness in 5:1–9 Paul used *katheudō*.
Some consider it unlikely that Paul would vary his usage of *katheudō*
suddenly in 5:10 without some explanation in the verse.[115]

An alternative way of reading 5:10 is to understand it as an attempt
to allow for human frailty. Might *katheudō* ("to sleep") signify not
unbelievers but Christians who are spiritually dull? Believers should be
vigilant and self-controlled. They are to persevere in the Christian life.

---

[115] See, e.g., T. R. Edgar, "The Meaning of 'Sleep' in 1 Thessalonians 5:10," *JETS* 22
(1979): 345–49.

But what if that vigilance wanes? Does believers' salvation hinge on their own vigilance or on the work of Christ? Paul was assuring his readers here of the security of those for whom Christ died. Human vigilance may flag, but Christ's sacrifice will not fail to deliver the believer from wrath, even believers who have fallen asleep at their post.

In summary, in 5:1–10 Paul reminded the church of the coming judgment. He did not do so to give them additional information regarding its timing or nature but to set the stage for ethical exhortation. In light of the coming parousia, the Christian was to watch expectantly and live responsibly. This is the purpose of this section—to encourage expectant and responsible Christian living. Eschatology presented as a basis for ethical exhortations is in fact the norm in the Pauline letters. Unavoidable judgment will come. Those in spiritual darkness will not expect it, but they will reap the wrath of God nevertheless. Because those who are children of the light expect the coming judgment, they should live appropriately. Vigilance, self-control, and perseverance in faith, love, and hope should characterize their lives. For through the work of Christ they are destined for life together with him. Even if they should falter, Christ will not fail.

5:11 The passage concludes with an admonition to mutual encouragement and edification similar to that in 4:18. Believers knew of the future judgment. They knew the character of the Christian life they were to live. But knowing and doing are two different things. Paraenesis functions to remind readers to do what they already are aware they should do. Paul encouraged his readers to help one another remain alert and self-controlled. Both imperatives, "encourage one another" (cf. 4:18, where the same imperative is used) and "build each other up," are positive. Paul instructed the Corinthians to "build up" others in the church by providing both examples (1 Cor 8:1; 10:23) and words (14:4), which would especially benefit the less mature Christian. The Ephesian churches were advised that the exercise of gifts for mutual benefit is how the church "grows and builds itself up in love" (4:16). In addition, these commands to engage in encouragement and in constructive ministry to one another are both present tense, implying consistency of action. The last clause of the verse, "just as in fact you are doing," affirmed the good already evident even as it encouraged the Thessalonians to continue doing the good work of mutually strengthening one another.

6. Exhortations Regarding Life in the Fellowship (5:12–22)

This final section of paraenesis is made up of several brief collections of exhortations. Each one is quite capable of standing on its own, and most exhibit similarities with other Pauline paraenetic passages (esp. Rom 12:12–18). These facts indicate that the content of vv. 12–22 is traditional Christian paraenesis that Paul could deliver to any number of churches. At the same time, however, the uniqueness of vv. 12–13a and the fact that Paul did select these particular exhortations for inclusion in this particular letter indicate that the material was selected and shaped with the Thessalonians in mind.

Although there is no *peri de* … formula (as in 4:9,13; 5:1) stating a central concern, these exhortations do orbit around a common theme. They are not a collection of Pauline afterthoughts or disjointed, last-minute instructions. Though the passage touches on several different points of life in the family of believers, all the exhortations deal with life in the assembly. Also (with the possible exception of one section, vv. 16–18) each piece of paraenesis gives advice regarding points of potential conflict in the assembly. The brevity of the exhortations and their generic nature indicate that the church was actively embroiled in a crisis of fellowship. But potential points of conflict did exist in Thessalonica, and Paul apparently intended to commend the kind of behavior that would prevent disruptions in the life of the congregation.

The Christian assembly in Thessalonica, indeed the church in most instances, is a complex entity including a great variety of personalities. There are leaders and followers (vv. 12–13), those who are weak in the faith and those who are strong (vv. 14–15), the optimists and the pessimists (vv. 16–18), the cynical and the gullible (vv. 19–22). These and others must coexist in the church. Even more they must learn how to love one another and work with one another for the encouraging and the building up of each other (4:9,18; 5:11).

(1) Leaders and Followers (5:12–13)

¹²Now we ask you, brothers, to respect those who work hard among you, who are over you in the Lord and who admonish you. ¹³Hold them in the highest regard in love because of their work. Live in peace with each other.

5:12–13 The first two verses of the section address the way the congregation should relate to its leaders. The sentence is structured as a request ("we ask you"). But the verb *(erōtōmen)* was used in 4:1 along with "we ... urge you" *(parakaloumen)* as a general call to live obediently to the instructions given by the apostles in the name of the Lord. Both verbs are common in the LXX, though *parakaleō* is more frequent. Paul also used *parakaleō* much more frequently than *erōtaō*.[116] In Hellenistic writers, however, the two words are synonyms; and Paul appears to have used them as synonyms as well.[117] Both words typically introduce transitions in the text, normally leading to a section of exhortations. The content of the exhortation in vv. 12–13 is introduced with two infinitives, "to respect" (v. 12) and "to esteem" (v. 13, RSV). Each infinitive is expanded.

"To respect" is literally "to know" *(eidenai)*. By itself it means to "identify" or to "take note of" those who are listed as its objects. The second infinitive *(ēgeisthai),* "to esteem" (NASB), complements the first.[118] In combination the two infinitival clauses exhort the church to acknowledge and respect those who ministered in their midst. If the congregation did not already think of their ministers in this way, how would they? Two likely alternatives to the attitude Paul encouraged are ingratitude and contentiousness. Assuming the exhortation in v. 13b concludes vv. 12–13a and should not be taken alone or with what follows (see below), "Live in peace with one another" may indicate that Paul was concerned to prevent needless conflict between the leadership and the congregation as a whole.

The church was to take note of "those who work hard," those "who are over you," and those "who admonish you." The three participles used *(kopiōntas, proistamenous,* and *vouthetountas)* are introduced by a single definite article indicating that Paul was thinking of these activities as emanating from a single group. Paul apparently listed laboring, leading, and admonishing as typical or basic ministry functions. All of the participles are present tense, implying that these were habitual or characteristic activities by the people concerned. These persons were not sporadic but consistent laborers in the congregation.

---

[116] Both in general and specifically in 1 Thessalonians. Cf. παρακαλέω in 1 Thess 2:12; 3:2,7; 4:1,10,18; 5:11,14; and ἐρωτάω in 4:1 and 5:12.

[117] See C. J. Bjerkelund, *Parakalō: Form, Funktion und Sinn der Parakalô—Sätz in den paulinissben Briefen* (Oslo: Universitetsforlaget, 1967), 125–40, 188–90; and O. Schmitz, *TDNT,* s.v. "παρακαλέω," 793–99.

[118] The infinitive is rather neutral, simply meaning "to consider" or "to regard" without the implication of esteem. The positive translation "hold them in the highest regard" is generated by three modifiers: "highly," "in love," and "because of their work."

Paul could have provided a much longer list of participles detailing various ministry functions or positions in the church. Romans 12, 1 Corinthians 12, and Ephesians 4 each provide longer and more varied lists of Spirit-inspired ministries exercised in the church. Paul also could have discussed the role of deacons, elders, overseers, or widows (cf. Phil 1:1; 1 Tim 3:1–13; 5:3–20; Acts 14:23) as he did elsewhere. That he did neither of these things indicates that this list of three functions was intended to be generic, encompassing a broad range of specific leadership functions in the church.

"Those who work hard" *(kopiaō)* translates a verbal form of the noun *(kopos)* found in 1:3. The Thessalonians as a whole engaged in the "labor" *(kopos)* of love. Paul used the same word to describe the strenuous physical labor required to support himself materially (2:9; cf. 1 Cor 4:12) and of his spiritual ministry in their midst (3:5; cf. Phil 2:16). The term indicates strenuous labor. At the same time it is broad enough to include all sorts of ministry activity. The laborer in the church (whatever specific task is involved) who has consistently exhibited a willingness to do the hard work of the ministry is one who has earned the respect of the congregation (cf. 1 Cor 16:15–16; 1 Tim 5:17).

"Those who are over you" translates a compound word that literally means "to stand before" *(proistēmi)*. Various metaphorical meanings derived from this. The verb might describe one who "surpassed others," who "presided over" or "directed" others, who "represented" others, or who "protected" and thus "cared for" others.[119] In general it does not depict an office but a task. The "one who stands before you" in Paul's letters is both a leader and a caregiver. Romans 12:8 uses the same verb of one whom the Spirit has given the gift of "caring for others."[120] In the same letter Paul used a noun form of the same word to identify the "servant" *(diakonos)* Phoebe as a caregiver *(prostatis)*, one who had been "a great help" to many people. The same verb occurs in 1 Tim 3:4–5, where the overseer must "manage" *(proistamenon)* his own household to demonstrate his ability to "take care of" *(epimelēsetai)* God's church, implying that the latter term interprets the former.[121]

---

[119] B. Reicke, "προΐστημι," *TDNT* 6.700–703.

[120] Cf. Reicke, who cites a context of "works of love" in Rom 12:8 to support his translation. A context of "pastoral care" in 1 Thess 5:12 demands the same emphasis on caregiving as the meaning of προΐστημι (ibid., 701–2).

[121] The only other occurrences of ἐπιμελέομαι are in Jesus' parable of the good Samaritan, who took care of the wounded Jewish traveler (Luke 10:34–35).

The one who leads also does so as an example to the church. *Proista-menous* must not be understood in a manner that distances the task of leadership from the *ethos* of the leader (cf. 2:1–12). Paul attempted to provide a model for the church to follow (1:6; cf. 2 Thess 3:7), and he praised the Thessalonians for doing the same for others (1:7). Elsewhere Timothy and Titus were encouraged to lead by example as well (1 Tim 4:12; Titus 2:7–8). The grouping of *proistamenous* in v. 12 with the participles "working hard" and "admonishing" indicates that Paul was not describing a position but an activity. All three depict general activities characteristic of leadership, not particular offices a person might attain.

Those who "admonish" is the last of the three participles. The term *noutheteō* may simply mean to instruct but normally also carried the implication of exerting a "corrective influence" upon a person who is not predisposed to accept the instruction.[122] In negative contexts it can carry the connotation of issuing a reprimand or a warning, but the desire was to correct "without provoking or embittering."[123] In the New Testament the word only occurs in Paul's writings and in the Acts account of Paul's address to the Ephesian elders (Acts 20:31). Admonition was an activity carried out by the apostle and by leaders of the church (cf. 5:12; 1 Cor 4:14; Col 1:28), but members of the church in general also were expected to admonish one another to proper behavior (see 5:14; Rom 15:14; Col 3:16; 2 Thess 3:15). In the context of idleness or unruly behavior (see v. 14 for a discussion of *ataktous*), Paul may have intended to call on the church to respect ministers who have the responsibility of issuing reprimands when Christian behavior is not what it should be. But the leaders of the congregation were not expected to carry this burden alone. The task of admonishing wayward Christians was a responsibility shared by all believers (cf. vv. 12,14).

The three participles grouped together identify leadership tasks within the Thessalonian church. But as we have seen, the tasks themselves were not unique to church leaders. In fact, Paul's letters in general demonstrate a remarkable sameness regarding tasks and character traits expected both of the leaders of the church and the congregation in general. That which marked certain ones as leaders was the exemplary nature of their Christian walk and the exemplary manner in which their gifts were exercised.

The descriptive phrases scattered throughout these two verses also

---

[122] G. Behm, "νουθετέω," *TDNT* 4.1019.
[123] Ibid., 1021.

depict responsible leadership. First, Paul instructed the brothers to note those who "work hard among you." The qualifying phrase "among you" implies that these were ministers who were a regular part of the congregation. These were proven, hard workers within the fellowship who had earned respect from the people who had seen the character of their ministry. Second, the Thessalonians were instructed to note and honor those who lead "in the Lord" (v. 12). This phrase *(en kuriō)* is frequent in the Pauline corpus. It places that which it modifies within the sphere of Christian commitment, goals, and/or character. A person in the Lord is simply a Christian (Rom 16:11). An attitude in the Lord is one that is consistent with the character of Christ, not the character of the world, for example, Paul's love for Ampliatus (Rom 16:8) or the Philippians' joy (Phil 3:1). A leader or worker in the Lord is one who functions guided by the character and will of the Lord (Rom 16:12; 1 Cor 9:1).

Thus a leader in the Lord gives Christlike guidance and care to the church. Such deserve recognition and great esteem, for not all lead "in the Lord." Later in this chapter the church was urged not to "treat prophecies with contempt" but also warned to "test everything" (v. 21). The implication is that the congregation must not allow itself to be misled by someone claiming falsely to lead in the name of the Lord. Indeed, in 2 Thess 2:1–3 Paul did deal directly with some who were attempting to mislead the church doctrinally. The church at Corinth likewise suffered at the hands of immature leaders who created divisions and abused spiritual gifts. Such were obviously not leading "in the Lord." Neither those who have the responsibility to labor in, stand before, and admonish the church of God nor the congregation as a whole can afford to take lightly their responsibility to live always in a way reflecting the character and will of their Lord.

Finally, the church should note and respect leaders for the work they have done. The noun "work" *(ergon)* in v. 13 derives from a different root from the participle used for labor in v. 12. Paul may have selected *ergon* as a signal that "their work" in v. 13 encompassed all three functions specifically mentioned with the participles of v. 12. Leaders of congregations could exercise a variety of gifts and respond to a variety of needs. The respect of the church was due not on the basis of a gift possessed but on the basis of a gift exercised properly. The respect of the church was due not on the basis of reputation or position but on the basis of ministry performed. The minister who thinks his position alone should earn him the respect of the church has not read the Scriptures.[124]

The actions of the church are modified in two additional ways. They were to esteem the leaders "very highly," and they were to esteem them "in love." The respect the church paid those in their midst who worked hard at ministering in the Lord was not to be half-hearted. "Highest" regard renders a compound word signifying the greatest degree possible, literally indicating regard "beyond measure."[125] Paul used the same word of the great earnestness with which he prayed to see the Thessalonians again (cf. Eph 3:20). The church also was to respect their leaders "in love." It is one thing to follow someone out of respect or out of tradition. It is another altogether to follow in love. The latter speaks of a binding relationship. The former might be nothing more than a formality easily discarded.

"Live in peace with each other" (v. 13b) is syntactically independent of the preceding (vv. 12–13a) and the following (vv. 14–15) exhortations. Paul may have intended this command to stand alone, using a brief unadorned admonition to make a pointed statement. A comparable command occurs in the writings of several New Testament authors (cf. Mark 9:50; Rom 12:18; 2 Cor 13:11; Heb 12:14), and a call for peace among followers of the God of peace is not surprising (Phil 4:7,9). Verse 14 contains a series of imperatives similar in structure to v. 13b. But it is unlikely that the command "live at peace" should be linked directly to vv. 14–15. The introductory statement "we urge you, brothers" (v. 14) marks the beginning of a new paraenetic section (cf. "we ask you, brothers," v. 12). Though there is no grammatical link, logi-

---

[124] Based on the works of Theissen and Meeks, Wanamaker accurately points out that the wealthy and educated in the church were those with the capability to minister, serving in effect as patrons and protectors of the congregation. This does not mean, however, that such persons deserved respect (and, by implication, obedience) apart from doing the hard work of ministry and functioning in a manner Paul would describe as "in the Lord." Wealth may enable one to exert influence, but it does not by itself make one an exemplary Christian leader. See Wanamaker, *1 and 2 Thessalonians,* 194–95. Cf. W. Meeks, *The First Urban Christians: The Social World of the Apostle Paul* (New Haven: Yale University Press, 1983), 51–73; and G. Theissen, *The Social Setting of Pauline Christianity: Essays on Corinth,* trans. and ed. J. H. Schütz (Philadelphia: Fortress, 1982), 96. For discussion of patronage in relation to the problem of the idle, see B. W. Winter, " 'If a man does not wish to work …' A Cultural and Historical Setting for 2 Thessalonians 3:6–16," *TynBul* 40 (1989): 303–15.

[125] BAGD, s.v. "ὑπερεκπερισσοῦ."

cally the command to live in peace may continue the discussion of the congregation and its leaders in vv. 12–13a. The act of admonishing implies at least the possibility of conflict. And the need to instruct the church to hold leaders in high regard at least contemplates the possibility of the opposite happening. Understood in this light "live in peace with each other" urges the people and their leaders to seek a relationship marked by "peace," that is, a relationship in which destructive conflict is absent and a sense of well-being pervades the church.

"We urge you, brothers" (v. 14) and "we ask you, brothers" (v. 12) are parallel, each introducing a paraenetic unit. The formula in v. 14 leads to a series of imperatives that continues through v. 22. Both vv. 12–13a and vv. 14–15 deal with relationships in the church. Both address matters that could cause considerable disruption in the fellowship if handled with a contentious spirit. If v. 13b is not connected with vv. 12–13a, it may function as a bridge between the two areas of concern. The church exists in relationship with its workers, leaders, and admonishers (the spiritually strong of vv. 12–13a) and in relationship with the idle, timid, and weak (the spiritually frail of v. 14). A command to "live in peace" may have been placed in the seam between these two sections because of the potential for conflict between each of these groups and the congregation as a whole.

(2) The Weak and the Strong (5:14–15)

14And we urge you, brothers, warn those who are idle, encourage the timid, help the weak, be patient with everyone. 15Make sure that nobody pays back wrong for wrong, but always try to be kind to each other and to everyone else.

5:14 Two pieces of paraenesis are cobbled together in these verses. Though vv. 14 and 15 could easily exist independently, their juxtaposition highlights their commonality. The exhortation to patience in the end of v. 14 flows naturally to the prohibition of retaliation in v. 15. Also v. 14 presents four brief exhortations that encourage the church to take proactive steps to assist troublesome or weak Christians. Then v. 15a forbids retaliation against those who do wrong and may refer specifically to those outside the church. The exhortation to pursue good for one another (cf. v. 14) and for all (cf. v. 15a) provides a concluding summary.

The introductory formula "we urge you, brothers" is identical to that found in v. 12 but for the use of "we urge" (*parakaleō*) rather than "we ask" (*erōtaō*). Both were used in 4:1, and Paul appears to have used them interchangeably in 1 Thessalonians. It is highly unlikely that v. 14 was addressed to leaders of the congregation (cf. v. 12) as the only ones responsible to warn, encourage, and help others. Throughout the letter "brethren" refers to the entire church, and there is no indication that Paul used it more narrowly (i.e., meaning "leaders") in this instance. Also a rigid division of duties is inconsistent with the flexible organization of the church indicated in Paul's letters as a whole. The exhortations in v. 14 are a series of imperatives roughly parallel in structure, each consisting of a three-word clause.

The sentence "warn those who are idle" includes the verb translated "admonish" in v. 12. The verb connotes confrontation. It implies that the "idle" had chosen their lifestyle, and so the church needed to confront them with the fact that their behavior was unacceptable. Second Thessalonians 3:6–13 reveals that persisting in such behavior eventually led to the exercise of church discipline. The word "idle" *(ataktous)* refers to someone or something that is out of order. In an active sense such a person is unruly or insubordinate. In a passive sense such persons are not doing what they ought and thus are lazy or idle. The brevity of this imperative makes it impossible to determine which meaning Paul had in mind. Appeal to 2 Thess 3:6–13 is not helpful at this point because the *ataktoi* there are criticized both because they will not work and for making trouble as busybodies.[126]

Some indications are present, however, that Paul was using the adjective in the passive sense of "idlers." The other characteristics mentioned in v. 14 (the timid and the weak) are rather passive images. *Ataktous* probably was intended to be parallel to them. Also if Paul intended to work a contrast between v. 14 and those who actively do wrong in v. 15, then we might assume that all of the references in v. 14 were intended to be relatively passive.

In addition to warning the lazy, the church was urged to "encourage the timid." Timid translates a compound of *oligos* (few, or little) and *psuchē* (life, or soul). It occurs only here in the New Testament. Perhaps the best English parallel is the archaic compound "faint-hearted." It may

---

[126] Wanamaker argues that the brevity of this exhortation compared with the extensive treatment of the ἄτακτοι in 2 Thess 3:6–15 is evidence of the priority of 2 Thessalonians (*1 and 2 Thessalonians,* 197). It is also conceivable, however, that between the writing of 1 and 2 Thess the minor problem addressed briefly in 1 Thess 5:14 became a major issue in the church resulting in a more detailed treatment and recommendations regarding the disciplining of the ἄτακτος in 2 Thessalonians.

indicate a person who is "timid" as a personality trait or one who is "discouraged" at a particular turn of events. The death of fellow Christians (4:13–18), persecution by non-Christians (2:14–16), attempting and sometimes failing to live according to a new ethic (4:3–8), the absence of the evangelists (2:17–20), and various trials and temptations (3:5) could have discouraged some of the believers. Whatever the difficulty, the church was to attempt to "encourage" such people. Paul used the same verb *(paramytheomai)* to describe the fatherly care he exhibited toward the Thessalonians (2:11–12). In this also they were to follow his example.

The "weak" also were in need of help. *Asthenōs* is a general word and could signify people who lack strength or were physically ill (Acts 4:9), as well as those who were spiritually weak or immature (Rom 5:6; 1 Cor 8:9). Also these two types of weakness (spiritual and physical) sometimes overlapped (1 Cor 11:30). The context here does not rule out the thought of physical weakness, but the paraenesis overall deals with the implications of the faith for life. The verb "help" *(antechē)* used literally implies holding on to someone or something. Metaphorically, Paul was calling for the strong to be supportive of those weaker than themselves. As in Corinth, a number of believers in Thessalonica probably had difficulty moving from the pagan to the Christian manner of thought and life (cf. 1 Cor 8; 10). The church should support these "weak" brothers as beloved fellow strugglers, not desert them as ignorant or unimportant stragglers.

The final exhortation in this series of four encourages the church to "be patient with everyone." A patient person is one who is not quickly or easily provoked to emotional outbursts or precipitous actions. As a characteristic of God, patience is linked primarily to his willingness to delay judgment upon a sinful humanity deserving of his wrath (Rom 2:4; 9:22). It is a virtue derived from love, and its presence is evidence of the work of the Spirit in the believer (Gal 5:22; 2 Cor 6:6; Eph 4:2). Paul did not identify any particular group toward whom the Thessalonians should be patient. He encouraged patience "with everyone." But "everyone" does not try the patience of others, so Paul must have been encouraging patience especially toward those in (and outside?) the church who were offensive or annoying. He probably had the "idle," the "timid," and the "weak"[127] in mind. But whoever the offender is, Christians should have

---

[127] See D. A. Black, "The Weak in Thessalonica: A Study in Pauline Lexicography," *JETS* 25 (1982): 307–22. Black argues that the three phrases "warn those who are idle, encourage the timid, help the weak" are in the context of the three sections of the epistle. The "weak," therefore, refers to those who are having a difficult time understanding the death of loved ones and the apparent delay of the parousia.

the same godly patience when dealing with troublesome or troubled persons as God has demonstrated in his dealings with sinful humanity.

5:15 In addition to dealing with people who are hurting, the church sometimes had to deal with people who hurt others. Vengeance is the natural reaction to an offense suffered. But vengeance is not the way of the Christian. Verse 14 appears to focus on the church's response to those who are hurting; v. 15, on its reaction to those who hurt others.

The commands again (as in v. 14) were directed toward those strong in the faith. Just as they were to help those in the fellowship with problems, so also were they to help with problems between believers. "Make sure" (lit., "see") continues the string of second-person imperatives. But the behavior commanded here is directed through the reader toward others in the church. Believers should see to it that "nobody pays back evil for evil."[128] The official, judicial side of such mediation is reflected in 1 Cor 6:1–11. The Corinthians were expected to mediate differences among themselves and if necessary suffer wrong rather than bring the church into disrepute.

Paul's advice echoes the teachings of Jesus (Matt 5:44–48) and must have been a common piece in early Christian paraenetic tradition. Later, in his letter to the Roman church, Paul also discouraged giving "evil for evil" (12:17) and did so in a fuller context than occurs here. The believer should bless, not curse, others, even persecutors. They should do what is noble and enhances the reputation of the church. They should shame the evil by returning to them good and leave the evening of accounts to God (see Rom 12:14–21). Returning "wrong for wrong" makes a wrongdoer of the Christian. Most of the ancient world may have considered retaliatory justice appropriate. But Christians were encouraged to emulate the remarkable love and patience with evildoers that God revealed in Christ.

Rather than give wrong for wrong, believers were to "always seek after that which is good" (NASB). "Try to be kind" fails to convey the urgency and effort implied in Paul's exhortation, *to agathon diōkete*, "pursue the good." The Christian must actively "pursue" (the same verb is used) virtues such as love (1 Cor 14:1; cf. "hospitality," Rom 12:13), maturity (Phil 3:12–14), the peace and edification of the fellowship

---

[128] The third-person form of this command may simply indicate the quotation of a piece of tradition. But Paul's choice to use the tradition in third-person form rather than change the wording (as in Rom 12:17) indicates his intent to make believers responsible to help one another resist the temptation of retaliation.

(Rom 14:19), and righteousness (1 Tim 6:11). Paul encouraged the Thessalonians to pursue the good "always," for "each other" and for "everyone else" as well. The adverb "always" along with the use of a present tense imperative calls for continuity in the believers' behavior. "One another" refers to the Christian fellowship, and "everyone else" is all those outside the fellowship. Together they call for the Christian to seek good for everyone, even as earlier Paul prayed that the church would grow in love for everyone (3:12).

(3) Optimists and Pessimists (5:16–18)

¹⁶Be joyful always; ¹⁷pray continually; ¹⁸give thanks in all circumstances, for this is God's will for you in Christ Jesus.

5:16 The next group of exhortations consists of three brief imperatives that are very general in character. The logic that links them to one another and to the surrounding paraenesis is somewhat obscure and in fact each could be treated independently. Wanamaker unites the three commands by categorizing them as "religious duties," observing that each of the three commands "either has its source in God ... or is directed toward God."[129] Best observes a link between vv. 16–18 and the preceding paraenesis. In his estimate vv. 12–15 concern behavior toward others, while vv. 16–18 address the inner life of each believer. Since the inner life (vv. 16–18) shapes the outer attitudes (vv. 12–15), the two passages are supportive of each other.[130]

Rejoicing, praying, and giving thanks, however, were not exclusively personal spiritual experiences. They were just as much, if not more so, public expressions characteristic of the church assembled. As a result, distinctions between the internal and external practice of religion seems rather unlikely. It is more defensible to argue that vv. 16–18 present activities directed toward God, whereas vv. 12–15 and vv. 19–22 deal with actions and attitudes toward others.[131] But such an emphasis still neglects the corporate nature of the practices commended in vv. 16–18 and also results in vv. 16–18 interrupting the flow of commands in vv. 12–15 and vv. 19–22 that deal with attitudes and actions of the brethren toward others (primarily other Christians).

---

[129] Wanamaker, *1 and 2 Thessalonians*, 199.

[130] Best, *1 and 2 Thessalonians*, 234.

[131] See the following discussion; vv. 19–22 deal with the church's attitude toward prophets and their teachings delivered in the assembly; cf. 1 Cor 14:26,29.

Once taken out of the realm of private expressions of faith and recognized as community activities, these commands may be seen as
expressions of a common faith. Paul was commending joyful worship
directed toward the one true God to whom the church owed ceaseless
thanks. Grumbling toward leaders (cf. vv. 12–13), impatience with the
immature (v. 14), and anger toward those who do wrong (v. 15) must
not tarnish the fellowship of the congregation (cf. 1 Cor 11:17–19). The
church must not let its problems create an atmosphere of gloom or pes-
simism. Rather, an optimistic atmosphere of joy, thanks, and praise
ought to characterize the assembly when believers gather (cf. 1 Cor
14:15–17; Eph 5:19–20; Col 3:16–17).

Continuity is emphasized with each of the imperatives. "Be joyful"
(chairete), "pray" *(proseuchesthe),* and "give thanks" *(eucharisteite)*
are all present tense, implying continuous or recurring activities.
"Always," "continually," and "in all circumstances" strengthen the message that these actions should consistently characterize the Christian life.

The frequent references in Paul's letters indicate that joy is a characteristic of a healthy Christian life.[132] Joy is produced by the work of the
Spirit in the believer (Gal 5:22). But Christian joy is not self-centered.
The believer rejoices in the good fortune of others (Rom 12:15) and
when others demonstrate obedience in the Lord (Rom 16:19; 1 Cor
13:6; 2 Cor 7:9; 13:9; Phil 4:10). The presence of good Christian company is a source of joy (1 Cor 16:17; Phil 2:28), as is the believer's
future hope in the Lord (Rom 12:12). So even in the midst of personal
tribulations Paul could find cause for joy (2 Cor 6:10; cf. 1:6). And Paul
could rejoice in the spread of the gospel, even when it involved the personal pain of self-sacrifice (Phil 1:18; 2:17–18; cf. 2:19–20; 3:6).

5:17 The word chosen for "prayer" *(proseuchomai)* is a general
one that implies a worshipful approach to God (cf. Rom 8:26). Paul
encouraged his churches to make prayer a part of their personal spiritual
discipline (Rom 12:12; Phil 4:6). He and his coworkers prayed together
regularly (1:2; 2 Thess 1:11; Rom 1:10) and valued the prayers of the
church on their behalf (5:25; cf. 2 Cor 1:11, where "prayers" are petitions, *deēsei).* But prayer was also a feature of the public worship of the
assembly. Paul linked public prayer with prophecy in his discussion of
propriety in worship in 1 Cor 11:4 and with the public exercise of gifts

---

[132] Paul encouraged or celebrated Christian joy dozens of times in his letters and for a
wide range of reasons. The greatest concentration of references to joy or rejoicing is found
in Philippians, written while Paul was under arrest.

and giving thanks in the assembly (1 Cor 14:15–17). Clearly, Paul expected Christians both privately and in the public assembly to approach God with praise, intercessions, requests, and thanksgiving.

5:18 "Give thanks" translates the same verb *(eucharisteō)* Paul used when he told the Thessalonians that he thanked God for them and for their faith (1:2; 2:13). His thanksgiving for the church was directed to God both for what God had done (cf. Col 1:12–14) and in response to the faith and godly actions of the Thessalonians (2 Thess 1:3; 2:13–15).[133] Paul's prayers of thanks for his churches were frequently expressed in his letters (not just in private devotion) and were clearly intended as public affirmations encouraging continued praiseworthy behavior. Public thanksgivings also serve as an example of gratitude toward others, which all Christians should follow, for ingratitude is characteristic of ungodliness (Rom 1:27). In addition, Paul's public expressions of thanks showed his genuine appreciation for the churches and strengthened the bonds between them (Rom 1:8; 1 Cor 1:4; Phil 1:3; cf. Phlm 4–5).

"In all circumstances" translates a phrase that could just as well mean "at all times."[134] But the difference in meaning is not great, and Paul may have chosen an ambiguous phrase to cover both time and circumstance (cf. Eph 5:20, "give thanks always and for everything," RSV). Paul never instructed the church to thank God for evil events but to thank God that even in evil times and circumstances our hope remains, and God continues his work in our lives (Rom 8:28).

The second half of v. 18 may look forward to vv. 19–22. But the "for" more likely connects the clause with what precedes in vv. 16–18a. The identical statement "this is the will of God" also occurs at the beginning of the paraenetic section of the letter (see the discussion on 4:3). Thus at the beginning and near the end of these two chapters Paul reminded his readers that the commands given are not of human origin but divine.

(4) The Cynical and the Gullible (5:19–22)

[19]Do not put out the Spirit's fire; [20]do not treat prophecies with contempt. [21]Test everything. Hold on to the good. [22]Avoid every kind of evil.

---

[133] For an example of thanks directed to individuals see Rom 16:3–4.

[134] Wanamaker argues that this "temporal understanding is to be slightly favored" (*1 and 2 Thessalonians*, 200).

The incomplete canon of Scripture, the ambiguities of charismatic revelation, and the activity of itinerant teachers created in the early church a setting conducive to conflict. The church struggled to know which leader to follow (1 Cor 1:12; Gal 1:6–7), which prophet was true, and which was false (Matt 7:15–23; 1 Tim 4:1; 2 Tim 3:6–9). Disagreements over doctrine and ethics seemed inevitable. Some theological controversies impacted the entire church and affected the understanding of the gospel itself (Acts 15; Gal 2). Other disagreements were more local in their impact (1 Cor 1:10–17; 3 John), affecting a single congregation.

In such a setting, how was a congregation to respond to the many and diverse voices that claimed to be the voice of God? The New Testament is full of warnings regarding false teachers and their erroneous teachings (e.g., 1 Tim 4:1–8; 2 Tim 3:6–9). False teachers are recognizable by their "fruit" (Matt 7:15– 23). They lack love (1 John 2:9–11), deny the humanity of Christ (1 John 4:1–3), or disobey the commands of Jesus (1 John 2:3–6). They contradict the teachings of the apostolic gospel (Gal 1:6–9; 3:1; 5:1–2,12–15).

The collection of five exhortations in 5:19–22 represents an attempt to help the church maintain its trim in the storm currents of conflicting truth claims (cf. Eph 4:14).[135] The first two exhortations (vv. 19–20) are

---

[135] W. Schmithals argues that the specific problem these verses address was an anti-charismatic backlash. Supposedly, in response to Gnostic charismatic abuses, the church had suppressed charismatic activity altogether. In response Paul urged them to guard against abuse without giving up the use of charismata altogether (*Paul and the Gnostics,* 172–75). Although it is unlikely that the offenders were Gnostics, a scenario of charismatic abuse and false teaching leading to skepticism regarding so-called prophecies is otherwise plausible. First Corinthians provides abundant evidence that charismata were abused (e.g., 12:1–3), and a variety of false teachers did plague the churches. Others (Jewett, *Thessalonian Correspondence,* 175–76; Wanamaker, *1 and 2 Thessalonians,* 202–3) see here evidence of a power struggle within the community. The leaders and/or patrons of the congregation might have discounted the authority of charismatics in order to retain control of the fellowship. A third possibility is hinted at by the contrast in 2:1–12 between Paul as a preacher of the gospel and Hellenistic rhetoricians (2:1–12). Paul presented himself as a sincere proclaimer of divinely revealed truth, not one who specialized in the oratorical polish of the sophists (cf. 1 Cor 2:1–5). As a result his detractors criticized his speech (2 Cor 10:10) and preferred more polished presentations (such as the Alexandrian-trained Apollos? 1 Cor 1:12; Acts 18:24–19:1). If Paul's Corinthian experience demonstrates a tendency for some Christians to evaluate proclamations in the church by secular rhetorical standards, then it stands to reason that prophetic utterances by unschooled preachers would be treated with contempt. If this is the situation behind vv. 19–22, then Paul was exhorting the church not to judge prophetic utterances superficially but to put all (i.e., the artful and the simple) to the test, judging them in terms of good versus evil, not eloquence versus artlessness.

negative. The last three (vv. 21–23) are positive. The only connective in the passage is the adversative *de* (which the NIV does not translate; cf. NASB "but"), which marks the transition at v. 21. Paul did not wish the church to become so cynical that they treated with contempt those who came with a word of prophecy (5:19–20). Neither was the church to be so gullible that they accepted whatever a so-called prophet said without carefully weighing it and determining that it was indeed a true word of God (5:21–22).

5:19 The first two exhortations warned the church against excessively cynical behavior. "Do not put out the Spirit's fire" attempts to convey the connotation of a verb *(sbennyte)* that was used literally of extinguishing a flame or figuratively of suppressing or stifling something. The present imperative of prohibition (used in vv. 19 and 20) generally forbids the continuing of an act already in progress. This is not always the case, however, and these verses may be preventative rather than curative. There is no word for "fire" in the text, but the Spirit is symbolized by fire in the New Testament (cf. Acts 2:3–4,17); the verb "put out" indicates that this probably was the image Paul had in mind. In what way might the Thessalonians have stifled the Spirit? The parallel exhortation in v. 20 provides the answer.

5:20 The church must not "treat prophecies with contempt." The verb *exoutheneō* implies dismissive disdain (cf. Rom 14:3,10; 1 Cor 1:28). One faction in the Corinthian church expressed contempt for Paul,[136] arguing that his letters were "weighty and strong but his bodily presence [was] ... weak and his speech of no account" (2 Cor 10:10).[137] The church was not to dismiss or reject words of prophecy *(prophēteias)*[138] as something unworthy of consideration.

The person with the gift of prophecy proclaimed the word of the Lord to the congregation for its "strengthening, encouragement and comfort" (1 Cor 14:3,6–7,22). A word of prophecy could also be evangelistic, leading to the conviction and conversion of unbelievers (1 Cor 14:24–25). The Spirit might be quenched by the prophet himself if he refused to speak the word the Spirit gave to him. But the exhortations in vv. 21–22 indicate that it was the community of faith that was evaluating the worth of the prophecy and determining whether to accept or

---

[136] And possibly Timothy also, 1 Cor 16:11.

[137] "Of no account" translates εξουθενεῖτε. Cf. Gal 4:14.

[138] This term may refer to the gift of prophecy or to the word of prophecy. The absence of the article and the use of the plural indicates the latter meaning in this context.

reject it, not the prophet himself. The church as a body might quench the Spirit by refusing to hear the word of the prophet.

5:21–22 The shift to positive statements and the presence of a *de* ("but," RSV) in the text at this point[139] marks the beginning of statements intended to balance out vv. 19–20. Rather than stifle the Spirit by the contemptuous rejection of the prophetic word, the church should give prophecy a careful hearing. However, Paul did not recommend a gullible acceptance of every message claiming divine authority. The presence of false teachers in the church from an early date made blanket acceptance of prophetic claims foolhardy.

The church was urged to "test everything." The word "test" *(dokimazete)* implies a careful examination. "Everything" (a neuter plural) is broad enough to include more than just prophecy and may allude to all the various charismatic ministries operative in the church. But in this context it probably refers to the various words of prophecy that might be delivered in the assembly. The apostle did not even exempt himself or the other apostles from such scrutiny by the congregation. He also did not limit scrutiny to visiting teachers and prophets. Those in the congregation, its members, and its leaders as well were apparently included in the apostle's command to examine "everything." With these few and simple commands the apostle acknowledged the great authority and responsibility of the congregation.

Rather than accept everything (leading to confusion and error) or reject everything (leading to the loss of true prophecies along with the false), the church was to examine carefully everything, using the criteria Jesus and his apostles provided for recognizing false prophets. Careful examination by the congregation as a whole would allow the church to discern that which was good and right. It would also enable them to recognize false prophets using "prophetic" claims to veil error or evil (cf. 2 Thess 2:2).

Testing all things, the church was then commanded to "hold on to the good" and "avoid every kind of evil" (cf. Isa 1:16–17). "Hold on" *(kateche)* may mean "to possess" (cf. Phlm 13), but here it has the connotation of "remember" the teaching. They should retain it with the intent of allowing it to shape their lives in Christ. "Avoid" *(apechomai)* means "to keep away from" or "abstain from a teaching or a practice," as in 4:3 they were commanded to "avoid *[apechesthai]* sexual immorality." The same word was used by the Jerusalem apostles when they wrote to

---

[139] Some ancient MSS also omit the δέ.

the Gentile churches that they should "abstain from food sacrificed to idols ... and from immorality" (Acts 15:20).

Every "kind of evil" translates a word *(eidous)* that refers to the outward appearance of a thing. But *eidous* is not used here in a superficial way. There is no intent to draw a contrast between appearance and substance in this verse. Whatever "appears" evil upon careful examination by the fellowship is assumed to be evil in fact. Thus the various "kinds" of evil, whatever their particular shape, are what the apostle admonished the church to avoid.

In 5:12–22 the apostle admonished the church to love and affirm those who minister in their midst (vv. 12–13) and to love and assist those in the congregation who are in need of support (vv. 14–15). He reminded them that they had cause for optimism in all circumstances, and their assemblies should be filled with joy, praise, and thanksgiving (vv. 16–18). A final word of warning is also an affirmation that the Spirit was in their midst and that they should accept and abide by the words of truth God sent them (vv. 19–22). Many exhortations could have been added to these. But at some point the people of God, those who are God-taught and Spirit-led, must ultimately be left in the hands of the God who faithfully sanctifies and keeps his church to the end (vv. 23–24). Appropriately Paul called upon the power of God to accomplish more than the lengthiest list of exhortations ever could.

IV. BENEDICTION AND CONCLUSION (5:23–28)
   1. Benediction (5:23–24)
   2. Concluding Exhortations (5:25–27)
   3. Epistolary Conclusion (5:28)

IV. BENEDICTION AND CONCLUSION (5:23–28)

The final verses of 1 Thessalonians contain a mixture of forms and content.[1] Several of the themes prominent in the letter are mentioned again in summary. A benediction (vv. 23–24) expresses again Paul's prayers for the faithful and his confidence in the Lord. It also provides transition from the final paraenetic section (vv. 12–22) to the epistolary conclusion (vv. 25–28).[2] In vv. 25–27 three brief exhortations request prayer, send greetings, and require the recipients of the letter to give it the broadest possible reading among the Thessalonian church. An epistolary conclusion ends the letter (v. 28).

1. Benediction (5:23–24)

[23]May God himself, the God of peace, sanctify you through and through. May your whole spirit, soul and body be kept blameless at the coming of our Lord Jesus Christ. [24]The one who calls you is faithful and he will do it.

In a prayer expressing Paul's wishes for the congregation,[3] two of

---

[1] Like much of the letter, vv. 23–28 contain elements common to the letter writing of the day (see W. G. Doty, *Letters in Primitive Christianity* [Philadelphia: Fortress, 1973], 43) as well as demonstrate an awareness of rhetorical conventions appropriate for concluding the presentation (see R. Jewett, *The Thessalonian Correspondence: Pauline Rhetoric and Millenarian Piety* [Philadelphia: Fortress, 1986], 76, and the chart comparing epistolary and rhetorical analysis on pp. 220–21).

[2] C. Roetzel, "1 Thess 5:12–28: A Case Study," *Society of Biblical Literature: 1972 Proceedings,* ed. L. C. McGaughy (n.p.: SBL, 1972), 377.

[3] For a discussion of this sort of "wish-prayer" in Paul's writings see G. P. Wiles, *The Significance of the Intercessory Prayer Passages in the Letters of Paul,* SNTSMS 24 (Cambridge: University Press, 1974).

the basic themes of the letter are again highlighted. The prayer utilizes two optative verbs, asking that God "may ... sanctify" the Thessalonians and that they "may ... be kept blameless." The prayer for sanctification reminds the readers of the exhortations in chaps. 4–5. In fact, the call for sanctification brackets these final two chapters. Chapter 4 begins with an exhortation to the people to lead sanctified lives (vv. 3–8), and chap. 5 ends with a prayer that God would sanctify his people (v. 23a). The prayer for the preservation of the saints until the coming of the Lord (v. 23b) reflects back on encouragements to persist in hope despite affliction (1:3,10; 2:14–16; 3:5; 5:10–11).

The first desire expressed in the prayer is that "the God of peace himself" might sanctify them "through and through." For the implications of "sanctify" see the discussion on 4:3 (cf. the prayer in 3:13). The term translated "through and through" *(holoteleis)*[4] is a compound that connotes the doing of something completely *(holos)* and carrying through to the finish *(telos)*. The "God of peace"[5] is the one requested to accomplish the complete and final sanctification of the church.[6] Only through his power does the church exist, and only through his power can it endure and be acceptable to him at the parousia. At the same time, it is evident from the presence of the exhortations in the letter (4:1–5:22) that for Paul's prayer to become reality, God's will to sanctify (in its ethical sense especially) must be matched by the believers' willingness to see their lives transformed.

Paul often referred to the "peace" of God. Peace may indicate simply the absence of discord (cf. 1 Cor 14:33). But most often, as in v. 23, it reflects its Old Testament usage stressing the well-being that God provides his people.[7] For Paul true peace was attained through Jesus by those justified by grace through faith (Rom 5:1; 8:6) and so always has a theological dimension and looks with hope to the peace that God will bring at the eschaton (Rom 2:5–10). But peace is also a present possibility for believers (Phil 4:6–9) and ought to characterize life in the community of faith (5:13; Rom 14:17).

The second request in the prayer is for the preservation of the

---

[4] Used only here in the NT.

[5] Cf. "God of love and peace" (2 Cor 13:11) and "God of hope" (Rom 15:13).

[6] The aorist ἁγιάσαι ("sanctify"), the completeness implied in ὁλοτελεῖς and ὁλόκληρον, and the temporal reference ἐν τῇ παρουσίᾳ indicate that Paul was thinking of the final sanctification of the church rather than the process of sanctifying it. However, the process and the final product can never be completely segregated.

[7] G. von Rad and W. Foerster, "εἰρήνη," *TDNT* 2.402–8.

church. It elaborates on the first prayer chiastically. "God," the subject of "sanctify" in v. 23a, is the understood agent of v. 23b, "be kept" (i.e., by God). The object of v. 23a, "you," parallels "your whole spirit, soul and body," which is the subject of "be kept" in v. 23b. In addition the temporal clause "at the coming ..." is added, which provides the time frame for the entire prayer.

Paul's use of the three terms "spirit, soul and body" raises the question of his anthropology.[8] "Body" obviously describes the physical being of a person. "Soul" *(psychē)* is the life force that all living things (including animals) possess and that distinguishes them from the inanimate or the dead. The word is used of life itself, as the seat of internal thoughts, desires, and emotions, or of that aspect of life that survives physical death.[9] "Spirit" *(pneuma)* refers to the "breath" characteristic of life and thus also to the immaterial aspect of life. It is roughly synonymous with "soul," and like soul it sometimes is paired with "flesh" or "body" to sum up the entirety of a living being. In one Pauline context, however, adjectives related to the nouns "spirit" and "soul" do seem to draw a distinction between the two concepts (1 Cor 2:14–15). The "spiritual" *(pneumatikos)* person is one enabled to commune with the divine. The "natural" *(psuchikos)* person lives apart from the knowledge and power of God (cf. 1 Cor 15:42–46).[10] The key distinction here is relational, not ontological. Paul was not describing the human person as a three-part conglomerate but as a being with material and nonmaterial existence who may or may not be spiritually enlivened in relation to God.

The three terms used in v. 23, "spirit, soul and body," occur in a context stressing wholeness. Paul was not emphasizing the threefold nature of humanity but the deliverance of the "whole" *(holoklēron)* person. The adjective "whole" is first in the clause. The term is qualitative, indicating something that has integrity, is intact, complete, and undamaged.

Paul also prayed that the Thessalonian Christians might "be kept blameless." To "be kept" renders a word *(tēreō)* with military connotations. It implies the guarding of something to keep it safe. "Blameless"

---

[8] See R. Jewett, *Paul's Anthropological Terms: A Study of Their Use in Conflict Settings,* AGJU 10 (Leiden: Brill, 1971).

[9] A wise cautionary note occurs in BAGD, "It is oft. impossible to draw hard and fast lines between the meanings of this many-sided word" (s.v. "ψυχή").

[10] The nouns "soul" and "spirit" are not always used in a way consistent with the distinction implied in 1 Corinthians.

(amemptōs) is used only twice in the New Testament (here and 2:10). It and the related adjective *(amemptos)* have both ethical (Phil 2:15) and cultic (Phil 3:6) connotations. Only sacrifices that were unblemished or "blameless" were acceptable to Yahweh.[11] Paul's prayer was that the believers might be kept "blameless" and so be acceptable "at the coming of our Lord Jesus Christ." The preposition "at" *(ev)* implies that it was the day of the parousia itself that Paul had in mind. Thus both clauses in his prayer for the Thessalonians asked that they might be a sanctified people, acceptable in the eyes of God at the day of judgment (cf. 3:13).

5:24 The prayer concludes with a word of assurance. The God who calls believers into his kingdom is a faithful God. He is not whimsical and arbitrary. He is a powerful God, capable of doing what he promises. The present tense participle "who calls" highlights the ongoing work of God among his people (cf. 2:12). God's calling through the gospel of his Son begins a good work that gives believers a future hope (cf. Phil 1:6). That hope is as sure as the God who provides it. The "faithful" God does what he has promised to do for those whom he has called into the fellowship of his Son (cf. 1 Cor 1:9). That which this God "will do" is left unstated in the text, but the reference is certainly back to the prayer. Believers will be sanctified and kept. For those who are in Christ, the future is secure.

2. Concluding Exhortations (5:25–27)

25Brothers, pray for us. 26Greet all the brothers with a holy kiss. 27I charge you before the Lord to have this letter read to all the brothers.

Three brief exhortations follow the prayer. The first asks for prayer. The verb used is the same as the one in v. 17, "pray continually," but here Paul's tone is more personal, "Brethren, pray for us."[12] Paul valued the prayers of others and commonly requested prayer for himself and his coworkers (see Rom 15:30–32; 2 Cor 1:11; Eph 6:19–20; Phil 1:19; Phlm 22).

5:26 Paul directed the exhortation "greet all the brothers with a holy kiss" to the church in general. There is no indication in the text that Paul had a particular group in mind (e.g., the leaders of v. 12) who especially needed to express their love for the rest of the congregation. Greeting with a "kiss" was common in the ancient world, just as it is in

---

[11] Cf. Josephus, *Ant.* 3.278–79.
[12] Some MSS add "also" (καί).

many cultures today. Paul also commanded the churches at Corinth and at Rome to greet "one another" with a holy kiss (see Rom 16:16; 1 Cor 16:20; 2 Cor 13:12).[13] That it was a "holy" kiss indicates its nature and motivation. It was not an erotic kiss and may well have been restricted to kissing others of one's own sex.[14] The holiness of the kiss may also imply that Paul had in mind a kiss given as a regular part of the eucharistic ritual of the church.[15] It is not certain, however, that the church at this early date engaged in the eucharistic kiss as it was practiced in the postapostolic era.

The command in v. 26 to "greet all the brothers" is often taken as a command to the church that they ought to greet "one another." But Paul may have been sending his own greeting to the church (as he did in Phil 4:21; Col 4:15), not commanding the church to practice the ritual of a holy kiss.[16] The command of a kiss, along with the designation "brothers," implies a warm familial relationship that included "all" in the church. Whether the kiss was one of greeting or a part of the church's ritual, it indicates a remarkable level of familiarity in an assembly that crossed over the lines of social and economic class.

5:27 Paul's next statement, "I charge you … to have this letter read," was made in the first-person singular. The change of person may indicate the point at which Paul began writing the text himself. The shift from the amanuensis's handwriting to the author's would have been evident and represented the author's validation of the letter. It served in effect as the author's signature (cf. 1 Cor 16:21; Col 4:18; and esp. Phlm 19, where Paul was committing himself to the repayment of a debt). That this was a Pauline practice is also indicated by his comment in 2 Thess 3:17, "I, Paul, write this greeting in my own hand, which is the distinguishing mark in all my letters, this is how I write."[17]

---

[13] Peter described the same kiss of greeting as a "kiss of love" (1 Pet 5:14).

[14] Cf. Luke 7:45; 15:20; 22:47; Acts 20:37. G. Staehlin, "φιλέω," *TDNT* 9.125–27, 138–40; cf. E. Best, *A Commentary on the First and Second Epistles to the Thessalonians* (London: A. & C. Black, 1977), 245.

[15] Cf. F. F. Bruce, *1 and 2 Thessalonians,* WBC (Waco: Word, 1982), 134.

[16] H. Windisch points out that a greeting (ἀσπασμός) "consists of such gestures as 'embracing,' 'kissing,'" and "'offering the hand'" (see "ἀσπάζομαι," *TDNT* 1.496). Thus a command to greet the brethren with a kiss may simply be a slightly more specific variation of a general command to greet the brethren.

[17] "This is how I write" (οὕτω γράφω) does not refer to the formula, "I, Paul, …" but to the sentence as a sample of Paul's handwriting. See S. K. Stowers, *Letter Writing in Greco-Roman Antiquity* (Philadelphia: Westminster, 1986), 61, for an example of the use of the author's handwriting as a signature.

"I charge you" translates a strong word *(enorkizō)* used to require an oath of someone. Paul in effect was requiring a pledge from the recipients of the letter that they would have it "read to all the brothers." The guarantor of the oath was "the Lord," who would be expected to exact judgment if the oath were not carried out. Requiring such a pledge was not a common feature in Paul's letters, occurring only here.

The command may assume nothing more than the illiteracy of numerous members of the church and as a result the need to read the letter aloud for the assembly. On the other hand, the language of the command is unusually strong and may imply that some in the church were active opponents of the apostle who would try to suppress his letter. However, it seems unlikely that the carrier of the letter would entrust it to such people. Also, if a serious conflict existed between powerful persons in the church and the apostle, some attempt to resolve it would certainly have featured prominently earlier in the letter; it would not have appeared here for the first time.

A. von Harnack explained the exhortation by assuming that the Jewish and Gentile church met separately,[18] but we have no evidence of such an arrangement in Thessalonica. E. E. Ellis speculates that Paul was exhorting the church at Thessalonica to have the letter read in other churches in the vicinity (cf. Col 4:16). But if that was what Paul intended, why did he not direct the recipients to read the letter "in all the Macedonian churches"?[19] Though the wording is strong, it seems adequate and simplest to assume that a single reading of the letter might not have been heard by all the brethren in Thessalonica. The church may have met in more than one location, thus requiring multiple readings of the letter. Even if the entire Thessalonian church did meet together, some members might have missed the first reading, necessitating a repeated reading until all had heard Paul's encouragements and exhortations.[20]

---

[18] See A. von Harnack, "Das Problem des zweiten Thessalonicherbriefs," *SAB* 31 (1910): 560–78.

[19] E. E. Ellis, "Paul and his Co-Workers," *NTS* 17 (1970–71): 451, n. 1.

[20] Bruce suggests that Paul feared that the "idle" (ἀτάκτοι) who most needed the teachings of the letter might have a tendency to miss the assembly. "The responsible leaders of the church should therefore see to it that they were made acquainted with its contents" (*1 and 2 Thessalonians,* 135).

3. Epistolary Conclusion (5:28)

[28]The grace of our Lord Jesus Christ be with you.

5:28 The typical conclusion to an ancient letter was a simple "farewell" (cf. Acts 15:29). Paul replaced the secular formula with a benediction. His letters show considerable uniformity at this point. Romans 16:20 and 1 Cor 16:23 for instance are virtually identical to v. 28.[21] However, Paul could also abbreviate (Col 4:18) or expand (2 Cor 13:14) the formula.

As with the epistolary introduction, the formulaic nature of the closing benediction should not be allowed to obscure the heartfelt theological content. The conclusion brings grace and the source of God's grace to center stage and reminds the readers that it applies to them. The letter's final word was one that lifted up the "grace of the Lord Jesus Christ" and its impact upon the reader.[22]

---

[21] In both letters some texts do not include "Christ" in the benediction.

[22] ἀμήν, which concludes some manuscripts, is a scribal addition.

V. PRESCRIPT (1:1–2)
  1. Recipients (1:1)
  2. Greeting (1:2)

V. PRESCRIPT (1:1–2)

The prescript of 2 Thessalonians is identical to that in
1 Thessalonians but for the addition of the pronoun "our" in the first
verse and a prepositional phrase, "from God the Father and the Lord
Jesus Christ," in v. 2.[1] For a note on the meaning of "church" (*ekklēsia*)
see the discussion of 1 Thess 1:1. The prescript directs the letter to the
assembly of Thessalonian Christians.

1. Recipients (1:1)

**[1] To the church of the Thessalonians in God our Father and the Lord
Jesus Christ:**

Here as in all his letters Paul followed the conventional Hellenistic
form of address.[2] At the beginning of a letter the senders identified
themselves first, then identified the recipients, and then expressed a
greeting. A wish for the well-being of the recipients typically followed
before moving into the main body of the letter. Although Paul followed
this basic form, he did so with a distinctly Christian flair.

In all of his letters except for his Thessalonian correspondence, Paul
added descriptive phrases to his name. These generally emphasized his
role as apostle or as a servant of Christ. In 2 Thessalonians his name
(and those of his coauthors) is unadorned. Although Paul did identify
Silvanus and Timothy as coauthors and the letter does use the first-
person plural "we" predominantly, it is clear that Paul was the dominant
force in the trio. Twice the first singular "I" is used in the letter. Once

---

[1] See 1 Thess 1:1 for a brief discussion.
[2] See W. G. Doty, *Letters in Primitive Christianity* (Philadelphia: Fortress, 1973).

Paul was reminding the Thessalonians of the instructions he gave them (2:5). In the second instance (3:17) Paul provided his signature and described the letter as his (not "ours," which would include Silvanus and Timothy).

The assembly *(ekklēsia)* to which he wrote is identified by city or region. Yet several assemblies would exist in a typical Hellenistic city. Paul used a variety of phrases (e.g., "in God" or "in Christ") to make it clear that the letter was to the Christian *ekklēsia*. Both the modifiers added to his and his coworkers' names, and the modifiers added to describe the church also foreshadowed the content of the body of the letter. In 2 Thessalonians, however, such thematic anticipation is lacking.

2. Greeting (1:2)

[2]Grace and peace to you from God the Father and the Lord Jesus Christ.

1:2   For discussion of "grace" and "peace" see 1 Thess 1:1. The source of grace and of peace for the Christian assembly is "God the Father and the Lord Jesus Christ."[3] An identical phrase is also found in Rom 1:7; 1 Cor 1:3; 2 Cor 1:2; Eph 1:2; Phil 1:2; 1 Thess 1:1; Phlm 3; and in textual variants of Gal 1:3; Col 1:2.[4] The repetition of the phrase indicates that it was somewhat formulaic. But even so, such a theological affirmation could never have become so routine for the apostle that it was lacking in content. God's gracious act in Christ and the well-being that can result is the basic tenet of the Christian faith.

"Father" as the first designation of God in the letter connotes both authority and benevolent concern. The term reminds readers not only that a relationship exists between the father and his children (cf. Rom 8:12–25; Gal 4:1–7) but also between the siblings. Children who share the same Father are bound together in a single family and should demonstrate familial love and care for one another.

---

[3] The variant reading "our" Father (which has strong MS support) may be a carryover from the use of the pronoun with "Father" in v. 1. It creates a reading identical to Rom 1:7.

[4] The Pastoral Epistles show more variation. "Mercy" is added to "grace and peace" in the addresses in 1 and 2 Timothy (but not in Titus), the word order within the prepositional phrase varies, and Titus 1:4 calls Jesus Christ "our Savior" rather than "our Lord."

Further, the assembly acknowledges Jesus as Messiah (Christ) and as Master (Lord). Although these words do not anticipate the specific content of the letter, they do remind the readers of the foundation on which the letter stands. It reminds them that their faith in Jesus is well placed, for he is God's Anointed One. Their place in the kingdom of God is secure, for the gospel is the message of what God himself has done through his Christ. And his gospel does not suffer from the vagaries and inconsistencies of human works and so-called wisdom. Therefore the believers' task is clear: they must continue to obey the Christ whom they have owned as Lord. Neither persecution (1:5–10) nor false teaching (2:1–11) nor human weakness (3:6–15) can be allowed to discourage the church from persevering in their commitment to the one who has called them into his kingdom. For their God is just (1:6), and their Lord is faithful (3:3), and faithful obedience to his call is not only right but also guards against divine wrath and brings eternal reward (1:12; 2:13–15).

VI. THANKSGIVING AND PRAYER (1:3–12)
1. Thanksgiving (1:3–4)
2. The Outcome of Perseverance (1:5–10)
3. Prayer (1:11–12)

VI. THANKSGIVING AND PRAYER (1:3–12)

As in most Pauline letters, the prescript is followed by a thanksgiving and a prayer for the recipients. In this letter, however, the thanksgiving (vv. 3–4) and the prayer (vv. 11–12) are separated by several verses. The mention of persecution as a part of the thanksgiving (v. 4) leads to a discussion of God's justice (vv. 5–10). The Thessalonians would receive a just reward for their faithfulness, and their persecutors would receive a just punishment at the parousia. The last two verses of the chapter (vv. 11–12) return to the regular Pauline pattern and express the apostle's prayer for the Thessalonians.

1. Thanksgiving (1:3–4)

³We ought always to thank God for you, brothers, and rightly so, because your faith is growing more and more, and the love every one of you has for each other is increasing. ⁴Therefore, among God's churches we boast about your perseverance and faith in all the persecutions and trials you are enduring.

The thanks Paul expressed for his readers in 2 Thess 1:3–4 and 2:13 varies from his normal expressions of thanksgivings. They are unusual in that they include a sense of obligation. "We ought" *(opheilomen)* implies that the following giving of thanks was not an option. The impact of *opheilomen* is strengthened by the assertion that words of thanks were only "fitting" (RSV) in light of the way the Thessalonians had conducted themselves. This sense of obligation expressed both by *opheilomen* (cf. 2:13) and the phrase "and rightly so" occurs in Pauline thanksgivings only in 2 Thessalonians. This unusual wording may be explained in several different ways.

For some the unusual wording is evidence that 2 Thessalonians is not Pauline. But such a conclusion would require evidence far beyond these few words.[1] Paul's expression that he was obligated to give thanks and the blandness of this thanksgiving when compared to that in 1 Thessalonians led von Dobschuetz to the conclusion that Paul's appreciation for the community had diminished, resulting in a less fervent thanksgiving. That is, he felt "obligated" to give thanks in spite of the church's shortcomings.[2] But the mention of obligation does not necessarily reflect diminished appreciation or fervency. Paul used a form of *opheilomen* of the obligation a husband has to love his wife (Eph 5:28) and of the love that believers owe to one another (Rom 13:8). In neither instance is it implied in the context that the love of the husband or of the church was anything other than heartfelt and ardent.

Several commentators suggest that Paul's statements in 1:3 and 2:13 are in response to a message from Thessalonica. According to this theory, following the reception of 1 Thessalonians with its effusive thanksgiving for the church, the Thessalonians objected that they were undeserving of such high praise. When Timothy communicated this to Paul, he responded in 2 Thessalonians by asserting that such thanksgivings were their due and he could do no other.[3]

Although this scenario is plausible, it is also chiefly speculation. In addition it presumes the traditional order of the letters, an assumption that not all share.[4] Reacting against such speculations, R. D. Aus has argued that indictments of the propriety of giving thanks were common in Jewish and Christian prayers and as a result it is unnecessary to construct a scenario that explains its presence.[5] Aus's evidence is persua-

---

[1] E. Best correctly observes that "in the variations here there is nothing that strongly suggests authenticity or inauthenticity: a conclusion reached on other grounds will not have to be revised in light of what we find here" (*A Commentary on the First and Second Epistles to the Thessalonians* [London: A. & C. Black, 1977] 250). See the discussion of the authorship of 2 Thessalonians in the introduction for a listing of evidence and proponents of various views regarding Pauline authorship.

[2] E. von Dobschuetz, *Die Thessalonicher-briefe* (1909; reprint, Göttingen: Vandenhoeck & Ruprecht, 1974), 235–36.

[3] See F. F. Bruce, *1 and 2 Thessalonians,* WBC (Waco: Word, 1982), 144; and J. E. Frame, *A Critical and Exegetical Commentary on the Epistles of St. Paul to the Thessalonians* (Edinburgh: T & T Clark, 1960), 221.

[4] E.g., C. A. Wanamaker, *Commentary on 1 and 2 Thessalonians,* NIGTC (Grand Rapids: Eerdmans, 1990), 216–17.

[5] R. D. Aus, "Liturgical Background of the Necessity and Propriety of Giving Thanks according to 2 Thess 1:3," *JBL* 92 (1973): 432–38.

sive, but it fails to explain why terms of obligation occur only in the thanksgivings of 2 Thessalonians and not in Paul's other letters. Surely some circumstance prominent in if not peculiar to Thessalonica must have called for its use.

Based on the evidence of 1 Thessalonians 2, it does not seem too speculative to assert that Paul's opponents in Thessalonica criticized him as a flatterer. Thus he may have used the obligation terminology in 1:3 and 2:13 to make it clear to the church that his praise for them was not flattery nor merely the biased appreciation of a loving father for his children (cf. 1 Thess 2:4–6,11–12). Rather, Paul assured them, they had earned the affirmation they were about to receive, and he was obligated to give them their due. He was not simply trying to ingratiate himself to them.[6]

The present tense of the verb and infinitive ("we ought … to thank"), along with the adverb "always," indicates the continuity of the act. Consistent thanksgiving for the Thessalonians was due not just because they were "brothers" but because of their faith, love (v. 3), endurance, and faithfulness (v. 4). The apostle's words of thanksgiving were not empty flattery; they were just and proper affirmation of believers who had persevered in spite of persecution.

Two reasons for thanks are stated in v. 3. First, the apostle was thankful because the faith (*pistis*) of the Thessalonians was "growing more and more."[7] The use of a present tense verb implies that Paul was thankful for the ongoing growth of the community. But the word itself does not signify progression (as "more and more" might imply) as much as it indicates a growth beyond the expected. Their growth was "abundant" or "wonderful" growth.[8]

Paul had heard about the confusion some of the Thessalonians were experiencing regarding the parousia (2:1–12) and about the problem of those in the congregation who were idle busybodies (3:6–13). But these did not blind him to the good news he also apparently received that the faith of the church continued to grow in spite of these difficulties. In typical Pauline style he began the letter with affirmation, not correction.[9]

---

[6] Although the same problem apparently existed at the time 1 Thessalonians was written, the same obligation terminology does not occur in its thanksgivings because the assertions in 2:1–6 made modification of the thanksgivings unnecessary.

[7] Cf. 1 Thess 1:3; 3:10.

[8] BAGD, s.v. "ὑπεραυξάνω." This is the only occurrence of the word in the NT.

[9] Galatians, which begins with rebuke rather than affirmation (1:6–10), is the only exception to this pattern.

Second, the apostle was also thankful that their love *(agapē)* was "increasing." Faith and love in conjunction reflect both the theological and the ethical aspects of the Thessalonians' Christian commitment. If "faith" is directed Godward (as is common in Paul's writings; cf. Gal 3:26; Eph 1:15; Col 1:4), "love" directed toward other believers serves to balance the affirmation of the Christian growth of the church. Special emphasis is placed on the inclusiveness of the love of the church in v. 3. In a clause that would sound redundant if translated literally, the apostle celebrated the love that each and every one of them had for one another. For the use of a command to love as part of the paraenesis in Paul's epistles see the comment on 1 Thess 4:9–10 (cf. 1 Thess 1:3; 3:12).

1:4 Paul continued the thanksgiving with a result clause *(hōste* plus an infinitive), "therefore ... we boast ...," indicating that the growing faith and increasing love of the church was cause for boasting.[10] Paul boasted partly because the Thessalonians' faith and love were growing in spite of persecution. The infinitive for "boast" *(enkauchasthai)* is only used here in the New Testament. Its compounded form gives it more emphasis than the uncompounded form *(kauchaomai)* Paul frequently used.[11] "We boast" translates an emphatic construction. "We ourselves speak proudly" (NASB) stresses that Paul and his coworkers themselves spoke with joy and pride in other churches about the "perseverance and faith" of the Thessalonians.[12] The apostle's stress on this boast before other congregations served two purposes. It intensified the affirmation and at the same time implied that the Thessalonians had a reputation to live up to, thus encouraging continued perseverance.

Paul's boast on behalf of the Thessalonians derived not only from their faith and love (v. 3) but also from their "perseverance"

---

[10] Cf. 2 Cor 8:1–5, which records a Pauline boast made to the Corinthians on behalf of the Macedonian churches regarding contributions to the collection for the saints in Jerusalem.

[11] Paul sometimes depicted boasting as a vice equivalent to arrogance (1 Cor 1:29,31; 3:21; 4:7; 13:3). But just as often it is the proper rejoicing in what God has done for his people (Rom 5:2,11; Eph 2:9; Phil 3:3) or what his people have done in his service and by his power (Rom 5:3; 2 Cor 5:12; 7:14; 9:2; 11:30–12:7).

[12] The stress on "we ourselves" may imply some unstated contrast. Did Paul mean to say that he boasted although he was the founder of the community and should not boast in his own work or that he boasted although boasting is sinful and he should not boast at all? While it is possible that Paul intended some such contrast, reading such unstated ideas into the text is hazardous and unnecessary. See Best, *1 and 2 Thessalonians*, 252, for references and a brief discussion on this point.

(hypomonē) and "faith" *(pistis)*. These latter two words are both objects of "about" *(hyper)* and are presented as parallel virtues in the face of persecution. *Hypomonē* is the same word used in 1 Thess 1:3 (translated "endurance"). There Paul linked it with their "hope in our Lord Jesus Christ," indicating that it was eschatological hope that inspired continued perseverance. Here he focused on that which the church endured: "persecutions and trials" inflicted by unbelievers (cf. vv. 5–10). "Faith" *(pistis)* in v. 4 is linked with perseverance, stressing not the church's growth in faith (v. 3) but their persistence in the faith. Thus *pistis* in this context is a reference to the "faithfulness" of the church in spite of the affliction they were suffering.

This prayer of thanks mirrors 1 Thess 1:2–3, which praises the virtues of faith, love, and hope. (Endurance is, in a sense, the act of maintaining hope in spite of difficulties.) The difference between the two is that in vv. 2–4 Paul placed a much heavier emphasis on perseverance. The use of *hypomone* and *pisteōs* as synonyms, the setting off of this virtue in a clause (v. 4) separate from the mention of love and faith (v. 3), the mention that Paul himself boasted of this particular virtue on behalf of the Thessalonians, and the relatively large amount of elaboration related to persecution all highlight the perseverance of the church in the face of persecution.

"Persecutions" *(diogmois)* is an infrequent word in Paul's letters (Rom 8:35; 2 Cor 12:10; 2 Tim 3:11) and especially connotes religious persecutions. "Trials" *(thlipsesin)* literally means "pressure" and metaphorically indicates some burdensome or chafing oppression (cf. 1 Thess 1:6; 3:3,7). The modifiers of these synonyms ("all your" persecutions and afflictions "which you are enduring," RSV) indicate that the persecutions of the church were numerous and were ongoing at the time the letter was written. For some this stands in contrast with the implications of 1 Thess 2:14, "You suffered ...," which speaks of suffering as a past event.

Had the initial persecution of the church lessened by the time 1 Thessalonians was written, only to worsen again by the time 2 Thessalonians was sent? Although such a scenario is possible, it should not be overdrawn. First Thessalonians 3:3,5 implies that the church was suffering when Paul sent the letter (at least he feared they were), and Timothy's report indicates that the church was "standing firm," not that persecution had ended (1 Thess 3:6–10). The denunciation of the persecutors in 1 Thess 1:14–16 is just as scathing as that in 2 Thess 1:5–10; both are

destined for divine wrath. The persecution apparently generated from
the inception of the church continued (though possibly in various forms
and with varied intensity) through the time of the writing of both letters.[13]

2. The Outcome of Perseverance (1:5–10)

**[5]All this is evidence that God's judgment is right, and as a result you
will be counted worthy of the kingdom of God, for which you are suffering.
[6]God is just: He will pay back trouble to those who trouble you [7]and give
relief to you who are troubled, and to us as well. This will happen when the
Lord Jesus is revealed from heaven in blazing fire with his powerful angels.
[8]He will punish those who do not know God and do not obey the gospel of
our Lord Jesus. [9]They will be punished with everlasting destruction and
shut out from the presence of the Lord and from the majesty of his power
[10]on the day he comes to be glorified in his holy people and to be marveled
at among all those who have believed. This includes you, because you
believed our testimony to you.**

These verses are not a digression. Rather, they are an elaboration that
addresses one of the great hopes the apostle had for the church—that
they would persevere. Paul encouraged their perseverance by pointing
out its end result as well as the end result of opposition to the faith. God
is just. Ultimately he will reward the faithful and punish the wicked. So
Paul encouraged the church to persevere by praising their faithfulness to
date (v. 4) and by reminding them of the outcome of genuine and persistent faith. The faithful "will be counted worthy of the kingdom" (v. 5) at
the parousia. Their persecutors, on the other hand, "will be punished
with everlasting destruction" (v. 9).

Syntactically, vv. 5–10 are a continuation of the sentence that began
with the thanksgiving of v. 3. After mentioning the persecution of the
church and his boast regarding their perseverance in spite of it (v. 4),
Paul went on to assert that this was evidence *(endeigma)* of the just
judgment *(kriseōs)* of God (v. 5). But to what does "evidence" refer?

1:5 The translation "all this is evidence" (NIV) renders a Greek
text that begins with *endeigma*, referring to a recognizable sign or

---

[13] Cf. the discussion in the introduction to the commentary regarding the order in which
1 and 2 Thessalonians were written.

"plain indication" of some fact.[14] Paul may have intended "evidence" to refer to the entirety of v. 4 as the NIV's addition of "all this" implies. But there is no word for "all this" in the Greek sentence, and *endeigma* is singular, which may imply a narrower focus than the NIV insinuates. The apostle may have meant that the persecutions and trials suffered by the church stand as evidence that God is right to condemn evil men who persecute the godly (cf. v. 6). But v. 5 places the emphasis first on God's evaluation of the church, not his condemnation of the ungodly. Yet assuming the "evidence" was the "persecutions and trials" (the phrase closest to *endeigma* in the context), in what way do they prove God is right to judge the church worthy? It is possible, as a few commentators have argued, that Paul thought of persecution as a refining fire that prepared believers to participate in the kingdom of God.[15]

On the other hand, "evidence" may refer to the perseverance and faith of the church that demonstrates that God is right to count them worthy of his kingdom for which they have suffered (cf. v. 5). Grammatically, the reference to perseverance and faith is more distant from *endeigma* than are "persecutions and trials," but not so distant as to make the link impossible. Also, Paul might have referred to his "boast" on their behalf as evidence, that is, as independent testimony of the worthiness of the Thessalonians, a testimony that truthfulness obligated (cf. v. 3) him to give.[16] The text that follows, however, does not develop the idea of Paul's boast. Since vv. 5–10 elaborate both on the

---

[14] ἔνδειγμα occurs only here in Paul's letters. But the related noun ἔνδειξις occurs in Rom 3:25–26; 2 Cor 8:24; Phil 1:28 (BAGD, 262). In Philippians the confidence of the church in the face of opposition is "a sign" (ἔνδειξις) of two things at the same time: (1) that the persecutors of the church will be destroyed and (2) that the church will be saved. Although Phil 1:28 is not an exact parallel to 1 Thess 1:5 and cannot settle the matter of the proper interpretation of 2 Thess 1:5 (see J. M. Bassler, "The Enigmatic Sign: 2 Thessalonians 1:5," *CBQ* 46 [1984]: 496–510), it does demonstrate a Pauline style that can draw multiple inferences from a single sign. Thus neither the complexity of the thought nor the "word order in the sentence" (as Wanamaker asserts, *1 and 2 Thessalonians*, 221) is a hindrance to understanding both "perseverance and faith" and "persecutions and trials" as antecedents of ἔνδειγμα.

[15] See Bassler, "Enigmatic Sign," and Wanamaker, *1 and 2 Thessalonians*, 220–23, for evidence supporting the existence of this "theology of suffering" and its implications for 2 Thessalonians.

[16] See Best, *1 and 2 Thessalonians*, 254–55, who reasons that the Thessalonians were "not sure of their position on the day of judgment; Paul said, 'I have boasted about you; this is a sign that God will count you worthy then.'"

reward of the faithful and the punishment of the persecutors, it probably is best to understand that the evidence Paul mentioned was both the persecution of the church and their perseverance in the faith in spite of it. Thus God is just when he punishes the wicked and when he rewards the faithful.

Both when he rewards the righteous (vv. 5,7,10) and when he punishes the wicked (vv. 6,8–9), God's "judgment" *(krisis)* is "right" *(dikaios)*.[17] *Krisis* is not necessarily a negative concept. Judgments may be favorable for those judged. In this context the judgment involves both reward and punishment in an eschatological time frame (vv. 7–10). The Lord will come, and the world will see a radical reversal. The afflictors of the church will reap affliction from the Lord, and those afflicted for the sake of the Lord will reap rest in his marvelous presence. Persecution by the wicked demonstrates not only that the wicked deserve punishment but also that the church is on the side of good. If this were not so, the world would not persecute them. Thus God is right when he counts the church "worthy of the kingdom." At the same time the perseverance of the church (their response to persecution) is also evidence of their genuine faith. Thus their willingness to suffer for the kingdom is evidence that God is right to declare the church worthy of the kingdom.

"As a result you will be counted worthy" *(eis to kataxiōthēnai humas)* is an infinitival construction that expresses a result clause. Does this imply that being counted worthy (i.e., salvation) is the direct result of the believers' perseverance through suffering (v. 4)?[18] Certainly, suffering for the kingdom is evidence of the genuineness of one's Christianity. It indicates a depth of commitment that could only be assumed in times of ease. It implies a oneness with Christ, who suffered at the hands of evil men. But Paul nowhere argued that suffering alone is redemptive and that by itself it could make one worthy of the kingdom.

The statement "this is a plain indication of God's righteous judgment" (NASB), which immediately precedes the result clause, stresses the justice of God. "As a result you will be counted worthy" is best understood in relation to the rightness of that judgment. The church was suffering for the kingdom, and their suffering was evidence that they were properly a part of the people of God. As a result they could depend on a just God to include them in his kingdom when he came to judge

---

[17] The same adjective is translated "just" in v. 6.

[18] Wanamaker argues for this understanding (*1 and 2 Thessalonians*, 223).

the world. Their membership in the kingdom was based on the certainty of God's justice, not the efficacy of their suffering. Since God's judgment is just and since their perseverance was evidence of a genuine faith, Paul could assure the Thessalonians that they would be counted worthy of the kingdom of God.

The clause "for which you are suffering" indicates that some form of persecution was a continuing reality in Thessalonica.[19] Yet the phrase is not merely repeating the statement of v. 4 that the church was "enduring" trials. Much less is it implying that the Thessalonian Christians were suffering as a way of earning their place in the kingdom.[20] Rather than either of these, Paul was encouraging the church by placing their suffering in context. Senseless, purposeless suffering is intolerable. But for a vital cause one may suffer and consider it a small thing (Rom 8:18; Phil 1:29; 2 Cor 4:7–12). To the unstated but perpetual question of the sufferer (why?), Paul provided the answer: for the kingdom of God (cf. Acts 14:22). In the New Testament as a whole, the present suffering of the godly is often balanced by a celebration of the glories to come and/or by an assurance that God will punish the persecutors of the righteous (Luke 6:21–23; Rom 8:17; Heb 12:1–2; Jas 1:12; 1 Pet 1:3–9; 4:12–19; Jude 10–13).

1:6 God is just both in his treatment of the faithful and in his condemnation of the persecutors of the church. A conditional particle *(eiper)* introduces v. 6, but since the truth of the condition is assumed, the NIV translates the verse as an assertion, "God is just." However, this obscures the connection with v. 5. Introducing v. 6 with "since" (RSV) makes it clearer that Paul was expanding on the thought of v. 5b. The persecuted will be deemed worthy of the kingdom (v. 5b), since *(eiper)* it is just in the sight of God[21] for the afflictors to reap affliction and the afflicted to be granted rest.

"God is just" in the NIV sounds like a statement about the nature of God. But the text of vv. 6–7a focuses on the act of appropriate repayment, not on the character of God per se. Paul asserted that it is just in the eyes of God for those who afflict the church to be repaid with affliction and for the afflicted to receive rest. This is not a repudiation of the

---

[19] See the discussion in v. 4 and in the introduction regarding persecution in Thessalonica and the sequence of the Thessalonian letters.

[20] See Bruce, *1 and 2 Thessalonians*, 149.

[21] "God" is not the subject of the clause but the object of the preposition παρα (cf. NASB marginal reading).

mercy of God in favor of a law of retaliation. Mercy is not only available to the church but also to the persecutors of the church, as Paul's own life illustrated. But the existence of mercy does not nullify the validity of justice, for those who reject God's offer of mercy in the gospel will receive justice at the hands of a just God.

It is just to "pay back trouble to those who trouble you." *Antapodidōmi* ("pay back") may be used in a negative context reflecting Isa 66:6 ("It is mine to avenge, I will repay, says the Lord," Rom 12:19; cf. Heb 10:30) or in a positive context indicating an appropriate response to some gift or benevolence (Luke 14:14; 1 Thess 3:9). In both instances it implies the fair and appropriate payment of a debt. In the context of the unjust suffering of the righteous it serves as an assurance that evil men ultimately will receive the punishment they deserve. For the righteous it is somehow easier to suffer at the hands of evil with the knowledge that the evil persecutor will not escape but will be brought to justice. The promise of a balancing of accounts in the future may not eliminate the pain of suffering, but it does reduce its insult. It confirms the innocence of the victim and limits evil's success. The victim's temporary affliction is easier to bear when viewed against the eternal suffering of the afflictor.

1:7a The just judgment of God will repay afflictors with affliction (v. 6) and give rest to the afflicted ("give relief to you who are troubled," v. 7a). "Those who are troubled" translates a participle of the same verb *(thlibō)* used in v. 6 (cf. 1 Thess 3:4 and the noun *thlipsis* in 1:4; 1 Thess 1:6; 3:3,7). Verse 7a contains no verb. Most likely Paul intended "pay back" in v. 6 to carry over to v. 7a but with a positive connotation. For their faith and perseverance the believers would receive "relief" or "rest" (RSV).

The exact implications of "rest" *(anesis)* are uncertain since it is used of eschatological reward only here in Paul's writings. But clearly it involves more than just the cessation of persecution. "And to us as well" indicates that this "rest" is a state that both the Thessalonians and the evangelists would share. Linked temporally to the parousia (v. 7b) it connotes the ultimate reward, the promised rest that represents the goodness of the realized kingdom of God (cf. the "rest" in Heb 3:7–4:13, where the author used *katapausis,* citing and developing the implications of Num 14:20–23 as recited in Ps 95:11).

These verses are not often included in the discussion of the eschatol-

ogy of 2 Thessalonians. Chapter 2 dominates the eschatological land-
scape of the letter. But one of the difficulties for the interpreter of
2 Thessalonians 2 is that of explaining why the Thessalonians were
tempted to believe that "the day of the Lord had already come" (v. 2) in
spite of the instruction Paul had given them on this very point (v. 5).

Discussion of these matters comes later, but at this juncture it is helpful to note a possible link between the experience of suffering and the
dawning of the day of the Lord. The similarities between our current
passage and Isa 66:6–9 are often noted. Aus suggests that Paul used this
passage to serve two purposes. On one level he was comforting the
church "by portraying in a judgment theophany in 1:7–10 how at the
Lord's coming they will receive rest … and their persecutors will be
repaid with affliction."[22] But Paul also was anticipating the discussion
of the day of the Lord and used the Isaiah passage because Isa 66:9
"provided him with the delaying factor he needed to convince his
addressees in chapter two that the Day of the Lord had not yet
arrived."[23]

If indeed the discussion of persecution is an integral part of the discussion of the parousia in 2 Thessalonians (and not a preliminary to it),
we may better understand 2:2. The Thessalonians may have interpreted
their intense experience of suffering as an indication that the day of the
Lord had dawned. A misleading word of prophecy or letter had compounded their misunderstanding. The combination of suffering and false
teaching created an eschatological confusion that both 1:5–10 and 2:1–
12 were intended to correct. That day was coming but had not yet
arrived.

1:7b   The punishment of those who "trouble" the church will occur
when the Lord "is revealed from heaven." For the coming of the Lord
"from heaven" see 1 Thess 4:16. The Lord's arrival on that day is here
termed his "revelation" *(apokalypsei)*.[24] The word indicates the dis-
closing of something previously hidden and is most often used in the
New Testament of the revealing of God's will or nature (1 Cor 14:26;
Gal 1:12,16). It is only used here in the Thessalonian correspondence.

---

[22] Aus, "Relevance of Isaiah 66:7," 265.

[23] Ibid., 264.

[24] The NIV paraphrases the temporal use of ἐν τῇ ἀποκαλύψει τοῦ κυρίου ("at the
revelation of the Lord") at the beginning of v. 7b, inserting "This will happen when" and
translating the noun "revelation" as the verb "is revealed."

Elsewhere the Lord's arrival was termed his *parousia* or *epiphaneia* (cf. 2:8).[25]

The focus of this passage is not on the gathering of the saints (as in 1 Thess 4:13–18). Nor were the saints exhorted to Christian living in preparation for the coming (as in 1 Thess 5:6,8,11).[26] Rather, here the focus is on the judgment of evil. The church was assured that God would repay their persecutors with eternal punishment. The tone of 1:7b–9 is unusually retributive, almost celebrating the judgment upon the wicked. It is a tone that a people suffering unjustly at the hands of wicked oppressors could well appreciate.[27] Largely it echoes the message of the Old Testament regarding the day of the Lord as a day of judgment and leaves unstated the message of grace, a message proclaiming the possibility of the redemption even of ungodly persecutors of the faithful. Paul, the former persecutor of the church, highlighted his own story for the Galatians (Gal 1:13–16) and clearly understood the full reach of God's grace (see also Rom 2:3–5; 3:23–26; 5:6–11; 11:28–32).

The Lord will appear "with his powerful angels" (v. 7b). Angels as a part of the parousia are mentioned frequently in the New Testament (cf. Mark 8:38; 13:27; 1 Thess 3:13; 4:16) and are commonly associated with the presence of the Lord in the Old Testament (Exod 19:13; Zech 14:15; Isa 6:1–3; Ezek 1:4–28). The translation of Paul's phrase here is difficult. "Powerful" translates a genitive noun, not an adjective, and is open to a variety of interpretations. Literally the text reads that the Lord will come "with the angels of the power of him." Power could modify either "angels" or "him." The word order of the Greek text and the context in general suggests that "of power" refers not to powerful angels but angels who are a part of and an expression of the power of the Lord. Best's suggestion that a preferable translation would be either "the angels by which he exercises power" or "which belong to his power" is a good one.[28]

---

[25] For the use of ἀποκάλυψις in eschatological contexts see Rom 2:5; 8:19; 1 Cor 1:7; 1 Pet 1:7,13; 4:13. Aus argues that the use of the term here may derive from Jewish traditional interpretations of Isa 66:7,14–15 ("Relevance of Isaiah 66," 267). For a broader discussion of ἀποκάλυψις see A. Oepke, "καλύπτω," *TDNT* 3.563–92.

[26] 1 Thess 5:3,9 does anticipate that day as a time of judgment for the ungodly, but overall 5:1–11 focuses on the preparation of the church more than the judgment on the pagans.

[27] Cf. the imprecatory psalm (Ps 137), full of sorrow and anger, in which the psalmist pronounces a blessing on the one who "repays" Babylon, who seizes Babylonian infants and "dashes them against the rocks" (v. 8).

[28] Best, *1 and 2 Thessalonians*, 258.

The placement of the phrase "in blazing fire" *(en puri flogos)* presents difficulties as well.[29] It occurs in the Greek text at the junction of vv. 7 and 8 and may be read along with either verse. It may modify Jesus and his angels (as the NIV indicates) and depict their coming as fiery. Angels are often associated with fire in Jewish tradition (Ezek 1:13), and fire is a common element in the theophanies of the Old Testament (Exod 3:2; 19:18; Ps 18:8; Ezek 1:27). Linked with what precedes it, "in blazing fire" is consistent with the presentation of the revelation of Jesus as the Old Testament day of the Lord and serves to emphasize the awesome grandeur of his appearance.[30]

1:8 A second option is to apply the phrase *en puri flogos* to v. 8 as a description of the judgment of rebellious humanity, asserting that God will punish them with "blazing fire." Appeal again to Isaiah 66 reveals the image of fire as an image of judgment. The Lord who comes with fire brings "his rebuke with flames of fire. For with fire and with his sword the Lord will execute judgment upon all men, and many will be those slain by the Lord" (Isa 66:15–16).[31] While the language of vv. 7–9 is that of theophany, the emphasis of the verses falls on the sure and terrible punishment of persecutors of the church. This fact along with the evidence of Isa 66:16 makes it most probable that the fire of his coming is better taken as depicting the punishment of those who will not know God or obey the gospel of the Lord Jesus (v. 8).

Verse 8 does not begin a new sentence. "He will punish" translates a construction (lit., "giving retribution") that continues the sentence begun in v. 3 (and especially the discussion of God's just judgment begun in v. 5). God will pay back the persecutors of the church (v. 6) at the revelation of Jesus (v. 7), "dealing out retribution to those who do not know God" (v. 8). Retribution *(ekdikēsin)* or "vengeance" (RSV) is the responsibility of the Lord God. "It is mine to avenge ... says the Lord" (Rom 12:19; cf. Deut 32:35). But here, as often occurs in Paul, no distinction is made between the prerogatives of the Lord of the Old Testament and the Lord Jesus (cf. v. 5, where it is God who pays back those who afflict the church). This vengeance is not a limited and tem-

---

[29] Some MSS read "in flames of fire"; cf. Isa 29:6; 66:15; Dan 7:9; Acts 7:30.

[30] See Best, *1 and 2 Thessalonians,* 258–59, and Aus, "Relevance of Isaiah 66," 266, as proponents of this perspective.

[31] Wanamaker (*1 and 2 Thessalonians,* 226–27) agrees with I. H. Marshall (*1 and 2 Thessalonians,* NCB [Grand Rapids: Eerdmans, 1983], 177) that "the phrase does not point simply to a theophany but underlines the fact of judgment, and it should probably be linked with the immediately following phrase."

poral punishment designed to be corrective (as in 2 Cor 7:11 and 1 Pet 2:14) but is the well-deserved and final judgment of the day of the Lord. Its finality is a terrible part of its sting and is cited explicitly in v. 9.

The recipients of the punishment *(ekdikēsis)* are those who "do not know God and do not obey the gospel." Both clauses begin with the definite article, and such a construction would normally indicate that the author was thinking of two distinct groups. The two groups could be interpreted as the Gentiles who do not know God and the Jews who know God but are disobedient to the gospel. Although this is possible, the Greek construction does not require it, and the distinction is misleading. "Know" in this context refers to obedience as much as knowledge, and given this sense of the word both Gentiles and Jews may not "know God" (see John 8:54–55; Jer 9:6). Both unbelieving Jews and unbelieving Gentiles were willfully disobedient to the gospel as far as Paul was concerned (Rom 1:18–20; 2:12–16). Thus either a Jew or a Gentile could be described as one who does not know and does not obey God. Rather than presenting two groups, these two parallel clauses probably reflect the Old Testament background of the passage and utilize parallelism to describe a single group: unbelievers of any ethnicity.

In support of both clauses referring to a single group it should also be remembered that both clauses apparently describe those who are troubling the church (v. 7). Thus the words "do not know God" could not apply to people who are ignorant of God and/or of the gospel but only to those who have rejected them.[32] The second clause in the parallel, "and do not obey the gospel of our Lord Jesus," adds emphasis and at the same time brings back into focus the thrust of the passage. God's judgment will fall on those who neither acknowledge God nor obey the gospel, and the ultimate expression of such rejection is the persecution of the church (cf. 1 Thess 2:14–16). Thus condemnation is earned not by ignorance or by an isolated act of persecution of believers but by the settled rejection of God inspiring the persistent persecution of God's people.

1:9 Such people (the "they" of v. 9 is qualitative) who reject God and the gospel "will be punished." Paul used a construction here that is common in classical texts but does not occur elsewhere in the New Testament. It means to "pay a penalty" and implies the just imposing of punishment for a person's misdeeds. An example of such a "penalty" *(dike)* as the ancients understood it may be observed in Acts 28:4. Paul lived

---

[32] The fate of persons who have never heard the gospel is not discussed in this passage (cf. Rom 1:18–32).

through a shipwreck only to be bitten by a viper on the shore. The people of the island decided that Paul had to be a notable murderer if the goddess "Justice" *(dikē)* was so determined that he should not live.[33]

The just penalty that must be paid by those identified in v. 8 is a terrible one: "everlasting destruction" *(olethron aiōnion)*. The phrase probably should be seen in contrast to the fate of the believer: everlasting life *(zōē aiōnion)*, with "everlasting" indicating something that exists without end. "Destruction" *(olethron)* translates a word that is not frequent in the New Testament. Paul used the same term in 1 Thess 5:3, where he asserted that the "destruction" of those in darkness on the day of the Lord will be unexpected (by unbelievers) and unavoidable. Here the destruction is described as everlasting and as banishment "from the presence of the Lord." In 1 Cor 5:5 and 1 Tim 6:9 *olethron* refers to physical death or some temporal disaster. Though the term could be used of total destruction, the New Testament concept of the fate of the wicked is not that of annihilation but of everlasting punishment as enduring as the everlasting life anticipated by the saved (Matt 25:46).[34]

In addition, the subsequent phrases descriptive of this "destruction" imply continued existence but exclusion "from" *(apo* implying spatial separation) the "presence of the Lord" and the "majesty of his power."[35] Thus the word should be understood as depicting extreme and disastrous punishment, but not the obliteration of the person punished. A similar fate is depicted in Matt 25:41, where the "cursed" are sent away from the presence of the Lord and banished to the "eternal fire prepared for the devil and his angels."[36] It is ironic that those who would reject God receive as punishment God's rejection.[37] It implies

---

[33] Unlike Paul's use here, "justice" sometimes was personified as a goddess. See BAGD, s.v. "δίκη."

[34] For a critique of annihilationism see L. Dixon, *The Other Side of the Good News* (Wheaton: Victor, 1992), and the discussion of the "dark side" of judgment by S. Grenz in *Theology for the Community of God* (Nashville: Broadman & Holman, 1994), 826–39. For proannihilation arguments see J. Wenham, *The Goodness of God* (Downers Grove: InterVarsity, 1974), and E. Fudge, *The Fire That Consumes* (UK: Paternoster, 1994).

[35] These two phrases are synonymous, indicating the majestic and terrifying presence of God on the day of judgment; cf. the LXX text of Isa 2:10,19,21. Continued existence may also be suggested by the active voice of the verb. The phrase is literally, "And these will pay the penalty of eternal destruction" (cf. NASB).

[36] If "in flaming fire" is understood as part of v. 8, then fire is also part of the punishment in this passage.

[37] Contrast this with the fate of the believer who will be "with the Lord forever" (1 Thess 4:17), sharing the indescribable and eternal glory of the Lord (2 Cor 4:16–18).

that the so-called freedom from God's influence that the rebellious desire is not freedom but condemnation. It is a hellish banishment from the true and only source of goodness and blessing.

1:10 A compound temporal clause (v. 10) that modifies "they will be punished" (v. 9) concludes Paul's rather lengthy sentence (vv. 3–10). The punishment of those who trouble the church will occur "when he comes … to be glorified … and to be marveled at" (RSV). The temporal note that begins the verse is matched in the Greek text with "on that day" (RSV), which is the final phrase of the verse. The compression of the two statements into "on the day" in the NIV should not obscure that the day in mind is the day of the Lord. That day is a day of revelation, a day of relief for believers (v. 7), and a day of punishment for the ungodly (vv. 6,8–9). With v. 10 Paul turned from the fate of the persecutors back to the fate of the persecuted believers. That day of shocking and terrible judgment for the unbelievers will be a marvelous day of celebration for the church. They celebrate not in the punishment of the wicked but in the grandeur of their Lord's revelation. It is a day in which the Lord will "be glorified in his holy people" and "marveled at among all those who have believed." These two clauses are another example of synonymous parallelism (cf. vv. 8–9).

The first clause uses an unusual compound verb *(endoxazomai)* that occurs in the New Testament only here and in v. 12. It probably is derived from the Greek rendering of Ps 89:7 (88:8 in the LXX), which tells of God being honored or glorified (the same verb is used) "in the council of the holy ones." The "holy" *(hagioi)* ones in the psalm are the angelic host, and Paul may have reference to them here as well (cf. 1 Thess 3:3). But he also frequently referred to the church as God's "holy ones" (cf. Rom 15:25; 2 Cor 1:1; Phil 1:1). Since *hagioi* is parallel to "all those who have believed" in the following clause, the NIV probably is right to take it as a reference to God's "holy people."

The second clause also echoes the Psalms (cf. 68:35; 67:36 in the LXX), but Paul used the verb "to be marveled at" *(thaumasthēnai)* rather than the adjective "awesome" *(thaumastos),* used by the psalmist, and replaced the psalmist's phrase "among his holy ones" ("in your sanctuary") with a reference to those who have "believed."[38] In both

---

[38] Πιστεύσασιν, an aorist participle, seems an unusual choice of tense. One would expect a present. It may indicate that Paul was thinking of the believers' entrance into the faith rather than their lives of faith. But if Paul was citing an existing tradition in these verses, the choice of tense may not have been his and may have had no special significance for him.

clauses the "holy" ones and "those who have believed" may either constitute the assembly among which the Lord is honored and marveled at
or the agents who give the Lord honor and awe. The preposition with
both is *en* and may introduce phrases expressing agency or sphere. If
the believers are not the agents expressing their respect for the Lord,
perhaps it is the unbelievers who must finally kneel and confess that
"Jesus Christ is Lord" (Phil 2:11). Although this is possible, v. 10 is presented as a contrast to the fate of the wicked in vv. 8–9. The contrast
works best if the banishment of the wicked is matched by the gathering
together of the holy ones and the punishment of the unbeliever is balanced by those who have believed celebrating the coming of their glorious Lord.

The mention of the fact that the Lord would "be marveled at among
all those who have believed" inspired a parenthetical comment[39] that
brings the Thessalonians back into the foreground of the letter. Paul
reminded them that they would be included among those glorifying and
marveling at the Lord "because you believed our testimony." The "testimony" believed was the basis for the Thessalonians' inclusion among
the saints, and so in this instance (in contrast to 2 Cor 1:12) "testimony"
is a reference to the apostolic proclamation of the gospel (cf. 1 Cor 1:6).
The NIV accurately clarifies the function of the causal clause by supplying "this includes you," which is not in the Greek text. This parenthetical statement personalized the tradition cited in the preceding
verses, but it did more that just that. It also reminded the readers that it
was the acceptance of the apostolic gospel that separated the church
from those who "do not obey the gospel" (v. 8). Thus the stark contrast
between the fate of believers (v. 10) over against that of unbelievers (vv.
8–9), together with the certainty of the coming of the day of judgment,
served as an eloquent argument for continued faith. For the alternative
to obedience is nothing less than certain condemnation.

Following the address and salutation, Paul began this letter in typical
form with a thanksgiving for the faith of the Thessalonians. Especially
he thanked God for their perseverance (vv. 3–4). He then elaborated on

---

[39] "In that day" (ἐν τῇ ἡμέρᾳ ἐκείνῃ) is the last phrase of the Greek text and fits neatly
with the first half of the verse (cf. the NASB, which moves the clause into the middle of
v. 10a). The causal clause "because you believed ..." (ὅτι ἐπιστεύθη ...) interrupts the
flow of the Greek text and is clearly an insertion. It may indicate that Paul was using (and
modifying) an existing tradition. The unusual vocabulary and frequent allusions to if not
quotations of the LXX, the shift from second person in vv. 3–7a to third person in vv. 7b–
10, and the parallelism in vv. 8–10 all support this possibility.

the theme of perseverance by assuring the Thessalonians that a terrible punishment was prepared for the ungodly who persecuted them (vv. 6,8–9), while the faithful could anticipate God's rest in the glorious kingdom of the Lord Jesus (vv. 5,7,10). The last two verses of the chapter supply the intercessory prayer one would normally expect to see immediately after the thanksgiving.

3. Prayer (1:11–12)

11With this in mind, we constantly pray for you, that our God may count you worthy of his calling, and that by his power he may fulfill every good purpose of yours and every act prompted by your faith. 12We pray this so that the name of our Lord Jesus may be glorified in you, and you in him, according to the grace of our God and the Lord Jesus Christ.

1:11 "With this in mind" has no clear antecedent. The neuter pronoun "this" probably looks back to the preceding passage as a whole and the Thessalonians' salvation and perseverance through persecution. The apparent disjunction between vv. 11–12 and what precedes is caused in part by a temporal shift. Verses 5–10 deal with God's future judgment, while vv. 11–12 primarily return attention (as in vv. 3–4) back to the believers' current Christian life. Thus the "this" that Paul had "in mind" probably was the Thessalonians' perseverance until and participation in the future glory of the day of the Lord (vv. 5–10). Mindful of achieving that goal, he prayed for the character of their current Christian lives.[40] Even as God had called them, so they must live as people worthy of his kingdom, anticipating its full and final coming (cf. 1 Thess 2:12).[41]

The apostle's consistent concern for the church is stressed by the use of "constantly" *(pantote)* along with the present tense of the verb

---

[40] Thus "with this in mind" has a mildly telic force, and indeed εἰς ὃ is translated by some "to this end" (NASB), which more clearly indicates the element of purpose. This does not mean that living a worthy life (vv. 11–12) serves the purpose of securing future salvation for the Christian. But as Frame has succinctly observed, while it is certainly true that "salvation is assured to those who are in Christ, ... the test of being in Christ is ethical" (*1 and 2 Thessalonians,* 239).

[41] Thus while the concern with being "worthy" of the kingdom in God's sight (vv. 5,11) is not the grammatical antecedent of εἰς ὃ, one could argue for being "worthy" as an overall theme of the introductory thanksgiving and prayer.

"pray" (cf. 1 Thess 1:2).[42] The content of the prayer is stated in two lengthy purpose clauses (the second begins in v. 12). The first clause requests that God would (a) count the church worthy of his "calling" and (b) fulfill every good purpose and deed of faith. This "calling" *(klēseōs)* of God is the call to participate in the glories of the kingdom. It was the call to salvation vocalized in the apostolic "testimony." The link between the two is not only consistent with the reference to the "testimony" believed by the Thessalonians in v. 10 but also with Paul's prayer in 1 Thess 2:12, which refers to the God "who calls you into his kingdom and glory," an act accomplished by apostolic evangelization. Today, as then, those who voice the gospel call must speak with boldness and awe. For their message is not a matter of personal opinion, and its power is not limited to their personal eloquence. They relay to humanity God's call into his kingdom. The privilege of participation in this divine purpose must ever instill humility and confidence in those entrusted by God with this vital task (cf. 1 Thess 2:4).

Paul prayed that the church may be worthy of that kingdom. The verb used *(axiōsē)* may mean "count worthy" (its normal meaning) or "make worthy" (a rare meaning). The former would focus on the determination of God to "consider" (NIV) the church worthy and would imply not so much godly living by the church as the application of the grace of God. On the other hand, the verb may focus on the growing Christian character of the church God is "making" (RSV) worthy. Although this is an uncommon use of the word, it is in line with the emphasis on ethical acts in the remainder of the verse. However, Paul may not have been making a sharp distinction between the two since the extension of grace and a resultant growth in godliness are inseparable in the apostle's teachings (cf. Eph 2:10). The absence of either makes a mockery of the other. In a sense, then, Paul's prayer requests that the kind of "evidence" (v. 5) of membership in the kingdom already displayed among the Thessalonians would continue in abundance and fur-

---

[42] The Greek text contains a καὶ before the verb "we pray" ("also," NASB). Its interpretation is uncertain. "We [in addition to others] also pray for you," "we pray for you also [i.e., in addition to others for whom we pray]," and "we [in addition to giving thanks] also pray for you" are all possible translations. But the first two options introduce unnamed others into the interpretive mix, and the latter expresses a link with a verb too distant (v. 3). While a case may be made for considering the word insignificant and dropping it from translation (see Best, *1 and 2 Thessalonians,* 268), the καὶ fits with both common usage and the tone of this passage if used as an intensive ("with this in mind, indeed, we constantly pray for you").

ther validate God's call in their lives.

The second part of v. 11 unambiguously expresses Paul's concern for ethical behavior. Paul asked that God might "fulfill" every good intention, every act of faith. The verb connotes bringing something to its fullest expression and so is a request for God to bring to maturity the faith that was already operative in the Thessalonians (cf. 1 Thess 3:10). The good purpose may be God's (cf. Phil 2:13)[43] but must also be owned by the believer if it is to be fulfilled. Whereas "purpose" in other biblical authors refers to the divine will, Paul also used it of the human determination or resolve to do something (cf. Rom 10:1; Phil 1:15). Since in this instance the phrase is parallel to "every act prompted by ... faith," it probably refers to the righteous resolve within the Thessalonians to live in a godly manner. This is supported by "good" (agathōsunē), which Paul used elsewhere of human goodness (cf. Rom 15:14; Gal 5:22; Eph 5:9). Yet this is not goodness as humans might define it but that which accords with the divine will. The believer guided by "good purpose" (eudokia) is the opposite of a person who would "delight in wickedness" (2:12).

An "act prompted by your faith" recalls the affirmation in the thanksgiving of 1 Thess 1:3. If a good resolve expresses the internal will to live a godly life, the fulfilling of every work of faith is the outward expression of that resolve. "By his power" is actually the last phrase of the verse and does not include a pronoun.[44] Although it may modify the verb "fulfill" and so apply to every good purpose and to every act of faith, its location argues for applying it primarily to the last phrase, "work of faith" (RSV). If this approach is taken, then the phrase stresses that the works of faith were not the accomplishment of the will of the Thessalonians alone but were the product of the power of God as well.

1:12 Following v. 11, "we pray this" does not occur in Paul's text, and v. 12 does not begin a new sentence. Rather, it continues Paul's prayer by placing a result clause ("so that ...") after the purpose statement of v. 11. The glorification of Christ's name and of the church in him was also Paul's prayer, but it results only if that which Paul prayed for in v. 11 is indeed fulfilled. A church that God counts "worthy" and

---

[43] The references to the Thessalonians in the NIV (every good purpose "of yours" and every act prompted by "your" faith) do not occur in the Greek text.

[44] It is also possible (perhaps preferable in the absence of a possessive pronoun) to translate the phrase ἐν δυνάμει as an adverb, "and that he may powerfully fulfill ..." or "that he may fulfill [in you] every ... work of faith powerfully."

in which God is powerfully working will as a result bring glory to the name of Christ and be glorified themselves in his name.

Paul prayed "that the name of our Lord Jesus may be glorified in you." To glorify a name is to praise and/or enhance the reputation of the person represented by that name. But when would this occur? Was Paul referring to the glorification of the Lord by his saints at the parousia? "Be glorified" does repeat the unusual verb from v. 10, which in that context is clearly a reference to the day of the Lord. Also it is true that "the whole tenor of 2 Th. 1:3ff is eschatological."[45] In addition, the prayer that God would consider the church worthy (v. 11) may refer to the final judgment. However, as we have already noted, the focus of the passage has shifted to the present in vv. 11–12, as is indicated both with the mention of works of faith (v. 11) and with the reference to grace in v. 12.[46] It is far from certain that the reference to the name of the Lord being glorified is another citation from Isaiah 66.[47] More likely it is an echo from v. 10, but in the context of vv. 11–12 Paul was concerned that the church in the present bring glory to the name of the Lord as a result of God's grace toward them and their works of faith. With this understanding, "in you" may be locative (meaning "in your midst") but more likely is instrumental, "by you," meaning as a result of your words and works. God may be "glorified" or praised for his great works (cf. Gal 1:24). He is also "glorified" by the actions of his people when they are obedient and generous (2 Cor 9:13), sexually pure (1 Cor 6:20), and when they live in harmony with one another (Rom 15:6).[48] In short, Christlike behavior is more important than words of praise in the glorifying of the Lord. For praise from a life transformed by the power of the Spirit rings true and sweet, but godless living makes a mockery of praise.

Paul prayed not only that the name of the Lord would be glorified, but also with the words "and you in him" he prayed that the church might be glorified in Christ. Glorification reaches its culmination at the

---

[45] Best, *1 and 2 Thessalonians,* 271.

[46] Cf. B. Rigaux, *Saint Paul: Les Epitres aux Thessaloniciens* (Paris: Jl. Gabalda; Gembloux: J. Duculot, 1956), 641.

[47] Isa 66:5 does refer to glorifying the name of the Lord, but the verb is the uncompounded form, not ἐνδοξάζω, and references to the name of the Lord are too common in Paul's writings to prove a link by itself.

[48] The references above are examples of the Pauline use of δόξαζω rather than ἐνδόξαζο, but the implications for the life of the church are unaffected by the variation in the verb.

parousia (Rom 8:17–18,30; Phil 3:21). But if that culmination means sharing the likeness of Christ, the present expression of glorification likewise must be the growing Christlikeness of the believer (2 Cor 3:18). That the Thessalonians should be glorified "in him" (as they glorify his name) and should be glorified "according to the grace of our God and the Lord Jesus Christ" expresses a necessary reciprocal relationship between the obedience that glorifies God and the growing Christlikeness of the true follower of Christ. Paul was not praying simply that the believers might receive honor through their association with Christ either in the present (cf. 1 Cor 12:26) or in the future at his coming but that through the grace of God they might be transformed in Christ.

The transformation of the believer, both in the present and in the future, is possible only through grace. The phrase that modifies grace, "of our God and the Lord Jesus Christ," is unique in Paul's letters in one respect. "God" and "Lord Jesus Christ" are both governed by a single article that occurs at the beginning of the phrase. This construction would allow both "God" and "Lord" to apply to Jesus (cf. John 20:28; 2 Pet 1:11). Although Paul frequently applied to Jesus certain Old Testament references to Yahweh and often ascribed to Jesus tasks that are divine prerogatives, it is unlikely that he intended to refer to Jesus as "God and Lord." The construction probably resulted from the combining of the phrase "according to the grace of God" (which normally has the definite article before "God," e.g., 1 Cor 3:10) with "and the Lord Jesus Christ" (which normally does not use a definite article, e.g., 2 Thess 1:1). Paul's intent was to link grace with both God the Father and the Lord Jesus, not to exclude the Father from the formula.

VII. REGARDING THE DAY OF THE LORD (2:1–17)

The coming of the Lord will be a day of judgment. The persecutors of the church will reap the harsh punishment of being banished from the presence of God. But when will that day occur? Has it already begun? The church was after all experiencing persecution appropriate to the end times. And some were asserting that day had already arrived. If that day had not arrived, how would the believers know this, and how would they recognize the day when it did arrive? Although there is no mention of a letter from the Thessalonians that requested that Paul supply answers to such questions, it seems highly likely that Paul was responding in chap. 2 to concerns addressed to him by the Thessalonian church.

The organization of this middle portion of the letter is complicated. The teaching that begins at 2:1 extends at least through v. 12. The NIV places a major break after v. 12 and inserts a new heading, indicating a shift to a different topic. But ending Paul's treatment of the parousia of Jesus at v. 12 leaves it unconnected from its concluding exhortation, "so then brothers stand firm," which occurs at v. 15 (cf. the exhortations that conclude 1 Thess 4:13–18; 5:1–11). Also, if a major break is assumed between vv. 12 and 13, it has the effect of isolating vv. 13–15, making it difficult to understand how they are integrated into the flow of chap. 2. Perhaps the most telling argument against assuming a major break at the end of v. 12 is the fact that v. 13 begins in the middle of a contrast.

The "but we" that begins the verse contrasts the believers in vv. 13–14 with those in vv. 11–12 who are destined for condemnation. "They perish because they refused to love the truth" (v. 10b) as "all will be condemned who have not believed the truth but have delighted in wick-

edness" (v. 12). By way of contrast Paul thanked God that God chose
the Thessalonian Christians "to be saved through the sanctifying work
of the Spirit and through belief in the truth" (v. 14). It seems unlikely
that a major break in topic would occur between vv. 12 and 13, dividing
such an emphatically stated contrast. A final indication that the passage
ends with v. 15 rather than v. 12 is the second mention of teachings
received "by word of mouth or by letter" (v. 15; cf. v. 2). The repetition
of these phrases forms an *inclusio* bracketing the entire passage.

Admittedly, vv. 13–14 express a thanksgiving. But this particular
expression of thanks is so entwined in the thought of the preceding passage that it is better understood as a part of that passage rather than indicating a formal thanksgiving. Rhetorical-critical analysis of the chapter
leads to much the same conclusion.[1] The introduction of the passage
(vv. 1–2, the rhetorical *partitio*) identifies two matters Paul should
address in the following section of proofs (the rhetorical *probatio*). One
is the assertion that the day of the Lord had not arrived. Proofs to this
point are provided in vv. 3–10. The second assertion in v. 2 is that the
Thessalonians were not to succumb to the false teaching. Verses 13–15
explain why the readers were not to allow false teachings to mislead
them. They were people of truth, not deception, destined for salvation,
not condemnation, and so were to adhere to the truth of the apostolic
gospel. Thus vv. 13–15 are an integral part of the discussion introduced
in vv. 1–2.

Taking 2:1–15 as a unit, we find that the first two verses of the chapter introduce the primary concern—attempts to delude the church
regarding the time of the parousia. Verses 3–10 provide proofs indicating that the day of the Lord could not have yet arrived. The proofs of
vv. 3–4 and 8–10 (derived largely from the OT) are interrupted by a
Pauline parenthesis (vv. 5–7) reminding the Thessalonians that Paul
taught them these things previously. Verses 5–7 highlight especially his
earlier teachings that the parousia was being delayed until the appropriate time. Verses 11–15 contrast the dangers of succumbing to delusion
and the blessings of holding to the truth, delivering a final encouragement to the church to stand firm in the apostolic traditions. The message
of 2:1–15 then called forth a concluding prayer (vv. 16–17) requesting
God's encouragement and assistance that the Thessalonians might
indeed remain firm in the faith.

---

[1] W. Hughes, "The Rhetoric of 1 Thessalonians," in *The Thessalonian Correspondence*,
BETL 87 (Leuven: University Press, 1990), 57.

The Issue Identified (2:1–2)

[1]Concerning the coming of our Lord Jesus Christ and our being gathered to him, we ask you, brothers, [2]not to become easily unsettled or alarmed by some prophecy, report or letter supposed to have come from us, saying that the day of the Lord has already come.

1:1 The first words of the Greek text are, "We ask you brothers." "We ask" *(erōtōmen)* or its synonym "we urge" *(parakaloumen;* cf. 1 Thess 4:1; 5:12,14) often marks a transition in Paul's writing. A direct address such as "brothers" is also a common part of the Pauline transition formula (cf. 2 Thess 1:3; 2:1; 3:1,6). But at the same time the reference to brotherhood is more than a formula to introduce a new admonition. It reiterated the familial bond that existed between Paul and the Thessalonians and helped establish the context in which he gave his exhortations to the church. He exhorted them as one who loved them, as their brother in Christ, as a spiritual parent giving guidance to his children in the faith (cf. 1 Thess 2:7–8,11–12).

The conventions of ancient rhetoric called for an author to announce his topic at the beginning of a presentation. In this instance Paul did so, and the formula he used for this purpose *(de … hyper),* "Now concerning …" (RSV), was a variation of the *peri de …* formula found in 1 Thessalonians and 1 Corinthians (see 1 Thess 4:9 for references; cf. 2 Cor 12:8 for the use of *hyper* in the same sense as *peri).* The topic is stated in two phrases: (1) "the coming of our Lord Jesus Christ" and (2) "our being gathered to him" (v. 1). The coming *(parousia)* of the Lord is a time of judgment upon evil (v. 8,10b; cf. 1:7b–10; 1 Thess 4:15; 5:3,9) and a time of celebration for those who will share the glory of their Lord (v. 14). Paul juxtaposed Jesus' coming and the gathering of the saints as coincident events that are part of a single happening (1 Thess 4:15–17).[2]

"Our being gathered to him" includes a word for gathering *(episyn-agōgē)* that is unusual in the New Testament.[3] The cognate verb *episyn-*

---

[2] G. S. Holland may well be correct that the two phrases had become "a dogmatic *locus,* a traditional way of referring to the events of the end" in general. See *The Tradition That You Received from Us: 2 Thessalonians* (Ph.D. diss., University of Chicago, 1986), 95.

[3] It occurs elsewhere only in Heb 10:25, where it refers to assembly for worship. D. E. Hiebert says: "These assemblies are a precious foretaste and anticipation of that future assembly of the saints 'unto him' when our Lord will be present, not as now by His Spirit only, but in the visible glory of His person" (*The Thessalonian Epistles* [Chicago: Moody, 1971], 301).

agō is slightly more common. In the Old Testament literature of the exile the verb is sometimes used of the future, glorious "gathering" of Israel (e.g., Isa 52:12). The gospel writers seem to reflect this eschatological use of the verb. It was used to express Jesus' desire to gather his people to him (Matt 23:37; Luke 13:34) and of the church's hope of a gathering together of all the people of God when the Son of man comes "in clouds with great power and glory" (Mark 13:27; cf. Matt 24:31). Thus the coming of the Lord and the gathering of his people are essentially two ways of referring to the day of the Lord, and this is the stated topic of 2:1–15.

2:2 The second verse of chap. 2 expresses Paul's specific concerns related to that day. The finite verb of v. 1, "we ask you," is completed in v. 2 by the two infinitives "not to become … unsettled or alarmed." The shift in tense between the two infinitives (the first is aorist; the second is present) implies an unsettling event that generates a state of alarm among the members of the church. Paul wanted to prevent the false teaching that "the day of the Lord has already come" from disturbing the church.

The infinitive "to become unsettled" *(saleuthēnai)* used literally refers to something that has been shaken by a storm (Luke 6:48) or caused to totter in an earthquake (cf. Acts 16:26). The addition of *apo tou noos* (not translated in the NIV but literally "from the mind"), meaning something like "in mind" (RSV), implies that Paul was worried about the believers becoming disoriented or confused by false teaching. The combination implies a spiritual instability that ought not characterize believers grounded in the truth and maturing in Christ (cf. Eph 4:14). The second infinitive, "alarmed," depicts a frightened or disturbed state. The same word occurs in Mark 13:7 as a caution against premature expectation of the end: "When you hear of wars and rumors of wars do not be alarmed. Such things must happen, but the end is still to come."

Such alarm and confusion in the face of false teaching is the opposite of standing firm in the faith (cf. v. 15). The word "easily" may imply that the church was immature and easy to lead astray. On the other hand, the same Greek word *(tacheōs)* can be translated "quickly" or "readily" in a temporal sense (cf. Gal 1:6). Whichever was intended, the word implies a mild reprimand. The faithful should be difficult to sway from the apostolic faith, even if the false teachers misrepresent themselves. The Pauline church was expected to test "prophetic" words spoken, clinging to the good and rejecting the evil (1 Thess 5:21–22).

How did the false teaching come to the Thessalonian church? The three phrases "by prophecy, report or letter" are not as precise as they may first appear. Also the statement "supposed to have come from us" may apply to all three sources mentioned or to the final two (which are repeated alone in v. 15) or to "letter" alone. Finally, "supposed to have come from us" may allude to a Pauline teaching that was misunderstood (i.e., they supposed Paul meant something that he did not intend to communicate)[4] or to a false teaching that someone else delivered to the church.

The first source mentioned, "by prophecy" *(dia pneumatos),* is literally "by spirit." It probably refers to a Spirit-inspired utterance of some sort with emphasis on the revelatory nature of the utterance. Prophecy, interpreted tongues (cf. 1 Cor 14:5,12), or any other exercise by which a speaker claimed to guide the church by Spirit-inspired insight could serve as the specific avenue of the teaching. Paul warned the church against the error of either dismissing such spiritual teachers out of hand or accepting their words uncritically (cf. 1 Thess 5:19–22; 1 Cor 14:36–37). The apostolic teaching regarding the day of the Lord in vv. 3–15 (also that in 1 Thess 4:13–5:11) is the kind of information the church could use to evaluate teachings claiming spiritual authority.

The second avenue of false teaching, "by report" *(dia logou),* is literally "by word." If it is intended as a contrast to "by spirit," it refers to speech emphasizing its rational nature. Arguments derived by reasoning from the Old Testament or from the life of Jesus might fall into this category. *Logos,* however, is a flexible term applicable to a wide range of utterances and not limited to the nonpneumatic. It may refer to the spoken word but often was used of a teaching passed on in the church either in oral or written form (e.g., Acts 1:1; "book," *logon,* refers to Luke). Although *logos* does not necessarily refer to an oral over against a written "word" or "teaching," in this context it probably was intended to contrast with "letter."

The final possible source of the church's confusion and anxiety regarding the day of the Lord was a "letter" *(epistolēs).* Several possibilities exist for identifying the letter. Was Paul referring to (a) that letter we now have as 1 Thessalonians, (b) another genuine Pauline letter that is no

---

[4] Such misunderstandings did occur, as 1 Cor 5:9–11 documents. Paul warned the Corinthians to stay away from immoral persons, meaning (but apparently not clearly communicating) that they were to avoid so-called "brothers" who lived immorally. He later explained that he did not mean withdraw from all who lived immorally since doing so would require retreating from the world altogether.

longer extant, or (c) a letter forged in Paul's name?[5] If Paul was alluding to 1 Thessalonians,[6] what in that letter might the church have misunderstood?[7] Could a reading of 5:1–11 have convinced the church that "the day of the Lord has already come"? This seems possible only if the "day" is not a reference to the parousia itself but to the period immediately preceding it (that time of persecution for the church during which the ungodly feel secure; cf. 5:3; 2 Thess 1:6–7). The event of judgment at the coming of the Lord on the day of the Lord (which 1 Thess 5:2–3 presents) is unmistakable. Since the "day" is so tightly connected with judgment, it seems unlikely that a misreading of 1 Thessalonians 5 would have caused the problem addressed in these verses.

Perhaps Paul was referring to an authentic letter from him and his coworkers that was misunderstood by the Thessalonians and is no longer extant. The theory of a lost letter, by its very nature, can never be disproven entirely. In this instance, however, it seems unlikely given the comments in the conclusion to the letter, where Paul felt it necessary to call special attention to his signature (see 3:17). The point of his comments there seems to be that the church should disregard any letters supposedly from him if they do not bear this mark. Such precautions assume the existence of spurious letters circulated in Paul's name, and thus it is not unreasonable to assume that he had such a false letter in mind when he composed the warning in 2:2. The reason for such forgery is evident. It would allow someone to usurp whatever influence Paul enjoyed in the churches.

If forgeries existed in the first century, how would the church know a particular letter was genuinely from Paul? Three ways are indicated in the Thessalonian correspondence. First, the carrier of a letter was a guarantor of its authenticity. Timothy, known and trusted by both the church and the apostle, apparently served as the courier between the

---

[5] If Paul did not have a particular false letter in mind, one might say he was referring to a "hypothetical" forgery. Such terminology, however, should not be used to minimize the very real threat of false teachers using any means available to promote their error.

[6] Which of course requires presuming not only the Pauline authorship of both letters but also that 2 Thessalonians was written after 1 Thessalonians.

[7] C. L. Mearns argues that 1 Thessalonians was not misunderstood but that Paul had changed his mind ("Early Eschatological Development in Paul: The Evidence of I and II Thessalonians," *NTS* 27 [1980–81]: 137–57). But too little time passed between the writing of these letters for such a development of Paul's eschatology. Also Paul explicitly disavowed responsibility for the erroneous teaching. Verses 2,5,15 make no sense if the overall passage is a Pauline correction of his earlier beliefs.

apostle and the Thessalonians (1 Thess 3:1–3,6). The carrier of a letter in antiquity commonly served as the envoy of the sender. He both delivered the document and if necessary interpreted the intent of the author. Often, as in the case of Timothy, the letter carrier also returned with a verbal or written reply.

A second assurance of genuineness was the signature of the author. Correspondence often was produced by an amanuensis, the first-century version of a personal secretary (cf. Rom 16:22). The amount of freedom allowed the amanuensis was determined by the person using his services. When it was deemed necessary, the author of the correspondence wrote a final word and in this way "signed" the letter personally. Second Thessalonians 3:17 is an example of just such a practice (cf. Gal 6:11; 1 Cor 16:21).

The third assurance of authenticity was the content of the letter itself. The teachings and the lifestyle of the apostle were known to the churches he established. Paul on occasion appealed to this knowledge as a guide for the believers (cf. 2:5; 3:7; 1 Thess 1:5). Teachings that were at odds with those they had from the apostle in person were to be rejected (cf. Gal 1:8–9). Even so in this instance the events Paul cited that would precede the parousia were not new to the church, as Paul reminded them (v. 5).

The false teaching is identified in v. 2. Somehow the church had heard that "the day of the Lord has already come." The day of the Lord in Scripture is a fairly flexible concept. The title could signify a specific event of judgment at the end of time or a complex of events that may somewhat extend its temporal scope. In this passage, however, Paul used "the day" of a climactic point of eschatological judgment concurrent with the "splendor of the coming" of the Lord Jesus (v. 8). The "rebellion" and the revelation of the "man of lawlessness" (v. 3) are presented as preliminary.

How then could the Thessalonians have believed that the day of the Lord had "come" (v. 2)?[8] Might they have believed that that day was near but that it had not actually arrived? The perfect tense verb *(enestēken)* means "has arrived," not "is imminent."[9] Elsewhere Paul

---

[8] The NIV inserts "already" as appropriate to the context. There is no corresponding Greek word in the sentence.

[9] Attempts to use the verb to mean that the day is at hand (but not actually here) run afoul of both the normal usage of the verb and the argument of vv. 3–8, which works as a refutation of the proposition that the day has arrived and could not refute the proposition that the day is near.

used *enestēken* to signify "present" in contrast to future events (Rom 8:38; 1 Cor 3:22) and to speak of the "present" distress in which the church lived (1 Cor 7:26). When Paul did wish to describe the imminence of the parousia, he used different terms (see Rom 13:12; Phil 4:5).[10] In addition, the apostle's argument presumes that the church had heard that they were living in the day of the Lord already, and it is this that he corrected. If the Thessalonians were saying simply that the day of the Lord was imminent, Paul should not have corrected them. For he himself taught the same thing repeatedly. It seems best then to allow *enestēken* its normal meaning and assume that the Thessalonians had heard that the day of the Lord had arrived in some immediate and climactic sense.

In what sense then might the Thessalonians have thought that the day had arrived? Those who succumbed to the erroneous teaching could not have understood the concept as referring narrowly to the climactic judgment of the world as described in 1:5–10. Such a physical and cosmic happening would be impossible to confuse with any other event, no matter how traumatic. Somehow they must have either spiritualized the event or misunderstood its character.

Schmithals has argued that it was Gnostic teaching that misled the Thessalonians.[11] In general, Gnostic thought held that the Lord had come with the coming of the Holy Spirit and that the spiritual self would ascend at the death of the body. Thus the day of the Lord was already present spiritually, and a future resurrection and judgment was both unwanted and unnecessary (cf. 2 Tim 2:18). The supposition of a Gnostic heresy, however, cannot explain the Thessalonian confusion. Gnosticism as a fully structured Christian heresy is not documented in the mid-first century, and even at a later date the teachings of Gnosticism were not uniform enough to state with certainty the effect they might have had among the Thessalonian Christians.[12] Even more to the point, if the problem was Gnostic teachings, Paul's argument in vv. 3–9 represents an unlikely and oblique response by an apostle who was

---

[10] ἤγγικεν and ἐγγύς respectively.

[11] W. Schmithals, *Paul and the Gnostics* (Nashville: Abingdon, 1972), 146.

[12] Adding to the improbability is the variety of thought within Gnosticism. M. L. Peel has pointed out that while in general within Gnostic writings "eschatological goals are conceived of as being realized in the present … certain aspects of Gnostic eschatological hope remain outstanding and futuristic in orientation. And … it can even be shown that some Gnostics did believe in a form of resurrection" ("Gnostic Eschatology and the New Testament," *NovT* 12 [1970]: 155).

capable of being much more direct.[13] It seems unlikely then that the Thessalonians had somehow spiritualized the resurrection (either through Gnostic teachings or as a result of a misunderstanding of some Pauline teaching such as those recorded in Rom 8:9–11 or 2 Cor 5:17) and as a result assumed that the day of the Lord had already fully come.

More likely the Thessalonians had presumed that the beginning of tribulation was the immediate predecessor of climactic judgment and that both were part of the day of the Lord (cf. the reference to both in Mark 13:9–26). Such a perspective could easily include the expectation that the parousia would come shortly after the tribulations began (cf. Mark 13:20). Mark 3:7 may have been intended as a warning against this very type of error. If the Thessalonians believed that the troubles they were enduring were the woes preceding the parousia,[14] an intense level of expectation would result. The delay of the parousia for a community convinced that it must occur in a very short time could spell the end of faith for many of its adherents. Paul sought to defuse the situation not by arguing that the parousia was distant (the events described in vv. 3–9 could occur in fairly short order) but by highlighting intermediate events that distanced their immediate suffering from the event of the parousia. In effect Paul struggled with the double-edged task of maintaining eschatological expectation and at the same time reducing its intensity in the interest of maintaining the health of the community. The emphasizing of intermediate events between the Thessalonian's current experiences and the parousia could serve such a purpose admirably.

1. Eschatological Error Corrected (2:3–10)

[3]Don't let anyone deceive you in any way, for that day will not come until the rebellion occurs and the man of lawlessness is revealed, the man doomed to destruction. [4]He will oppose and will exalt himself over everything that is called God or is worshiped, so that he sets himself up in God's temple, proclaiming himself to be God.

[5]Don't you remember that when I was with you I used to tell you these things? [6]And now you know what is holding him back, so that he may be revealed at the proper time. [7]For the secret power of lawlessness is already

---

[13] Cf. his refutation of those who denied a physical resurrection in 1 Cor 15:1–12 or the condemnation of those who teach "that the resurrection has already taken place" in 2 Tim 2:18.

[14] As R. D. Aus, "God's Plan and God's Power: Isaiah 66 and the Restraining Factors of 2 Thess 2:6–7," *JBL* 96 (1977): 263–64.

at work; but the one who now holds it back will continue to do so till he is taken out of the way. [8]And then the lawless one will be revealed, whom the Lord Jesus will overthrow with the breath of his mouth and destroy by the splendor of his coming. [9]The coming of the lawless one will be in accordance with the work of Satan displayed in all kinds of counterfeit miracles, signs and wonders, [10]and in every sort of evil that deceives those who are perishing. They perish because they refused to love the truth and so be saved.

2:3 The statement that begins in v. 3 is lengthy and complex. The intent of the author was to list events that refute the teaching that the day of the Lord had arrived (v. 2). The sentence, however, is incomplete. Paul listed and elaborated upon proofs in a conditional structure. The negative conditions are stated first, lest "the rebellion occurs and the man of lawlessness is revealed" (v. 3b). The "then" clause, however, was left unstated. The NIV clarifies the sentence by adding "that day will not come," which does not occur in the Greek text. Paul's intent was to assert that if the things listed have not occurred, then the day of the Lord could not have arrived.

The three things that must take place before the day of the Lord are (1) the rebellion must occur (v. 3), (2) the man of lawlessness must be revealed (v. 3), and (3) the restraint/restrainer must be removed (vv. 6–7). It should be noted at the outset that the discussion of these includes few if any temporal references. The "first" (RSV) of v. 3 and the occasional "then" scattered in the passage may have more to do with the sequence of the list than with sequence in time. There is also no indication how soon these things might occur or how long the process would take once it began. Also the description of the events is not very detailed. The assumption on the part of the apostle was that the church knew about these things (v. 5). Thus his intent was to remind the church of teachings already given, not present new teachings in a full and detailed fashion.

Listing three proofs required that they be placed in some sort of sequence, but the sequence says little about the relation of the three events to each other. They may be understood as three facets of a single event, three separate events, or any combination in between. What was important for Paul's argument was that the visible elements of these happenings were not evident; therefore the day of the Lord had not arrived.

Paul was concerned that no one "deceive" the church. Along with the ambiguities of v. 2, the rather general character of this third-person imperative[15] may indicate that Paul did not know precisely who was misleading the church or how they were disseminating their teachings. But it seems unlikely that news of such an error could reach Paul without some accompanying information about its source(s).[16] Although concern over false teachers is apparent in many of Paul's letters, the idea of deception does not necessarily indicate the intrusion of some malevolent force from outside the church. The deceivers may have been well-meaning but self-deceived members of the congregation (cf. Rom 16:17–18 and 1 Cor 3:18, where the same verb was used).

"In any way" probably refers to the various ways that deception might invade the church, as listed in the preceding verse. The danger of false revelations, false teachings, and false letters existed. Thus the church could not accept at face value the claim that certain teachings were spiritual revelations, or established church teaching, or apostolic communication. The presence of false teachers in the church required the constant exercise of discernment on the part of the congregation (cf. 1 Thess 5:21).

The NIV indicates that the clause "that day will not come" is not in the Greek text by putting the words in small brackets. But there is no doubt that some statement such as this must fill the ellipsis and complete what would otherwise be an incomplete sentence.[17] Paul's flow of thought is indicated by the preceding statement of his topic. Verses 3–4 refute the proposition that "the day of the Lord has already come." So Paul likely intended readers to complete the negative conditional clause ("unless the apostasy come first and the man of lawlessness is revealed," NASB) in vv. 3–4 with some such statement as "then the Lord has not (or will not) come."[18] Thus the Thessalonians were not to allow anyone to deceive them regarding the presence of the day of the

---

[15] Paul normally used the more personal and direct second-person imperative, leading F. F. Bruce (*1 and 2 Thessalonians,* WBC [Waco: Word, 1982]) to insert βλέπετε or ὁρᾶτε and read "[see to it] that no one deceives you," but the third-person imperative may be a part of the citation of traditional material and also is not unknown in Paul's writings (1 Cor 16:11; Gal 1:8–9).

[16] Cp. also the Gal 1:8–9 pattern of reasoning from the broadest possible conception of the offender to the narrower and more specific.

[17] Such incomplete sentences (*anacolutha*) are not uncommon in Paul's letters and are indicative of the dictation of lengthy and complex sentences to an amanuensis (cf. Gal 2:3–5; 2 Cor 8:12–14; Rom 5:12–14).

[18] See C. H. Giblin, *The Threat to Faith: An Exegetical and Theological Reexamination of 2 Thessalonians 2,* AnBib 31 (Rome: Pontifical Biblical Institute, 1967), 122–39, for an alternative to the apodosis suggested by the majority of interpreters. See also Wanamaker, *Thessalonians,* 244, for a critique of Giblin's suggestions.

Lord. That day has not arrived unless certain observable events have taken place. The rebellion must occur, and the man of lawlessness must be revealed (v. 3). The revelation of this man follows the removal of the restrainer (vv. 7–8) and precedes the day of the Lord (v. 8). If the man of lawlessness has not been revealed, then the day of the Lord cannot have arrived.

The temporal relationship between the rebellion and the man of lawlessness is not certain. Because of the sequence of the statements in the verse, one may assume that a general apostasy as a distinct event would precede and set the stage for a second event, the appearance of the lawless one. The adverb *prōton* ("first" in the NASB, not translated by the NIV) seems to support this temporal sequence. Its placement in the sentence slightly favors the understanding that the apostasy comes "first" and then the lawless one is revealed. But this is not necessarily the case. If Paul were intentionally presenting the events leading up to the day of the Lord in a strict temporal sequence, the removal of the restrainer should have been mentioned in v. 3 as well as in vv. 7–8. Alternately, the syntax of the sentence could mean that both the apostasy and the revelation of the man of lawlessness comes "first," that is, before the arrival of the day of the Lord. Understanding "first" in this fashion also opens up the possibilities that (a) the two events mentioned in v. 3 could occur simultaneously, representing two facets of a single happening, or (b) the deceptions of the lawless one (vv. 9–10) will precede and/or bring about the apostasy rather than follow it. Paul's comments here are simply not detailed enough to make a certain determination on this point.

Neither did Paul elaborate on the nature of "the rebellion" *(apostasia),* which therefore must already have been a well-defined concept for the Thessalonians. *Apostasia* indicates an act of abandoning or moving away from a position formerly held.[19] Cognate forms of *apostasia* were sometimes used in the LXX of political revolt. Similarly, Josephus used it of the Jewish revolt against Rome.[20] If the word is understood in its political sense here, it could allude to a general rebellion against Rome (God's appointed authority for maintaining order, Rom 13:1–7) as a

---

[19] Hiebert mentions but rejects the view of some that ἀποστασία here means "departure" and refers to the rapture. The rapture, he notes, is not an act of departure but of being "caught up" (1 Thess 4:17; see *The Thessalonian Epistles,* 306).

[20] Josephus, *Life,* 43.

sign of the end of the age.[21] In the New Testament, however, verbal forms related to *apostasia* are commonly used in religious contexts rather than political (Luke 2:37; 8:13; 1 Tim 4:1; 2 Tim 2:19; Heb 3:12; but see also Acts 5:37). Religiously it means to desert one's faith. The Jews for instance charged Paul with inciting the *apostasia* of Jews on the grounds that he encouraged them to desert the teachings of Moses (Acts 21:21).[22] Jewish apocalypticists expected a general rebellion against the teachings of Moses at the end of the age (*Jub* 23:14–23; *1 Enoch* 91:3–10; *1 QpHab* 1:5,12–13; 2:1–8). It is possible that the apostasy Paul was referring to was not a Christian apostasy but this expected Jewish apostasy[23] that would signal the end and lead to the coming of the man of lawlessness.

As noted earlier, however, it is possible that the coming of the lawless one does not follow the apostasy but is coincident with it or even antecedent to it. If either is the case, than we probably should understand the deception of vv. 9–10 (produced by the lawless one) as the engine driving the apostasy. The apostates in such a scenario would have been those who fell away from the worship of the true God in favor of following the deceiver. If Paul was expanding on Jewish apocalyptic thought, these who apostasize would most logically be Jews, not pagans (since pagans have no relationship from which they could apostatize). But the church also expected an unusually difficult time near the end of the age when false teachers would entice many of its members to desert the apostolic faith for more palatable but false teachings (Matt 24:11–13; 1 Tim 4:1–5; 2 Tim 3:1 9; Jude 17–19). Paul also, though he expressed confidence that all the elect will be saved, allowed for the

---

[21] Bruce sees the apostasy as a "general abandonment of the basis of civil order" (*1 and 2 Thessalonians,* 167). J. E. Frame sees it as the "apostasy of the non-Christians as a whole," but if this is what Paul meant, "ungodliness" would have been a far better word (*A Critical and Exegetical Commentary on the Epistles of St. Paul to the Thessalonians* [Edinburgh: T & T Clark, 1960], 251). Apostasy assumes a relationship that is deserted. The non-Christian has had no such relationship.

[22] This is the only other use of the noun in the NT.

[23] Wanamaker cites the reference to the temple in v. 4 as an indication that Paul was working with "a traditional apocalyptic understanding ... that many of the people of God, that is the Jews, would rebel against God and the Law at the time of the end" (*1 and 2 Thessalonians,* 244). Best seems to lean this way too, asserting that "it is hard to believe that as early as 2 Th. Paul was so pessimistic as to envisage an apostasy of Christians" (*1 and 2 Thessalonians,* 282). But see 1 Thess 3:5.

possibility of some in the church deserting it (1 Thess 3:5). Thus it seems likely that the apostasy Paul had in mind expanded on Jewish apocalyptic expectations and envisioned a dramatic and climactic falling away from the worship of the true God (by both Jews and some portion of the Christian church) as a part of the complex of events at the end of the age.[24]

The remainder of vv. 3–4 is given over to a description of the man "of lawlessness" *(anomias),*[25] who is further described as a "man doomed to destruction" (lit., "son of destruction").[26] Both "man of lawlessness" and "son of destruction" are Hebraisms that use "lawlessness" and "destruction" adjectivally. Later in the passage (v. 8) he is termed (in a more typically Greek construction) "the lawless one" *(ho anomos).*[27] Law *(nomos)* itself may refer to civil or religious regulations, but here the lawless one is destined for condemnation by God, making it clear that it was God's law that was in mind. This person is a rebel who is neither constrained by nor respectful of the law of God.

"Son of destruction" is parallel but adds another element to the reader's understanding of the man of lawlessness. He is doomed, destined to be destroyed (cf. Rom 9:22). In the Gospel of John, Judas Iscariot is identified with the same phrase (John 17:12). But this "man doomed to destruction" is not just doomed personally. Verses 9–10 depict him as one who deceives and contributes to the destruction of others. He himself is doomed, and those influenced by him are as well. Though not the root cause, he is an instrument of destruction for those who do not love the truth and so will not be saved (v. 10).

---

[24] L. Morris includes pagans in the rebellion, arguing regarding ἀποστασία that "in the present passage the emphasis is on the revolt against God rather than on the falling away from the church" (*The First and Second Epistles to the Thessalonians,* NICNT, rev. ed. [Grand Rapids: Eerdmans, 1991], 219, n. 17). But pagans are already in revolt against God, and ἡ ἀποστασία seems to indicate a radical new event, not simply a continuation of existing animosity.

[25] A number of later MSS contain not ἀνομίας but the variant ἁμαρτος, i.e., man "of sin," the reading reflected in the KJV. Note that in v. 8 it is the "lawless (ὁ ἄνομος) one" who is revealed (using the verb ἀποκαλύπτω, "reveal" as in v. 3).

[26] In the LXX, Ps 88:23 contains the phrase υἱὸς ἀνομίας, which may lie behind both of Paul's terms here. See R. D. Aus, "God's Plan and God's Power: Isaiah 66 and the Restraining Factors of 2 Thess 2:6–7," *JBL* 96 (1977): 538.

[27] Wanamaker argues that the description of Pompey's conquest of Palestine in 63 B.C. in *Pss. Sol.* 17 provides much of the imagery Paul used here of the revelation of the ultimate "lawless one" (*1 and 2 Thessalonians,* 245).

The man of lawlessness will be "revealed."[28] The same verb, *apocalyptō*, is used for the revelation of Jesus in 1:7. The repetition of the verb may imply that the man of lawlessness will be a pseudo-messiah (cf. Matt 24:4). This impression is strengthened with subsequent references to his "coming" *(parousia)* in v. 9a; the miracles, signs, and wonders that support his claims (v. 9b); and his assumption of the place and title of deity (v. 4). Those who are not deceived by him will recognize that he is not the Christ but is anti-Christ (cf. 1 John 2:18; 4:1–3). He will be a deceptive and satanic opponent of the true Christ who will ultimately destroy the pretender at the genuine parousia (v. 8).

2:4 The grandest delusion of this lawless agent of destruction is his pretention to deity. It is the ultimate expression of his rejection of divine law and the most eloquent justification of his ultimate destruction. Two parallel participles[29] in v. 4 describe his attitude. The lawless one "opposes" all other objects of worship. This same term occurs in 1 Tim 5:14 referring to Satan, "the enemy" of the church, and in the LXX, translating the Hebrew verb behind the name "Satan" or "the adversary" (1 Kgs 11:25; Zech 3:1). Thus it is no surprise that this opponent of God functions "in accordance with the working of Satan" (v. 9). He "will exalt himself" translates a second participle descriptive not just of his action but of his character. The image is one of extreme arrogance,[30] the ultimate in megalomania, installing oneself not just as a god but as the greatest of the gods, the self-proclaimed ruler of all.

The man of lawlessness places himself above "everything that is called God or is worshiped." The participle translated "that is called" may refer only to the "so-called" (RSV) gods of the pagans as in 1 Cor 8:5 (the construction is the same). But the lawless one in this passage is presented especially as the opponent of the true God and his Christ. Thus the opponent exalts himself above all that people call god, whether falsely or accurately. While in Athens, Paul observed many "objects of worship" *(sebasmata),* including an altar inscribed "TO AN

---

[28] Paul gives no indication where this one is before he is revealed. If Paul thought of him as a human being who would be empowered and used by Satan, then his revelation is tantamount to a secular (though spectacular) rise to power. If he is more than human, his revelation itself would be a miraculous event.

[29] The one article preceding ἀντικείμενος καὶ ὑπεραιρόμενος indicates they comprise a dual description of a single activity. He opposes and sets himself above everything else that humanity worships.

[30] 2 Cor 12:7 contains the only other NT use of the verb.

UNKNOWN GOD"; and in his sermon at the Areopagus he proclaimed the true God to them as the one whom they worshiped "as something unknown" (Acts 17:23). With his reference in this letter to every "god" or "object of worship" *(sebasma),* the apostle summed up the whole world of things revered in the religious lives of humanity. Paul's image of this arrogant but doomed ruler is similar to that in Dan 11:36–37. But whereas Daniel's great king worships a foreign god (see Dan 11:38–39), the man of lawlessness is even more arrogant, deifying himself (cf. v. 4b).[31]

A result clause completes v. 4. As an expression of his self-deification, the son of perdition will assume the place and claim the name of God. He "sets himself up in God's temple."[32] The word for "temple" *(naon)* was a common word that could refer to any temple (e.g., Acts 17:24) as well as to the temple in Jerusalem (e.g., Matt 26:61; Luke 1:9). It could also be used in the narrower sense of "sanctuary," indicating the high holy place in which the very presence of God resides either in an earthly temple (cf. Acts 19:24; Matt 23:35) or the heavenly sanctuary (Rev 14:15). Paul commonly used *naos* metaphorically of the believer as the dwelling place of the Holy Spirit (1 Cor 3:16–17; 6:19; 2 Cor 6:16). But here it must be used literally if the passage is to depict an observable, symbolic event the church could recognize as an indication of the nearness of the day of the Lord. In Eph 2:21 the church is called the temple, and some argue that Paul taught that the son of perdition would claim preeminence in the church.[33] But the scope of the lawless one's actions seems much broader than just the church. He will press a claim of absolute preeminence over all people and all gods. Such breadth of influence implies political and/or military might, not just religious megalomania.

Although Paul did not identify this *naos* unambiguously (by adding "in Jerusalem," for instance), it is most likely that he was thinking of an event similar to the desecration of the holy place accomplished by Antiochus Epiphanes, who placed an altar to Zeus in the sanctuary, and again by Pompey, who defiled the sanctuary by entering it but did not

---

[31] S. R. Miller equates the two and explains the "god of fortresses" he will honor as figurative of "military power and might" *(Daniel,* NAC [Nashville: Broadman & Holman, 1994], 308).

[32] Several MSS contain variants stating explicitly that this one sets himself in the place of God, "as God" (ὡς θεὸν). The addition is a scribal clarification that is unnecessary considering the last clause of v. 4.

[33] See Giblin, *Threat to Faith,* 76–80.

attempt to assert himself or change the character of Jewish worship. In A.D. 40, only a few years before Paul wrote this letter, Gaius Caesar (Caligula), who had declared his own divinity, attempted to have his image set up in the holy of holies in Jerusalem. Paul, in line with Jesus' teaching (Mark 13:14; cf. Dan 9:27), expected some such event to occur again as a part of the trauma of the end times and as a precursor of the day of the Lord itself. Yet it should not be forgotten that the location of the temple (and whether he meant the reference literally or metaphorically) is not an essential element in Paul's argument about the coming of the day of the Lord.[34] All that is necessary for Paul's purpose in this passage is that the man of lawlessness express his presumption of pre-eminence through some sort of clear demonstration for all to see and understand[35] and that this must occur before the coming of the day of the Lord.

Taking the seat of God, the lawless one in effect proclaims himself to be God. The participle "proclaiming" implies a demonstration as much as an announcement (cf. Acts 2:22; 1 Cor 4:9) and expresses the implications of one sitting in God's sanctuary. Taking such a place and posture would be allowed only to God himself. Pretensions to divinity were far from unheard of in antiquity. The prophets condemned both the king of Tyre (Ezek 28:1–10) and the king of Babylon (Isa 14:9–19) for assuming godlike status. According to Josephus, Herod Agrippa I presented himself at a festival in Caesarea in a manner calculated to impress the masses. Dressed in a silver robe, he entered the theater at daybreak to deliver an oration. The sun played off the silver, making a spectacular display to accompany his speech. Agrippa was lauded as not a mere man but a god. He did not reprimand the people but accepted their praise. As a result he was stricken by God and died after five days

---

[34] Bruce argues that Paul was referring to the Jerusalem sanctuary but was doing so metaphorically as "a graphic way of saying that he (the man of lawlessness) plans to usurp the authority of God" (*1 and 2 Thessalonians*, 169). But a metaphorical interpretation of the passage leaves one wondering how the lawless one will express, in a public and recognizable manner, the fact that he has usurped God's authority if not through some grand symbolic act. The Thessalonians would have known what Paul meant on the basis of his earlier oral teachings (v. 5). In the absence of such teachings, for us the nature of the temple will remain a debatable matter.

[35] Even if the details of the coming of the son of lawlessness were (and are) not fully known, his arrival on the scene will be recognized, for he "will be revealed" by God. The verb ἀποκαλυφθήσεται in v. 8 is passive, not middle, and so does not mean that the lawless one "will reveal himself."

of severe abdominal pain.[36]

The people of the Hellenistic age would not have found a claim to divinity so outrageous as would a person today. The boundary between human and divine was rather porous in the mind of the ancient. Homer wrote of numerous exchanges between gods and mortals, as well as the movement of a few mortals into the ranks of the divine. Since the time of Augustus emperors had been deified at death. Since the time of Caligula deity had been claimed by living emperors. The cult of emperor worship was an active and important part of Roman society by the time Paul wrote this letter. Of course the presumption of anyone, even an emperor, claiming divinity was scandalous blasphemy in Jewish eyes. It was the height of rebellion against God. It is not surprising then that the ultimate and final rebellion should feature this most extreme example of pretensions to divinity.

2:5 At this point Paul inserted a parenthetical comment that interrupts the flow of the sentence begun in v. 3. The interrogative "don't you remember" chides the church. The things they already knew were sufficient to refute this false teaching about the day of the Lord. "I used to tell you these things" translates an imperfect verb tense that implies ongoing or recurring instruction. "These things" (the teachings of vv. 3–4) were not presented only once, a situation that might excuse the Thessalonians' failure to remember them. Rather, they were matters addressed repeatedly (and presumably in far greater detail than was recorded here), and the church should have remembered them. The brief lapse into the first person implies that Paul personally felt responsible for the initial instruction given the church as well as for the writing of this letter (as was also indicated in 1 Thess 5:27), although he did both in conjunction with Timothy and Silvanus. Thus apostolic instruction already possessed by the church could have served as a basis for refuting the false teaching without any additional instruction from Paul.

2:6 In addition to the "things" (v. 5) mentioned in vv. 3–4 (the rebellion and the man of lawlessness), the Thessalonians also knew that the lawless one was being restrained (vv. 6–7). Lawlessness of the type that would be epitomized by the son of perdition was already active. The ultimate demonstration of such lawlessness, however, would not come to pass until the proper moment. Until then it is restrained. Restraint is mentioned twice in these verses. The first time (v. 6) the NIV translates a neuter present participle *(to katechon)*, "what is hold-

---

[36] Josephus, *Ant.* 19.343–52; cf. Acts 12:21–23.

ing him back." The translation, like the neuter tense, implies not a person but a force that restrains. The second time (v. 7) the translation is "the one who now holds it back," reflecting a change in the Greek to a masculine participle *(ho katechōn)*. Why did Paul change the gender, and how should we think of the restraint on the man of lawlessness? This is the most difficult, but not the only interpretive dilemma in these two verses.

"And now" at the beginning of v. 6 may modify the verb "you know" as the NIV implies. If this is the case, "now" *(nun)* is best understood as "resumptive rather than temporal,"[37] indicating that as things stood (in light of the earlier instruction, v. 5), the Thessalonians knew about the son of perdition and that he would not be revealed until the appointed time. The word order of the Greek text, however, has *nun* adjacent to "what is holding him back" *(to katechon),* not the verb. If taken as a modifier of *to katechon,* it produces a translation like the NASB's "and you know what restrains him now." Either understanding of *nun* is possible, but the latter leads more naturally into vv. 6b–8 and the idea that the current restraining force is now in place. The man of lawlessness will not be revealed until the proper time in spite of the fact that lawlessness is already at work.

This assumes (as does the NIV translation) that the restrainer is a godly force that presently limits the influence of evil. However, the verb *katechō* itself implies neither good nor evil, meaning either "to hold down or suppress something" or "to hold fast, retain control, or rule."[38] Given these two possibilities, suggested interpretations of *katechon* (v. 6) and *katechōn* (v. 7) can be divided into two broad categories (with various refinements possible within each category). The participle *katechon* may refer to either a positive force (person in v. 7b) that is suppressing evil and delaying the onslaught of the lawless one or an evil force currently ruling the world whose ultimate expression is the coming of the lawless one.

Suggested identifications of this power/person understood as a force for good include, for example, the Holy Spirit, God's plan/God himself,[39] some unknown spiritual being, the apostolic gospel/Paul,[40] or the

---

[37] Bruce, *1 and 2 Thessalonians,* 170.

[38] BAGD, sv. "κατέχω."

[39] See Aus, "God's Plan," 544–52.

[40] See, e.g., J. Munck, *Paul and the Salvation of Mankind,* trans. F. Clark (London: SCM, 1959), 36–42.

Roman Empire (i.e., human government) as the enforcer of good.[41] On the other hand, *katechon* may refer to the evil force of lawlessness that retains control of the world currently (v. 7a) and will ultimately reach its climax at the revelation of a supremely evil "lawless one" who will be destroyed at the coming of Jesus. In this case the specific identifications suggested include both spiritual powers such as the powers of the air or Satan himself (2 Cor 4:4; Eph 2:2)[42] and earthly powers such as a pagan Roman Empire. The fact that scholars through the ages cannot even decide whether the *katechon/katechōn* is an evil or a godly force/person should lead the reader to respect the ambiguities of the passage from the outset; it implies that even when conclusions are reached, they can never have the ring of certainty.

Indecision regarding these alternatives is the result of ambiguity at several points in vv. 6–8. First, in v. 6a the participle *katechon* is not followed by an object. This either creates an ellipsis the author intended the reader to fill logically (by inserting an object) or indicates that the verb is intransitive and should not have an object. The NIV rendering "and now you know what is holding him back" inserts a pronoun, "him," that is not present in the Greek text. Without the pronoun the participle translates more smoothly with an intransitive rendering such as "and you know that which now holds sway." Such a translation seems to look toward v. 7a and the "secret power of lawlessness" as that which is in control of the present age.

The second clause of v. 6, "so that he may be revealed at the proper time," expands on the role of the *katechon*. Unfortunately it does not limit the interpretation of *katechon*. If it is a restrainer, then it restrains the evil one (or the power of evil in general) and prevents it from breaking out with full fury until the time God has designated. If the *katechon* is the force that rules the present age, then its exercise of power has the purpose of setting the stage for the revelation of the lawless one when the time is right. In either instance the "he" who will be revealed refers back to vv. 3–4 and the son of perdition. The verb "revealed" (*apokalyphthēnai*, cf. 1:7) implies that this one is a false messiah. It is possible (in light of v. 9) that the unexpressed agent who will reveal the son of perdi-

---

[41] See Tertullian, *De resurr. carn.* 24; Chrysostom, *Hom. 4 on 2 Thess.;* Bruce prefers this alternative and argues that "even after the Roman Empire passed away, the principle of the wording did not become obsolete, for when the secular power in any form continues to discharge its divinely ordained commission, it restrains evil and prevents the outburst of anarchy" (*1 and 2 Thessalonians,* 188).

[42] See Giblin, *Threat to Faith,* 230–34.

tion is Satan,[43] but the New Testament consistently represents God as the one in ultimate control of the events of the end times. For the "times and dates" are in God's hands (*kairos* is used here and in 1 Thess 5:1).

2:7 The following sentence, "For the secret power of lawlessness is already at work," is explanatory. Unfortunately, it also does not clarify *katechon* because it may explain either the need for restraint or the character of that which is now in control of this age. The "secret power" ("mystery," NASB) translates a word *(mysterion)* that Paul used elsewhere in relation to the gospel. A "mystery" in Hellenistic religions referred to secret knowledge revealed only to initiates of a cult. Paul used the word with a different nuance, representing the gospel as a "mystery" that was formerly hidden but that had been revealed in Christ and is now available to all (Rom 16:25; 1 Cor 2:1,7). But the mystery was not all good news. Part of the story of the gospel was for Paul the rejection of the gospel by Israel and their ultimate fate (Rom 11:25). We probably should understand the "mystery of lawlessness" (RSV) not as a "secret power" but as a reference to those evil forces exposed by and opposed to the power of the gospel. These are the evil powers of this age (cf. Eph 2:1–2), the many anti-Christ forces that are "already at work" (cf. 1 John 2:18).

The second part of v. 7 contains a masculine singular participle from *katechō*. It (similarly to the neuter form in v. 6) could be translated "he who now restrains" (NASB) or "he who now controls." The former personalizes the restraining force that either prevents the unchecked growth and influence of lawlessness in general (cf. v. 7a) or prevents the revelation of the man of lawlessness specifically (cf. v. 8a). The object of *katechōn* is not stated. The NIV supplies "it," implying that the "secret power of lawlessness" is that which is restrained. It is possible, however, that the lawless one himself is intended as the object, and "him" should be supplied. On the other hand, if *katechōn* means "he who now rules," it needs no object and refers to the ruler of the current age of lawlessness. Whether the *katechōn* is a restrainer or a controller, when he is "out of the way," the lawless one will be revealed.

The restrainer (or the ruler) "will continue to do so[44] until he is taken

---

[43] So Wanamaker, *1 and 2 Thessalonians,* 254.

[44] A verbal idea similar to "will continue to do so" is supplied in most translations to fill an ellipsis in the Greek text. It is possible to understand v. 7b as a single temporal clause (eliminating the need to supply a verb) and read with v. 7a, "The mystery of lawlessness is already at work, but only until the one who is now prevailing is out of the way" (see BDF, 475.1). If κατέχων is a "restrainer," however, the assumption of an ellipsis makes better sense of the verse and is consistent with Pauline style.

out of the way." If that which the restrainer restrains is the lawlessness of v. 7a, his removal would allow lawlessness to run rampant, preparing the way for the lawless one. If, on the other hand, the restrainer restrains the lawless one himself (v. 8a), we would understand that the removal of the restrainer sets the lawless one free to be revealed and fully exert his influence.[45] On the other hand, if *katechōn* refers to a "ruler" of the present lawlessness, then the removal of this one creates a void that the revelation of the lawless one fills.

Given the brevity of Paul's statements and the ambiguities of the text, it is unlikely that the *katechōn* can ever be identified with certainty. Fortunately, precise identification is not essential to an understanding of the message of vv. 1–15. Verses 5–7 are a parenthesis inserted into the larger passage. Thus the identity of the *katechon/katechōn* was (and still is) tangential to Paul's argument in vv. 1–15. The *katechōn* was not one of the signs of the end. Its/his removal would be demonstrated only in the revelation of the son of perdition, an evident and unmistakable event.

The son of perdition will "be revealed at the proper time" (v. 6). This will not happen until the *katechōn* is "taken out of the way" (v. 7). Though both statements are temporal, neither provides any concrete temporal references. Yet they do predict the future in one sense. Both clauses assume that God is ultimately in control of the end times. And if this is true, then God is also in control of the events themselves. For the people of God, then, peace and assurance come not from a full knowledge of the times and seasons but from a personal knowledge of the God who rules the times and seasons.

The coming of the lawless one is the central feature of Paul's argument in vv. 1–12. It was the fact that he was not on the scene that assured Christians that the day of the Lord had not arrived (vv. 3–4). After the parenthesis of vv. 5–7, Paul returned in v. 8a to the revelation of the lawless one he began describing in v. 4. Verses 8b–10 then elaborate on the coming of the lawless one, the effect it will have on unbelievers, and the final judgment upon him and all those who follow him.

2:8–9 "And then …" follows on the statement that the restrainer will be taken out of the way (v. 7b). After the restrainer's influence is

---

[45] This would imply that the lawless one is a spiritual being already in existence but held in custody in some fashion until the proper time for him to be unleashed (cf. M. Barnouin, "Problems De Traduction Concernant 2 Thess 2:6–7," *NTS* 23 [1977]: 482–98).

removed, the lawless one "will be revealed." The same verb *(apoka-lyphthēsetai)* was used of the coming revelation of the Lord (cf. vv. 3,6). The predicted miracles and signs (v. 9) also parallel that which would be expected of a messiah. The lawless one's power to deceive coupled with these signs and wonders implies that his arrival will be lauded as a marvelous event (v. 11). It is little wonder that such a figure could assume an exalted status (v. 4).

His glory will be fleeting, however; for the Lord Jesus[46] will "over-throw" *[anelei]* him "with the breath of his mouth." Paul here echoed Isa 11:4, which asserts of the coming descendant of Jesse that "with the breath of his lips he will slay *(anelei,* LXX) the wicked." In a parallel clause Paul asserted that the Lord Jesus will "destroy" *(katargēsei)* the lawless one "by the splendor of his coming."[47] The destruction of the lawless one signifies more than the punishment of a singularly wicked individual. It is a part of the destruction of all "dominion, authority and power" (1 Cor 15:24; cf. 1 Cor 15:24–26, where the verb *katargeō* is used twice), clearing the way for the establishing of the Lord's reign.

The "splendor" *(epiphaneia)* of his "coming" *(parousia)* uses two terms for appearance. "Splendor" is used only here and in the Pastorals, where it refers to the "appearing" of Christ (1 Tim 6:14; 2 Tim 1:10; 4:1,8; Titus 2:13). The term implies a visible demonstration of the presence of a formerly unseen deity. It may consist of a revelation of the deity himself or a revelation of his power through some visible act. The latter term, *parousia,* emphasizes personal presence. The combination here is a redundancy that lends emphasis to the phrase. But even more Paul probably intended it to stress the glory of the Lord's coming while making sure the reader was aware that the occasion of judgment (which event by itself could be termed an *epiphaneia* of the Lord) will be the parousia of the Lord Jesus.

In vv. 8–9 Paul turned back from the final phase of the career of the lawless one (v. 8) and considered again his arrival on the scene of human affairs. Before the Lord comes to reveal and to judge, the law-

---

[46] A number of MSS do not contain "Jesus," reading somewhat ambiguously "whom the Lord will overthrow." Though Paul's intent was certainly to refer to Jesus, it is most likely that the shorter reading was the original.

[47] Best *(1 and 2 Thessalonians,* 303) and Bruce *(1 and 2 Thessalonians,* 172) both speculate that the image of Yahweh as a warrior and the breath of God as a powerful weapon is behind Paul's references here. If this is so, it played no major part in Paul's argument at this point since he did not develop the image.

less one will have his day. His coming *(parousia)* is elaborated upon in a series of prepositional phrases.[48] It will be "in accordance with the work *[energeian]* of Satan." By contrast, the gospel of Jesus operates by the working *(energeia)* of God (Eph 1:19; 3:7; Phil 3:21). The powers displayed by the lawless one will be impressive but will originate from an evil source. The belief that Satan as well as God had the power to do amazing deeds was reflected by the Pharisees, who when they could not deny the works of Jesus attributed them to the power of Beelzebub (Matt 12:22–24). Jesus himself warned that false messiahs and false prophets would come displaying "signs and miracles" *(sēmeia kai terata*, see below) in an effort to deceive even the elect (Mark 13:22). The implication is that these will be genuine works of power but that the power will be satanic (cf. Rev 13:2).

These works of Satan will involve "all kinds of counterfeit miracles, signs and wonders." All three of these terms are used in the Gospels of the miracles performed by Jesus. "Miracles" translates a singular noun *(dunamei)* indicating great ability.[49] "Signs" *(sēmeiois)* are deeds that point beyond themselves and indicate a greater truth than the sign itself. "Wonders" *(terasin)* are works that inspire awe. Peter used the same three words in his sermon on the Day of Pentecost as he affirmed Jesus as "a man accredited by God to you by miracles, wonders and signs, which God did among you through him" (Acts 2:22).

The combination of the three for Paul also (cf. Rom 15:9; 2 Cor 12:12) seems to constitute a convincing argument for the validity of the gospel and specifically for the validity of the apostolic proclamation of that gospel. The lawless one will seek to convince as well, but he will

---

[48] The syntax of vv. 9–10 is complex. The clause "the coming of the lawless one will be (ἐστιν)" is followed by three prepositional phrases (κατ'... σατανᾶ, ἐν... ψεύδους, and ἐν... ἀδικίας) and a participial clause (τοῖς ἀπολλυμένοις...). Paul most likely intended the phrase nearest ἐστιν, "in accordance with the work of Satan," to be a complement. The prepositional phrases in vv. 9b,10a modify and elaborate on the "work" of Satan: it will incorporate (a) "counterfeit miracles, signs and wonders" and (b) "every sort of evil that deceives." The participle "those who are perishing" modifies "evil that deceives" by identifying those who are taken in by the deception. These persons do not perish because they are deceived; they are deceived because they are among the perishing, i.e., among those who have already rejected the truth of the gospel.

[49] Δυνάμει along with the adjective πάσῃ may mean "every sort of miracle," and so the NIV translates it "miracles" in conjunction with "signs and wonders" as if it were a plural noun. (All three nouns are grouped together and governed by the preposition ἐν.) On the other hand, the singular δυνάμει more commonly refers to the "power" (cf. NASB) that can express itself in "signs and wonders."

be an apostle of Satan. "Counterfeit" *(pseudous)* comes at the end of the clause, but Paul probably intended it to apply to all three words since they appear to be used as a threefold description of the misleading miracles of the son of perdition. The term may indicate that Paul thought of the miracles as deeds accomplished by trickery and not true acts of amazing power. But the emphasis on satanic power, on the persuasive deceptiveness of the lawless one, and his implied status as the preeminent false messiah all imply that Paul believed the "miracles, signs and wonders" would be genuine. Nevertheless the deeds are false in the sense that they will be used to validate a figure whose message is a lie and whose end is destruction (v. 11).[50]

2:10 The deception perpetrated by the lawless one is stressed in v. 10. The coming of the lawless one according to the working of Satan will be "in all kinds of counterfeit miracles, signs and wonders" (v. 9b) and "in every sort of evil that deceives." The NASB translation of v. 10a is more literal: the evil one comes "with all the deception of wickedness."[51] Deception is the alluring mask worn by evil. Those deceived are led to destruction (cf. Matt 13:22; Eph 4:22; Col 2:8; 2 Pet 2:13). "Every sort" (of evil) translates the same preposition and adjective rendered "all kinds" (of counterfeit miracles) in v. 9b. Paul seems to explain the success of the lawless one by stressing the multitude of counterfeit signs and the varied deception he will use. But the lawless one's effectiveness is also explained by the fact that his audience has already rejected the truth.

Paul repeatedly drew a contrast between *adikia,* "wickedness," and adherence to God's truth (cf. v. 12, Rom 1:18; 2:8). The genitive noun "of wickedness" (NASB) may be adjectival as the NIV indicates (so "evil that deceives"). But considering the contrast between truth and wickedness in v. 12, Paul probably intended to indicate the source of the deception ("deception" arising from "wickedness"). That is, the message of the lawless one springs not from truth or even from honest error but from a satanic and conscious intent to mislead. It is self-consciously contrary to God's truth and will find its greatest audience among persons already hostile to God's truth, that is, among "those who are per-

---

[50] The genitive ψεύδους in this case would indicate the falseness of the source and imply that the object of the deeds is deception.

[51] The two phrases are parallel in structure so that "with ... deception" is the fourth substantive (following "with ... power, and signs and ... wonders) characterizing the "activity of Satan" (NASB).

ishing" *(apollymenois).* This particular present participle is the antithesis of those "who are being saved" *(sōzomenois)* in 1 Cor 1:18 and 2 Cor 2:15. Those who are perishing already have rejected the truth of the gospel (cf. 2 Cor 4:3). It is then no surprise that son of "perdition" *(apōleias,* v. 3) will find his ranks filled by those already on their way to perdition *(apōleias* is a cognate noun of the participle *apollymenois).*

The NIV simplifies Paul's rather lengthy sentence (vv. 8–10) by beginning new sentences at v. 9 and v. 10b, where they also supply, "They perish." Paul's sentence runs directly from "those who are perishing" to the causal clause "because they refused to love the truth."[52] The perishing do not suffer their fate because of the deceiver. The causal clause makes clear that they suffer their fate because they have "refused to love the truth" (lit., "have not received the love of the truth").

The phrase "love of the truth" (NASB) occurs only here in the New Testament. But Paul apparently was using "truth" as a synonym for the "gospel" (cf. v. 12; Gal 2:5,14; 5:7; 2 Cor 4:2; Col 1:5). The "love" of the truth is the acceptance of and obedience to the gospel. Paul may have used the aorist verb "refused" either speaking from his own time frame or from the perspective of the future deception. If the former, then he was stating that those who had already rejected the gospel will in the future be deceived by the lawless one. If the latter, then Paul was asserting that those who have not received the love of the gospel by the time the lawless one arrives on the scene will be deceived by him. Either way, the perishing inevitably accept the deception because that is all that is left to them once they have rejected the truth. On the other hand, the acceptance of the love of the truth would result in their salvation.

The arrival of a self-proclaimed deity, a person of immense deceptive power, is hardly the kind of thing that anyone would fail to notice. When he arrives, the church will know it. Then they will know that the day of the Lord is at hand, for it is this false messiah that the Lord will destroy at his parousia. As captivating as the imagery of the lawless one is, it was not Paul's intent to detail his coming and his character at this point. We might wish that Paul had written much more about this figure, but evidently he did not think it necessary to elaborate on a matter about

---

[52] Cf. Luke 1:20; 19:44; Acts 12:23 for other examples of ἀνθ᾽ ὧν initiating a causal statement. See BAGD, s.v. "ἀντί" for extrabiblical references.

which he had repeatedly given the Thessalonians oral instruction. That simply was not necessary to meet the concerns of the moment.

Paul's intent in this part of his letter was to prove that the day of the Lord had not begun and to warn the church to beware of those who would deceive them (cf. vv. 1–2). The description of the coming of the son of perdition is important in this context because it addresses the first concern. The Lord will not arrive until after the lawless one is revealed. He has not been revealed; therefore the day of the Lord has not arrived. The recounting of the sad destiny of those deceived by the lawless one serves two purposes. First, it fills out the description of the lawless one by detailing his effect. Even more importantly, however, it serves as a warning against deserting the truth and succumbing to deception—a path that can only lead to condemnation (vv. 11–12).

2. Rejection or Acceptance of the Truth (2:11–15)

[11]**For this reason God sends them a powerful delusion so that they will believe the lie** [12]**and so that all will be condemned who have not believed the truth but have delighted in wickedness.**

[13]**But we ought always to thank God for you, brothers loved by the Lord, because from the beginning God chose you to be saved through the sanctifying work of the Spirit and through belief in the truth.** [14]**He called you to this through our gospel, that you might share in the glory of our Lord Jesus Christ.** [15]**So then, brothers, stand firm and hold to the teachings we passed on to you, whether by word of mouth or by letter.**

2:11 "For this reason" links the unbelievers' rejection of the truth (v. 10b) with their subsequent deception and ultimate condemnation (vv. 11–12). Specifically, it explains that God's act of sending a "powerful delusion" to "those who are perishing" is the result of their choice to reject the truth. Once the truth is rejected, the only alternative is to trust in that which is false. By refusing to receive the truth (v. 10) and then choosing to "believe the lie" (v. 11), unbelievers compound their culpability and make plain the justice of their condemnation. God does not cause their unbelief, but he does set the stage for them to demonstrate it and thus openly earn their own condemnation. Genuine believers will not be deceived in this way (vv. 13–14). Paul expressed confidence in the salvation of the Thessalonians through their "belief in the truth" (v. 13). As a result of adherence to the truth, they will share in the glory of the Christ (v. 14) rather than in the condemnation of the son of perdition.

Thus the exhortation that concludes vv. 1–15 reiterates the importance of standing firm against deception. The believers were to maintain the apostolic traditions they had received. The reference to apostolic "word" *(logos)* and "letter" *(epistolos)* in v. 15 draws a final contrast between truth and deception. The false "report *(logos)* or letter" *(epistolos)* in v. 2 is a part of the error that is already at work in the world. The believers must not fall prey to such deception, for the end result is a fully deserved condemnation. Thus believers must stand firm and hold on to the truth as those destined for salvation, not wrath (1:6–10; 1 Thess 5:9).

Because those who are perishing have "refused to love the truth and so be saved" (v. 10), God "sends[53] them a powerful delusion." Both in the Old Testament (2 Sam 24:1–25; 1 Kgs 22:19–23) and in Paul (Rom 11:7–12), God is presented as using human evil for divine purposes. The hardening of the Pharaoh's heart, for example, is attributed alternately to Pharaoh's own rejection of God's message and to the active intervention of God (Exod 9:34–35; 10:20). When pagan Gentiles refused to acknowledge God (Rom 1:28–29), he "gave them over to a depraved mind," permitting unrestrained exercise of "every kind of wickedness" *(adikia;* cf. v. 10). Although the thought of God permitting or even capitalizing on the performance of evil is on the surface disturbing, it is consistent with the absolute sovereignty of God. A sovereign God must be sovereign over evil as well as good, otherwise he is not really sovereign at all. Christianity (as Judaism before it) does not present a dualistic struggle between good and evil gods. It presents the working out of the divine will so that even those who exercise their freedom to do evil will ultimately discover that their actions have paradoxically served the divine economy. In this light it is not surprising that Paul should tell the Thessalonians that as the plan of God unfolds, he sends a "powerful delusion" to those who have rejected the truth.

This "powerful delusion" may be understood in two ways. It is most commonly taken as a new element in the passage, a revelation that God,

---

[53] God "sends" (πέμπει) is replaced in some MSS with the variant "will send" (πέμψει). The variant probably was a scribal attempt to clarify the sentence by applying the delusion unambiguously to the end times. It is clear from the context that the coming of the lawless one was in the future, and if the delusion refers to this event, "sends" is a dramatic present intended to add realism to the reading of the passage. If Paul thought of the delusion as a separate event prior to the coming of the lawless one and if Paul was convinced that the parousia would occur soon, he might have used the present tense of those who were deluded by the spirit of lawlessness already at work.

in the last days, will actively confuse the reasoning of the lost and guarantee their condemnation. Thus the delusion sent by God represents
some sort of mental and spiritual confusion that prevents the lost from
recognizing the truth as truth, changing their minds, and being saved as
a result. It is also possible, however, to see the "powerful delusion" as a
reference to the coming of the lawless one. In Paul's sentence it is not
"delusion" *(planēs)* but *energian* (translated "work" in v. 9 but used in
v. 11 as an adjective, "powerful") that is the object of the verb "sends."
Planēs ("of error") is a genitive modifying "work." Thus the phrase
(energeian planēs) indicates that God sends to those who have rejected
the truth a "work of error."[54] The phrase is reminiscent of the earlier
comment that the coming of the lawless one will be according to an
energeian tou satana, "work of Satan" (v. 9). The lawless one as an
agent of deception makes any further "delusion" redundant. The perishing have rejected the true Messiah already. A deceptive, satanic messiah
arises. The unbelievers' decision to follow this one whose coming is
according to the working of Satan, whose intent is to deceive, confirms
their rejection of the truth and fully justifies their condemnation.

"So that they will believe" translates an infinitive expressing the
intended result of the act of sending. The use of "believe" here highlights the contrast between those who believe Jesus and those who
believe the lie. "The lie" *(tō pseudei)* of which Paul was thinking is not
specified. But his terminology echoes the earlier reference to "counterfeit" *(pseudous)* signs and wonders (cf. v. 9) the lawless one would use
to bolster his claim to divinity. The lie itself, then, probably was the
claim to be a god greater than all other gods. Believing the lie or believing the truth are presented in this passage as the only two alternatives
available. Those who reject God's truth are destined to "exchange the
truth of God for a lie" (Rom 1:25). One must either trust in Jesus or
trust in a lie. The presence of the man of lawlessness forces the issue
and makes the choice unambiguous.

2:12 A final clause presents the ultimate fate of those who choose
to trust the lie (v. 12). All who have not believed the truth "will be condemned" *(kriqw'sin)*. This verb does not require in itself a negative
judgment (cf. the translation "may be judged," NASB). But most often

---

[54] Cf. Morris, who with Frame understands the phrase as a reference to an energy or
working that has as its object the deluding of humanity *(First and Second Epistles to the
Thessalonians,* 234). The lie that the deceived accept as truth is "the lie that the Man of
Lawlessness is God."

condemnation is implied when *krivnw* is used, and the description of those who will be judged make clear that in this case judgment will result in condemnation. Paul described those judged with a negative and then a positive clause: they "have not believed the truth" but have instead "delighted in wickedness." The "truth" they have rejected is the gospel of Jesus Christ (cf. 1:8). Those for whom the day of the Lord is a day of glory rather than condemnation are those who have believed the testimony of the apostles (cf. 1:10). Those who will receive condemnation have not only rejected the truth but have delighted in wickedness. The verb used in this second descriptive clause, "delighted," implies the exercise of personal judgment and will. But delighting in wickedness in this context implies far more than finding a particular sinful act enjoyable. It represents one's basic attitude toward God. Faced with the opportunity to follow God's truth, those who delight in wickedness are those who have chosen to reject God and follow the path of "wickedness" (*adikia,* cf. v. 10; Rom 1:18,32), a choice that destines them for condemnation.[55]

2:13–14 In terms of form these verses begin with a thanksgiving, "We ought always thank God for you" (cf. 1:3), inserted in a rather odd location. One might expect the beginning of such a thanksgiving to introduce a change of theme.[56] This particular expression of thanks, however, does not mark a major change of topic. Rather, it marks a transition within the discussion of the deception threatening the church (cf. v. 2). Paul was thankful because he knew that the church would not succumb to deception and eventual destruction (vv.11–12) "but" (the adversative *de* contrasts vv. 11–12 with vv. 13–14) was destined for sal-

---

[55] The use of two aorist participles, πιστεύσαντες ("believed") and εὐδοκήσαντες ("delighted"), strengthens the impression that Paul was thinking of the path these had chosen (when they rejected the gospel) more than the lifestyle that resulted from that choice.

[56] Best notes an abrupt change of theme here, asserting that "Paul has answered the explicit and implicit questions of the Thessalonians about the parousia" (*Commentary on the First and Second Epistles to the Thessalonians,* 310). What Paul had not emphasized in vv. 1–12, however, was the vital importance of rejecting deceptive claims made by false teachers. The church must not be unsettled or alarmed (v. 2). They must persist in their "belief in the truth" (v. 13), for that alone will allow them to "share in the glory" of the Lord Jesus Christ (v. 14). Therefore they must "stand firm" in the apostolic teachings (v. 15). Although Paul utilized a thanksgiving formula in v. 13, we cannot consider that he had completed his treatment of the topics stated in vv. 1–2 until vv. 13–15 are added to the discussion of the day of the Lord in vv. 3–12.

vation "through belief in the truth" (v. 13).[57]

A second time (cf. the discussion of *opheilomen* at 1:3) Paul stressed his obligation to give thanks as a way of emphasizing the veracity and the appropriateness of his affirmation of the church. The condition of the "brothers" is indicated first by the fact that they are "loved by the Lord" (cf. 1 Thess 1:4). The perfect tense participle rendered "loved" implies a settled condition. The phrase as a whole was no doubt especially meaningful for Paul the Benjamite since it was part of Moses' blessing of the tribe of Benjamin (Deut 33:12). The Thessalonian believers were reminded that they had entered into a loving relationship with the Lord (they had not rejected the truth) and were assured that they continued to be the beneficiaries of that love.

The reason for giving thanks stated in 2:13 stands in contrast to the reasons stated in 1:3–4. In an unusual statement for a Pauline thanksgiving (but cf. 1 Cor 1:4–9), the causal clause of 2:13 places far more emphasis on God's activities than on those of the Thessalonians. Paul told the Thessalonians that he gave thanks to God because "God chose you to be saved." Though the verb "chose" *(eilato)* is uncommon in the New Testament (used only here, Phil 1:22 and Heb 11:25), Paul apparently used it in this context as a synonym of the more common *eklegomai* (cf. 1 Thess 1:4; Eph 1:4), meaning to "select" or "elect." Salvation is always the result of the active grace of God. No one earns it on the basis of works or beliefs. Salvation is the result of God's choice to make salvation available. Yet the fact that God chooses is not presented as an act that limits the availability of salvation. There is no direct statement

---

[57] The δέ itself could be understood to resume the statement of thanksgiving from 1:3 (see Bruce, *1 and 2 Thessalonians*, 189; Dibelius, *Neun Kleinen Briefe*, 34). Paul did repeat the same thanksgiving formula, but 2:13–14 is too far removed from 1:3–4 for a logical link to be convincing. And as P. T. O'Brien observes, 2:13–14 "does not have an epistolary function" but "is evidence of Paul's pastoral concern for the addressees and his desire to encourage them" (*Introductory Thanksgivings in the Letters of Paul,* NovTSup 49 [Leiden: Brill, 1977], 184). Comparisons with the extended thanksgiving of 1 Thessalonians are unconvincing since 2 Thess 2:13–14 does not expand on 2 Thess 1:3–4 in the same fashion as 1 Thess 2:13 and 3:9–13, which provide additional thanksgiving elements to the truncated thanksgiving structure of 1 Thess 1:2–5. Δέ could serve as a transitional particle (such as "now") without any indication of contrast (cf. Best, *1 and 2 Thessalonians,* 311). But a contrast is present between the condemned "who have not believed the truth" (v. 12) and those destined for salvation "through belief in the truth" (v. 13). The contrast is only obscured if one fails to recognize that 2:1–15 is a coherent unit.

in the New Testament to the effect that the option of salvation is unavailable to certain persons or that God has chosen some for damnation. But sadly, the passage overall gives ample evidence that some people will choose not to avail themselves of God's salvation.

The presence of a textual variant complicates the interpretation of the next phrase. Did God choose the Thessalonian believers *(ap archēs)* "from the beginning" (NIV, RSV) or *(aparchēn)* as "firstfruits" (NAB, GNB)? Both readings have strong manuscript support, and internal arguments can also be made for both readings. Against reading *archēs* is the fact that Paul never used *ap archēs* in a temporal sense.[58] Even if one assumes that Paul did intend to say that the believers were chosen "from the beginning," we still must ask which "beginning" he had in mind. He may have meant that God chose the Thessalonian believers "from the beginning of time" (cf. Rom 8:28–30, note the differences in vocabulary), but Paul never used *archē* of eternity past. His only temporal use of *archē* (Phil 4:15) refers to the beginning of the proclamation of the gospel in Macedonia (translated "in the early days" in the NIV). Used in a similar sense in v. 13, the phrase might affirm the believers as some of the earliest (and by implication most spiritually responsive?) converts in Macedonia. This appears at first glance to make sense of the clause but does not mesh well with the larger context of vv. 13–14, which celebrates the chosenness of the Thessalonians, not the Thessalonians' responsiveness. The reading *ap archēs* is also unlikely considering copyists' apparent tendency to misread *aparchē* and insert *ap archēs* in its place (cf. Rom 16:5; Rev 14:4).

But if the original reading was "firstfruits" *(aparchē)*, what was meant? In the Old Testament firstfruits was a cultic technical term. It was that first portion that was dedicated to God and served to consecrate the remainder (cf. Rom 11:16). Used of persons it might indicate the firstborn of each family consecrated to Yahweh or the Levites (as a portion of the entire nation) consecrated to God's service. Thus the word has the temporal connotation of that which comes first in a sequence and/or the qualitative connotation of that which is holy and consecrated to the Lord. Twice Paul used *aparchēn* temporally of the first converts of a region. Epaenetus was the first convert in Asia (Rom 16:5), and the household of Stephanus were the first converts in Achaia (1 Cor 16:15). But the Thessalonians were evangelized after the Philippians. They

---

[58] Paul almost always used ἀρχή of rulers or spiritual powers. His only temporal phrase involving the word is ἐν ἀρχῇ τοῦ εὐαγγελίου (Phil 4:15).

were not the first converts in Macedonia. "Firstfruits" in v. 13 is unmodified, however, and Paul could have used *aparchēn* meaning that Thessalonian believers were the firstfruits in Thessalonica. Such a statement could serve to encourage the church by implying that more converts would yet follow from their city in spite of the persecution they were experiencing.[59]

Yet the context of vv. 13–14 seems to encourage the church not by stressing the evangelistic potential of their city but by emphasizing that God chose them and they are destined to share the glory of the Lord. This implies a qualitative rather than a temporal use of "firstfruit."[60] Used qualitatively *aparchēn* highlights for the readers their status as persons chosen by God for consecration to his service. This fits well with the statements that they are "loved by the Lord" (v. 13a) and called to "share in the glory of the Lord Jesus Christ" (v. 14). It also makes sense of a reading that is difficult on the surface (explaining the scribal tendency to change it) but does fit the flow of Paul's sentence.

God's selection of the Thessalonian believers "to be saved" (or more lit., "for salvation," NASB) is modified by two phrases that express the means of salvation.[61] The preposition "through" *(ev)* occurs only once in the Greek text of v. 13 and has as its objects both "sanctification by the Spirit" and "faith in the truth" (NASB). "Spirit" may refer to the spirit of the believer (cf. 1 Thess 5:23), but with a singular noun and in the absence of a possessive pronoun it seems unlikely that Paul meant "sanctification of your spirits." Elsewhere Paul (using the same preposition, *en*) described sanctification as the work of God's Holy Spirit (cf. Rom 15:16; 1 Cor 6:11), and he probably intended the same here.

God's choice to consecrate a people to himself is balanced by the people's act of exercising "faith in the truth." The "truth" is the apostolic gospel (cf. vv. 10–12). Paul's choice of vocabulary was the result of the contrast he was working between those who believe the truth and are saved and those who believe the lie (rejecting the truth) and are con-

---

[59] G. D. Fee argues for this option ("On Text and Commentary on 1 and 2 Thessalonians," in *SBL Seminar Papers* 31, ed. E. H. Lovering, Jr. [Atlanta: Scholars Press, 1992], 179–80).

[60] The qualitative element of the ἀπαρχή is prominent (if not dominant) in several Pauline passages (see Rom 8:23; 11:16; 1 Cor 15:20,23).

[61] The noun σωτηρία occurs only here in 2 Thessalonians; the verb σώζω, only in 2:10 (cf. 1 Thess 2:16). "Salvation" involves both present and future deliverance, and in this instance (more so than in 1 Thess 5:8–9) it should be allowed enough breadth to connote both meanings.

demned. Faith in this context goes beyond its English connotation of believing the truth of a proposition and includes committing or entrusting oneself to this truth. In this way Paul both affirmed and reassured the church while at the same time reminding them of the vital importance they should attach to fidelity to the apostolic gospel. They must stand firm in the truth of the gospel, for confusion and deception are the tools of Satan, and those who succumb ultimately are destined for perdition.

2:14 Salvation through sanctification and faith is further modified by the clause that begins in v. 14. The neuter relative pronoun translated "to this" indicates Paul had the preceding clause in mind, not just the term "salvation." God "called" the Thessalonians to this salvation "through our gospel," that is, through the apostolic message. God's choice (*eilato*, v. 13) of the Thessalonians differs from his call (*ekalesen*) in v. 14 in that the former is a timeless event within the mind of God. The call, on the other hand, refers to the temporal event at which the apostle proclaimed the gospel, and the Thessalonians had the opportunity to respond to it (cf. Rom 10:14). There could be no ambiguity regarding the avenue by which the Thessalonians heard the call of God. They heard it through the gospel of the Lord Jesus (1:8) preached by Paul and his coworkers (cf. 1 Thess 1:5). If God's initial call to them was expressed through the preaching of the apostle and obedience to that same message was the only means of salvation, then it would make no sense at this stage to give credence to false teaching that contradicted the words and writings of the apostle.[62]

The call of God to the Thessalonians and their positive response should lead to living as people of God in the present, as well as to sharing in the glories of the kingdom of God in the future (cf. 1 Thess 2:12; 4:7; 5:24). Paul's thought in this verse, however, leaps from contemplation of the Thessalonians' past conversion (v. 14a) directly to their future glorification (v. 14b). God called them through the apostolic gospel in order that they might "share in the glory of our Lord Jesus Christ" (v. 14b). The lostness of humanity can be described as falling "short of the glory of God" (Rom 3:23). Obtaining that glory (in other words, the glorification of the believer) is a reality that is initiated with conversion

---

[62] Gal 5:1-5 contains a similar argument. The gospel through which the readers entered into Christianity is the gospel they must maintain. Deserting the apostolic gospel is tantamount to deserting the faith. Rejecting the truth for the lie means joining the ranks of those destined for destruction.

but that will not reach its fullness until the coming of the Lord and the resurrection of believers to share his presence. Thus to "share" *(peripoiēsin)* or "obtain" (RSV) salvation stands in contrast to suffering the wrath of God at the final judgment in 1 Thess 5:9 (the only other occurrence of *peripoiēsin* in the Thessalonian letters; cf. Eph 1:14). Sharing the "glory *[doxēs]* of our Lord" is a phrase that looks toward that day in the future when the Lord Jesus "will transform our lowly bodies so that they will be like his glorious *[doxēs]* body" (Phil 3:21; cf. Rom 8:17; 1 Cor 15:43). Obtaining this ultimate glory, then, requires a genuine and abiding commitment to the apostolic gospel. Paul's thanksgiving is based on the conviction that the Thessalonians genuinely had responded to God's call in the gospel and possessed a faith that leads ultimately to the sharing of the glory of the Lord at his coming. All that remained was to encourage them to persevere.

2:15 The passage concludes with a summary exhortation.[63] "So then" indicates that the two imperatives that follow grow out of the preceding verses. In light of the error of the teaching that the day of the Lord had arrived (vv. 2–3), and in spite of present and future satanic attempts at deception (vv. 3,7,9), and considering the terrible cost of preferring the lie rather than adhering to the truth (v. 12), the church must "stand firm."

The exhortation to "stand firm" is often followed in Paul's writings by a clarifying prepositional phrase, for example, "in the faith" (1 Cor 16:13) or "in the Lord" (1 Thess 3:8). But here (as in Gal 5:1) it is followed by a second imperative that expands on the nature of the "stand" maintained. The call to stand firm was made more specific as Paul warned the church that they must "hold to the teachings we passed on to you." The church must not be deceived either in the present (vv. 3,7) or in the last days when a great deceiver will come on the scene. They must not be deceived by false prophecy (v. 2) or by false reports (vv. 2,15) or by forged letters (vv. 2,15). They must stand firm in the truth already received through the apostolic gospel because to fail to do so could lead to condemnation (vv. 11–14; cf. 1 Cor 15:1–2).

The "teachings" to which the church was to cling were those central religious truths or "traditions" (RSV) that were passed from believer to believer. Used in this context "tradition" *(paradoseis)* does not refer to mere human teachings or to the traditions of Judaism to which Paul previously devoted himself (cf. the use of *paradoseis* in Col 2:8 and Gal

---

[63] Cf. 1 Thess 4:18; 5:11.

1:14).[64] Rather, it refers to apostolic tradition delivered in the name of Christ (cf. 3:6; 1 Cor 11:2,23).

The various confessions (e.g., 1 Cor 15:3–5), hymns (Phil 2:6–11; cf. Col 1:15–20), exhortations for Christian households (e.g., Eph 5:22–6:9; cf. Col 3:18–4:1), and ethical instructions in general (e.g., 1 Thess 4:1–8), including vice and virtue lists (e.g., Gal 5:19–23), reflect the type of tradition that was circulated in the churches[65] and had been "passed on" to the Thessalonians (cf. 1 Thess 4:1). The "traditions" contained in vv. 1–14 had to do with eschatology. But no teaching is totally compartmentalized, and error in one matter often leads to error in another.[66] It was therefore imperative that the church remain true to the traditions they were taught either "by word" when he was with them or "by letter" while he was apart from them.

The reference to "word" *(logos)* and "letter" *(epistolēs)* is interesting at several points. First, the reference to instruction the Thessalonians had received by letter implies that this was not the first letter they had received from Paul. However, identifying the earlier letter remains an exercise in speculation. Assuming the traditional sequence of the extant correspondence, the *epistolē* Paul had in mind could be 1 Thessalonians. If 2 Thessalonians were written first, Paul could refer to this very letter from the perspective of the reader. If Paul wrote letters to Thessalonica that are no longer extant, as is the case with two of his four known letters to Corinth, then the "letter" to which v. 15 refers could be lost to us.

Second, "whether by word of mouth *[logou]* or by letter *[epistolēs]*" appears to echo "by prophecy *[pneumatos]*, report *[logou]* or letter *[epistolēs]* supposedly from us" in v. 2. If this is so, then why was *pneumatos* not repeated? This may indicate that "by some prophecy" referred to prophetic utterances within the assembly. Such utterances deserved respect but also were subject to evaluation by the assembly (cf. 1 Thess 5:19–22). The most likely criteria by which they would be evaluated is the apostolic traditions delivered orally or by letter. By giving priority to apostolic words and letters, the apostle had in effect

---

[64] Cf. the reference in Mark 7:3 to the "tradition of the elders" adhered to by the Pharisees.

[65] See also 1 Tim 6:20; 2 Tim 1:13–14; 2:1–2; Titus 2:1; Jude 3.

[66] It is possible, for instance, that the eschatological error treated in vv. 1–14 is connected to the problem of the idle in 3:6–15. Consider also the implications that table fellowship had for the very essence of the gospel (Gal 2:11–16).

brought prophecy (from any source) under the control of apostolic tradition.

Third, and more importantly for our understanding of this passage, the recurrence of these two terms (cf. v. 3) helps mark the boundaries of Paul's discussion and together with the imperatives in v. 15a highlight his primary concerns. The intent of the apostle was to encourage the church to hold to established apostolic instruction and not be confused, alarmed, or (worst of all) won over by contradictory teachings. The context in which he did this is the appearance of false teachings regarding the day of the Lord. But the message delivered by the passage was applicable to a broad range of situations. It was a warning that to deviate from divinely revealed truth is to deviate onto a path that can only lead to condemnation.

3. A Concluding Prayer (2:16–17)

[16]May our Lord Jesus Christ himself and God our Father, who loved us and by his grace gave us eternal encouragement and good hope, [17]encourage your hearts and strengthen you in every good deed and word.

The exhortation to "stand firm and hold to the teachings" received from the apostles (2:15) is followed by a prayer requesting divine encouragement and assistance for the Thessalonians that they might do this very thing. In this way the prayer serves as a conclusion to 2:1–15.[67] Although it added the element of divine assistance to the preceding encouragement to endure (vv. 13–15), the prayer also expressed Paul's aspirations for the converts. This blended with Paul's request for prayer for himself and his coworkers (3:1–2) highlights the bond between Paul and the church. They shared a responsibility for one another. Mutual concern and mutual intercession should characterize their relationship as each faces the challenges of the wicked and faithless persons who would inhibit the faith and the work of both the church and the apostle (cf. 3:1–3).

2:16 The core of the prayer is the request, "May our Lord Jesus

---

[67] F. W. Hughes observes, regarding vv. 16–17, that "since the two-part proof in 2.3–15 seems primarily directed towards the doctrinal orthodoxy of the readers and their personal and doctrinal stability, it is not at all surprising that the *peroratio* which sums up this two-part proof should be an intercessory prayer for the readers" ("The Rhetoric of 1 Thessalonians," in *The Thessalonian Correspondence*, BETL 87 [Leuven: University Press, 1990], 62).

Christ himself and God our Father … encourage your hearts and strengthen you" (vv. 16–17).[68] "Himself" *(autos)* emphasizes the Lord Jesus Christ as does the placement of the name of Jesus before "God our Father."[69] One should not make too much of this, however, since an emphatic *autos* was a common stylistic element in wish-prayers (cf. 3:16; 1 Thess 3:11; 5:23). The placement of the name of Jesus before that of God is unusual but does occur elsewhere in Paul (see Gal 1:1; 2 Cor 13:14) and probably reflects the way in which actions of Jesus and of the Father were so closely identified as to be attributable to either.[70]

"God our Father" together with the two participial clauses that modify God highlight both his authority and his benevolence. This depiction of the Father God added to the image of a Jesus who is both Lord and Christ sets the stage for prayer. It presents God as one who has both the power and the inclination to help his children. God is a Father "who loved … and gave."[71] These two participles share a single article, indicating that they should be understood as a compound statement, perhaps referring to a single reality. That they are aorists makes it unlikely that Paul was thinking of God's constant love and care for his children. Rather, Paul probably had in mind God's loving gift of his Son Jesus (cf. Rom 5:8; 8:39). It is that which was given by grace and which provides hope and eternal comfort to believers. A Father God who would demonstrate such love is one to whom his children can pray with confidence.

"Eternal encouragement" ("comfort," NASB) may refer to the comfort God gives his people on a regular and unending basis, but the aorist tense of the participle "gave" weighs against this. Considering the eschatologi-

---

[68] For a description of the development and structure of this type of "wish-prayer" see G. P. Wiles, *The Significance of the Intercessory Prayer Passages in the Letters of Paul,* SNTSMS 24 (Cambridge: University Press, 1974), 22–107.

[69] The uniqueness of ὁ θεὸς ὁ πατὴρ ἡμῶν is highlighted by variants in some MSS reflecting scribal attempts to make Paul's prayer conform to more common patterns.

[70] B. Rigeaux asserts that Jesus is given prominence in the prayer as a part of the Christological orientation of the passage overall (2:13–3:5), but the emphasis in God's election and salvation of the believers in vv. 13–14 weakens his argument (*Saint Paul: Les Epitres aux Thessaloniciens* [Paris: Jl. Gabalda; Gembloux: J. Duculot, 1956], 690).

[71] Both participles are singular (as are the verbs in v. 17). But it is inadvisable to distinguish too sharply between the acts of the Father and the Son. Both love humanity, and both give comfort and hope (see Gal 2:20; Rom 8:35,38). The participles may attach primarily to the Father syntactically, but theologically they attach to both just as both are the subjects in Paul's prayer.

cal focus of the larger passage, what God gave was assurance regarding the character of the age to come. The day of the Lord brings distress and condemnation for those who have rejected the truth (v. 12). But for the followers of Jesus it brings deliverance as they share in the glory of the Lord (v. 14). At the same time, the assurance of eternal comfort also provides temporal encouragement. "Hope" (only here in 2 Thess) also looks to the future in Paul's writings (cf. 1 Thess 2:19; 4:13; 5:8). The phrase "good hope" was used by non-Christian writers to refer to life after death.[72] God gave believers "eternal encouragement and good hope," not on the basis of merit but "by his grace." Thus Paul directed his prayer to a God of love who had given salvation by grace to those who had not earned it. Who better to pray to than a God of power, love, and grace?

2:17 The two main verbs expressing Paul's prayer are in v. 17. He prayed that the Lord Jesus and God the Father might "encourage" *(parakalesai)* and "strengthen" *(stērixai)* the Thessalonians. Paul used infinitives of these same two verbs (in reverse order) in 1 Thess 3:2 to describe Timothy's goals in his mission to the church. "Encourage" translates a verbal form of the noun in the earlier phrase "eternal encouragement." This verb, however, in conjunction with the prayer for God to strengthen "every good deed and word" of the church, looks to the present condition of the believers rather than their eschatological hope. In their present distress (1:5–7) and alarm (2:2), the church needed divine encouragement. In the context of encouraging the doing of a task, *parakalesai* has the connotation of gentle and positive urging. Encouraging the "heart" does not stress the doing of a task but rather the giving of comfort. "Heart" was used of various facets of a person, the center of the emotion, or will, or thoughts. In this context "heart" is balanced by "deed and word" in the following clause. If the latter signify the external expressions of a person, the former ("heart") likely was intended to signify the internal life in general without drawing any finer distinctions.

The second request is that God might "strengthen" the church "in every good deed and word."[73] "Strengthen" in this context may mean

---

[72] P. Otzen, "'Gute Hoffnung' bei Paulus," *ZNW* 49 (1958): 283–85.

[73] "Strengthen" does not have a stated object in the Greek text. As a result some assume the object "you" (NIV), while others assume that "heart" was intended as the object of both verbs, resulting in a sentence like "comfort and strengthen your hearts" (NASB). This latter option, however, obscures Paul's dual concern (a) that the church not be unsettled and alarmed (2:2) but (b) continue with appropriate Christian behavior (cf. 3:1–15).

"to confirm as good or to establish as a pattern." In effect Paul's prayer affirmed the good deeds and words of the church and asked that such should continue as a consistent pattern of behavior. The strengthening or establishing of the church was a concern also expressed in the prayer in 1 Thess 3:11–13 and is the church's appropriate response to the challenges and persecutions intended to weaken or destroy it (cf. 3:3; 1 Thess 3:2). Paul did not pray for the elimination of the wicked who afflicted the church. That was a task to be accomplished at the parousia. But in the midst of wickedness he prayed that the church would persist in "every good deed and word." The two terms together are intentionally broad and nonspecific, encompassing all Christian behavior. A church certain of its future in Christ (v. 16), at peace within itself, and well established in Christian patterns of belief and behavior (v. 17) is a church that can stand firm (v. 15) in the face of error and opposition.

VIII. PRAYERS OFFERED AND REQUESTED (3:1–5)
1. A Request for Prayer (3:1–2)
2. A Prayer of Encouragement Offered (3:3–4)
3. A Concluding Benediction (3:5)

VIII. PRAYERS OFFERED AND REQUESTED (3:1–5)

"Finally *[loipon],* brothers," which initiates chap. 3, marks the beginning of the last major division of the letter, a section of ethical exhortations (3:1–15). Although *loipon* could be used inferentially,[1] it commonly indicates transition in Paul's letters (cf. 2 Cor 13:11; Phil 3:1; 4:8; 1 Thess 4:1). A transition in Paul's thought also is indicated by the fact that 3:1–2 turns the reader's attention away from the false eschatological teachings troubling the Thessalonians (2:1–17) and toward Paul's task of spreading the word of the Lord in spite of the evil, faithless persons who opposed him and his coworkers. Although the call to perseverance (v. 5) may echo the concerns of 2:1–17, the bulk of vv. 1–5 is too general to be an outgrowth of the preceding chapter. Paul's confident assertion that the Thessalonians would "continue to do the things we commanded" (v. 4) sets the stage for vv. 6–15.

1. A Request for Prayer (3:1–2)

[1]Finally, brothers, pray for us that the message of the Lord may spread rapidly and be honored, just as it was with you. [2]And pray that we may be delivered from wicked and evil men, for not everyone has faith.

The third chapter begins with a request for prayer. But the passage overall also highlights the bond between Paul and the church. They shared a common faith and a common Lord (v. 1). They also had in

---

[1] Cf. R. Jewett, *The Thessalonian Correspondence: Pauline Rhetoric and Millenarian Piety* (Philadelphia: Fortress, 1986), for arguments supporting translating Τὸ λοιπὸν "therefore" and the impact this has on the passage overall.

common the experience of suffering at the hands of evil (vv. 2–3). The Thessalonians were not alone in the faith and were not to so focus on their own difficulties that they failed to recognize the need to pray for others. Neither was their suffering to lead to despair because their common God is faithful, and through his gift of strength and protection both Paul and the Thessalonians would persevere in the faith.

Paul's plea for prayer for himself and his associates ("brothers, pray for us") uses the same terminology found in 1 Thess 5:25.[2] Paul considered prayer one means by which the church could participate with him in his ministry, and he frequently asked for prayers that his ministry might be accomplished and that those who would hinder him might be overcome (cf. Rom 15:30; 2 Cor 1:11; Phil 1:19). Here in vv. 1–2 Paul's request is twofold.

First, he asked the Thessalonians to pray that "the message of the Lord may spread rapidly and be honored." The phrase "message [or "word," *logos*] of the Lord" was not common in Paul's letters, occurring only in 1 Thess 1:18; 4:15 and here. Paul may have chosen it as a contrast to the false teachings (cf. *logou* in 2 Thess 2:2,15), the spread of which would inhibit the true "word of the Lord" (NASB). This "message" is the gospel (as in 1 Thess 1:8). "Spread rapidly" translates a verb *(treche)* that means "to run." Used with a human subject the image of the runner often symbolized the effort required to do well in some endeavor (1 Cor 9:24,26; Gal 2:2; 5:7; Phil 2:16).[3] Since the subject in this instance *(logos)* is impersonal, however, *treche* connotes not the effort required to make progress but rapid and unhindered progress itself.[4] Paul requested prayer not for himself but for the gospel that it might be spread even more rapidly than it had to date. But the proclamation of the word widely and rapidly does not guarantee its acceptance. Thus Paul also urged prayer that the gospel that spread rapidly also would be accepted ("honored") by those who heard it.

"Be honored" uses a word frequently translated "to be glorified." In this context it indicates the response Paul desired from those who would hear the rapidly spreading gospel. He asked the church to pray that the

---

[2] The word order differs, and some MSS add καὶ in 1 Thess 5:25.

[3] Athletic imagery in general and the image of the runner especially was a popular, positive image in the first century applicable to the struggles of life. See V. C. Pfitzner, *Paul and the Agon Motif* (Leiden: Brill, 1967).

[4] The LXX text of Ps 147:15, "[The Lord] sends his command to the earth; his word runs swiftly," uses the same verb for "run" (τρέχη).

hearers would respect the gospel. Similar terms describe the response of the Gentiles in Antioch of Pisidia who heard that the gospel was also for them. They "were glad and honored the word of the Lord, and all who were appointed for eternal life believed" (Acts 13:48). If the gospel is respected, it will be effective. At least it will not be perceived as a threat and actively opposed. Paul requested that the Thessalonians pray for a rapid and effective spread of the gospel. If everyone "honored" the gospel "just as it was" honored among the Thessalonian brethren, the gospel would spread rapidly indeed. Unfortunately, such was not the case.

3:2 The second prayer request is for deliverance from evil and wicked men. This verb for deliverance was used both to indicate eschatological future deliverance (e.g., Rom 11:26; Col 1:13; 1 Thess 1:10) and deliverance from dangers in this present age (e.g., Rom 15:31; 2 Cor 1:10).[5] The latter is what the apostle had in mind in v. 2. Paul had once been an opponent of the gospel (Gal 1:13–14). He had witnessed the death of Steven and knew the lengths to which persons opposed to the gospel might go (Acts 8:1; 9:1–2). It is certainly reasonable to fear such persons. Yet the prayer for the deliverance of the evangelists sprang not from timidity but from Paul's desire for the unhindered advance of the gospel.

"Wicked" *(atopōn)* and "evil" *(ponērōn)* appear to be used synonymously in this context, though the few times the former word is used elsewhere in the New Testament (Luke 23:41; Acts 25:5; 28:6) it generally describes actions that violate the laws of humankind. *Ponērōn* occurs much more frequently and may describe actions improper by human or divine standards. In the LXX *atopōn* is often linked with "lawless."[6] Some commentators argue that the Jewish opposition Paul faced in Corinth and the omission of the term "lawless" (because he did not wish to appear to exclude the Jews) together imply that Paul had "wicked and evil" Jewish opposition in mind.[7] But the wicked and evil

---

[5] The Judean opposition anticipated in Romans was subsequently encountered when the Jewish leaders in Jerusalem attempted to put an end to Paul's work (Acts 21:27–30; 22:30; 23:12; 24:1–9). The opposition from which Paul was delivered in Asia probably was related to the Gentile attack on his ministry by the followers of Artemis (Acts 19:23–41).

[6] The concurrence of ἄτοπος with ἄνομος should not be overstated. The two are linked on occasion, but not consistently; see Job 27:6; 34:12; Prov 30:20.

[7] See Marshall, *1 and 2 Thessalonians,* 214, who reflects the work of E. von Dobschütz, *Die Thessalonicherbriefe* (Göttingen: Vandenhoeck & Ruprecht, 1974), 306. Compare the caution expressed by Best, *1 and 2 Thessalonians,* 325–26.

ones who had opposed Paul in the Acts account of his Corinthian ministry were a mixture of Jews and Gentiles (Acts 16:16–24; 17:5; 17:18,32). And neither *atopōn* nor *ponērōn* was used exclusively of Jewish opponents of the faith (nor exclusively of Gentile opponents). It seems hazardous as a result to assert that Paul had Jewish opposition in mind in this passage based on the omission of "lawless" from the text.

Paul's prayer request operates on the conviction that "not everyone has faith," implying a direct connection between wickedness and faithlessness. Whether Jews or Gentiles, the faithless who oppose the gospel are evil persons. By characterizing the faithless negatively, Paul implied a positive characterization of the faithful. They are the good and just who are persecuted for no valid cause and who will ultimately be vindicated by God. The evil of the faithless, on the other hand, will ultimately lead to destruction (cf. 2 Thess 1:5–10).[8]

Paul was asking the church to pray that he and his coworkers would be delivered from those who were not persons of faith and who would use any means, even illegal and immoral, to stop the spread of the good news.[9] Even by non-Christian standards it was improper to make false accusations at court; it was illegal to jail or beat a person without just cause as happened to Paul in Philippi (Acts 16:20–24,37–39). And yet the opponents of the faith did engage in just such improper methods in their attempt to hinder the advance of the word. In Thessalonica, Jason faced the threat of punitive legal action for nothing more than giving aid and comfort to Paul and his coworkers (Acts 17:5–9).

Since such "evil and wicked" persons existed, rejection and opposition were an inevitable experience for any evangelist. If the message would not be honored, at least the messenger might be spared. Ridicule, physical punishment, or imprisonment (cf. 2 Cor 6:3–10) were not just unpleasant. They could rob the evangelist of the opportunity to spread the gospel. Thus Paul's prayer for deliverance from evil men was an extension of his prayer that the gospel might go forward unhindered (cf. Acts 28:31).

Finally, believers need to be reminded that they do not face opposi-

---

[8] For the role that the negative characterization of one's opponents can play in argumentation and in self-definition, see A. Y. Collins, "Vilification and Self-Definition in the Book of Revelation," *HTR* 79 (1986): 308–20.

[9] The article with πίστις, "the faith," and the use of the genitive πάντων, "of all," may imply that Paul was not lamenting a lack of "faith" on the part of some but a rejection of "the faith" by some who thus became its opponents.

tion in their own strength. They meet the opposition of the faithless assured that "the Lord is faithful" (v. 3).

2. A Prayer of Encouragement Offered (3:3–4)

³But the Lord is faithful, and he will strengthen and protect you from the evil one. ⁴We have confidence in the Lord that you are doing and will continue to do the things we command.

3:3 A shift occurs at this point in the text. Paul turned from concerns regarding the persecutions his own band of missionaries would experience ("pray for us," vv. 1–2) to the difficulties his readers would experience ("the Lord ... will strengthen you," vv. 3–4). It is appropriate that the transition between these two areas of concern is linked by two truths that impacted both Paul and the Thessalonians. "Not everyone has faith. But the Lord is faithful" (vv. 2b–3a).[10] Independently the two statements are somewhat obvious and abstract. Stated together and in this context the wordplay provides a needed word of encouragement to believers.

Persecution by faithless persons was a stark, indisputable reality. Persevering in the face of persecution required recognizing an equally genuine reality that one might forget in the midst of suffering—that the Lord is faithful.[11] His faithfulness guarantees that (a) our suffering has meaning, (b) our persecutors will reap their just reward, and (c) our future is secure in him. The conviction that God is faithful enables believers to look beyond the persecution of the faithless and continue in the faith.

The remainder of v. 3 consists of a relative clause that further describes the Lord. It is the Lord who "will strengthen [*stērixei*] and protect [*fulaxei*] you from the evil one." His faithfulness is seen not only in judgment but also in his care for the church. That which is strengthened is firmly established and is capable of withstanding the

---

[10] The punctuation in the English should not obscure the link between these two statements. The wordplay (πίστις ... πιστός) is obviously intentional. In the Greek text the two words are side by side, with πίστις the last word of v. 2 and πιστός the first word of v. 3.

[11] The more common phrase in Paul's letters is "God is faithful," which occurs three times in the Corinthian correspondence (1 Cor 1:9; 10:13; 2 Cor 1:18). Similar is "the one who calls you is faithful" (1 Thess 5:24). The use of "the Lord" here may imply an emphasis on judgment at the Lord's return (cf. 2 Thess 1:5–10). He can be trusted to exact a just judgment at the proper time.

onslaughts of its opponents.[12] Paul sent Timothy to the church with this same goal, to "strengthen and encourage" them so that "no one would be unsettled by these trials" (1 Thess 3:2–3).

"Protect" *(phylaxei)* is used elsewhere by Paul of guarding or keeping God's commandments. The use of the word here, however, is consistent with its occurrence in the LXX, where it describes God guarding his people,[13] and in John 17:12 of Jesus' keeping his disciples safe so that none were "lost except for the one"—Judas. As with the twelve, divine protection does not imply the absence of conflict but preservation through conflict. "The evil one" translates an adjective *(tou ponērou)* that may be either masculine and personal (as the NIV and NRSV translate) or neuter as a general reference to "evil" (as in the KJV and RSV). Satan was referred to in the early church as *ho ponēros,* "the evil one" (Matt 6:13; Eph 6:16). Likewise Paul did refer in a personal manner to the activity of Satan in these letters, both in the future (2:9) and in the present as a hinderer of his work (1 Thess 2:18) and as a tempter attempting to short-circuit the faith of the church (1 Thess 3:5).

Paul may have had Satan in mind in 3:3 as well. In the immediate context of 3:3, however, the references to the evil afflicting the Thessalonian believers are more general in nature. Paul's prayer for the strengthening of the church utilizes the same verb *(stērizō)* found in the prayer of 2:17—a prayer related to the church resisting the false teachings about the day of the Lord. In addition, Paul's request for prayer in v. 2 (which is balanced with his prayer for the church in v. 3) requests deliverance from "wicked and evil men." It seems likely then that the evil Paul had in mind was not "the evil one" specifically but those varied manifestations of evil that already were afflicting and would continue to afflict the church.[14]

---

[12] The strengthening of believers may focus on firmly establishing their Christian character, making Christian deeds natural characteristics of their lives (cf. the use of στηρίζω in Rom 1:11; 16:25). Such a putting on of the faith is at the same time the putting on of the armor of God (cf. Eph 6:10–20). The Christian soldier must be well established in the faith in order to survive the conflict with the opponents of the faith.

[13] See, e.g., Pss 11:8 (Eng., 12:7); 120:8 (Eng., 121:8).

[14] The future tense στηρίξει and φυλάξει refer not to the distant future but to the immediate future in which the present distress was sure to continue since the church is "destined" to experience trials (1 Thess 3:2–4; cf. Wanamaker's assertion that these are "progressive futures" (*1 and 2 Thessalonians,* 276). Also see Best, *1 and 2 Thessalonians,* 327–28, for a listing of arguments regarding the proper interpretation of τοῦ πονηροῦ in response to Dibelius and others.

Confidence in the Lord as the one who strengthens and protects his people leads to a confidence in the church and the sure perseverance of the faithful. A chiastic *(A B B A)* relationship may be observed between vv. 1–2 and vv. 3–4. Paul asked for prayer *(A)* that his missionary work might continue unhindered (v. 1) and *(B)* that he and his associates might be delivered from evil men (v. 2). Paul's prayer for the church in turn was that *(B)* they might be strengthened and guarded from evil (v. 3) so that he might have confidence *(A)* that they would continue in their Christian endeavors. Paul's intent was to call the church to perseverance in the walk and the mission given by the Lord even as he himself persevered based on confidence in the Lord. The prayer that concludes this section (v. 5) quite appropriately reflects this same concern for the living of a life of Christian love and endurance as well.

3:4 Paul's confidence in the perseverance of the church did not blind him to its flaws and its needs. He was aware that some in the congregation were not living in a way consistent with the apostolic message they had received (see v. 6). His expression of confidence, however, was not hollow. It was praise directed to the church as a whole, and the church as a whole was persisting in the faith and in its devotion to the apostles and their gospel (cf. 1:3–4; 1 Thess 3:6–8). Even those within the congregation living inappropriately were not beyond hope. They were still brothers (v. 15) whom the church should discipline in the hope that they would repent and change their behavior (vv. 12–14).

The praise expressed in v. 4, then, served not as a description of the church as a whole but as an affirmation intended to strengthen the bond between the faithful and the apostle as well as to encourage them to continue following and enforcing apostolic commands. The "things that we command" may refer to apostolic instruction of any sort, but the same verb *(parangellō)* occurs later in the chapter (vv. 6,10,12) urging ethical Christian living (see also 1 Cor 7:10; 11:17; 1 Thess 4:11; 1 Tim 5:7; 6:17). Paul seems to have had in mind already the exhortations regarding Christian behavior that he was about to deliver (vv. 6–15).

3. A Concluding Benediction (3:5)

⁵May the Lord direct your hearts into God's love and Christ's perseverance.

3:5 A final intercession on behalf of the Thessalonians concludes this series of prayers. The church as a whole was still obedient to the instructions previously given by the apostles (v. 4). A faithful people empowered by God and protected by God (v. 3) only need guidance. Thus Paul prayed that the Lord would "direct" the church in love reflective of God's love and in perseverance like that Christ had exhibited in the face of his persecutors.

"God's love" (lit., "the love of God," cf. the NASB) may refer to God's love for the Thessalonians (so the NIV) or the Thessalonians' love for God. If the former (i.e., "of God" as a subjective genitive), Paul was praying that the Thessalonians might live and act in a loving manner reflective of the love that God had exhibited in his dealings with them. If the latter (i.e., love "of God" depicts God as the object of love), then Paul was praying in effect that the church's love for God would endure and grow.

Elsewhere in Paul's letters (e.g., Rom 5:5; 2 Cor 13:13) this phrase is subjective, and considering the context it most likely is here as well. Just as God had exhibited love for them, they (who were "taught by God to love each other," 1 Thess 4:9) were to behave in a loving fashion. They should love without growing weary (v. 13) or giving up on errant fellow believers (v. 15). Thus Paul's emphasis on Christian behavior in vv. 4–5 sets the stage for a more specific focus on the Thessalonians' treatment of one another in vv. 6–15.

"Christ's perseverance" (lit., "the steadfastness of Christ," NASB) likewise translates a phrase in which Christ may be an objective or subjective genitive. As an objective genitive, Christ would be that toward which the Thessalonians' perseverance is directed. The prayer then would ask the Lord to help the Thessalonians to persevere or be patient as they await the coming of Christ (cf. the use of *hypomonē* in 1:4 and 1 Thess 1:3).

In 1 Thessalonians, however, Paul lauded the church for following the example of Christ (1:6). He also told them that their suffering was a common Christian experience. Their opponents' aim was to stop the spread of the gospel, just as Christ's crucifixion and the persecution of the Jerusalem church was intended to stop the spread of the message of Christ (1 Thess 2:14–16; cf. Jas 5:11). It also seems likely that the reference to Christ was intended to parallel the reference to God earlier in the sentence. All these things considered, the prayer most likely was a request for the Lord to guide the Thessalonians to exhibit the same perseverance Christ exhibited when he suffered persecution.

"May the Lord direct your hearts" utilizes a verb *(kateuthunē)* that occurs only twice in Paul's writings. It is used literally in 1 Thess 3:11. The metaphorical use as occurs here, however, is found frequently in the LXX. David, for instance, prayed to the Lord for his people that the Lord would "keep *[kateuthunon]* their hearts loyal to" him (1 Chr 29:18). Conversely, King Rehoboam did evil "because he had not set *[kateuthunen]* his heart on seeking the Lord" (2 Chr 12:14). Paul used the phrase similarly to pray for a genuine inward disposition on the part of the church to live in a manner consistent with "God's love and Christ's perseverance." Consistent Christian behavior can result only from genuine inward commitment.

IX. REGARDING CHURCH DISCIPLINE (3:6–15)
  1. Apostolic Exhortation and Example (3:6–10)
  2. Commands to the Idle (3:11–12)
  3. Commands to the Church (3:13–15)

IX. REGARDING CHURCH DISCIPLINE (3:6–15)

After offering and requesting prayers both for himself and his coworkers and for the gospel, Paul introduced a new topic. In a series of exhortations accompanied by supporting arguments, Paul advised the church how to deal with some of its members who were living in an idle *(ataktōs)* manner. As we will see, the exact nature of the improper behavior is a matter of debate. *Ataktōs* was used outside the New Testament to describe a variety of behaviors. In the following verses the *ataktoi* appear to be persons who not only did not work but also were a disruptive force in the church (v. 11). What motivated them to act as they did also is debatable.

As important as it is to identify the cause and nature of the problem behavior addressed in vv. 6–15, we should not ignore the fact that our passage both begins (v. 6) and ends (vv. 14–15) with exhortations, not to the idle but to the rest of the church. The admonition addressed directly to those Christians who were living improperly (v. 12) is, in fact, rather brief. The bulk of the passage contains Paul's advice to the church about how to deal with disruptive persons who were not following apostolic examples or instructions. Thus the passage deals as much (if not more) with the exercise of church discipline as it does with the specific problem of the *ataktoi*.

1. Apostolic Exhortation and Example (3:6–10)

⁶In the name of the Lord Jesus Christ, we command you, brothers, to keep away from every brother who is idle and does not live according to the teaching you received from us. ⁷For you yourselves know how you ought to follow our example. We were not idle when we were with you,

[8]nor did we eat anyone's food without paying for it. On the contrary, we worked night and day, laboring and toiling so that we would not be a burden to any of you. [9]We did this, not because we do not have the right to such help, but in order to make ourselves a model for you to follow. [10]For even when we were with you, we gave you this rule: "If a man will not work, he shall not eat."

3:6 In 3:4 Paul stated that he was confident the church would faithfully do the things the apostles commanded. With the actual issuing of commands in vv. 5–16 (using the same verb, *parangellomen,* in vv. 4 and 6), Paul's confidence and the church's obedience are put to the test. The specific command given in v. 6 ("keep away from every brother who is idle and does not live according to the teaching you received from us") is directed to the "brothers."

E. Ellis has argued that Paul used the term to address not the congregation as a whole but a smaller group of his Christian coworkers (perhaps the leaders mentioned in 1 Thess 5:12) who were responsible to exercise discipline in the church.[1] However, the frequent use of "brothers" in these letters in a wide variety of contexts makes it improbable that it should be understood in this instance as a technical term for the leaders of the congregation.[2] Such an interpretation would be justified only if the context required that the word be used in this way. But the context of vv. 6–15 requires just the opposite. The exercise of discipline was the responsibility of the church as a whole. Joint action by the entire congregation was especially imperative, considering that the only punishment authorized was the ostracism of the offender(s). If the whole congregation did not take a unified stand, such action would be ineffective either as punishment or as a symbolic statement that the *ataktoi* were not living according to Christian standards.

Paul delivered his exhortation to the church "in the name of the Lord Jesus Christ." Since Christians are those who have called on the name (1 Cor 1:2) of Jesus for salvation, he deserves their absolute obedience as Lord (cf. Phil 2:10). Yet obedience is not always easy. Also in the

---

[1] E. Ellis, "Paul and His Co-Workers," *NTS* 17 (1970–71): 450–51.

[2] Cf. 1 Thess 1:4; 2:1,9,14,17; 3:2,7; 4:1,6,10,13; 5:1,4,12,14,25–27; 2 Thess 1:3; 2:1,13,15; 3:1,6,13,15. The word ἀδελφοί is frequently used stylistically as a signal to the reader (or the one hearing the letter read) that a change of topic is occurring. At the same time the repeated use of ἀδελφοί was intended to emphasize the spiritual familial bond between Paul and the church, predisposing believers to obey commands they should understand as expressions of spiritual love and familial concern meant for their benefit.

Corinthian correspondence difficult issues involving factions and church discipline faced the congregation (1 Cor 1:10; 5:4). Likewise the idle believers who were disrupting the Thessalonian church were a faction the church was obligated to discipline. In both instances Paul evoked the authority of "the name" in an effort to remind the church of their obligation of obedience to the Lord and to ensure obedience by emphasizing that the important commands they were about to receive were not Pauline opinion but the commands of Christ (cf. 1 Cor 1:10,12,25).

Paul commanded the church "to keep away from every brother who is idle." The infinitive *(stellesthai)* means "to avoid or hold oneself apart from something or someone." The only other time it occurs in Paul's letters is when he was expressing his desire to "avoid" any criticism about the offering entrusted to his care by the Gentile churches for the poor in Jerusalem (2 Cor 8:20). In the present context Paul was instructing the members of the church to refuse to associate with fellow believers who persisted in living in a way contrary to "the teaching" *(paradosin;* cf. 2 Thess 2:15; 1 Cor 11:2) they had received from Paul and his coworkers.[3] Several years later Paul would instruct the Corinthian believers also to withdraw fellowship from persons who claimed to follow Christ yet persisted in (and defended as a valid Christian lifestyle) some unchristian behavior (1 Cor 5:9–11). By ostracizing such persons the church as a body was able to express its disapproval in a manner that the offender could not dismiss lightly. Ultimately the goal of the church was to see the errant one repent, return to a Christlike lifestyle, and return to the fellowship of believers (vv. 14–15; cf. 2 Cor 2:6–8).

The offense in this particular instance was that of living in an "idle" *(ataktōs)* manner. The participle used in conjunction with "idle" indicates that the offense was not a single occurrence but an activity characteristic of the offender.[4] The term *ataktōs* itself contains implications the English word "idle" does not convey. It occurs only once in the LXX, where it refers to a "disorderly mob" (NOAB) rushing about in a city (3 Macc 1:19). Philo used the term to refer to the chaos preceding

---

[3] Παράδοσις indicated the teachings sanctioned by and regularly passed on by a group. Elsewhere Paul used the same word of Jewish traditions (Gal 1:14) and the teachings of various philosophies (Col 2:8). The word could encompass teachings regarding both beliefs and behavior, but here the latter is clearly emphasized (in contrast to 2:15).

[4] Cf. Rom 8:4; 2 Cor 4:2; Phil 3:17.

creation,[5] and Josephus used it of a disorderly military retreat.[6] Clearly the dominant connotation of *ataktōs* is that of someone or something "out of line" or "acting in a disorderly manner."[7] The exact nature of the improper behavior must be determined on the basis of the immediate context in which the word occurs. In these verses we find that the *ataktoi* were brothers (v. 15) who were living contrary to apostolic teaching (vv. 6,10), contrary to the apostolic example of hard work and self-support (vv. 7–9), and disrupting the church as "busybodies" (v. 12).

Who specifically were these "idle" brothers whom the church was to discipline, and why were they living as they did? The answer most commonly given is that the *ataktoi* were Christians whose belief in an imminent parousia led them to abandon what they considered mundane material pursuits. They may have reasoned that working for material gain was to commit the error of building up treasure on earth at a time when all such material stuff was about to pass away. In support of this scenario we might observe that some of the Thessalonians were indeed persuaded that the day of the Lord had already arrived (2:2). In addition, eschatological concerns appear to dominate 2 Thessalonians, a letter that has the treatment of the *ataktoi* as its primary ethical concern. Similarly, in 1 Thessalonians it is concern that believers work (4:11–12) and not be idle (5:12–14) that brackets Paul's eschatological discussions in 4:13–5:11. Finally, the connection between the *ataktoi* and an eschatological motivation seems both logical and true to human nature.

However, the text never states what motivated the *ataktoi*, and assuming they had succumbed to an aberrant eschatology is only one of the viable options for explaining their behavior. Neither letter explicitly connects the expectation of an imminent parousia and the actions of the "idle." Ellis has suggested that the *ataktoi* were a small group of Christian workers who were living off the church rather than working at other jobs to supply their needs. If such were the case, it certainly would have been appropriate for Paul to cite his own example of self-support as evidence that his coworkers in Thessalonica should

---

[5] Philo, *Op. Mund.*, 22.

[6] Josephus, *Bell.* 3.113.

[7] C. Spicq, "Les Thessaloniciens 'inquiets' etaient-ils des paresseux," *ST* 10 (1956): 1–13. Ἄτακτος derives from τάσσω; for discussion of which see G. Delling, "τάσσω," *TDNT* 8:27–48, and particularly the discussion of its negated forms on pp. 47–48.

support themselves as he had (vv. 7–9).[8] Such persons might be characterized as "idle," but as we have already seen, "disorderly" or "insubordinate" probably would be a better characterization of the *ataktoi* than "idle."

Another possible explanation of the motivation of the *ataktoi* is that these persons simply considered manual labor demeaning, as did many in Greco-Roman society.[9] Although this is possible, R. Russell has argued in a helpful article that disdain for manual labor reflects "upper class Hellenistic life," yet Paul's churches were not predominantly populated with high-born or wealthy persons.

Rather than posit a general disdain for manual labor, Russell suggests that unemployed lower-class poor in the church had become accustomed to being the beneficiaries of the church's generosity to the point that they were comfortable accepting support and made no effort to work or offer any "reciprocal response" to their benefactors in the church.[10]

Refining Russell's article, B. W. Winter has suggested that the particular social convention that created the situation Paul addressed was the client/patron relationship common in Hellenistic cities. Wealthy patrons maintained their status in a city partly by supporting a sizable number

---

[8] Ellis, "Co-Workers," 450–52. This suggestion depends on the occasional use of "brothers" as a technical term for Christian ministers. If the "idle" were ministers supported by the church, one still must explain why they all should be denounced as "busybodies" (v. 11). Certainly not all church-supported ministers were so labeled by Paul. On the contrary, he recognized that those supported by the church could be diligent, effective Christian workers (as apparently were Peter, the brothers of the Lord, and other apostles who received church support; 1 Cor 5:5–12).

[9] I. H. Marshall asserts for instance that "the motives for the idleness at Thessalonica did not lie merely in heightened expectation of the End, when work would be unnecessary, but rather in a general attitude to manual labor which was current in the Hellenistic civilization of the time" (*1 and 2 Thessalonians,* NCB [Grand Rapids: Eerdmans, 1983], 223). A. Malherbe puts a finer point on the matter, arguing that some Thessalonian believers had adopted a position similar to that of the Epicureans, who withdrew from public life preferring the fellowship of other Epicureans (*Social Aspects of Early Christianity* [Philadelphia: Fortress, 1983], 24–27.

[10] R. Russell, "The Idle in 2 Thess 3:6–12: An Eschatological or a Social Problem?" *NTS* 34 (1988): 113. Russell provides an excellent survey of the history of interpretations for this passage. M. Menken critiques Russell's article and concludes that a "causal relationship" between eschatological expectation and the behavior of the ἄτακτοι "is at least a very plausible hypothesis" ("Paradise Regained or Still Lost? Eschatology and Disorderly Behavior in 2 Thessalonians," *NTS* 38 [1992]: 271–89).

of clients. Clients were social and economic inferiors who were supported by their patron in various ways. The poorest of the clients depended on their patron even for daily sustenance. It is conceivable that a client/patron relationship existed between some fellow believers in the church. If certain of the clients were choosing not to work at all and as a side effect of their idleness were creating problems in the fellowship, Paul may well have recommended that the church discipline them.[11]

This scenario certainly is plausible and may well lie behind vv. 6–15. Even if it is accepted, however, one is left wondering if Paul were rejecting the patronage system altogether or only the abuses of the system.

The command "if a man will not work, he shall not eat" (v. 10) seems to run contrary to patronage itself, yet Paul made no specific reference to it. In the Hellenistic world idleness alone would not necessarily have been condemned, and Paul would not fear that being "idle" (i.e., someone's client) would result in the community not respecting believers as 1 Thess 4:11 and 5:14 seem to imply.

If Paul were opposed to patronage in general, why was the issue not featured in any of his other letters? It seems then that while patronage could provide the general background for our passage, it was not patronage itself that motivated his comments but the disorderly (*ataktōs*) behavior of some believers who may have in patronage found the leisure to engage in disruptive behaviors.

R. Jewett has argued that if meals "were being provided by upper class patrons, it would be relatively immaterial whether particular guests were gainfully employed or not."[12] Such would not be the case, however, if the Thessalonians were not supported by a patron. If the church were composed of lower-class laborers who shared a common meal in the tenement or *insula* in which they lived, then they would not

---

[11] B. W. Winter concludes that Paul sought to teach that "it was not possible for some of the Thessalonians to opt out of work simply because others would support them. While in secular society 'it was less disgraceful to depend idly on the state or on a patron for subsistence than to earn it by sordid labor,' it was not so in the Christian community—those who did not wish to work were not permitted to be supported by their fellow Christians acting as patrons" (" 'If a man does not wish to work ...' A Cultural and Historical Setting for 2 Thessalonians 3:6–16," *TynBul* 40 [1989]: 303–15).

[12] R. Jewett, "Tenement Churches and Communal Meals in the Early Church: The Implications of a Form-Critical Analysis of 2 Thessalonians 3:10," *BR* 38 (1993): 38.

have had an abundance.[13] The failure of a few to work and contribute to the meal would work a significant hardship on their fellow Christians. Paul could have reprimanded the *ataktoi* in this scenario because they were exploiting the church's communal meals, cynically abusing the benevolence of a loving community. Such people would not need the motivation of eschatological expectation. Their failure to work would be a personality flaw, not a theological error. If such a person also disrupted the fellowship as a "busybody," it would be no great surprise.

We may never know the motivation of the *ataktoi*, but we do have a description of their behavior. These "brothers" were exploiting and disrupting their Christian family (vv. 10–11). While the church clearly was not in the business of exercising discipline on their society as a whole (cf. 1 Cor 5:9–11), they were expected to address problem behavior in their own fellowship. As a result Paul occasionally exhorted a congregation to discipline one of its members—even an apostle could not exercise discipline by himself. By its very nature church discipline as prescribed by Paul had to be an action taken by the entire congregation, or it would not be effective.

3:7 Paul reminded the Thessalonians that neither the example (vv. 7–9) nor the instructions (v. 10) of the apostolic band could justify the behavior of the idle. "You yourselves know" is emphatic and served to remind the Thessalonians of the apostolic example and the ethical instructions that were doubtless a part of the body of teachings previously given the church. The community had received the commands; it remained for them to "do the things" (v. 4) they had already been commanded by word and example to do.[14]

The disciples were obligated[15] "to imitate *(mimeisthai)*" (RSV, NASB margin) those who had established them in the faith. Imitation was not used here in a shallow sense, implying a lack of genuineness. Nor does it

---

[13] Jewett cites several studies of urban living conditions in imperial Rome, pointing out that "90% of the free population and an even higher percentage of the slave population in the cities of the empire lived in apartment blocks called *insulae*. The upper floors of the four- and five-story apartment blocks typically contained tiny cubicles of about 10 square meters representing the space for one family." Workshops occupied the ground floor. Occupants either cooked in their rooms or ate in a common kitchen (Jewett, "Tenement Churches," 26).

[14] The γάρ indicates that what follows serves as the basis for the command to keep away from fellow believers living in a disorderly manner.

[15] "Ought to" does not simply indicate what one should do but what one is obligated to do. It translates the impersonal verb δεῖ, which implies a compulsion rather than an option.

indicate any arrogance on the part of the apostle (see the discussions of *mimētai* in 1 Thess 1:6 and 2:14). Teachers of the day were expected to instruct their disciples both with their words *(logos)* and with their manner of life *(ethos)*. Disciples were expected not only to understand the wisdom of their teachers but to emulate their wise behavior as well.[16]

Paul reminded the church, "We were not idle when we were with you." This is the only place in the New Testament where the verbal form *atakteō* (the cognate of the adverb *ataktōs*) occurs, and as a result its meaning is drawn mainly from context. Outside the New Testament the verb connotes acting in a manner that is out of step with proper behavior.[17] The missionaries, Paul reminded the Thessalonians, did not act in an unseemly way while living in Thessalonica. They did not refuse to work, did not take advantage of the generosity of others, and were not troublemakers (vv. 8–12).

3:8 By describing the missionaries' conduct among the Thessalonian church, Paul gave specific content to the matter of not living in an "idle" manner. He and his coworkers did not "eat anyone's food without paying" (v. 8). The clause literally states that the missionaries did not "eat bread" from anyone "freely." Eating bread in this context relates to more than just food. The same verb and noun are used in the LXX at Gen 3:19, "By the sweat of your brow you will eat your food," signifying the necessity for man to work to supply his needs. Paul did not accept anything as a gift from the church (he did not eat "freely") and apparently did not allow the church to remunerate him for the gospel ministry he performed for their benefit.

It was common for teachers of the day to receive remuneration from those they taught. This often resulted in charges that the teachers cared nothing for their disciples or their disciplines but did what they did solely for the adulation and material gain it brought them. Paul certainly faced similar criticisms as an itinerant missionary of the gospel. Indeed, 1 Thess 2:3–12 implies that he had critics in Thessalonica who were attempting to convince the church that Paul was motivated by greed to say whatever would earn him human approval and financial support. Paul answered these charges with the evidence of his life. He routinely refused church support in favor of working to supply his own needs so that he could supply the gospel to the church freely (cf. 1 Cor 9:13–

---

[16] See A. J. Malherbe, *Moral Exhortation, A Greco-Roman Sourcebook,* LEC 4 (Philadelphia: Westminster, 1986), 135.

[17] See F. F. Bruce, *1 and 2 Thessalonians,* WBC (Waco: Word, 1982), 205, for several nonbiblical references for ἀτακτέω and its cognates.

18).[18] This not only allowed him to refute his critics but also was consistent with his understanding of the gospel. God gave it freely, and Paul had received it freely. It was appropriate then that he share freely what God had given him without cost.

Earning their own living and establishing a church at the same time while in Thessalonica was not an easy assignment. Working "night and day" implies that they worked a trade in addition to conducting their evangelistic work; thus long hours and exhausting schedules were the norm.[19] Paul also described the missionaries' work with the phrase "with toil *(en kopō)* and labor *(kai mokthō)*" (RSV). Paul remembered the *kopos* of the Thessalonians and expressed thanks for it (1 Thess 1:3). It seems little to ask that they remember his labors as well. *Kopos* and *mokthos* are synonyms Paul also used in tandem in 2 Cor 11:27 to describe the rigors of his lot as an apostle. These two terms paired with "night and day" convey the image of a difficult and demanding ministry. (Paul used the same four terms to describe himself and his coworkers in 1 Thess 2:9.) Why would anyone choose to live this way?

Paul's description of the way he supported himself is followed by a purpose statement, "so that we would not be a burden to any of you" (v. 8). Here, as in his correspondence with the church at Corinth, Paul attempted to explain his motivations so his readers would not draw erroneous conclusions from his actions (cf. v. 9a). One reason for not demanding support from the church was that he did not wish "to burden" them.[20] Requiring support might indeed have worked a hardship

---

[18] Paul's particular situation and missionary strategy seems to have called for him to refuse the support of new churches in cities where he was residing. At the same time he clearly asserted that it is proper for a minister to receive support from the congregation to which he ministers (1 Cor 9:7–12). In addition, he gratefully accepted support from churches he had established earlier and considered their gifts a form of participation in his ministry (2 Cor 11:7–9; Phil 4:14–18).

[19] Hock provides an informative discussion of Paul's comments regarding his trade and their implications regarding his daily life and social status (*The Social Context of Paul's Ministry: Tentmaking and Apostleship* [Philadelphia: Fortress, 1980]).

[20] The identical statement, νυκτὸς καὶ ἡμέρας ἐργαζόμενοι πρὸς τὸ μὴ ἐπιβαρῆσαί τινα ὑμῶν ("working night and day in order not to burden any of you"), occurs in 1 Thess 2:9. Although some have found here evidence of literary dependence, Wanamaker observes correctly that the broken grammatical construction of v. 8 (which does not occur in 1 Thess 2:9) makes it improbable that this is a quotation from 1 Thess (*1 and 2 Thessalonians,* 284). More likely, given the evidence here and in the Corinthian correspondence, Paul often was forced to explain why he did not do the expected and require support from his converts. It is easy to envision Paul repeatedly using the clause πρὸς τὸ μὴ ἐπιβαρῆσαί τινα ὑμῶν, which would both explain his unexpected actions and endear him to his hearers/readers.

on a church, especially if it were a church made up predominantly of persons from the lower classes of society.[21]

Even if the church were capable of supporting Paul without feeling burdened, the apostle might well have reasoned that if anyone had to work unusually long hours to feed the missionaries, then why should it not be Paul himself? Also Paul might have feared erecting financial barriers (the obligation to contribute to the apostle's support) to membership in the church that could discourage the poor from responding. Whatever his motives, Paul's decision not to require support from the Thessalonians was a wise one. Apparently the credibility of his message would have suffered if opponents could have cited his remuneration as "evidence" that he was an opportunist selling a man-made product. Since he gained no financial advantage from his missionary work, however, he was not vulnerable to charges of greed.

3:9 Paul's motive is clarified further in v. 9, first with a negative statement and then with a positive. First, he pointed out that his refusal to live off the church did not result from a lack of authority. He did in fact have the authority as an apostle to expect the church to care for his physical needs. He chose, however, not to exercise this right.[22] In the second half of the verse Paul explained that the missionaries worked long hard days to support themselves rather than accept support given by the church in an effort to "give" (RSV) themselves to the church as examples for the church to imitate.[23] What kind of example did Paul have in mind? His actions might illustrate generosity, humility, self-sacrifice, a willingness to work hard for the kingdom, acceptance of personal responsibility, and/or numerous other virtues. This context, however, calls for an example of one who is not disruptive (v. 11) and who provides for his own needs rather than attach himself like a leech to the vein of kindness he finds in others (v. 10).

3:10 In addition to reminding the church of the way in which he lived, Paul also reminded them of his teaching. While with them he had instructed them, "If anyone will not work, let him not eat" (RSV). To

---

[21] Paul himself observed that few of his converts were high born, well educated, or wealthy (1 Cor 1:26). But both Acts and Paul's letters agree that Paul's churches did include some persons of considerable means (Acts 16:14; 17:7,9,34; Rom 16:23; 1 Tim 6:17). Cf. Malherbe, *Social Aspects of Early Christianity,* 29–31; and W. Meeks, *The First Urban Christians* (New Haven: Yale, 1983), 51–53.

[22] In the Corinthian correspondence some years later Paul explained that love sometimes motivates one to forgo rights in the interest of others (1 Cor 8:1–11:1).

[23] See discussions of μιμετής at 1 Thess 1:6 and 2:14 and μιμέομαι at 2 Thess 3:7.

describe this as a "rule" sounds more absolute than the context justifies.[24] The use of the verb *parēngellomen* (lit., "we were commanding") both links this exhortation to the apostolic injunctions mentioned in vv. 4 and 6, where the same verb is used, and (as an imperfect tense) implies that this injunction was one given repeatedly.

The saying addresses the case of one who is able but unwilling to work, not the person who is willing but unable to work. Similar advice is found in rabbinic literature.[25] The *Didache* likewise encourages the church to assist travelers, but one who settles in their midst must exercise his craft and "work for his bread." If the person has no craft, some provision must be made that will prevent him from living as a believer "in idleness." The church is warned that if such a person refuses to work, "he is making merchandise of Christ; beware of such people."[26]

The rather harsh sounding remedy to the situation, "he shall not eat," should not be understood punitively but as an incentive to work. The intent of church discipline in the Pauline letters is consistently redemptive and constructive. The actions recommended are always designed as a corrective to improper behavior. The hope is that this "brother" will heed the "warning" (v. 15), correct his lifestyle, and be restored to the full fellowship of the church.

The earlier verses (vv. 6–10) were addressed to the church members who were not idle. They reminded them that idle or disorderly behavior could not be justified in light of the example and instructions given them by the apostles. Thus the church was to shun any believer who acted in such a blatantly unchristian way. But this is not the end of the apostle's instructions in this matter. In the following verses Paul summarized the problem again (v. 11), addressed the idle directly (v. 12), and then gave the church a series of general instructions regarding church discipline (vv. 13–15) that expand on the initial command to "keep away from" the errant brother (v. 6).

2. Commands to the Idle (3:11–12)

[11]We hear that some among you are idle. They are not busy; they are

---

[24] The sentence is rendered more exactly by the NRSV, "Even when we were with you we gave you this command." We should understand that any unable to work could be fed by the church. It was those able but unwilling to work who should not be allowed to abuse the church's generosity.

[25] *Gen. Rab.* 2.2.

[26] *Did* 12:2–5.

busybodies. [12]Such people we command and urge in the Lord Jesus Christ to settle down and earn the bread they eat.

3:11 "We hear" is a present tense implying that ongoing reports indicated that this was a persistent problem the church needed to address.[27] A string of three present participles further illustrate both the persistence and the nature of the problem. The NASB translation preserves the structure of the Greek clauses: the apostles had heard that certain believers were (1) "leading an undisciplined life," (2) "doing no work at all," but (3) "acting like busybodies." The first of these, translated "living in idleness" in the RSV, repeats the charge stated in v. 6.[28]

The next two participles elaborate on this improper lifestyle adopted by certain members of the church. "They are not busy; they are busybodies" attempts to duplicate a wordplay in the Greek. These people were not "busy," that is, engaged in productive activities *(ergazomai),* but were "busybodies," that is, engaged in unproductive activities *(periergazomai).*

The addition of the preposition *peri* to the verb implies activity that lies outside the sphere of constructive or productive labor. Such "busybodies" could disrupt the work of the church either with their passivity or with their activity. First, the idle's refusal to support themselves would damage the ministry of the church because supporting them required the church to expend some of their limited resources. The inevitable result was that it was less able to help others who genuinely could not support themselves.[29] Second, they were a disruptive influence in the church. *Periergazomai* occurs only here in Paul's letters but seems to indicate persons who had ignored the apostolic admonition "to lead a quiet life" and to "mind your own business" (1 Thess 4:11). Such persons likely would have found rationalizations for their behavior. The

---

[27] Paul did not identify the source of these reports. It is clear from 1 Thessalonians and Acts that Timothy made several trips between Thessalonica and Athens or Corinth (1 Thess 1:1; 3:2,6; 2 Thess 1:1; Acts 18:5). It is also possible that other believers traveled between these cities periodically as certain Corinthians traveled between Corinth and Ephesus (1 Cor 1:11; 16:17).

[28] The adverb again is ἀτάκτως, and the translations in the NASB and the RSV reflect the related problems of idleness and disruptive behavior that Paul addressed in the larger context.

[29] Cf. 1 Tim 5:3–16, where the church is instructed to assist only widows who are genuinely in need and have no other means of support, "so that the church can help those widows who are really in need" (v. 16).

meddler would claim to help, the gossip would purport to share needed information, and the lazy always would consider "supervision" their preferred form of participation. Such persons raise to an art form the ability to justify unchristian behavior and disguise obstructionism behind a mask of cooperation.

3:12 The situation led Paul to "command and urge" the idle to eat their own bread, working quietly. The use of two verbs to introduce the command gives it an extra measure of emphasis. The second of these verbs (*parakaloumen*, cf. 1 Thess 4:1,10; 5:14) is milder than the first and sometimes connotes a request or encouragement rather than a demand. Used in tandem with "command" (*parangellomen*, cf. 1 Thess 4:11), *parakaloumen* may give the combined statement a softer tone. In the context of a mandate to the church to shun and to withhold food from the idle, however, the use of this word alone does not weaken what is a clear and forceful call for repentance and revised behavior.

Even more stress is given the command by reiterating that these exhortations are delivered "in the Lord Jesus" (cf. v. 6). The primary command is that the idle must "eat their own bread" (NASB). Thus they must emulate Paul, who did not eat bread he had not earned (cf. v. 8). The command to eat one's own bread is modified with the participial clause "working with quietness."[30] (The NIV translates the combination of the two clauses, "settle down and earn the bread they eat.")

"Working" (*ergazomenoi*) repeats the verb translated "busy" in v. 11 and is intended to stand in contrast to it. Those who are not working (v. 11) are exhorted to support themselves by working (v. 12). Even as they returned to work, they were also to adopt a demeanor of "quietness" (*ēsuchias*), a term evidently intended to stand as an alternative to both "disorderly" behavior and acting as a "busybody." The idle must not only work but they must also repent of their disorderly behavior. A heavy work schedule may give a troublemaker less opportunity to cause trouble, but it does not necessarily alter his penchant for creating conflicts. "Quiet" behavior is peaceful (Acts 22:2) and appropriate (1 Tim 2:11–12). Persons who work "quietly" to "earn their own keep"[31] will not only avoid depleting the church's resources unnecessarily but also are more likely to earn the respect of those outside the church and less likely to find themselves in need (1 Thess 4:12).

---

[30] Cf. Wanamaker, *1 and 2 Thessalonians*, 287.
[31] Best, *1 and 2 Thessalonians*, 341.

3. Commands to the Church (3:13–15)

[13]And as for you, brothers, never tire of doing what is right. [14]If anyone does not obey our instruction in this letter, take special note of him. Do not associate with him, in order that he may feel ashamed. [15]Yet do not regard him as an enemy, but warn him as a brother.

3:13 Balancing the command to the idle is a series of commands to the church (vv. 13–15). "And as for you, brothers" marks a shift in focus, but not in topic. "You" is stated in an emphatic manner and clearly stands in contrast to "they" and "such people" in v. 12. The transition of the apostle's attention from the exploiters (the idle) to the exploited (the responsible members of the church) begins with an encouragement. Those in the church who are not idle must "not be weary in welldoing" (RSV).[32]

The verb *enkakeō* means "to grow weary" physically, or "to despair" emotionally. The latter is intended here. The participle "in welldoing" may signify "doing what is right" (in general)[33] or "doing good toward others" (i.e., toward the *ataktoi*). Since the encouragement is a part of the larger instruction about the disciplining of the *ataktoi* (beginning in v. 6) and the following verses (vv. 14–15) continue this theme, it is best to take v. 12 in the more narrow sense of instruction about the church's reaction to the idle busybodies' misbehavior. Paul may have feared that exploitation by the idle might so discourage the church that they would cease all benevolence. Certainly when "doing well" results in being exploited, it can be a discouraging experience. It was bad enough that the idle had robbed the church of resources. It would be worse still if their actions also robbed the church of its willingness to engage in Christian benevolence.

Equally possible is that Paul feared the church would react with a harsh and unchristian manner toward the idle. If this was the case, the encouragement to "do what is right" would mean that the church should react with Christian love even toward those believers who would abuse

---

[32] A similar clause occurs in Gal 6:9. The context there is more general, encouraging doing good "to all people" (6:10) with the conviction that evil actions reap "destruction" while a life pleasing to the Spirit reaps "eternal life" (6:8).

[33] W. Trilling has argued that v. 13 begins a new section and is a general exhortation to proper Christian living rather than a specific reference to the ἄτακτοι (*Der zweite Briefe an die Thessalonicher* [Neukirchener-Vluyn: Neukirchener, 1980], 154). Few commentators have followed him in this.

their generosity. They must not lash out at them as though they were enemies (cf. v. 15). Although the context of the idle is definitely in mind, this encouragement and the instructions that follow (vv. 14–15) could apply to a multitude of situations in the early church and today. What could be more Christlike than persisting in well-doing even when the beneficiaries of love in action do not deserve or appreciate the sacrifice made on their behalf?

3:14 At the same time, the church was not to ignore the abuses of immature or unscrupulous believers. Christians should continue doing well. But allowing a believer to persist in blatantly unchristian, exploitive, and disruptive behavior is not a kindness—neither to the church nor to the errant believer nor to the watching non-Christian public. Similar advice was given to the Roman church: "Watch out for those who cause divisions and put obstacles in your way that are contrary to the teaching you have learned. Keep away from them" (Rom 16:17). In extreme cases Paul even called down the judgment of God upon any so-called believer whose actions or teachings threatened the purity of the gospel or the welfare of the church (Gal 1:8–9; cf. 1 Cor 16:22). Thus for both the good of the person and the good of the church, if any member of the Thessalonian church persisted in abusing the church's kindness he must be disciplined.

The conditional clause at the beginning of v. 14, "If anyone does not obey . . . ," is structured in a way that assumes there were indeed some who were not obeying the teachings of the letter. The "instruction [logō] in this letter" is a sufficiently ambiguous phrase to cover a multitude of apostolic commands. *Logō* is singular but could easily refer to the entire body of apostolic instruction contained in the letter. Second Thessalonians, however, does not contain an abundance of exhortation. The church is admonished not to give credence to false teachings about the day of the Lord (2:3) but "hold to the teachings" delivered by Paul and his coworkers (2:15). But would failure in this area call for the exercise of church discipline? Such seems highly unlikely. The exercise of discipline in other Pauline letters consistently relates to ethical, not doctrinal, issues. The only ethical issue addressed in the letter that might require such extreme action is that of the behavior of the *ataktoi*. As a result it is most likely the word delivered in v. 12, "Such persons [as the *ataktoi*] we command and exhort in the Lord Jesus Christ to do their work quietly and to earn their own living" (NRSV), which the church was directed to enforce.

The church was to identify the *ataktoi* in order to disassociate from them. For such an action to be effective, the congregation as a whole would have to participate.[34] "Take special note," as a command to the church, refers to the process of identifying (perhaps publicly) a person as a serious offender and securing the joint action of the congregation.[35] Once identified the church was to "not associate" with the person. The same command was later given to the Corinthians regarding the extraordinary case of immorality in their midst (1 Cor 5:9,11).[36]

The reason for ostracizing the person is stated in the following clause, "in order that he may feel ashamed." The punishment was not intended to alienate the person and make him an enemy of the church but to make the person aware of the wrongness of his actions by demonstrating the church's unanimous condemnation of his behavior. One who had been "shamed" successfully would have realized the error of his own position and come to respect the truth of the criticism leveled against him (cf. 1 Cor 4:14; Titus 2:8).[37] Such a change of mind should have led the person to repent and genuinely change his ways. Understanding that the intent of the church's action was redemptive, not punitive, is key to understanding the whole of vv. 5–16.

Both the timing and the exact nature of the shunning of the idle is somewhat ambiguous. If the idle were excluded completely from association with believers, what occasion would there be to admonish them? Best suggests that the idle were excluded from table fellowship (cf. 1 Cor 5:11) prior to the assembly for worship but that they attended the assembly at which they would hear the word of admonition.[38] Wanamaker, responding to Best's suggestion, argues against such a limited understanding of the shunning and asserts that "there is no reason to think that admonishing someone excluded from the community could not take place outside the communal meeting."[39] It seems more likely, however, that admonition was preliminary to disassociation and that the shunned brother was excluded from all association with the church until

---

[34] Requiring congregational action (rather than action by a small group charged with maintaining order) might also have avoided the inappropriate application of discipline.

[35] The verb σημειοῦσθε occurs only here in the NT (and only in Ps 4:6 in the LXX).

[36] These are the only three instances of the use of this verb συναναμείγνυμι in the NT. Josephus used it of mingling in with a crowd (*Ant.* 20.165); and Philo, of the Jews' refusal to mingle with other nations (*Mos.* 1.278).

[37] See also the use of this verb (ἐντρέπω) in the middle voice to mean "respect" in Heb 12:9.

[38] Best, *1 and 2 Thessalonians,* 343–44.

[39] Wanamaker, *1 and 2 Thessalonians,* 290.

such time as he repented and came to be restored to the fellowship.

Admonition apparently was a common feature of fellowship as the church sought to maintain an acceptable Christian character. Shunning represents a clear escalation, as the church found it necessary to remove from its midst one who refused to respond to admonition. In the case of the Thessalonian *ataktoi,* previous warnings both by word and by example (vv. 7–10; 1 Thess 5:14) had no effect. The church apparently had hesitated to exercise discipline, necessitating the reminder (v. 6) and the renewed command (v. 14), "If anyone does not obey our instruction ... do not associate with him."

3:15 The church was not to consider the idle one (or any other fallen Christian) "an enemy," either during or after the exercise of discipline. Rather, they should "warn" *(noutheteite)* the sinful Christian "as a brother" (cf. 1 Thess 5:14). The leadership of the Pauline church was responsible for warning or admonishing the fellowship (the same verb occurs in 1 Thess 5:12 and 1 Cor 4:14). But the leaders were not the only ones who shared this responsibility. Paul called on all believers to exercise mutual admonition (see Rom 15:14; Col 3:16) for the benefit of one another (presumably with members admonishing even their leaders when the situation merited it). Such admonition in the Pauline letters consistently has a positive intent. It was meant for the benefit of the one admonished. Here as well Paul reminded the church that their goal was not the imposing of a harsh and unrelenting punishment but the restoration of a beloved but errant brother.

X. CONCLUSION (3:16–18)
   1. A Prayer for Peace (3:16)
   2. Authenticity Assured (3:17)
   3. Benediction (3:18)

X. CONCLUSION (3:16–18)

The letter concludes with an intercessory prayer (v. 16),[1] a signature (v. 17),[2] and a benediction (v. 18).

1. A Prayer for Peace (3:16)

¹⁶Now may the Lord of peace himself give you peace at all times and in every way. The Lord be with all of you.

3:16 The intercessory wish-prayer for the congregation stands between the instruction regarding church discipline (vv. 6–15) and the signature and concluding benediction of the letter (vv. 17–18). As a result it is impossible to know whether Paul intended it as a conclusion for the section dealing with church discipline or as a conclusion to the entire letter.[3] A prayer for peace is certainly a fitting conclusion to a passage instructing the church to discipline some of its members. But such a prayer is just as fittingly a conclusion to the letter as a whole with its concerns that the church persevere in the face of persecution (1:3–12), maintain the faith in spite of false eschatological teachings (2:1–17), and deal redemptively with the problem of the *ataktoi* (3:6–

---

[1] For the form of the wish-prayer see G. P. Wiles, *The Significance of the Intercessory Prayer Passages in the Letters of Paul*, SNTSMS 24 (Cambridge: University Press, 1974), 22–107.

[2] For the use of an amanuensis and the need for a personal signature by the author see R. Longenecker, "Ancient Amanuenses and the Pauline Epistles," in *New Dimensions in New Testament Study*, ed. R. Longenecker and M. Tenney (Grand Rapids: Zondervan, 1974), 281–97.

[3] See R. Jewett, *The Thessalonian Correspondence: Pauline Rhetoric and Millenarian Piety* (Philadelphia: Fortress, 1986), 222–25.

15). These and any number of other problems are capable of shattering the peace of a congregation. Whichever threat to peace Paul had in mind, the source of peace and the church's need for peace remains the same.[4]

The one whom the prayer addresses is the "Lord of peace." This is the only occurrence of this exact phrase in the New Testament. Quite common, however, is reference to the "God of peace" in prayers (Rom 15:33; 1 Thess 5:23; Heb 13:20) and in various pronouncements made to the church (Rom 16:20; 1 Cor 14:33; 2 Cor 13:11; Phil 4:9).[5] The use of "Lord" in this context rather than "God" reflects the unity of the two in the mind of Paul. The phrase here also is consistent with the linking of God and the Lord in numerous salutations as the grantors of "grace and peace" (Rom 1:7; 1 Cor 1:3; 2 Cor 1:2; Gal 1:3) and Paul's encouragement to the Colossians to "let the peace of Christ rule in your hearts."

Assessed negatively, peace is the absence of conflict. But Paul's prayer involved much more than a temporary truce in the conflicts troubling the church. In Paul's Jewish heritage peace was a broad concept encompassing both the absence of conflict and the presence of well-being. That Paul prayed for a peace granted by the Lord of peace makes clear that he was thinking of a spiritual reality that goes beyond human peace, one that can exist even in the midst of temporal turmoil (cf. Phil 4:6–9). It arises from the knowledge that all that is rests in the hands of the Father. And so it is possessed only by those who have learned to trust their Lord and God.

Paul prayed for peace "at all times and in every way."[6] With the turmoil generated by the idle and the conflict likely to arise from attempts to discipline them in mind, it is understandable that the apostle's prayer

---

[4] C. A. Wanamaker offers the suggestion that v. 16 was the original conclusion to the letter as it was written by Paul's amanuensis and that Paul then penned vv. 17f. himself (*1 and 2 Thessalonians*, 292).

[5] Several of these passages show that the peace God would give his people can be disrupted by forces not only external but also internal to the church.

[6] The variant reading ἐν παντὶ τόπῳ, "in every place," which replaces ἐν παντὶ τρόπῳ ("in every way") in some manuscripts, likely resulted from the similarity of the two words together with the "more usual" use of the former expression in Paul; cf. B. Metzger, *A Textual Commentary*, 638. Here, however (in contrast to passages such as 1 Cor 1:2 and 2 Cor 2:14), Paul was not contemplating multiple congregations or locations but the multiple trials of the Thessalonian church. The less common and contextually more appropriate "in every way" is to be preferred.

for the church should plead for peace. Yet the phrase implies a multitude of troubles, and the letter has revealed a persecuted, doctrinally confused, and socially troubled church. Thus the plea for peace should be understood as broadly as this phrase and the larger context demand. Clearly Paul was convinced that believers could experience the peace of God in any and all situations. For any who were cognizant of Paul's turbulent past and ongoing trials, such a statement from the apostle was not just a theological assertion but a testimony from one who had tested its truth and found his trust well placed.

"The Lord be with you all" echoes Jesus' promise to be with his disciples (cf. Matt 28:20). Similar prayers occur in Rom 15:33 and Phil 4:9 with (as in the prayer in v. 16a) "God" as the subject rather than the "Lord." Bruce probably is correct to identify this as a "liturgical benediction." Such benedictions would have been familiar to the church but not so routine as to lose any of its impact. The presence of the Lord of peace with "all" in the church should serve both to encourage and to unify the entire fellowship.

2. Authenticity Assured (3:17)

[17]I, Paul, write this greeting in my own hand, which is the distinguishing mark in all my letters. This is how I write.

3:17 It is reasonable that a letter that warns the recipients about forged letters (2:2,15) should conclude with a guarantee of authenticity. However, a signature at the conclusion of a letter, as here in v. 17, is not an uncommon feature in Pauline letters. There is an abundance of evidence demonstrating that Paul wrote his letters using the services of an amanuensis (a secretary who assisted with the writing of a document).[7] The amanuensis who assisted in the writing of Romans included his own greeting at its conclusion: "I, Tertius, who wrote down this letter, greet you in the Lord" (16:22).

The amount of freedom given the secretary in phrasing ideas varied depending on the author's inclination. Even when an amanuensis was utilized, the document produced remained the property and responsibility of the author. Thus it was not uncommon for the author to write a final word himself as a personal signature validating the letter as his

---

[7] See Longenecker, "Ancient Amanuenses," for a fuller discussion of the amanuensis in general and Paul's utilization of such in his letters.

own. Though no amanuensis other than Tertius is named in Paul's letters, he repeatedly made reference to the fact that certain lines of a letter were written by his own hand (see 1 Cor 16:21; Gal 6:11; Col 4:18; Phlm 19), clearly indicating that some other "hand" had written the bulk of the document. In some instances multiple senders are named at the beginning of a letter, and one of these cosenders could have served as Paul's amanuensis on occasion.[8]

Paul's statement that the final greeting in his "own hand" was "the distinguishing mark [lit., "sign"] in all my letters" raises some questions. First, to what "mark" was Paul referring? The author's name was not a normal feature at the conclusion of Hellenistic letters but at the beginning. What is common, however, is an evident change in handwriting style, indicating that the author rather than the amanuensis wrote the concluding lines of a document. Paul most likely was referring to this practice as one typical of the letters he wrote.

Second, how many letters had Paul written at this point? The Thessalonian correspondence is generally accepted as the earliest of Paul's extant letters. But it is reasonable to assume that Paul had written numerous letters, including some to churches, prior to the production of 2 Thessalonians. Paul had, as Best points out, "been an active missionary for many years before this."[9] And it is evident from Paul's extant epistles that some of his letters have not been preserved (see 1 Cor 5:9–11; 2 Cor 2:3–4; Col 4:16). It is reasonable to believe that Paul wrote instructions and encouragements to the churches he founded (e.g., those recorded in Acts 13–14) well before the middle of his second missionary journey.

3. Benediction (3:18)

[18]The grace of our Lord Jesus Christ be with you all.

3:18 The letter concludes with a benediction that is identical to that in 1 Thess 5:28 except for the addition of "all" *(pantōn).* Concluding benedictions requesting grace for his readers are common in Paul's letters (cf. 1 Cor 16:23; Gal 6:18; Phil 4:23; Col 4:18) but can show a fair

---

[8] See references to Sosthenes (1 Cor 1:1), Timothy (Col 1:1; Phlm 1), and Silas (2 Thess 1:1).

[9] E. Best, *A Commentary on the First and Second Epistles to the Thessalonians* (London: A & C Black, 1977), 347.

amount of variety regarding the persons addressed (the Lord, the Father, and/or the Spirit, by various titles) and the blessings requested (e.g., grace, peace, love, fellowship; cf. Rom 15:33; 16:24, NIV margin; 2 Cor 13:14). Though some such formula was routine at the conclusion of a Pauline letter, it should not be dismissed too quickly as a simple matter of form. The variety demonstrable in the concluding benedictions of Paul's letters indicates that he did craft them with some thought and intent, and perhaps the simple inclusive nature of this final word was the message he desired to convey. Even considering the doctrinal and ethical confusions in the church, his knowledge of the power of the grace of God was such that his final word sought the power and the blessings of grace for all.

Selected Subject Index

Person Index

Scripture Index

Ancient Sources Index